ADVANCED HOME GARDENING
CUTTING-EDGE GROWING TECHNIQUES FOR GARDENERS

CRE**A**TIVE
HOMEOWNER®

ADVANCED HOME GARDENING

CUTTING-EDGE GROWING TECHNIQUES FOR GARDENERS

Miranda Smith

CREATIVE HOMEOWNER®, Upper Saddle River, New Jersey

Editorial Director: Timothy O. Bakke
Art Director: W. David Houser
Production Manager: Stanley Podufalski

Editor: Nancy T. Engel
Copyeditor: Ellie Sweeney
Photo Researcher: Amla Sanghvi
Editorial Assistants: Stanley Sudol, Laura DeFerrari
Development Editor: Neil Soderstrom
Editorial Intern: Lisa Amelio
Consulting Copyeditor: Anne Halpin
Technical Reviewers: Elizabeth P. Stell, Joe Smillee
Indexer: Ellen Davenport; Glossary: Victoria Mattern

Design and Layout: Virginia Wells Blaker
Assistant Graphic Designer: Chuck Van Vooren
Principal Illustrator: Mavis Augustine Torke
Front and Back Cover Design: Robert Strauch
Front Cover Photography: Background, Foreground Left, Walter Chandoha; Foreground Right, John Glover
Back Cover Photography: Photos Horticultural
Author Photo: Brian Nieves

Advanced Home Gardening
Library of Congress Catalog Card Number 00-101559
ISBN:1-58011-073-8

CREATIVE HOMEOWNER®
A Division of Federal Marketing Corp.
24 Park Way, Upper Saddle River, NJ 07458
Web site: **www.creativehomeowner.com**

METRIC EQUIVALENTS

All measurements in this book are given in U.S. Customary units. If you wish to find metric equivalents, use the following tables and conversion factors.

Inches to Millimeters and Centimeters

1 in = 25.4 mm = 2.54 cm

in	mm	cm
1/16	1.5875	0.1588
1/8	3.1750	0.3175
1/4	6.3500	0.6350
3/8	9.5250	0.9525
1/2	12.7000	1.2700
5/8	15.8750	1.5875
3/4	19.0500	1.9050
7/8	22.2250	2.2225
1	25.4000	2.5400

Inches to Centimeters and Meters

1 in = 2.54 cm = 0.0254 m

in	cm	m
1	2.54	0.0254
2	5.08	0.0508
3	7.62	0.0762
4	10.16	0.1016
5	12.70	0.1270
6	15.24	0.1524
7	17.78	0.1778
8	20.32	0.2032
9	22.86	0.2286
10	25.40	0.2540
11	27.94	0.2794
12	30.48	0.3048

Feet to Meters

1 ft = 0.3048 m

ft	m
1	0.3048
5	1.5240
10	3.0480
25	7.6200
50	15.2400
100	30.4800

Square Feet to Square Meters

1 ft^2 = 0.092 903 04 m^2

Acres to Square Meters

1 acre = 4046.85642 m^2

Cubic Yards to Cubic Meters

1 yd^3 = 0.764 555 m^3

Ounces and Pounds (Avoirdupois) to Grams

1 oz = 28.349 523 g
1 lb = 453.5924 g

Pounds to Kilograms

1 lb = 0.453 592 37 kg

Ounces and Quarts to Liters

1 oz = 0.029 573 53 L
1 qt = 0.9463 L

Gallons to Liters

1 gal = 3.785 411 784 L

Fahrenheit to Celsius (Centigrade)

$°C = °F - 32 \times 5/9$

°F	°C
-30	-34.45
-20	-28.89
-10	-23.34
-5	-20.56
0	-17.78
10	-12.22
20	-6.67
30	-1.11
32 (freezing)	0.00
40	4.44
50	10.00
60	15.56
70	21.11
80	26.67
90	32.22
100	37.78
212 (boiling)	100

Author's Acknowledgments

This book could never have come into being without the wonderful work by everyone at Creative Home-owner, from Neil Soderstrom, whose idea it was, to those people listed in the credits, opposite. Additionally, I'd like to thank the many students who have taught me what needs to be taught and how to do it. This book was written while I was teaching at Lampson Brook Farm at the New England Small Farm Institute in Belchertown, MA, and then at Thanksgiving Farm in Harris, NY. A special thank you goes to all of my students and colleagues at both locations; you provided a great deal of needed inspiration.

—*Miranda Smith*

HEALTH AND SAFETY CONSIDERATIONS

All projects and procedures in this book have been reviewed for safety; still it is not possible to overstate the importance of working carefully. What follows are reminders for plant care and project safety. Always use common sense.

■ **Always** consider nontoxic and least toxic methods of addressing unwanted plants, plant pests, and plant diseases before resorting to toxic methods. Follow package application and safety instructions carefully.

■ **Always substitute rock phosphate and gypsum** for bonemeal when amending soil. Authorities suggest that there's a hazard in using bovine-based products such as bonemeal, blood meal, and cow manure because they could harbor the virus that causes Mad Cow disease in cattle and humans.

■ **Always** read labels on chemicals, solvents, and other products; provide ventilation; heed warnings.

■ **Always** wear eye protection when using chemicals, sawing wood, pruning trees and shrubs, using power tools, and striking metal onto metal or concrete.

■ **Always** wear a hard hat when working in situations with potential for injury from falling tree limbs.

■ **Always** wear appropriate gloves in situations in which your hands could be injured by rough surfaces, sharp edges, thorns, or poisonous plants.

■ **Always** wear a disposable face mask or a special filtering respirator when creating sawdust or working with gardening dusts and powders.

■ **Always** protect yourself against ticks, which can carry Lyme disease. Wear light-colored, long-sleeved shirts and pants. Inspect yourself for ticks after every session in the garden.

■ **Always** determine locations of underground utility lines before you dig, and then avoid them by a safe distance. Buried lines may be for gas, electricity, communications, or water. Contact local utility companies which will help you map their lines.

■ **Always** read and heed tool manufacturer instructions.

■ **Always** ensure that the electrical setup is safe; be sure that no circuit is overloaded and that all power tools and electrical outlets are properly grounded and protected by a ground-fault circuit interrupter (GCFI). Do not use power tools in wet locations.

■ **Always** keep your hands and other body parts away from the business end of blades, cutters, and bits.

■ **Never** employ herbicides, pesticides, or toxic chemicals unless you have determined with certainty that they were developed for the specific problem you hope to remedy.

■ **Never** allow bystanders to approach work areas where they might by injured by workers or work site hazards.

■ **Never** work with power tools when you are tired or under the influence of alcohol or drugs.

■ **Never** carry sharp or pointed tools, such as knives or saws, in your pocket.

CONTENTS

INTRODUCTION

Advanced Home Gardening will teach you how to grow flowers, vegetables, herbs, and fruit with less effort and more yield; and how to make the process of gardening as enjoyable as the finished product. You will learn how to create a restful haven, without more work than is absolutely necessary, where you and your family can work, play, and relax.

New gardeners should start at the beginning of this book. If you have some experience and consider yourself an intermediate-level gardener, just skim the first two chapters. Although you might already know most of the information there, you still may learn a few new tricks.

Both time efficiency and environmental sensitivity are emphasized in the book. Smart Tips are liberally sprinkled throughout the book and highlighted in colored boxes. Look for these proven techniques in each chapter.

Tools, Materials, and Plants

In the beginning of each chapter is an illustrated box of tools. Please keep in mind that these are only suggestions; it is not necessary to buy every tool shown. With some field experience, you will soon know which tools are the most helpful to you, as well as those you can do without. Many of the tools, materials, and plants mentioned are specialty items and may not be readily available at the home-and-garden center. To locate the source for a particular item, either shop on the Internet or try the more old-fashioned, but still effective, mail-order catalogs.

The Mailorder Gardening Association (MGA) produces a booklet to help gardeners sort through the myriad catalogs to focus in on the items they need. The MGA's *Garden Catalog Guide* lists catalogs by product category and includes a glossary of garden catalog terms. The Mailorder Gardening Association's Guide costs $2. Contact the MGA for information. Address: P.O. Box 2129, Columbia, MD 21045; Phone: (415) 730-9713; Web address: mailordergardening.com.

About the Plant Directories

Illustrated Plant-by-Plant Directories in Chapters 3, 5, 6, 7, and 8 provide specific, detailed information on more than 100 plants. The entries in the directories are written for gardeners in USDA Hardiness Zones 5, 6, and 7. However, if you live in Zones 3, 4, 8, 9, or 10, you may have to modify this information slightly, particularly in reference to size, planting time, soil, and exposure.

Chionodoxa luciliae — BOTANICAL NAME
Glory-of-the-Snow — COMMON NAME

PLANT PORTRAIT

Related Species: None used in garden.
Zones: 3 to 8.
Appearance: Leaves are strap-shaped and die back early. The 6-petaled, star-shaped, 1-inch-wide flowers grow in sprays above the foliage.

SPECIFIC PLANT INFORMATION

Each directory entry includes a photograph of the plant and information such as the hardiness zone, bloom time, propagation, and notes. In chapters 3, "Flowers, Flowers, and More Flowers" and 5, "Vines;" the entries are alphabetized by botanical name. But in chapters 7, "Herb Gardens" and 8, "Fruits," the entries are alphabetized by common name because that is the way most people refer to these plants. In Chapter 6, "Vegetable Gardens," the entries are grouped by botanical family names, but a few are listed by common names. On pages 311 to 317, the plants are indexed by both botanical and common name to make it easier for you to find every plant in the book.

Chapter 9, "Preventing Weeds, Pests, and Diseases," contains preventive techniques and ecologically benign control methods.

CHAPTER 1

PREPARING TO GARDEN

Location, location, location. It matters as much for a garden as for a retail store. But unlike a retail business, there is almost no such thing as a bad garden location. You just need to match the plants to the locations where they will grow best. If one plant doesn't thrive in a particular spot, another will.

You may also find that some of the spots that once seemed difficult are where your most interesting gardens grow. A yard with a variety of areas, ranging from wet and boggy to dry and sandy, gives you the opportunity to create several specialized gardens. But don't despair if your property lacks this kind of diversity. With a little forethought, you can create very interesting plantings in any situation.

A well-designed yard, complete with gardens and recreational areas, is as much a part of your living space as the kitchen or dining room. If you remember that while you design the property, you're more likely to create a space that suits your needs, pleases your senses, and supports the kind of plants you want to grow.

Most people create new gardens on old lawns. When they are in the planning stages, the actual process for turning lawn into garden is not likely to be something they think very much about. They assume that you can just dig up the lawn and plant a garden in its place. Sometimes, this is true. But more frequently, getting rid of the lawn isn't that easy. In addition, the soil under the sod layer may not be appropriate for garden plants.

Soil is as important to your plants as temperature or sunlight. A good garden soil gives your plants the oxygen, moisture, and nutrients they need and protects them from some pests and diseases. But don't be surprised to discover that the soil in your backyard is not quite up to the standard of "good garden soil."

This chapter can help you through the mundane, but necessary, process of preparing to garden, from design through caring for your soil.

ADDING COMPOST to the garden every spring helps to keep soils fertile while it discourages some pests and diseases.

PLANTS IN THIS GARDEN are all accessible from the central pathway or the surrounding pavement, making weeding, troubleshooting, and deadheading possible.

DESIGN GARDENS FOR EASY CARE by mulching to keep weeds down, spacing plants so air can circulate around them, and making pathways so all areas are accessible.

DESIGNING FOR EASY CARE

GARDENS THAT ARE EASY to maintain are usually well maintained. In contrast, gardens with crowded planting schemes are usually the first ones to get out of control. Remember, no matter how beautiful the concept, you're more likely to maintain the garden if it's easy to do so.

Soil is healthier if you never compact it by stepping on it, so the plan should allow you to reach around every stem and every branch without stepping in the bed. Check your reach from both a standing position and kneeling. The average woman has a 3-foot working reach; and men can often reach slightly further. Measure your reach; then construct pathways at the correct intervals through the bed so that you can reach all parts of the planting area and never feel uncomfortable while you're working.

Choose Appropriate Plants

Choose plants according to each plant's suitability to your environment, including the soil; maintenance requirements; and pest and disease resistance. Learn about the growing conditions in your garden, and select plants that thrive in those conditions. While it is possible to grow plants that are marginally hardy, it makes for extra work. Each fall, you'll need to build windscreens or wrap the plants in burlap to protect them from the cold. In the spring, you'll need to unwrap them and take down the windscreens. Similarly, you can also alter the pH in a particular spot to grow a cherished plant. But again, this is extra work. It's worth the effort to create a lower-pH bed if blueberries are your favorite fruit, but if your soil is not naturally acid, you might think twice about surrounding the front door with azaleas.

SMART TIP

3 KEYS TO AN EASY-CARE GARDEN

1. Design so the whole garden is accessible.

2. Choose plants suited to your climate.

3. Give plants a good growing environment.

A few pest and disease problems are normal. However, you'll be much happier, and your garden will look much better, if your problems are few rather than many. As you'll soon discover, some plants simply attract problems while others, often in the same family and sometimes even the same genus, repel them. Whenever you are buying seeds or plants, read the description carefully, looking for the magic words, "pest (or disease) resistant."

Site plants with room to grow. In addition to choosing plants with a genetic resistance to problems, you can also influence their health with cultural techniques. The third element of designing for easy maintenance—locating plants wisely—can help. Plants sited where they have adequate growing space, the correct exposure to light, appropriate soil nutrition and drainage, good air circulation, and protection from drying winds stay healthier.

Less experienced gardeners tend to space plants too tightly. For one thing, it's hard to believe that the scrawny

SPACE PLANTS so they have room to grow to their mature size without crowding.

little stem you're planting will really turn into a 3-foot mound of greenery in a year or so; and for another, you don't want to look at the bare spaces between plants while you're waiting.

Plant annuals with perennials. The best way around this problem is to plant perennials at the spacing recommended on nursery labels and interplant annuals between them. This approach eliminates the bare-looking spots and minimizes the open area that weeds can easily colonize. You can either remove the annuals as the perennials fill in or plant early-blooming annuals such as pansies (*Viola*) which come out of the garden in the summer. An annual with a dense leaf canopy, such as nasturtium *(Tropaeolum majus)*, will shade the soil all through the season and discourage weeds from sprouting.

TOOLS

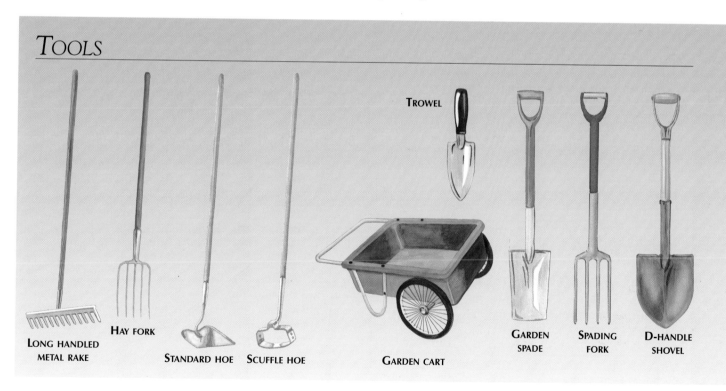

LONG HANDLED METAL RAKE

HAY FORK

STANDARD HOE

SCUFFLE HOE

GARDEN CART

TROWEL

GARDEN SPADE

SPADING FORK

D-HANDLE SHOVEL

LAYING OUT THE GARDEN

PLAN TO DEVOTE A weekend or more to laying out a design for a whole yard. If you are designing a smaller area, such as a perennial border or an herb garden, it may take only a few hours to accomplish. But whether the area is big or small, complex or simple, the more care you take with the layout, the lovelier the final garden will look and the easier it will be to maintain.

In gardens, lines should be straight and circles should be round. Don't worry that crisp, well-defined lines will look too rigid. As soon as the stems grow beyond the boundaries and leaves spill over pathways, the lines will soften.

It's easiest to mark off the largest dimensions first and then refine your measurements. Stakes and string make valuable visual aids while you work. A bag of lime, or rock phosphate, is another essential marking tool. Once you are satisfied with a particular outline, use the powder to draw it on the grass or soil. If you change your mind, you can wash it away, but until then it will give you a good idea of the dimensions of various elements in your garden plan.

THE 3, 4, 5 RULE is invaluable for making square angles. Measure 3 feet on one side, 4 feet on the other side, and then 5 feet on the diagonal line that connects the sides.

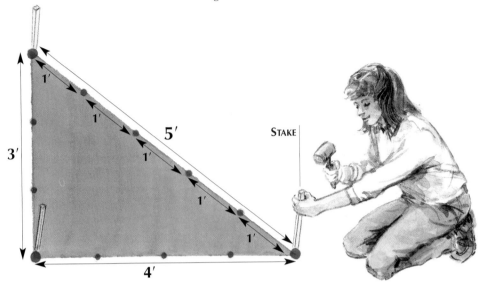

Create right angles with "3, 4, 5 ." One of the most useful tricks for gardeners is the "3, 4, 5" rule. As illustrated, you can create 90° angles with this technique. Not only does this allow you to square the corners of beds, it also helps when you are trying to align a garden with another feature of the yard. For example, if you want the back of a flower border to line up with the back of the house, you can use the side wall of the house as one side of your measuring triangle. By working from the square angles you can create with the "3, 4, 5" principle, you'll be able to set the bed exactly where you want it.

Informal borders often have irregular shapes, with widely varying widths from one part of the border to another. To be effective, the curves should be graceful. It's also important that the border look as if it belongs to the natural landscape. If the area is slightly sloped, one side of the border can be formed to follow the contour of the land, while the other can become wider or more narrow as the plants within it dictate. On flat ground, try to echo the line of something else in the area, such as the curve of a nearby tree line or roadway. In either case, lay out the curves and look at them for a few hours before tearing up the sod.

MEASURE and use stakes and string when you want to create straight rows in the garden.

FORMAL GARDENS are often built on right angles, as shown here. This detail makes the garden look tidy and well-maintained.

Preparing Garden Sites

If you plan to remove a lawn, begin by digging up a small patch and examining the roots of the grass. You want to determine whether the grass reproduces from long underground stems, or rhizomes, or spreads from a central, fibrous root system. More than likely, there will be a combination of grass types in the lawn. Fibrous-rooted grasses such as yellow foxtail (*Setaria glauca*) are the easiest to eliminate; it is usually possible to simply roll up the sod layer and remove it, or till. But if the lawn contains a significant quantity of rhizomatous grass, such as quack grass (*Agropyron repens*) or Kentucky bluegrass (*Poa pratensis*), it is best to smother it with sheet mulching (as described on the next page) or till it first and then plant a cover crop. No matter how you get rid of the grass, test the soil afterward as soon as possible. You'll want to adjust the pH and add appropriate nutrients before planting a cover crop or a garden.

THE REPRODUCTIVE STRATEGIES OF A GRASS PLANT include an underground rhizome and an aboveground stolon as well as a tiller, or offset growing from the crown of the plant.

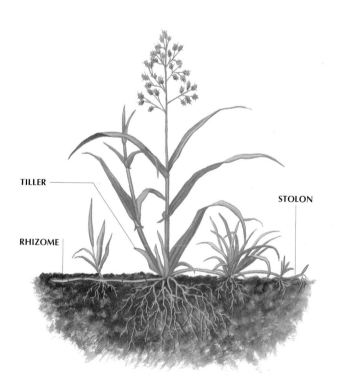

TILLER

STOLON

RHIZOME

HOW TO GET RID OF QUACK GRASS FOREVER

QUACK GRASS IS A COMMON problem, especially during the first few years after a new garden is established. But you really can get rid of it. Begin by tilling the soil in early spring and walking the area, pulling up all the rhizomes you see. Repeat the tilling and rhizome removal every week until the weather is frost-free. Then plant buckwheat (*Polygonum fagopyrum*). The broad leaves will shade out some of the emerging quack grass and many other weed seedlings. Let the buckwheat grow until the seeds at the bottom of the flower panicles have turned brown. Then till it under. The ripe seeds will germinate, giving you a second crop. Let that crop grow until early fall. Till it under and plant winter rye (*Lolium*). The rye will grow through the fall and into the next spring. Till it under as soon as the soil can be worked. As the rye decomposes, it will release compounds that are *phytotoxic*, or poisonous, to quack grass rhizomes and many weed seedlings. Protect your garden plants by waiting at least two weeks before planting or transplanting into the area.

Sheet Mulching: Slow and Easy

Sheet mulching is one of the easiest ways to create a new garden area in a lawn. It also creates soil with excellent nutritional capacities. In fact, the only disadvantage to this system is that it requires a full year to work.

Begin by testing the soil pH. To test the soil under a lawn, use a spade to slice through the roots. Take your sample from a slice of soil that starts just under the roots to 6 inches below. Sift out any roots. If grass has been growing reasonably well, the nutrients are probably adequate. Sheet mulching contributes enough nutrition to make up for all but the most serious deficiencies.

It's best to start the mulching process early in the spring before the grass has been mowed. If you need to adjust the pH, sprinkle limestone or sulfur on top of the sod. Then mulch with layers of newspaper, compost, and straw. If you can't get straw, use autumn leaves or another organic mulch such as rice or buckwheat hulls. If the mulch is in danger of blowing away, cover the area with a tarp. The garden will be ready for planting the following spring. To keep it weed-free, continue to mulch after the plants are in place. If the lawn contained rhizomatous grasses, you can prevent their migrating back into the area by sinking plastic or metal barriers along the garden edges.

Working with a Tiller

Tillers can make fast work of a heavy job. But you must know how to use them properly, or you run the risk of damaging the soil. Do not till if the soil is wet, or you risk creating clods that are impenetrable to roots through the season. Test the soil by taking up a handful and squeezing it together. Consider it too wet to till if beads of moisture form on its surface or if it does not immediately break apart when you strike a handful with the edge of your other hand. No matter how frustrating it seems to wait until the soil dries, the long-term health of the garden is worth it.

Tines wear out on tillers. In heavy or rocky soils, you'll find that they can wear out in only a couple of seasons. Replace them when they have lost their edge. This expense is justified by more efficient tilling. Safety is also a concern.

From bare ground to gardens. New houses are often surrounded by bare ground. More often than not, the contractors gave little thought to treating the soil kindly while they were working. In some cases, the topsoil has been scraped off and sold to other developers. Other locations may still have the topsoil, but it has been so badly compacted by the weight of all the heavy machinery that nothing much will grow in it.

If the soil in your future garden space is overly compacted, try to get some air into it by poking it with a spading fork. After you've been over the whole area a couple of times with the spading fork, spread 1 to 2 inches of compost or fully aged manure over the whole planting area. Depending on the results of your soil test, adjust the pH—and fertilize for nutrient deficiencies while you're at it. Then sow a cover crop. If you plan to leave the cover crop in place for at least 18 months, include a nitrogen-contributing legume, such as alfalfa, in the mix.

POWER TILLERS make fast work of cultivation. But, too much tilling can create a problem. Avoid damaging the soil by tilling only until soil clods are two or three inches in diameter.

FOUR STEPS OF TILLING

FIRST PASS

SECOND PASS

THIRD PASS

FOURTH PASS

BEGIN TILLING NEW GROUND by setting the tines only deep enough to cut through the layer of sod.

MAKE A SECOND PASS by working perpendicularly to the direction of the first one.

SET THE TINES to their maximum depth for the third and final pass with the tiller.

RAKE THE SURFACE of the beds smooth to create a fine seedbed for planting.

Soil

THE IDEAL SOIL HAS a loose, crumbly texture; holds both air and water well, yet drains quickly; is teeming with numerous kinds of microorganisms and soil-enhancing creatures; has an acid/alkaline (pH) balance appropriate for the particular plants being grown; and has an adequate and balanced nutrient supply.

But since few garden soils start out fitting this description, you'll have to learn how to improve what you have. Most people need to work on their soil's structure, its nutritional qualities, the pH, and drainage. But on a small garden scale, it doesn't take long to turn poor soil into good. Best of all, as the soil improves, so does the garden.

What Is Soil?

Most soils are composed of about 45 percent inorganic minerals, 20 to 30 percent air, 20 to 30 percent water, and 5 percent organic matter. The inorganic minerals, or rock particles, are classified according to their size. Sand is composed of the largest particles, clay the smallest, and silt falls in between (see photograph below).

Air and water are held in the spaces between the rock particles. Ideally, soil contains equal amounts of both. After a heavy rain, it contains more water, of course. But within only a few hours, some of the water evaporates into the air, some drains into lower soil depths, and some is taken up by roots and other organisms. As all of this happens, air replaces the lost water. The quantity of water that can move through a soil as well as the speed with which it does so determine the soil's drainage characteristics.

Organic matter in a soil can be living or dead. Soil animals, microorganisms, plant debris, and roots are all part of the soil's organic matter. As you'll see later, the organic

matter has a profound effect on the way a soil behaves and on the health of plants.

Soil texture and soil structure. *Soil texture* is a term soil experts use quite often. It describes the percentages of sand, silt, and clay. Loams, which are the "ideal" for most gardening, contain some of each. But here again, few are so lucky as to have a deep, rich loam in the backyard, so you have to work with whatever you have.

The texture of the soil influences the availability of air, water, and nutrients to all soil life, including plant roots. For example, a very sandy soil drains quite quickly, while a soil containing a large percentage of clay can retain too much water. Plants in sandy soil tend to suffer more during a drought (or require more watering) than those in soil with a heavy clay content. However, the plants growing in sandy soil fare far better during a rainy spell. No matter what you do, short of importing truckloads of sand or clay, you'll never be able to change the texture of your soil. If it starts out sandy, it will end up sandy. But you can change its structure. One of the keys to creating a good garden is to improve the structure of your soil.

Structure refers to the way that a soil's particles group together. In a soil with good crumb structure, for example, a random handful looks like a slice of perfect chocolate cake. You can see numerous air spaces between clumps of glistening particles.

Many of these clumps, or soil aggregates, are literally glued together. As soil animals and microorganisms live and die, they excrete sticky substances which bind soil particles together. The long bodies of microscopic fungi grow between and around soil particles, grouping them into aggregates. Earthworms also contribute soil-binding substances. As they move through soil, some of the mucilagenous substances on their skin are left behind, enclosing the channels where they travel. The channels created by earthworms stay in place for some time, giving air and water a good pathway. Plant roots do this, too. After the plant dies, its roots decompose leaving open channels behind. Both air and water occupy these spaces.

SAND **LOAM** **CLAY**

SAND (left) is composed of large particles. Clay (right) is made of smaller particles. Loam (center) contains sand and clay and is ideal.

TESTING FOR SOIL TYPES: TEXTURE AND STRUCTURE

Difficulty Level: **EASY**

A FEW SIMPLE TESTS can tell you a great deal about the texture of your soil. Do these tests when the soil is damp, not wet. Dry soil will fall apart, and soggy soil may not crumble.

1 Make a ball of soil, but press only hard enough to make it stick together.

2 Gently bounce the ball up and down in your hands with a rocking motion.

3 Loamy soils crumble partially, but sandy soils fall apart, and clay soils stick together.

4 Feel the texture. Sand is gritty, silt feels silky, and clay is slippery.

Plant health depends on the structure of the soil. If the pore spaces are large, water and air easily move through the soil, assuring good drainage. And *capillary action*, the rising of water from lower soil depths up to the root zone, is enhanced, so plants can better cope with lack of rain.

Drainage

Drainage can affect plant health as much as any other factor. And drainage improves dramatically over a period of just a year or two as you add compost and other organic matter to the soil. However, for improved drainage, soils with a high clay content may need some extra help. Try adding about 50 pounds of gypsum per every 1,000 square feet; this will promote crumb formation to improve soil

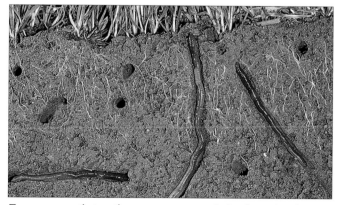

THE CHANNELS that earthworms create remain in place after the earthworms have moved on. These channels provide an easy path for both air and water.

structure. In addition to improving the soil's structure, gypsum supplies some minor nutrients. It provides calcium in a form that doesn't raise soil pH (unlike limestone), and it's an excellent source of sulfur.

Serious drainage problems may require pipes or trenches.
If the garden is situated where it gets huge quantities of snow and rain runoff or if a spring erupts in the middle of it, you must take stronger measures than adding organic matter. For severe drainage problems, ask a landscape professional about installing underground pipes or digging trenches or swales. Check with your town or city before you dig; you may need a permit.

Improving Structure and Nutrient Content

The more living creatures your soil hosts, the healthier your plants are likely to be. The number of organisms in a good soil are staggering. Researchers tell us that there are billions of microbes in every teaspoon of soil, and that the total weight of the living organisms in the top 6 inches of an acre of soil ranges from 5,000 to 20,000 pounds. These creatures—fungi, bacteria, protozoa, nematodes, mites, springtails, worms, grubs, and even viruses—make up the soil community and, as such, help to create good soil structure.

They do much more than that, however. Soil microbes also decompose organic matter, making nutrients available to plants. They prey on certain pests and diseases in the soil, create vitamins and other beneficial compounds, and supply some nutrients directly to your plants.

Keep the soil organisms healthy. New gardeners are sometimes surprised to learn that one of their most important jobs is to keep the soil organisms healthy. Fortunately, you don't need to be a doctor of tiny things to do this. All it takes is a little common sense. Soil flora and fauna require food, air, and water. They are active when soil temperatures are above 50°F, and they die if exposed to a poison such

SWALES shown here at the left of the photo are easy to build and maintain and can make a huge difference in the way your garden drains.

as a fungicide, pesticide, or herbicide. Even a large application of strong, concentrated fertilizer (a typical synthetic) will slow or stop microorganism activity and may actively harm these hard-working soil creatures.

Organic matter in and on the soil is food for soil organisms. As these microorganisms live, eat, and die, they also take in air and moisture. Organic mulches on the surface provide one of the best food sources for soil life. Even in a soil without good structure, mulch on the surface of the soil is perfect, as long as air is abundant and dew (if not rain or irrigation water) is fairly certain. Other ways to supply organic matter include mixing in compost or aged manure, or growing cover crops, which are discussed later. As soil organisms break down the organic matter, they produce *humus*.

What is humus? Humus makes the difference between "good" and "poor" soils. This magical stuff contains decomposed organic matter as well as microbial organisms and their by-products. Humus is forming around us all the time. In nature, it takes many years to produce results. But fortunately for gardeners, there's a much faster system, called *composting*. An average gardener, with an average amount of yard and kitchen waste, can create at least a cubic yard of humus-rich material a year, with scarcely any work.

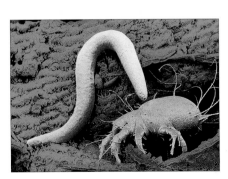

THIS BENEFICIAL NEMATODE is investigating a mite to determine whether it will devour it.

COMPOSTING

COMPOSTING IS SIMPLY CREATING the optimal conditions for very fast microbial decomposition of organic matter. You can make your own compost area as shown on pages 22 and 23. To create compost, begin by building a pile that includes about 6 inches of dry plant material, such as old cornstalks or shredded autumn leaves. Then add a 2- to 4-inch layer of moist green material.

Sprinkle on a half-inch layer of good garden soil before you begin again with the dry material. If you have manure, add it with the green layer. Manure adds nitrogen and microorganisms. Another way to supply microbes is to substitute compost from a previous batch for the garden soil. Or buy a canister of compost-activator (which is full of microorganisms) and sprinkle it between the green and dry layers. This proportion of dry to green materials gives the decomposing microorganisms the optimal blend of carbon (dry stuff) to nitrogen (green stuff), roughly 25 to 40 times as much carbon as nitrogen. To start, try to make

> ## SMART TIP
> ### LEAN COMPOST
> Never include meat, dairy, or fats in your compost; these materials will only attract rodents, making your compost a neighborhood problem.

the pile at least 3 feet tall. If the materials are very dry, sprinkle them with water until they glisten in the sunlight. Properly moist compost should be damp, never wet, about the consistency of a wrung-out sponge. As the materials begin to decompose, the interior of the pile will get hot, simply from the microorganisms working. Oxygen on the inside of the pile will be depleted; soil organisms consume oxygen (O_2) and give off carbon dioxide (CO_2), just as we do. To keep them active, introduce more air by turning or poking holes in the pile. For the very best final product, turn the pile so that you reverse the outside and inside portions. That way, disease-causing fungi and bacteria, as well as most weed seeds, will be exposed to temperatures hot enough to kill them. A hayfork (a pitchfork with curved tines), is an excellent tool with which to turn compost in a pile. To be on the safe side, avoid adding diseased plants or weeds with seeds to the compost pile; that way you won't have to worry whether all parts of the pile got hot enough to kill them. Compost is considered "finished" when it no longer

Continued on page 23

FULLY FINISHED COMPOST can be left in an uncovered pile (above) until you are ready to apply it to the garden soil or a garden bed, as shown here at right.

BUILDING A WOODEN COMPOST BIN

A FEW HOURS of simple carpentry is all it takes to build a sturdy compost bin that will serve you for many years. You can build a single bin, as shown below, or a row of bins, as shown to the right.

Forego the temptation to use pressure-treated wood; the chemicals used to treat it may kill many of the beneficial organisms that transform garden waste products and kitchen scraps into life-supporting compost.

1 Side panels of a compost bin can be made by attaching 1x6 boards to 4-feet long 2x2 wooden stakes set 2 inches apart so they form a channel.

2 After cutting off the excess length of the stakes, pound them into the soil with a mallet. Protect them from splitting with a piece of scrap wood.

3 Make certain that the panels are plumb before you finish driving the stakes into the soil. Get help if you need it to make them plumb.

4 After setting both side panels in place, attach the first of the back boards. Make certain it is level before going on to add the remaining boards.

5 Slide the boards for the front of the bin into place in the channel formed by the two 2×2 wooden stakes on the side panels.

6 Begin filling your compost bin. As you add materials, you can add boards to the front. When you want to turn the pile, remove boards.

Difficulty Level: **CHALLENGING**

Tools and Materials: **Saw, mallet, level, drill, hammer, 1×6 boards, 2×2 wooden stakes, 1-in. pipe-clamps, ¾-in. electrical conduit, screws.**

ADDING A COVER

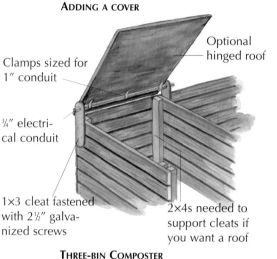

Clamps sized for 1″ conduit

¾″ electrical conduit

1×3 cleat fastened with 2½″ galvanized screws

Optional hinged roof

2×4s needed to support cleats if you want a roof

Add a top to the bin to keep rainwater out. Make it from plywood and use 1-in. pipe clamps to hold electrical conduit in place. Drill 1-in. holes in supporting boards for the conduit.

THREE-BIN COMPOSTER

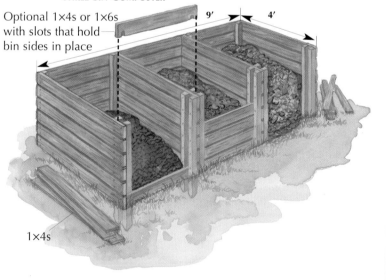

Optional 1×4s or 1×6s with slots that hold bin sides in place

9′

4′

1×4s

Three bins placed side by side allow you to turn compost into a new area as it decomposes. To hold the front boards in place, cut slots into a 1x4 where the top boards can fit.

heats up after it is turned and most materials are decomposed. Look at the finished product closely; if you can still recognize some of the plant materials, it's likely that the microorganisms need more nitrogen to finish the job.

Wait for compost to cure. While it is decomposing, compost can produce compounds that are phytotoxic, or poisonous to plants. Also, instead of supplying plants with nutrients, unfinished compost can actually cause a deficiency. This is because soil microorganisms attack the undecomposed bits as soon as you put the compost within reach. But these organisms need nitrogen to complete the job, and they take it from the surrounding soil. Plants growing in the area may suffer from a temporary nitrogen deficiency until the composting is complete. Finished compost, on the other hand, slowly releases nitrogen to plants. Consequently, you're wise to let your compost cure awhile before you apply it to be certain that decomposition is really finished.

To cure compost, pile it in an out-of-way spot, cover it with a tarp to keep the rain or snow off, and let it sit—undisturbed—for one to three months. If you plan to use it in a vegetable garden in the spring, you can also cure the compost by spreading it over the bare soil in late fall after the crops are finished; the compost will cure in place over the winter and be ready for spring planting.

Nutrients

Plants use simple mineral elements, such as magnesium, and more complicated compounds, such as nitrates (nitrogen combined with oxygen), as nutrients. Plant nutrients are generally classified as major (or macro) nutrients, minor nutrients, and trace (or micro) nutrients, depending on the quantity of each that most plants need. Nitrogen, phosphorous, and potassium are considered major nutrients; calcium, sulfur, and magnesium are considered minor nutrients; and copper, iron, manganese, zinc, boron, and molybdenum are some of the many trace elements.

Good garden soils contain all the nutrients necessary for plant growth, in roughly the correct proportions. Balance is essential. If the soil lacks enough of a particular nutrient, plants will weaken or die, while excess amounts of particular nutrients can prevent plants from taking up other needed elements, even if they're abundant. Humus-rich compost is crucial to the nutrient balance in the soil. It not only supplies nutrients in balanced proportions, it also holds them where plant roots can find them and keeps them from being washed out of the soil in a heavy rain.

COMPOST BINS

A DETERMINED COMPOSTER can find a way to compost in almost any situation. Drill holes in the bottom and lower sides of an old garbage pail to turn it into an unobtrusive compost bin. Remember to fluff up the material to add oxygen. Secure the lid to keep animals out.

WORM BINS provide entertainment as well as lots of the very best compost—worm castings.

USE FINISHED COMPOST or soil to cover composting ingredients layered into trenches in the ground.

TESTING YOUR SOIL

BEFORE YOU BEGIN A new garden, have the soil tested. Different laboratories conduct different kinds of tests. In general, tests done by laboratories associated with your Cooperative Extension are less expensive than those done by private labs. The Extension office is also the place to find the latest horticultural research tailored to your region. You will find your county's Extension service listed in the phone book under "Cooperative." However, private labs usually give more detailed soil reports. Look on the Web under "Soil Testing" for a list of private labs.

Take your samples at the same time every year. The test measures the nutrients that are currently available, and that availability changes with the soil temperature and season. It's best to test in mid- to late-summer, because that tells you what is available at the peak of the season. Test the soil every year for the first two years of the garden; every other year for the next four to five years, if all is well; and only every third or fourth year thereafter.

pH

pH is the measure of the acid/alkaline balance in the soil. Technically, it's a measurement of the concentration of hydrogen ions. Pure acids contain lots of hydrogen ions, so the more hydrogen ions in your soil, the more acid it will be. Lower numbers on the pH scale indicate greater acidity; pH numbers above 7 indicate alkaline soil. Areas with high rainfall tend to have acid soils. Dry regions tend to be alkaline.

The pH level is important because it determines which nutrients are available to plants. As shown on the table to the right, the majority of nutrients are most available when the soil is slightly acid. Either excessively acid or alkaline conditions will cause availability problems, locking nutrients out of plants' reach even when large amounts are present. In very acid conditions, for example, manganese can become so accessible that it can cause problems. In alkaline soils, plants usually suffer from severe micronutrient deficiencies which can stunt or kill them. If your soil is too acid or alkaline, you can waste a lot of money on fertilizer, and your plants may still suffer from nutrient deficiencies.

Adjusting the pH. Correcting the soil pH is the first step toward creating fertile soil. As already discussed, if the pH of the soil is off, no amount of fertilizer can solve the plants' nutrient problems. The nutrients will simply become locked up if the soil chemistry is out of balance.

When you receive your soil test results, you'll learn how

to adjust your soil's pH if necessary. If the test results show a pH of 6.2 to 7.5, you won't have to do anything. Most garden plants require a pH of 6.2 to 6.7, with 6.5 being ideal. If the test results indicate a pH above 7.5, you will need to bring it down by adding elemental sulfur. If you are lowering the pH more than half a unit, apply only half the recommended amount initially. Then, two to three months later, apply the balance. If your test results show a pH lower than 6.2, the lab will suggest a particular quantity of ground limestone. But you can't just add a standard amount of lime to raise the pH to an acceptable level. A sandy soil low in

SOIL pH

This table shows the availability of plant nutrients; the narrower the band width, the less available the nutrients.

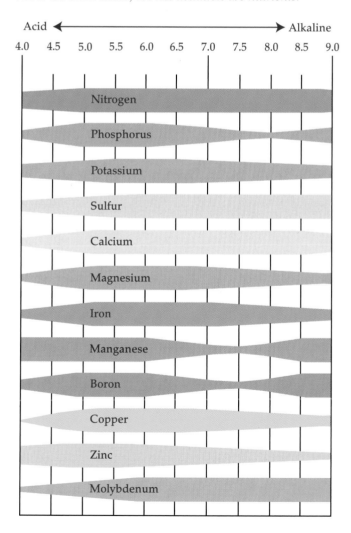

Acid ← → Alkaline

4.0 4.5 5.0 5.5 6.0 6.5 7.0 7.5 8.0 8.5 9.0

Nitrogen
Phosphorus
Potassium
Sulfur
Calcium
Magnesium
Iron
Manganese
Boron
Copper
Zinc
Molybdenum

HOW NUTRIENTS MOVE THROUGH SOIL TO PLANTS

HERE'S HOW NUTRIENTS ARE CARRIED by soil particles, and how plant roots can capture them: All of the nutrient elements in soil, called ions, carry an electrical charge. The positively charged elements, called cations, include calcium, magnesium, ammonium, and potassium, as well as many of the trace elements. Mineral elements are present in rocks and are released as these rocks weather in the process of becoming soil particles. They also enter the soil in organic matter or in amendments such as limestone or other rock powders. Mineral cations are water-soluble; when dissolved they make alkaline substances, called bases, rather than acids. Because they are so soluble, water can leach, or drain, them from the soil. One of the first nutrients to wash out is N (in the ammonium form), which is one of the most useful forms for plants.

Fortunately, another mechanism comes into play, preventing many nutrients from just running off into the nearest stream. Both humus and clay particles have huge numbers of negatively charged ("cation exchange") sites on their surfaces. Because cations are positively charged, they are attracted to these sites. They are held there until one of two things happens. A nearby plant root can release a positively charged hydrogen ion in exchange for a nutrient ion on one of the sites, or a huge rainstorm can flood the soil with water, forcing many cations to leach away.

The negatively charged particles are called anions and include phosphorus and sulfur, the nitrate form of nitrogen, and some forms of carbon. Most of the anions are stored in organic matter in the soil and become available to plants through microbial decomposition. Humus contains the ideal proportion of the anion nutrients for most plants: 100 parts carbon: 10 parts nitrogen: 1 part phosphorus: 1 part sulfur. In the soil solution, anions change their form quite readily, often making acids. Plant roots pick up anion nutrients from the soil solution.

TESTING SOIL | *Difficulty Level:* **EASY**

SOME HOME TESTS for your soil are easy and reliable enough that you can count on their results. Wait to perform these tests until the soil has warmed, and ideally, do them at the same time every year.

Tools and Materials: **Trowel, pH test kit, soil life test kit.**

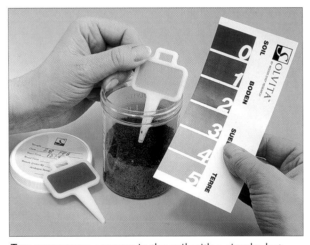

TEST BIOLOGICAL ACTIVITY in the soil with a simple, but accurate test called the soil life test. If the soil tests low, you can add compost to remedy it.

TEST pH IN SEVERAL LOCATIONS in your garden. If your soil is like most, you'll find slight variations from place to place. Amend accordingly.

organic matter with a pH of 5.5 will require less limestone than a loamy clay at the same pH with lots of organic matter, because both clay and humus can absorb more calcium. (Because the rich loamy clay holds more in reserve, it can go longer before needing additional limestone.)

Alkaline soils are usually high in salts, sometimes as a result of irrigation and sometimes from leftover fertilizers that contained a lot of salts. No matter what the cause, the salt problem must be addressed, too, or plant roots will be unable to take in adequate water. Your lab will recommend a certain quantity of elemental sulfur or gypsum. When you apply these materials, work them into the top couple of inches of the soil, and keep the area moist for a few weeks. It is best to apply these materials in the winter to allow the soil to rest for at least three to four weeks. In extreme southern regions, this resting period may be in midsummer.

If your test results show a pH over 7.5, the lab will suggest a particular quantity of sulfur to help neutralize your alkaline soil. Sulfur is best applied in spring, or a few weeks

SMART TIP

LIME IN THE FALL

The best time to apply lime is in the fall. But spread the lime before the ground freezes, applying it over a cover crop or under a mulch. It will break down over the winter. By spring, the soil should be alkaline ("sweet") enough so that fertilizers will be effective. If you must wait to apply lime in spring, try to do it at least two weeks before planting so that it leaches down in time to do some good. Don't spread lime and fertilizer at the same time, as you'll cause some of the nitrogen in the fertilizer to evaporate.

before planting. The lab may also suggest specific fertilizers to acidify the soil. If you are lowering the pH more than half a unit, apply half the recommended amount initially. Apply the balance three months later.

Test the soil again at the same time you did the year before, to verify that the pH has been corrected. If the correction was a unit or less, you should have been able to adjust it in a single year. However, greater corrections usually require two years. Very alkaline soils may require annual doses of sulfur. Adding compost every year keeps the pH corrected for a much longer time, simply because the compost adds cation exchange sites as well as materials that neutralize the soil.

HOW TO BUILD AN IN-GROUND BED

Difficulty Level: MODERATE

BUILD AN IN-GROUND BED in areas where a raised bed would be obtrusive or if summer droughts are common. Choose a site where the soil has good drainage, or add a layer of pea gravel to the bottom of the bed. The bed shown here is 4×8.

Tools and Materials: **Shovel, spading fork, two 8-ft. long 1×8s and two 4-ft. long 1×8 boards, saw, hammer, topsoil, rockpowder, tarp, four 12-in.-long 1x3 wooden stakes.**

1 After digging down to the correct depth, set stabilizing boards in place, and pound in four 12-inch-long 1x3 wooden stakes.

2 Continue removing soil from the bed until it is level throughout. To aid your eventual cleanup, place all the soil you are removing on a tarp.

3 Use a spading fork to aerate the bottom of the bed. Work from the middle to the edges of the area so you don't step on aerated soil.

4 Fill the bed with top-quality topsoil or compost, bagged or homemade. Fill the area completely, but do not compress the medium.

5 Add rockpowders such as this azomite to the medium for added nutrition. If you're using homemade compost, amend it as necessary.

6 Fill the gap between the side boards and the surrounding soil and then use a shovel to level off the medium in the new bed.

EVERY TIME YOU REMOVE A MAJOR PART OF THE PLANT, you've removed nutrients that could have been returned to the soil. Make up for this by adding a general-purpose fertilizer.

Choosing and using fertilizers. Gardeners often use the terms "fertilizer" and "soil amendment" interchangeably. It's true that both increase the fertility of the soil, but technically there is a difference between the two. A soil amendment is used primarily to improve soil (as by changing soil pH) or benefit microbial life, while a fertilizer is meant to provide plants with nutrients. Sometimes an amendment can act as a fertilizer and vice versa. For example, the compost you spread to improve the soil's drainage may also contribute important nutrients to your plants, and the fish emulsion you feed the spinach may help microorganisms break down a mulch.

The distinction between soil amendments and fertilizers is really only important when you are buying fertilizers. By law, soil amendments do not need to be labeled with their minimum analysis (the amount of nutrients guaranteed to be supplied), but fertilizers do. When you buy a bag of fishmeal, you'll find a series of numbers, such as 9-3-1, printed on the bag. These numbers mean that the product is guaranteed to contain at least 9 percent nitrogen, 3 percent phosphate (a form of phosphorus), and 1 percent

continued on page 30

Soil Amendments and Fertilizers

ALL GARDENS REQUIRE SOME kind of fertilization. How much and what kinds of fertilizer, and how frequently they need it depend on both the soil and the plants. As a general rule, if you remove a significant part of the plant, as you do when harvesting produce or cutting flowers, or if you're gardening in containers, the soil will need greater amounts of fertilizers more frequently. Vegetables and fruits usually require the highest levels of feeding, while herbs and shrubs (except roses) require the least. But there is wide variation within these categories. The plant directories in Chapters 3, 5, 6, 7, and 8 give information about the fertility needs of individual plants.

NET WEIGHT 40 LBS.

QUIK GREEN 5-10

GUARANTEED ANALYSIS

Total Nitrogen (N) . . . .
Available Phosphate (P_2O_5) . . . .
Soluble Potash (K_2O) . . . .

FERTILIZERS derived from chemical treatment give larger amounts of immediately available nutrients but can injure delicate roots and benefical soil organisms.

NUTRIENT CONTRIBUTIONS OF COMMON SOIL AMENDMENTS AND FERTILIZERS

Soil amendments and fertilizers derived from natural sources often contain much more than simply mineral nutrients. The table below lists some of their other benefits as well as giving application rates.

MATERIAL	PRIMARY BENEFITS	ANALYSIS (N-P-K, PLUS MINOR & TRACE NUTRIENTS)	AVERAGE APPLICATION RATE PER 1,000 SQ. FT. WHEN SOILS TEST:			NOTES
			LOW	MODERATE	ADEQUATE	
Alfalfa meal	Organic matter, nitrogen	5-1-2	50 lbs.	35 lbs.	25 lbs.	Contains a natural growth stimulant plus trace elements
Aragonite	Calcium	96% calcium carbonate	100 lbs.	50 lbs.	25 lbs.	Can replace limestone
Calcitic lime		65-80% calcium carbonate 3-15% magnesium carbonate	Use soil test; quantity depends on soil type as well as pH			Use in soils with adequate magnesium and low calcium
Colloidal phosphate	Phosphate	0-2-2	60 lbs.	25 lbs.	10 lbs.	Adds to soil reserves as well as available quantity
Compost	Organic matter, soil life	0.5-0.5-0.5 to 3-3-3	200 lbs.	100 lbs.	50 lbs.	Adds balanced nutrients & the soil life to make them available
Dolomitic lime	Calcium, magnesium	51% calcium carbonate 40% magnesium carbonate	Use soil test; quantity depends on soil type as well as pH			Use in soils with low magnesium and low calcium
Epsom salts	Magnesium, sulfur	10% magnesium, 13% sulfur	5 lbs.	3 lbs.	1 lbs.	Use when magnesium is so low that other sources won't work
Fish emulsion	Nitrogen	4-1-1; 5% sulfur	2 oz.	1 oz.	1oz.	Can be used as a foliar feed too, mix 50/50 with liquid seaweed, and dilute to half the recommended strength
Granite meal	Potash, trace elements	4% total potash; 67% silicas, 19 trace elements	100 lbs.	50 lbs.	25 lbs.	Rock powders add to long-term soil fertility and health
Greensand	Potash, trace elements	7% potash, 32 trace minerals	100 lbs.	50 lbs.	25 lbs.	Excellent potash source
Kelp meal	Potash, trace elements	1.5-0.5-2.5	20 lbs.	10 lbs.	5 lbs.	Best for spot applications where extra potash is needed
Rock phosphate	Phosphate	0-3-3; 32% calcium, 11 trace elements	60 lbs.	25 lbs.	10 lbs.	Apply when you start the garden and every four years once soil phosphate levels are adequate
Soybean meal	Nitrogen	7-0.5-2.3	50 lbs.	25 lb.	10 lbs.	Excellent soil amendment during the second half of the season
Sul-Po-Mag	Sulfur, potash, magnesium	0-0-22; 11% magnesium, 22% sulfur	10 lbs.	7 lbs.	5 lbs.	Use only if magnesium levels are low & never with dolomitic lime
Worm castings	Organic matter	0.5-0.5-0.3	n/a	n/a	n/a	Use in potting soils and for spot fertilizing

continued from page 28

potash (a form of potassium). Fishmeal also contains a certain amount of calcium, but the law does not require companies to label percentages of minor and trace nutrients. The table on page 29 lists the average nutrient content of many of the most common fertilizers and amendments, including minor and trace nutrients. If you correlate the table with the results from your soil test, you'll be able to add the nutrients your plants need.

Nutrients are spoken of as "being available" or "being in reserve." This refers to the present form of the nutrient. For example, several commercial fertilizer blends contain about 4 percent phosphate in a form that plants can take up. However, they also contain close to the same quantity of phosphate that won't be available until soil microorganisms decompose and transform it. If you add this blend to a soil with low organic matter, you can't really count on getting more than the nitrogen and phosphate that is immediately available. However, if you also add compost or large quantities of organic mulches to boost the activity of soil microbes, more phosphate from that source will slowly become available over the next few years.

Fertilizers in the bag. Numerous companies make blended fertilizers from natural ingredients. These fertilizers do not usually burn plant roots or injure soil life because they release their nutrients more slowly than most synthetic blends. (This also means they last longer.) However, such natural ingredients as Chilean nitrate can burn plants and harm soil organisms. When looking for a fertilizer, check the label. It should contain ingredients such as dried or composted animal manures, alfalfa meal, feather meal, soybean meal, rock phosphate, and kelp meal. The analysis of these fertilizers is lower than that of fertilizers made from synthetic chemicals; it may range from 2-1-2 to 8-5-5, often in the 5-3-4 range. If you compare them with the synthetic 10-10-10 sorts of fertilizers, it may seem as if you are paying far more per unit of nutrient. However, the organic fertilizers actually contain more than is indicated on the package. As microorganisms break down the materials, additional nutrients are released over time. Organic fertilizer blends also contain many valuable trace elements, which are missing from synthetic blends.

Using fertilizers and soil amendments. In most cases, the best results come from fertilizing in the early spring. Exceptions to this rule are noted in the plant directories. Your soil test and the table will help you select appropriate fertilizers. In most cases, a soil that is deficient in one nutrient is defi-

cient in others too. And, because you want to apply the proper proportion of one nutrient to another, the safest course is to start by adding a "complete" fertilizer that contains major, minor, and trace elements. Compost or one of the natural blends discussed above are your best bets. Follow suggested application rates on the label; avoid overfertilizing because it makes plants more prone to pests and diseases.

Sometimes a plant is more deficient in one nutrient than the others. If the lab that tested your soil recommended natural fertilizers, all you have to do is follow its directions. But if you want to create your own mixes, you'll need to do some math. You should strive for a proportion of two to four times as much nitrogen to phosphate, and one to two times as much potash as nitrogen. However, most perennial fruiting and flowering crops require slightly less nitrogen relative to phosphate and potash; and perennial herbs require even less nitrogen.

FOR PRECISION'S SAKE, mix amendments and fertilizers such as this leaf mold, woodash, rockpowder, compost, and organic fertilizer blend before applying it to the soil.

A LIVING MULCH of clover on these pathways keeps weeds down and adds nutrients.

LOW WHITE DUTCH CLOVER is an excellent choice for a living mulch crop.

COVER CROPS AND GREEN MANURES

COVER CROPS AND GREEN manures make the garden healthier by adding specific nutrients, increasing the supplies of organic matter available to soil organisms, and bringing up minerals from the subsoil. They also smother weeds, prevent erosion over the winter, and break up hard pans that the tiller might have created.

The difference between cover crops and green manures is a matter of both timing and purpose. If a spring-planted crop will be tilled under because it will add needed nutrients to the soil, it's a green manure. If it's planted in late summer through early fall to hold the soil from eroding during winter snows, rains, and runoff and will be tilled under the following spring, it's more correctly called a cover crop. But even so, green manures left in place over the winter prevent erosion, and cover crops add both nutrients and organic matter.

Both types of crops are most useful in the vegetable garden, where whole plants are removed every year and plantings are staggered through the season. Cover crops are wonderful where annual bedding plants are routinely grown. They not only improve the soil, they also look neat and tidy through the fall and winter, giving the garden a finished look. In the perennial flower garden, they are most useful if they are used before the garden is planted. Green manures

SMART TIP
PLANTING COVER CROPS

A GOOD TRICK WITH cover crops is to plant a non-hardy crop in areas of the garden that are slow to dry in the spring or where you want to make the first plantings of the season. The winter-killed cover crop will hold the soil over the winter, and by spring, it will have left a nice mulch behind. Pull the dead crop aside where you want to plant— you'll find that it breaks down within only a few weeks during warm weather.

COVER CROPS AND GREEN MANURES

CROP	LIFECYCLE	PRIMARY PURPOSE	SEEDING RATE LB/1000 SQ. FT.*	PLANTING TIME	TIME TO TURN UNDER	SOIL TYPE
Alfalfa *Medicago sativa*	Perennial	Contributes nitrogen	3	Spring	After 2 years	pH 6.5–7; well-drained
Buckwheat *Fagopyrum esculentum*	Annual	Contributes phosphorus/ smothers weeds	3	Early-mid summer	Late summer- early fall	Widely adaptable
Clover, Dutch white *Trifolium repens*	Perennial	Contributes nitrogen	0.25	Spring-late summer	Fall or following year if at all	pH 6.5–7; well-drained
Clover, Mammoth red *Trifolium pratense*	Biennial	Contributes nitrogen	0.5	Spring-fall	After 1–2 years	Well-drained, tolerates pH of 6.0 if limed at seeding
Clover, Crimson *Trifolium incarnatum*	Annual	Contributes nitrogen	0.5–0.66	Late summer in south/ spring in north	Late spring in South/ midsummer in north	Well-drained, pH 6.5–7
Marigold, 'Sparky' *Tagetes erecta*	Annual	Controls nematodes	2–3 oz.	Mid-late spring	After flowering	Adaptable
Oats *Avena sativa*	Annual	Prevent erosion	3–4	Early spring or fall	At flowering; winter-kills in north	Adaptable
Peas, field, 'Trapper' *Pisum sativum*	Annual	Contributes nitrogen/ smothers weeds	3	Early spring	After pods form	Well-drained
Rapeseed *Brassica napus*	Annual	Alkalizes soil	3 oz.	Mid-spring	After flowering	Adaptable
Ryegrass *Lolium multiflorum*	Annual	Adds organic matter	2	Early spring-late summer	At flowering; winterkills in north	Adaptable
Sweetclover *Melilotus officinalis*	Biennial	Contributes nitrogen; breaks up hardpan	0.5	Mid spring-summer	After flowering or following spring	pH close to 7, well-drained
Vetch, Hairy *Vicia villosa*	Annual	Contributes Nitrogen	1–3	Spring-late summer	After flowering or early following spring	Adaptable
Winter Rye *Lolium*	Annual	Adds organic matter; phytotoxic to weeds	4–6	Spring through mid-fall	At flowering or early following Spring	Adaptable

*Decrease seeding rate appropriately when using the seed in a mix.

and cover crops loosen the soil and greatly reduce weed populations.

Try to plant a fast-growing crop such as oats, buckwheat, field peas, or ryegrass whenever soil will be bare of plants for a month or more. For example, an early planting of oats will prepare the soil for midseason greens or cabbage-family crops.

Many gardeners use white Dutch clover as a "living mulch." After they have transplanted a crop such as broccoli, they broadcast the clover seed between the plants, which prevents weeds from growing. Dutch clover also makes good garden pathways. In the fall, prepare by making beds and marking off the pathways. In very early spring, when the snow has gone but frost is still common, toss clover seed on all the paths. By the time you want to get into the garden, the clover will be large enough to tolerate being lightly walked over. Once it is established, mow it once a month to prevent its seed from creating a weed problem.

TOPOGRAPHY AFFECTS MICROCLIMATES

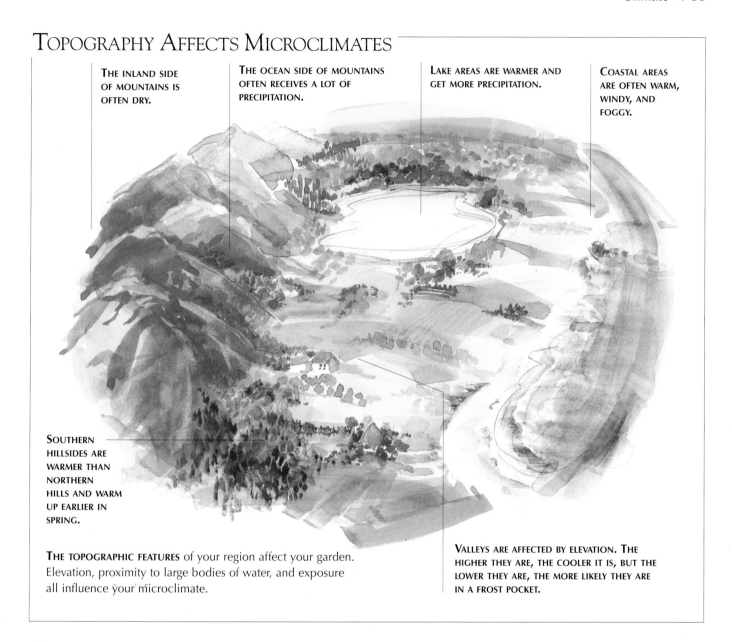

THE INLAND SIDE OF MOUNTAINS IS OFTEN DRY.

THE OCEAN SIDE OF MOUNTAINS OFTEN RECEIVES A LOT OF PRECIPITATION.

LAKE AREAS ARE WARMER AND GET MORE PRECIPITATION.

COASTAL AREAS ARE OFTEN WARM, WINDY, AND FOGGY.

SOUTHERN HILLSIDES ARE WARMER THAN NORTHERN HILLS AND WARM UP EARLIER IN SPRING.

THE TOPOGRAPHIC FEATURES of your region affect your garden. Elevation, proximity to large bodies of water, and exposure all influence your microclimate.

VALLEYS ARE AFFECTED BY ELEVATION. THE HIGHER THEY ARE, THE COOLER IT IS, BUT THE LOWER THEY ARE, THE MORE LIKELY THEY ARE IN A FROST POCKET.

CLIMATE

BEGIN PREPARING FOR YOUR garden by learning about the climate in your area and then the microclimates in your yard. If you are new to the area, ask the Cooperative Extension or a gardening neighbor when the first frost date is in the fall and when the last frost date is in the spring. Look at the Hardiness and Heat Zone maps on page 34 and 35 to determine the zones of your garden.

Use your powers of observation. Study the light patterns in your garden at different times of the year and different times of day; then make note of it. Look at the tree canopy to determine whether some judicious pruning will give you more light. Walk your property to get a sense of places that stay wet and those that don't. Be aware of high spots and dips, and where the wind whistles through as well as "dead spots," where there is little air circulation.

Make notes in a journal, and keep track of all these pre-existing factors as you plan your garden. Unlike the soil and drainage, there is little you can do to change the climate where you garden. But you can adapt your plantings to suit the existing climate.

HARDINESS ZONE MAP

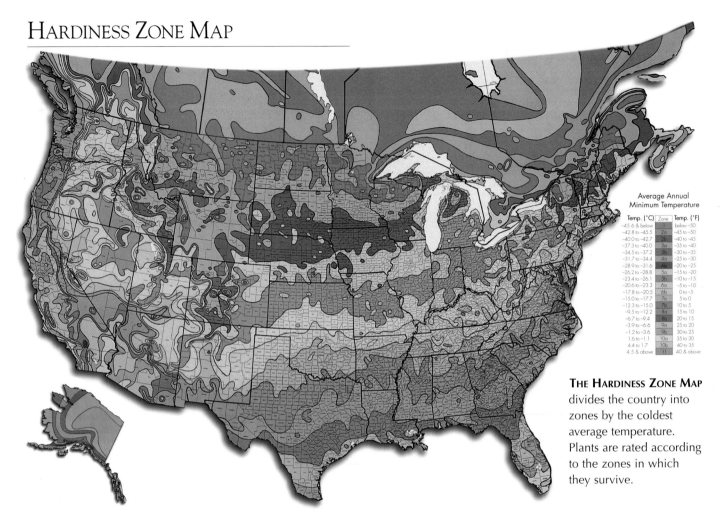

Average Annual Minimum Temperature

Temp. (°C)	Zone	Temp. (°F)
-45.6 & below	1	below -50
-42.8 to -45.5	2a	-45 to -50
-40.0 to -42.7	2b	-40 to -45
-37.3 to -40.0	3a	-35 to -40
-34.5 to -37.2	3b	-30 to -35
-31.7 to -34.4	4a	-25 to -30
-28.9 to -31.6	4b	-20 to -25
-26.2 to -28.8	5a	-15 to -20
-23.4 to -26.1	5b	-10 to -15
-20.6 to -23.3	6a	-5 to -10
-17.8 to -20.5	6b	0 to -5
-15.0 to -17.7	7a	5 to 0
-12.3 to -15.0	7b	10 to 5
-9.5 to -12.2	8a	15 to 10
-6.7 to -9.4	8b	20 to 15
-3.9 to -6.6	9a	25 to 20
-1.2 to -3.6	9b	30 to 25
1.6 to -1.1	10a	35 to 30
4.4 to 1.7	10b	40 to 35
4.5 & above	11	40 & above

THE HARDINESS ZONE MAP divides the country into zones by the coldest average temperature. Plants are rated according to the zones in which they survive.

Hardiness and Heat Zone Maps

The best place to start planning is with the USDA Hardiness Zone Map and the American Horticultural Society's Heat Zone Map. The Hardiness Zone Map is based on records of the average minimum temperatures all over the U.S. and Canada. If you learned what your zone was long ago, you might want to check it again. The boundaries of many of the zones were changed in 1990, based on actual changes in the climate since 1965. The "A" and "B" divisions in each zone are a further refinement. For example, even though both the Berkshire Mountain area and the Pioneer Valley of Massachusetts are listed as Zone 5, the mountains are 5A while most of the valley is 5B. The higher altitude makes mountain winters significantly colder than they are in the valley, only a few miles away.

The Hardiness Zone Map is invaluable when you are shopping for seeds and plants. All perennials are rated according to the zone to which they are winter hardy. In general, you are safe if you stick with plants having the same rating as your zone. But you'd be wise to make an exception to this rule when choosing very expensive stock, fruit trees that bloom early in the season, and any plants that will be a focal point in your yard. In these cases, choose plants that are rated for the next colder zone. This is when the "A" and "B" ratings come in handy, too. As an example, Chinese wisteria (*Wisteria sinensis*) is listed as hardy to Zone 5. If you live in a Zone 5B area, you can be fairly certain that it will survive in your yard. However, if you live in Zone 5A, you might be better off growing the Japanese wisteria (*Wisteria floribunda*), because it is hardy to Zone 4.

Heat Zone Map. Researchers have recently discovered that plants begin to suffer cellular damage at temperatures over 86°F. The American Horticultural Society's Heat Zone Map, introduced in 1998, divides the United States into 12

HEAT-ZONE MAP

THE HEAT ZONE MAP divides the country into zones according to the average annual number of days that temperatures exceed 86°F.

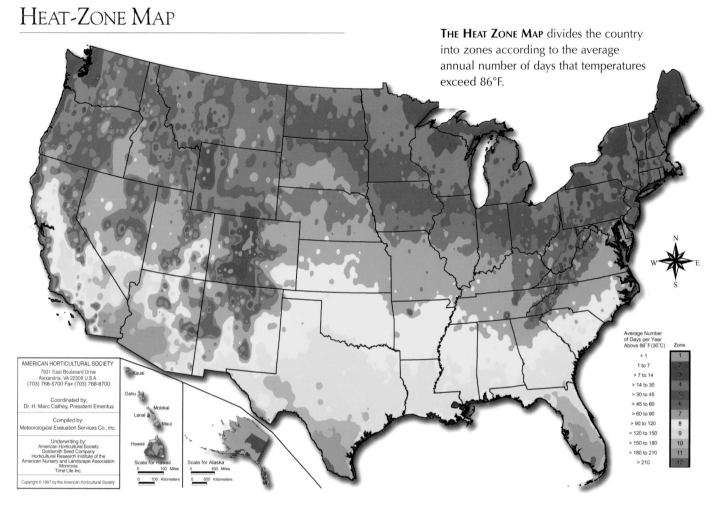

AMERICAN HORTICULTURAL SOCIETY
7931 East Boulevard Drive
Alexandria, VA 22308 U.S.A.
(703) 768-5700 Fax (703) 768-8700

Coordinated by:
Dr. H. Marc Cathey, President Emeritus

Compiled by:
Meteorological Evaluation Services Co., Inc.

Underwriting by:
American Horticultural Society
Goldsmith Seed Company
Horticultural Research Institute of the
American Nursery and Landscape Association
Monrovia
Time Life Inc.

Copyright © 1997 by the American Horticultural Society

Average Number of Days per Year Above 86°F (30°C)	Zone
< 1	1
1 to 7	2
> 7 to 14	3
> 14 to 30	4
> 30 to 45	5
> 45 to 60	6
> 60 to 90	7
> 90 to 120	8
> 120 to 150	9
> 150 to 180	10
> 180 to 210	11
> 210	12

Scale for Hawaii
0   100 Miles
0   100 Kilometers

Scale for Alaska
0   500 Miles
0   500 Kilometers

zones based on the average number of "heat days," or days over 86°F, that a region experiences. The zones range from Zone 1 (no heat days) to Zone 12 (210 heat days a year). More and more plant breeders are now labeling plants with both USDA Hardiness Zones and American Horticultural Society Heat Zones. Just as various factors affect a plant's ability to survive cold, so are there factors which affect a plant's ability to survive heat, including humidity. Use both maps as starting points. Then allow your own experience and the experience of other gardeners in your area to guide you in your choice of plants.

Learn your frost-free dates. Frost damage can be a threat to plants at both ends of the season. In the spring, late frosts often kill the blossoms of fruiting plants. Peaches, apricots, nectarines, and early strawberries are the most vulnerable, but apples, pears, and plums can also be harmed by an extremely late frost. Here again, location matters. If your fruit trees are positioned on a slope, it's likely that a light frost will roll right over your garden, doing only minimal damage. However, if the fruit trees are planted at the bottom of a hill, the frost may settle on your plants, causing serious problems.

In the fall, early frosts end the growing season for many of the fruiting vegetable crops. Tomato, pepper, eggplant, snap bean, summer squash, cucumber, and melon plants all blacken and die if their leaf temperature falls below 32°F. But often, the first autumn frost is only a teaser. After that one clear, cold night, you may have several more weeks of good growing weather. In Chapter 6, Vegetable Gardens, page 150, you'll learn how to protect your crops from light frosts with season-extending products and techniques. But as a first step, you can also position your less hardy vegetable plants so that frost is less likely to damage them. If possible, place them near the crest to halfway down a south-facing slope.

Optimize Sun Exposure for Fruiting Crops

South-facing slopes "see" more sunlight than north-facing slopes. Consequently, plants growing there experience more daylight hours, or growing hours, in a season. That's why sun-loving vegetable crops that fruit, such as tomatoes, do best in this location. However, a slope is rarely the best spot for growing fruit. The same south slope that does so much for tomatoes and melons can decimate your fruit trees and even your strawberries, which flower early in the season. The warmer temperatures early in the season encourage these crops to bloom too soon, making them vulnerable to sudden late frosts.

Northern slopes protect against spring frosts. Place fruiting plants and trees on north slopes whenever possible, so they bloom a bit later in spring, when there's less chance of a late cold snap. The week or so delay in their blooming can make the difference between having fruit or not in a year when the last spring frost comes late. In Chapter 8, "Fruit," page 218, you'll learn additional ways to protect plants from frost damage, but location is the best defense.

Very tender fruiting plants benefit from being planted behind a windscreen or hedgerow for protection against the wind. Air movement, whether gentle breezes or strong winds, also affects plants. Because of the reasons explained above, commercial fruit growers try to plant their crops on a north-

facing slope in rows that run parallel to the prevailing winds. This orientation means that a wind can blow through the leaves from one end of the row to the other. In humid conditions, wind helps to disperse water vapor around the leaves. As explained in Chapter 9, "Preventing Weeds, Pests, and Diseases," page 266, this simple wind action can help to prevent many of the most destructive plant diseases.

Winter wind chills can be devastating to plants. If you choose plants known to be hardy in your zone, you may never lose so much as an azalea to the weather. But then again, extreme winters are always possible. To be on the safe side, protect your most treasured plants through the worst of the year. You'll find instructions for creating windscreens and wrapping plants in the Winter Care section of Chapter 4, "Specialty Flower Gardens," page 120.

Heating and Chilling Hours

Most fruiting plants require a certain number of hours above and below specific temperatures to perform well. "Heating hours" are calculated as the number of hours above 65°F to which a plant is exposed. Plants with high heating-hour requirements include some types of sweet corn, jujube trees, and many citrus cultivars. In the case of corn, choose a cultivar that's recommended for your area. If you do, the corn

TENDER TOMATOES AND SQUASH die in freezing temperatures, while the more cold-hardy mums, beets, cabbage, and salad greens can survive temperatures into the mid 20s.

PLACE FRUIT TREES on a northern slope so that blooming is delayed as long as possible.

Avoid problems with heating or chilling requirements by choosing plants that are recommended for your area. For example, if you live where winters are mild, plant fruit cultivars with low chilling requirements. If you want to grow peaches, you might opt for a variety such as 'Flordawon', which needs only 50 hours of chilling, instead of 'Polly', which needs 1,100 hours of cold. If you do choose to experiment a bit, ask the supplier about the requirements of the plant you are buying. Your Cooperative Extension Service will be able to tell you the average heating and chilling hours required for particular fruits as well as the average numbers of heating and chilling hours in your location. Stay on the conservative side when you choose plants, and you won't have a problem.

APPLE TREES can provide beauty and bounty, but choose them according to their temperature requirements.

All Sunlight Is Not Equal

Besides temperature, many other factors determine whether or not plants thrive. These include the intensity and duration of the sunlight; moisture, drainage, and fertility characteristics of the soil; average relative humidity; length of the day; as well as the length of the growing season. Unfortunately,

should make ears well before frost in all but the wettest, coldest summers. Local nurseries can tell you whether particular citrus and jujube cultivars are appropriate to your location. It's wise to follow that advice so you don't suffer the frustration of watching unripe fruit succumb to winter cold. Other than these plants, you won't need to worry about heating-hour requirements if you choose plants rated to grow in your zone or colder.

Chilling hours break dormancy.

Many plants cannot break winter dormancy until they have been exposed to a certain number of hours with temperatures below 45°F. Apple trees and daffodils are two examples of the many plants that need a cold winter dormant period. If a cultivar is hardy in your area but requires a longer cold period than your garden receives, the plant may not be able to break bud and start growing in the spring.

SUN-SHADE PATTERNS

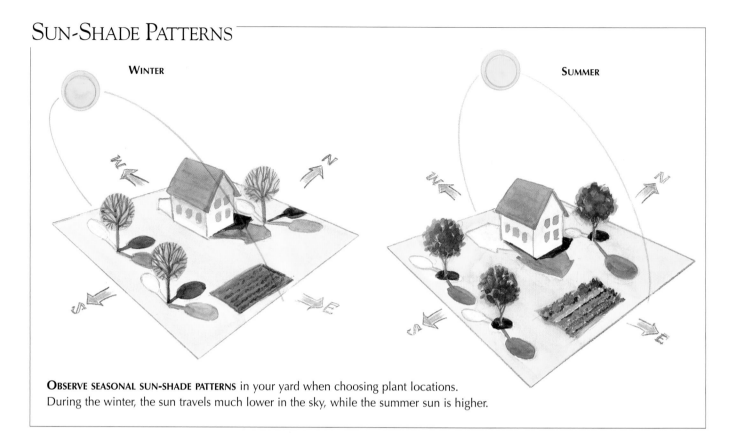

WINTER

SUMMER

OBSERVE SEASONAL SUN-SHADE PATTERNS in your yard when choosing plant locations. During the winter, the sun travels much lower in the sky, while the summer sun is higher.

no maps provide this information. Instead, you must rely on advice from experienced gardeners, local garden clubs, horticultural societies, and your own experience.

Full-sun plants need six hours of sun. Plants vary in their light requirements. When you read plant descriptions here and in other gardening books, you'll see terms such as "full sun," "partial sun," "filtered light," "semi-shade," and "shade." Without explanation, these terms can be confusing. For example, it would be easy to assume that "full sun" plants needed bright light from dawn to dusk every day. Fortunately, that isn't true. "Full sun" plants prosper in as little as six hours a day of bright, unobstructed sunlight. For the rest of the time, they can happily live on filtered light or dappled shade. They'll do well with much more light than six hours, too, but they absolutely require a minimum of six.

Shade plants need just two hours of sun. On the other side of the light requirement spectrum, the term "shade" means that the location gets at least two hours of full sun a day or dappled shade all day long. The terms "dappled" and "filtered" mean just about the same thing. Sunlight filtering

through leaves that are small and lacy rather than large and dense is "filtered light." But if the sun falls intermittently on an area, as it passes through openings in an upper leaf canopy, it may produce a "dappled" effect. In either case, the plants below receive moderate levels of light.

The term "filtered light" means that the plant must receive a minimum of four hours of full sun a day, preferably in the morning. The rest of the day, it needs light filtered through a canopy of leaves or reflected from a nearby wall.

The terms "semi-shade" and "partial shade" are used interchangeably. These mean about three hours of sun a day. If the light is filtered, the time can increase to four hours. Too long an exposure to unfiltered light may cause plants that thrive in partial-shade to dry out, while the measly two hours of bright sunlight that the shade-lovers thrive under might cause them to develop fungal diseases.

Finally, when a plant is listed as "versatile" or "adaptable," you can be certain that it can tolerate a wide range of conditions, generally doing well in light conditions ranging from filtered light to full sun.

It is relatively easy to add some shade to your yard. If you are building a garden for the long term, you can plant a tree or some shrubs, placing them so that they will create shade where you want it in years to come. While you are waiting for trees and shrubs to grow, you can create some instant shade with annual plants. For example, you can set up a trellis or fence to support fast-growing vines, like morning glories, or even plant a patch of tall annuals such as sunflowers or corn.

It is a bit harder, but not impossible, to increase sunlight. If you have an established yard, with many mature trees and shrubs, you may find little space to plant full-sun-lovers. In that case, consider some creative pruning. It's surprising how much light you can gain by selectively removing branches from trees. One way to accomplish this is to limb up—remove lower branches to raise the canopy of leaves higher off the ground. If pruning won't be enough, you'll either need to give up on full-sun plants or take more drastic action. But think long and hard before removing a huge tree; it could be providing some necessary shade to cool your home in summer, as well as being a handsome focal point. Or just concentrate on growing the many beautiful plants that love the shade.

LIMBING UP, or removing the bottom limbs, from trees allows more light into a landscape. If shade is problem, try this before cutting down the trees.

SUN/SHADE LOG

Use a chart like this to keep track of the number of hours of direct sun a particular area receives. By filling it out once a month during the growing season, you'll know which plants will be suitable for the spot.

Hour	Full Sun	Partial Sun	Full Shade
6:00 a.m.			
6:30 a.m.			
7:00 a.m.			
7:30 a.m.			
8:00 a.m.			
8:30 a.m.			
9:00 a.m.			
9:30 a.m.			
10:00 a.m.			
10:30 a.m.			
11:00 a.m.			
11:30 a.m.			
12:00 noon			
12:30 p.m.			
1:00 p.m.			
1:30 p.m.			
2:00 p.m.			
2:30 p.m.			
3:00 p.m.			
3:30 p.m.			
4:00 p.m.			
4:30 p.m.			
5:00 p.m.			
5:30 p.m.			
6:00 p.m.			
6:30 p.m.			
7:00 p.m.			
7:30 p.m.			
8:00 p.m.			

CHAPTER 2

GARDENING BASICS

Creating and maintaining a garden can be one of the most enjoyable things you'll ever do. It's satisfying partially because of the results and partially because of the process itself. Gardening calls on and develops skills that might otherwise lie dormant. For example, designing a garden brings out the artist in almost everyone.

When you create the overall plan and then the specific plantings, you are working with space, mass, and volume much as a sculptor does. The plants allow you to work as a painter; your palette is composed of all the wonderful colors and textures of foliage, bark, and bloom. And the best thing about garden design is that the plants are so beautiful that they will compensate for any but the most outrageous schemes.

You don't need to be physically strong to gar-

THESE BEAUTIFUL SEEDS contain miniature leaves, stem, root, and the nutrients they need to begin growing.

den. In fact, if the thought of heavy work discourages you, you can plan an almost maintenance-free garden. Yet for some people, the hard work involved in double-digging a bed is half the fun. Most people fall somewhere in the middle. While they appreciate the exercise, they don't push it into a marathon sport.

Quiet, meditative time is certainly part of gardening. Special are the early mornings when you're out there alone, and the evenings when a garden walk is the last thing you do.

In and of itself, gardening is not too demanding. Yet, it can be a wonderful source of mental stimulation. The more experienced you get, the more stimulated you'll become. The more you see, the more you'll want to know. Don't be surprised to find yourself reaching for a garden book to learn about the life cycle of a pest. Before long, you'll probably be rattling off arcane horticultural facts as if you'd known them all your life.

But to get the most from your garden, to learn to enjoy it to its fullest, you'll need to get off to a good start. The information in this chapter should help. So before you take shovel to soil, please sit and read a bit.

TOOLS

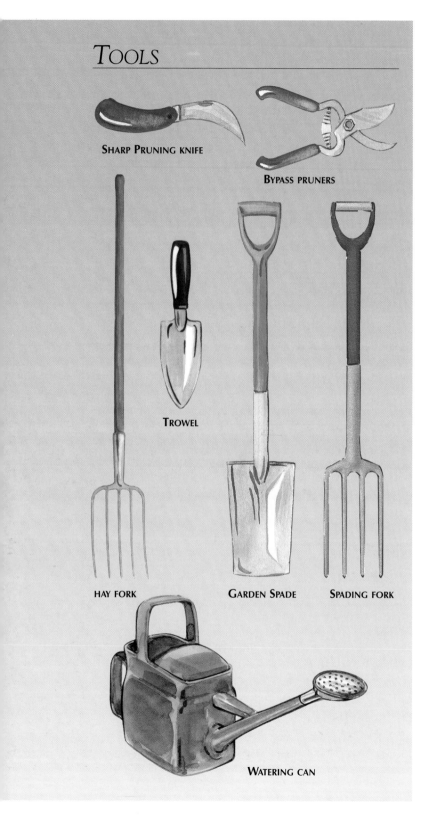

SHARP PRUNING KNIFE

BYPASS PRUNERS

TROWEL

HAY FORK

GARDEN SPADE

SPADING FORK

WATERING CAN

CAMPANULA PERSICIFOLIA (PEACH-BELLS), FROM THE GENUS CAMPANULA, is a favorite garden perennial.

PLANT BASICS

AS YOU GAIN GARDENING EXPERIENCE, you'll gain familiarity with the plants themselves. You'll know how various leaves should be formed, what color they should be, and how far apart on the stem they should grow. With this knowledge, you will be able to step in quickly when something's amiss.

Botanical Names

Plant names can be confusing. When you buy a perennial, it's likely to be labeled with two Latin names in italic print, such as *Campanula persicifolia*. The first of these is the genus name, and the second is the species name. Going further, there are several types of *Campanula persicifolia*, including one called 'Grandiflora Alba' and another called 'Telham Beauty'. These third names, always within single quotation marks, designate particular cultivars of the species. Cultivars are varieties that have been developed while the plant was in cultivation, either naturally or through breeding. Yet, if you're like most people, you'll use a common name to refer to this plant. Many people call it peach-bells, although it is also known as tall bell-flower. Common names can be misunderstood inasmuch

A MEMBER OF THE LARGE *COMPOSITAE* FAMILY, 'Tequilla Sunrise' tickseed belongs to the *Coreopsis* genus.

ALTHOUGH *CAMPANULA GLOMERATA* BELONGS TO THE SAME GENUS as peach-bells, left, you would never know from its appearance.

as two very different plants can share the same common name. No matter where you're from or what language you speak, there will be no confusion if you refer to a plant by its botanical (Latin) name.

Plant families. Only one more category of plant name is important to gardeners, and that's the family name. *Campanula* belong to the *Campanulaceae*, or Bellflower family. Many plants belong to larger, more encompassing families, though, and it's helpful to know about the family to understand the plant better. For example, both *Artemisia* and *Coreopsis* belong to the *Compositae* family, while *Baptisia* belongs to the *Leguminosae* family.

Flower forms. Some plants, such as Kiwi vines, are *dioecious*, meaning that they have male and female flowers on different plants. If you want fruit from them, you'll need a male plant within bee-flying or wind-carrying distance to ensure pollination. Other plants, such as tomatoes, have *perfect* flowers, with male and female parts in the same bloom, and still others, such as squash, are *monoecious* and have both male and female flowers on the same plant.

ANOTHER MEMBER OF THE *COMPOSITAE* FAMILY, 'Powis Castle', shown above, belongs to the *Artemisia* genus.

BUYING PLANTS

BUYING PLANTS IS EASY. But choosing them is another thing altogether, especially when you are trying to fit them into various spots in your yard. Even so, you'll need to know how to pick out the healthiest plants and how to keep them healthy until you plant them.

BUYING LOCAL is the best policy with nursery crops. You'll know that plants can tolerate your climate if they have been propagated and/or grown for at least a season in the neighborhood.

Local Versus Mail Order

Gardeners tend to develop strong opinions about nurseries. Some refuse to buy anything that isn't grown locally, while others insist on buying only from catalogs. There are advantages and disadvantages to both types of shopping.

Buy from local nurseries, if possible, when you are choosing a fruiting plant or a perennial that is marginally hardy in your area. You'll know that the plant has a chance of surviving the worst possible weather you're likely to get. And the growers at the nursery are more likely to have an answer to your question if they are familiar with the plant.

On the other hand, many garden outlets simply buy and sell plants. Even though these stores might be just down the street, they don't qualify as "local." The advantages to buying plants from home and garden centers are the selection and the immediate availability. Wherever you buy your

BUYING HEALTHY PLANTS

Although it is sometimes possible to rescue a sick plant, it can be more trouble than it's worth. In addition to having to carefully nurse it back to health, you also run the risk of infecting other plants in your yard with pests or diseases.

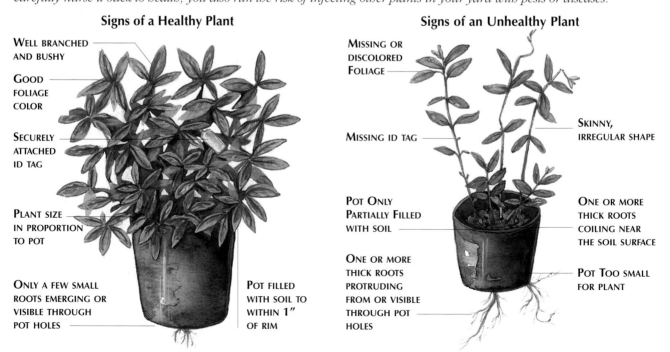

Signs of a Healthy Plant

- WELL BRANCHED AND BUSHY
- GOOD FOLIAGE COLOR
- SECURELY ATTACHED ID TAG
- PLANT SIZE IN PROPORTION TO POT
- ONLY A FEW SMALL ROOTS EMERGING OR VISIBLE THROUGH POT HOLES
- POT FILLED WITH SOIL TO WITHIN 1″ OF RIM

Signs of an Unhealthy Plant

- MISSING OR DISCOLORED FOLIAGE
- MISSING ID TAG
- SKINNY, IRREGULAR SHAPE
- POT ONLY PARTIALLY FILLED WITH SOIL
- ONE OR MORE THICK ROOTS COILING NEAR THE SOIL SURFACE
- ONE OR MORE THICK ROOTS PROTRUDING FROM OR VISIBLE THROUGH POT HOLES
- POT TOO SMALL FOR PLANT

PAY ATTENTION TO THE PLANT'S LIFE SPAN

ANNUAL PLANTS germinate, live, and die in one season. Most live from spring to fall. But some, such as shepherd's purse (*Capsella bursa-pastoris*), are "winter annuals." They germinate in the summer, live through the winter, and then make seeds and die in the late spring.

Biennials live for two years. The first year, most form a leafy rosette. In the spring of the second year, they send up flower stalks, form seeds, and die. Sweet William (*Dianthus barbatus*) and foxglove (*Digitalis purpurea*) are biennials.

Perennials live for three or more years. Some, such as peonies (*Paeonia* species), can live a hundred years, while others, such as delphiniums, can be hard for you to keep robust beyond the usual three years.

BIENNIALS such as this mullein develop a rosette of leaves during their first year and send up a seed stalk in their second.

---

plants, make certain they are hardy to your zone and are in good health. Avoid any plant that appears to be diseased or stressed.

Mail-order nurseries tend to offer a wider selection of plants because they sell a greater volume. However, if the nursery's prices seem too inexpensive to be true, you'll probably be getting very small plants that have been mass-produced. Sometimes you can get a bargain. Sturdy plants, such as daylilies, are so tough that you're usually safe buying them at cut-rate prices. Fruit trees, on the other hand, are vulnerable to so many problems that you'll want to buy them from the best possible source, no matter what the cost.

Between Buying and Planting

To keep mail-order plants in good shape until you plant them, first check to see that the soil or the peat moss around the roots is only as moist as a wrung-out sponge. If the roots are slimy, call the supplier immediately; plants rarely recover from root rot. If the roots are dry, the plant may survive if you sprinkle the roots with water and rewrap.

Heeling-in plants. This practice provides the most protection, but you need to prepare for it in the fall before you buy. In fall, till an area that will drain well in the spring.

Then dig a trench 2 feet deep and 2 feet wide, and fill it with mulch. Place the soil removed from the trench along the edge, and add another foot of mulch over the trench and the loose soil. When your plants arrive in spring, remove the mulch. After checking that the roots are moist enough, rewrap them in the plastic or burlap they came in, and lay them in the trench, with the stems at an angle. Cover them with a foot of soil. You can leave them this way for several weeks, by which time the soil will be workable. Heeling-in works best with woody plants.

SMART TIP

HOW TO STORE PLANTS

If the plants are small, pop them into the vegetable drawer of the refrigerator. You can keep them there for a week or more. Larger plants can be stored in an unheated garage, in a garden shed, or even on a protected porch. If temperatures threaten to plunge below freezing, wrap the roots in old blankets. You can keep them like this for several weeks as long as you check every few days to ensure that the roots are moist. Or you can heel-in the plants as described at left and above.

PROPAGATION

PROPAGATING YOUR OWN PLANTS is thrilling, especially when you have success with a plant or technique that is new to you. It's practical, too. You can start all your spring annuals as well as many herbs and perennials. Once you learn how to propagate vegetatively (from a part of the plant such as the stem or the roots), rather than from seed, you can raise a potentially unlimited number of identical plants from one stock plant, at almost no cost. Good propagation skills can make all the difference between a good garden and a great one, enabling you to develop the garden you might not otherwise be able to afford.

Vegetative Propagation

Vegetative propagation is surrounded by an undeserved mystique. In some ways, it's easier than starting plants from seed. But you do need to learn the techniques as well as match the technique to the plant you're propagating. For example, not all plants will root from a stem cutting, and some die if you divide the roots. The entries in the many directories found in this book include information about the best ways to propagate each plant listed.

You can often figure out the best way to propagate a plant just by looking at it. If a plant produces seeds in your garden, you can probably start it from seed. If it forms a clump, root division will usually work. Plants with many

MOST GARDEN PLANTS, even perennials, reproduce from seeds as well as vegetatively. You can save seeds, as shown here, from nonhybrid plants as long as they have not cross-pollinated with close relatives.

SERPENTINE LAYERING

Many plants, including this clematis, can be vegetatively propagated from branches still connected to the bush.

SERPENTINE LAYERING depends on burying small portions of the branch. After a few months, they will root and you can separate the new plants.

LAYER PLANTS in pots as shown here or directly in the soil, anchoring the slit stem with a ground staple.

stems often root from cuttings. And woody plants can be successfully propagated by layering a stem or a branch tip. These techniques are covered in this chapter.

Stem cuttings. If you have ever rooted the stem of a houseplant in a glass of water, you've worked with a softwood cutting. There are two other kinds of stem cuttings from which you can propagate plants: semi-ripe cuttings and hardwood cuttings. The accompanying illustrations on page 48 and 49 show how to handle each type of stem cutting.

ROOT DIVISION is one of the easiest ways to propagate plants. When plants get crowded for space, simply dig them up and divide the root ball into two or more sections.

TIP LAYERING

If left untrellised, bramble canes, such as those of a blackberry plant, often root themselves. New, rooted plantlets will grow at the base of the plant.

TIP LAYERING depends on burying just the tip of the branch. It too will root in a few months and be ready to be separated from the parent plant.

TO ENCOURAGE BRAMBLE vines to form new roots, anchor the stem with a ground staple and cover with soil; then weigh the stem down with a rock.

Root cuttings. This vegetative method can also be used to propagate many plants. Take root cuttings when the plant is dormant but while the ground is not frozen solid, in the mid- to late-autumn in most parts of the country. It's generally best to leave the plant in place while you take the cutting. Pretend that you are an archeologist and gently scrape the soil aside far enough down so that some new roots are exposed. Make clean cuts with a sharp knife. Take only young, relatively thick 2- to 4-inch-long pieces of roots, but don't take more than three cuttings from a plant. Put the pieces of roots immediately into a plastic bag to keep them moist before you plant them in the medium. Set them upright in the bag because you'll need to know later which end is the "top," that is the end closest to the aboveground portions of the plant.

Prepare the cuttings by slicing them into 2-inch pieces with a straight cut at the top and a slanted cut at the bottom for thick roots. Give thin roots straight cuts at each end. Fill a pot with soilless medium; half vermiculite and half peat moss works well. Plant thick roots upright in the pot, leaving an inch of medium under them. Place thin roots horizontally in the medium. Cover the roots with about ½ inch of medium. Overwinter the root cuttings in a cold frame. Once the roots sprout in the spring, transplant them to pots filled with a good soil mix and continue to grow them until the following fall, when you can transplant them to permanent places.

PROPAGATING CUTTINGS

Working with cuttings is an easy way to propagate your favorite plants. While this kind of propagation might seem intimidating at first, you only have to do it a few times to learn that it is actually easier in many cases than starting plants from seed. However, just as beginning gardeners have to learn that not every seed will germinate and not every seedling will thrive, beginning plant propagators have to learn that not all cuttings produce roots, nor do all rooted cuttings become vigorous plants. Consequently, it's wise to try to root more cuttings than you will eventually use. If you

Propagating with Softwood and Semi-ripe Cuttings

1 Take cuttings from stem tips; take softwood cuttings in late spring and semi-ripe cuttings in early summer. Take pieces that are 3 to 4 inches long. Remove the lower leaves, keeping a few at the tip.

2 Pour a bit of rooting hormone in a small dish. Dip the cuttings into the hormone, and shake off the excess. Throw out any unused hormone in the dish to avoid possible contamination of the powder in the bottle.

3 Make deep holes in the prepared medium with a pencil or dibble, and set the cutting into them, burying at least two nodes of the stem. Firm the medium around the buried stem, and water well. You can fit several cuttings into one pot.

4 Place thin stakes in the pot, and then cover it with a clear plastic bag. Place the pot in a bright, warm location, but out of direct sun. The plastic bag will keep humidity levels high around the cuttings. Open the bag daily to let in fresh, CO_2-laden air.

Difficulty Level: **MODERATE**

have too many, you can always give them away.

Begin by learning what kind of cuttings are appropriate for the plant you are trying to propagate. Specific propagation instructions are given in the Illustrated Plant-by-Plant Directories included in Chapters 3, 5, 6, and 7 of this book.

Tools and Materials: **Bypass pruners, pencil or dibble, thin stakes, pot, plastic bag or wrap, rooting hormone, rooting medium.**

Propagating with Hardwood Cuttings

1 Take hardwood cuttings from stem tips; cuttings should have at least three nodes. Make an angled cut just below a node. Roots will grow from the cut tissue. Remove all the leaves from the cutting.

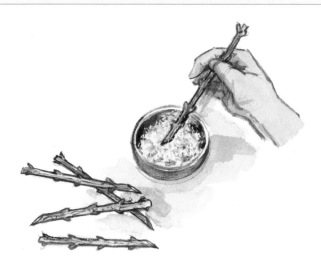

2 Pour some hardwood rooting hormone into a small container, and dip the bottom of the cutting in it. Use the angled cut to remind yourself which end is the bottom.

3 Make deep holes in the prepared rooting medium with a pencil, and place the cuttings in them, burying at least two nodes. Firm the medium around the cuttings.

4 New leaves indicate that roots have developed. Wait until the cutting has several leaves before gently tugging on it. If there is resistance, it is rooted. Pot up the young plants and continue to grow before transplanting them to the garden.

STARTING PLANTS FROM SEEDS is inexpensive and allows you to grow cultivars that are well-adapted to your environment as well as those that are too exotic for your local nursery to carry.

are often kept below 70°F during the winter, you may also need to create a warm seed-starting area.

The essential equipment for starting seeds includes: fluorescent lights, small electric heaters, heating mats, and polyethylene film. Lights are necessary to start some seeds. They are also essential for growing healthy seedlings if you don't have unlimited windowsill space. Daylight tubes will suffice if you plan to use lights only for germination, but you'll need tubes that give off a wide spectrum of light waves if you also want to grow plants under the lights.

As shown in the photograph of the homemade propa-

PROPAGATION BOX

This simple box makes an ideal germination chamber for seeds. Make a frame out of 2x2 boards. Screw 1x2 boards at 4-inch intervals along the sides, back, and front of the box. Then tack lathing strips across these boards to act as supports for growing flats. Staple clear, 6-mil, construction-grade polyethylene film to the sides and back of the box. Staple a separate sheet on the front side so that it can be raised or lowered as necessary. Place the prop box over a heating mat, and it will keep all your flats warm while they germinate.

SEEDS

STARTING PLANTS FROM SEEDS becomes a yearly routine, particularly if you grow vegetables, herbs, or flowers. By growing plants from seeds, you can choose the varieties you want and also have plants at different stages of growth throughout the season. More than likely, you will be starting plants indoors in the winter.

The important considerations for starting seeds indoors are tools, timing, technique, and control over temperature, relative humidity, and lighting. Seeds are fairly picky about germination temperatures. Some germinate best at 40°F to 50°F, while others require a minimum of 70°F and a maximum of 90°F. If you are starting many seeds that require cool germination temperatures, you may need to create a seed-starting area in the basement, where temperatures remain cool throughout the year. In the North, where homes

FLUORESCENT LIGHTS allow you to start plants in plenty of time for spring transplanting. As long as the lights are no more than 5 inches from the tips of all the leaves, one fixture can be used to start a wide variety of plants in different kinds of containers.

keep air circulation high, diseases won't be a problem.

The soilless recipe given earlier for starting root cuttings also works for seeds. Most compost-based potting soils will supply your seedlings with nutrients for about six weeks, after which you'll have to fertilize the plants in order to keep them thriving. Water with either a half-strength dilution of liquid seaweed and fish emulsion or compost tea starting in the sixth week. Fertilize the seedlings every week thereafter until they have been safely transplanted.

Seed-starting containers range from traditional wooden flats to plastic inserts; plastic, cardboard, or clay pots; compressed peat pots; and soil blocks. Each of these containers has both pros and cons, and each is more appropriate for certain plants than others. Fast-growing small plants that transplant well can be started in any kind of container. Slow-growing perennials and herbs are best started in deep plastic or wooden flats and transplanted to clay, cardboard, or plastic pots once the first true leaves, or *cotyledons,* have sprouted. Use a plastic pot if the seedling must be kept moist, but use clay or cardboard if the starting area is humid or the plant needs superior drainage.

Soil blocks. As illustrated on the next page, soil blocks are wonderful for fast-growing flowers, herbs, and veg-

gation box, left, an electrical heating mat for seedlings can heat a number of flats at once. If you start more than a few flats at a time, it will be worthwhile to buy or make a shelving unit for plant lights. To make your own shelving unit, attach light fixtures to the undersides of the shelves on an old bookcase. Place a small electric heater on the floor at least a foot under the bottom shelf to prevent possible fire hazard, and drape the whole bookcase with polyethylene sheeting. While the seeds are germinating, open the plastic several times a day to let in fresh air. Once plants are growing, take off the plastic because the humidity it traps can promote fungal diseases.

Air circulation is the best insurance against diseases such as *damping off,* a condition that kills seedlings just before or just after they germinate. To prevent damping off, set up an oscillating fan, and run it day and night if necessary.

Timing is everything when you are starting seeds. Consult the plant directories throughout this book to learn how many weeks before the spring frost-free date to start various plants.

Seed-Starting Media

Plants are usually healthiest if started in a mix containing compost. But some people are afraid compost carries diseases. If you water just enough to keep the soil moist and etables as well as plants that are difficult to transplant. You can maintain plants at top health in a 2-inch soil block for six to eight weeks if the mix contains quality compost. The beauty of using a soil block system is its efficiency. You seed into the mini blocks and then pop these into the 2-inch blocks after germination. When transplanting time comes, simply plant the whole soil block. The one problem with soil blocks, however, is the minuscule amount of medium. Once it's dry, it's forever dry, and the seedlings will probably die.

Planting medium. Soil blockers are available from several seed companies and some garden-supply shops. They require a specialized mix for the medium to hold together well. You can buy a commercially prepared mix or make your own by adding ½ part peat humus to 1 part compost, 1 part peat moss, and 1 part vermiculite.

Specialized Techniques

Just as seeds require particular temperatures to germinate, many of them also require either light or dark conditions. Additionally, some have such hard seed coats that you need to scratch them deeply (*scarify*), while others need to be subjected to fluctuating temperatures or a period of freezing or cooling (*stratification*). Still others germinate best if you wash them in clear water several times a day for a few days before you plant them (*flushing*).

Unfortunately, not all seed catalogs or packets inform you about these specialized needs. If you plan to start seeds with which you are not familiar, ask the supplier whether preplanting treatments are required. Fortunately the individual plant descriptions in the directories give this necessary information.

STARTING SEEDS IN SOIL BLOCKS

Difficulty Level: **EASY**

By using soil blocks, you can grow seedlings without a container. Soil blocks have several strong advantages: seedlings don't suffer transplant shock when you move them to the garden; transplanting is much faster; and there are no seed-starting containers to discard or wash and store.

The system depends on your making a somewhat sticky soil mix. Do this by adding at least ½ part of peat humus to a soil mix containing 1 part fully finished compost, 1 part vermiculite, and 1 part peat moss. If this mix doesn't hold together, increase the amounts of peat humus and compost until it does. Once you find a formula for your particular compost, write it down so you remember it.

Tools and Materials: **Soil blockers, tray, seed-starting medium, mister bottle**

1 Use a mini soil block maker to make 20 tiny soil blocks. Plant one seed in each of these blocks. If a seed doesn't germinate, you won't be wasting much medium.

2 Use the 2-inch blocker with inserts to make blocks where your seedlings can grow. Set the blocks on old foam trays from the grocery store to hold water and keep them warm.

3 Transplant the mini blocks into the 2-inch blocks as soon as the seedlings germinate. You don't have to wait until true leaves form because you are not disturbing the roots.

PLANTING

PLANTING IS ALWAYS FUN, no matter whether it's putting seeds in the soil or setting two-year-old trees into holes. Although planting is pretty straightforward, some tricks can make it more efficient and ensure the health of your plants.

Seeds in Containers

Depending on what you grow, you could spend many hours a year seeding into flats, pots, and other containers. The more seeding you do, the more efficiently you'll want to do it. Many people plant two seeds in every cell or pot as insurance in case one seed doesn't germinate. Once the plants are up, you can *thin*, or cut, the weaker extra plant. But because it's unusual to get less than 80 percent germination (provided you plant fresh seeds), double-planting and thinning actually costs you time. Instead, it's more efficient to plant about 25 percent more cells or pots than you need, with only one seed in each. In flats, space the seeds far enough apart so that the young plants will be easy to remove when the time comes to transplant them into large containers.

The chopstick seeding trick mentioned at right doesn't work well with seeds the size of specks of dust, such as those of lobelia and petunia. Mix these

PLANT SEEDS no deeper than two times their diameter. In the case of pointed seeds such as these pumpkin seeds, place the pointed end down; the root will emerge from this end.

tiny seeds with a pinch of thoroughly dry sharp sand or fine vermiculite, right in the seed packet. If you have extraordinarily good control of your hands, you can tap out the sand or vermiculite and seeds from the corner of the packet onto the growing medium. Otherwise, empty the packet onto a plate, and spread out the material. Use the moistened tip of the chopstick to pick up teeny bits. When you are finished, dust off the plate over the flat or other seed-starting containers.

Germination with light or in darkness. Check the plant directories or the seed packet to learn whether the seeds need light or darkness to germinate. If they need light, place them on the surface of the medium. To keep light lovers from drying too quickly, cover them with a thin layer of vermiculite, and then mist with a hand sprayer. Cover the container with a sheet of kitchen plastic wrap, and place it on a windowsill or under a plant light. Try to find an airtight window for your seeds because drafts can hamper germination.

Dark lovers should be placed just under the soil surface, no more than twice the width of the seed. Cover the container with plastic wrap and then with a section or two of newspaper to prevent light from reaching the seed. Most annuals germinate in about a week, but herbs and perennials can take much longer.

Seedlings growing in flats must be transplanted when the first set of true leaves has grown to full size. Move them into a container that is roomy enough so that they can grow quickly until you transplant them into the garden. If the growth of seedlings is slowed because of limited root area or lack of nutrients, they will never reach full potential as mature plants. If you give your plants enough room, they will always be superior to those you can buy, partially because of the ample size of your starting containers.

If you are removing plants from a flat, dig under a section and lift it out. Set it on a moistened terry-cloth towel or an old T-shirt so that you can fold the material over the roots and soil. Remove only a few plants at a time, and keep the rest covered while you work.

> ## SMART TIP
> ### CHOPSTICKS AND TINY SEEDS
> Tiny seeds can be really difficult to space well. Here is a trick that can make the job easier: Tap out the seeds onto a smooth, clean plate. Then moisten the tip of an unpainted wooden chopstick, use the chopstick to pick up the seeds, one by one, and place them on the potting soil surface or push them just under it.

Once the plants are potted in new containers, water them well; then place them in a partially shaded area for the rest of the day. By the next morning, they should have recovered from transplanting enough so that you can return them to full light.

WATER GENTLY using a misting nozzle or fine rose to deliver a stream that won't injure delicate seedlings.

> ## SMART TIP
>
> ### HANDLE WITH CARE
>
> Handle seedlings as if they were premature babies. Try to touch only the root ball, but if you must touch another part of the plant, let it be only the seed leaves. Do not touch the stem.

Seeds Outside

Planting seeds in an outside garden is much less complicated than planting inside. Use a soil thermometer, wait until the ground is warm enough for the particular seed, make a smooth seedbed, and start seeding. Seed spacing is critical. Some seeds, such as calendula, cosmos, and turnips, are so viable that you can count on close to 100 percent germination outside. If you plant twice as many of these seeds as necessary for the space you've allotted them, you'll later be faced with a thinning nightmare. And if you don't thin them right away, the plants will probably suffer. So think twice before overplanting. You might be better off seeding the correct number of plants and then going back to fill in any gaps where some seeds haven't germinated.

Seeds need moisture. Seeds must remain moist while they are germinating. In spring conditions in most regions, the soil will be so wet from winter snows or rains that you won't even need to think about watering. But in the summer and in arid locales, you'll need to water. In dry conditions, try to sprinkle the seedbed every morning and early afternoon until the seeds germinate. If you plan to be away during the day, cover the seeds with a layer of vermiculite rather than soil when you plant. If the soil is dry, cover the vermiculite with a layer of floating row cover material. Or if the seeds germinate in the dark, cover them with several sheets of newspaper. Water the coverings well every morning. Unlike a layer of soil, these coverings will keep seeds moist all day. Seeds and seedlings are fragile and should be watered gently. Misting is the best way to water seeds so that they don't get dislodged or flooded. If

you are tending many flats of seeds or watering seeds planted outside in the ground, try a water rose or fan nozzle to break up the droplets. A low-tech option is to use your hand to break up the water coming from a hose. The idea is to protect the delicate seedlings from being flattened by a hard spray of water.

Transplanting Seedlings to the Garden

Indoor seedlings must be *hardened-off*, or gradually acclimated to outside conditions, before being transplanted. Begin the process a week before you transplant by taking seedlings outside every day. For the first couple of days, place them in a spot protected from wind, where they get filtered light. After that, place them where they are exposed to the wind and receive full light. During this time, cut back on watering, and don't fertilize them.

TRANSPLANT seedlings to the garden late in the day or when it is overcast. This decreases transplant shock because the plants lose less water from their leaves.

Transplant in the late afternoon or on a cloudy day. Most seedlings should be transplanted at the same depth they were growing in the pot. Exceptions to this rule are noted under the individual plant descriptions in the directories. If you are planting a group of seedlings, mark the locations before you begin, measuring if necessary. Then dig the holes, place the plants, and gently pat down the soil to remove air pockets from around the roots. Water the plants deeply, step back, and let them grow.

Transplanting Plants, Trees, and Shrubs

Purchased plants can arrive in containers, with bare roots, or balled-and-burlapped. Each requires different handling. But no matter how the roots are packaged, they need a good planting hole.

Most plants don't need soil amendments. Gardeners often wonder whether to amend the soil for a large tree or shrub. In general, plants that don't bear fruit make a better adjustment if you don't improve the soil. But fruit-bearers need to be fed regularly, so you might as well start them out with a good nutrient boost. Add no more than 50 percent compost to the soil used to backfill the planting hole.

Dig the hole the proper depth. Planting depth is important. You want the plant to grow at the same depth that it grew at the nursery. To accomplish this, position the plant so that the former soil mark is an inch or so above the ground when you finish planting. This allows for the inevitable sinking of roots into the soil during the first year or so, without having the plant drop so low that the crown will be suffocated. Add or remove soil as necessary to adjust the level. Now lower the roots or root ball into the hole, and gently backfill the hole with soil. Pack the soil firmly throughout the process to eliminate air pockets. When the hole is half full, water well to make the soil settle. Finish filling the hole with soil, and water again. With fall planting, when the ground is drier, dig the hole a day before, and fill it with water before planting. In the spring, when the ground is already wet, you can skip this step.

TRANSPLANTING CONTAINER-GROWN PLANTS

Difficulty Level: MODERATE

Plants grown in containers transplant well. The plant here is still dormant, making it even easier to transplant.

Tools and Materials: **Shovel, tarp, hose, table knife.**

1 Dig the hole before you remove the plant from its pot. If it sticks, run the blade of a table knife between the root ball and the pot.

2 Set the plant at the same depth it was growing in the pot. Check that it is level with the soil by laying the shovel handle across the hole.

3 After the plant is in place, press on the soil with your foot to firm it. The roots must be in good contact with the soil.

4 Water the plant well after you have added soil to about midway up the root ball. This eliminates large air holes and settles the plant.

WATERING

EXPERIENCED GREENHOUSE GARDENERS HAVE a saying, "The person who waters the plants makes the profits." Absolutely true! Good watering techniques keep plants healthy and thriving, while poor watering habits can encourage diseases or kill plants outright.

Watering is crucial. Good planters water transplants three times. Dig the hole at least a day before you plant, and fill it with water. On planting day, roughen the surface of the hole, position the plant, and start backfilling. When the hole is half filled with soil, water again and let the soil settle before resuming backfilling. The final planting step is to make a watering basin and fill it with water.

How Much Water Is Enough?

Overwatering is the most frequent mistake made by beginning gardeners. Their enthusiasm can lead them to water every day. This is generally necessary for container-grown plants, but daily watering is too much in most situations, even under drought conditions.

Because each layer of soil becomes fully saturated before water can drip down into the next layer, it's possible to unwittingly create a "dry-soil sandwich." The soil surface and 3 inches down can be wet, while the soil 3 to 6 inches below the surface is dry and the soil below that still contains a moist residual. If this happens, most of the roots, which grow in the 3- to 6-inch-deep layer, won't be able to find enough moisture. Subsequently, new growth will be concentrated in the top 3 inches, making the plant too shallowly rooted to stand up well to wind. The easiest way to avoid a dry-soil sandwich is to water deeply, slowly, and thoroughly.

Sometimes less is more. There are two cases in which you shouldn't water deeply: one is newly planted seeds that have not yet germinated, and another is young plants in the garden, whose root systems are still delicate. Keep both uniformly moist. Depending on the weather, you may have to water twice a day. If this becomes difficult, try covering seeds with a layer of vermiculite, row cover, and/or newspapers as discussed on page 54.

Morning is the best time to water, in any season. Leaves will have a chance to dry before nightfall, even if it's humid.

> ### SMART TIP
> #### WATERING
> Remember this: Water deeply, but water infrequently. Water so that the entire root zone is wet, but let the top of the soil dry a bit before you water again. Before turning off a watering system, always check to see that the soil is wet throughout the root zone. You can check by sticking your finger into the hole and seeing how far down it is wet.

This is crucial for disease control since many fungal spores require a film of water to germinate. If plants go into the evening wet, they are more likely to suffer.

Obviously, when using an overhead sprinkler, there is no way around getting the leaves wet. If your timing is good, you may never experience a problem. However, if there are any fungal diseases in the garden, it's best not to wet the leaves. Instead, hand-water the soil around the plant. Just as diseases can spread through water dripping from leaf to leaf, they can also be spread by splashes from the soil surface.

Nozzles. Make it a practice to use the nozzle that gives the softest practical droplet size for each application. Misting nozzles come in various sizes. The most versatile is the "fine" nozzle. If you use a misting nozzle to water fragile seedlings, you'll never damage them with rough watering.

Waterbreakers and roses also come in various sizes. By breaking the water into 200 to 400 little streams, they make the flow considerably more gentle. These nozzles are appropriate for potted plants or established plants in the garden.

Specialized Watering Systems

Sophisticated watering technology has become so inexpensive in the last few years that it has become a practical investment for gardeners in all but the rainiest parts of the country.

WATER ELEMENTS add a touch of romance to any garden.

DRIP IRRIGATION increases yields and plant health, while it also saves you time and trouble.

Not only do these systems save you work and worry, they can also increase yields, simply because they never forget, nor do they overwater.

Drip systems can be set up on a timer so that they automatically water, with or without you. If you have a large garden, you can "zone" the system so that it waters in different areas at different times. A fertilizer injector makes the system truly versatile. Simply dunk one end of a hose in a bucket of fish emulsion. The fertilizer injector will siphon it up, dilute it to the correct concentration, and deliver it to the root zone. Talk to your supplier about this option if you are installing a drip irrigation system.

WATERING EQUIPMENT

Good watering equipment can make a tremendous difference both to the health of your plants and the ease with which you garden. Invest in a few inexpensive pieces of equipment right at the beginning. You'll never regret it.

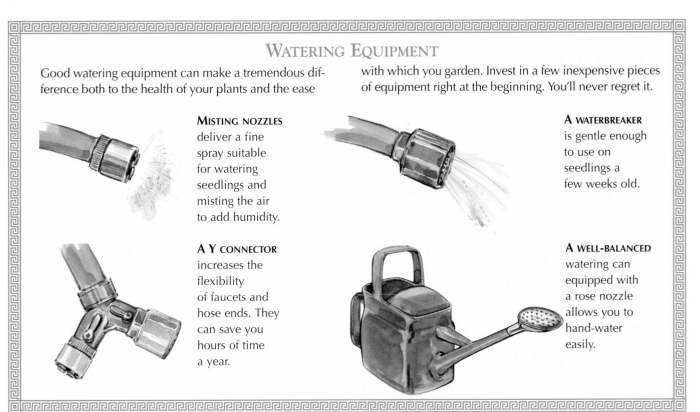

MISTING NOZZLES deliver a fine spray suitable for watering seedlings and misting the air to add humidity.

A Y CONNECTOR increases the flexibility of faucets and hose ends. They can save you hours of time a year.

A WATERBREAKER is gentle enough to use on seedlings a few weeks old.

A WELL-BALANCED watering can equipped with a rose nozzle allows you to hand-water easily.

CHAPTER 3

FLOWERS, FLOWERS, AND MORE FLOWERS

*F*lowering plants can bring a property alive. They are as important to the feeling of a site as any architectural element of your garden. Yet they have the virtue of being far less permanent. You can redesign flower beds over the years, experimenting with colors, placement, and style until you achieve just the right look.

Near the doors, well-chosen flowers offer a welcome. Visitors instinctively feel more light-hearted when they are greeted by the colors and fragrances of a lovely planting.

Flowering plants can also define spaces in the yard or lead the eyes, and the feet, to another area. For example, to invite visitors to the backyard, border the pathway with flowering plants. If you want to hide an area, screen it with a row of tall, bushy perennials such as golden glow (*Rudbeckia lacini-*

ata), or install a trellis and flowering vines.

People who hate mowing lawns soon discover another joy of flower gardens. The more flower beds you have, the less mowing you have to do. Flowering plants can also prevent erosion while creating a trouble-free area. For example, plant a steep rocky bank with a ground cover such as creeping thyme (*Thymus praecox*). For added interest, interplant it with daylilies (*Hemerocallis* species). As different as these plants are, they hold the soil in place and don't need mowing or more than a little annual maintenance.

One or another flowering plant may solve other environmental problems in your yard, too. Bog-loving plants will turn a soggy eyesore into an attraction, and a collection of desert plants becomes a beautiful solution to arid conditions.

The right flowers will attract birds, bees, and butterflies to your yard, and even a small flower bed can give you flowers to cut throughout the season as well as blooms to dry for winter arrangements.

But all these advantages aside, one of the best things about a flower garden is the endless fascination it gives as a succession of flowering plants comes into bloom throughout the season.

WALL-TO-WALL FLOWERS CREATE a visual feast. Hanging baskets of ivy geranium complement the potted annuals on the ground below.

START SMALL when developing gardens. Here, a corner of the lawn has been transformed, and though it makes a big statement, it's small enough to care for easily.

Planning Flower Beds

PLANNING A FLOWER GARDEN can be as involved as designing a house or as simple as opening a can of soup for supper. The very best advice you'll ever hear—to start small—is also the hardest to follow. It's natural to want to put in gardens all over the property. But think twice before you give in to this desire; major plantings require major commitments. It is more sensible to begin with one portion of a yard at a time, eliminating weeds before planting and learning how to deal with problems as they arise before expanding your garden.

By the time you sit down to plan your individual flower gardens, you should be well along in the visualization process. The garden you see in your mind's eye will have a color scheme and general style, formal or informal. Now is the time to translate the vision into reality.

From Vision to Reality

Begin by focusing on the aspect that is most important to you, whether it's color, season of bloom, or style. If color or season of bloom is what matters most to you, make a list of plants, like the table on page 63, that have the appro-

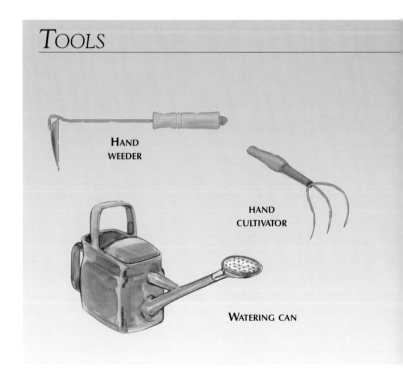

TOOLS

HAND WEEDER

HAND CULTIVATOR

WATERING CAN

priate hues or that bloom at the right time. If a particular style is what you are after, begin by sketching a plant placement map, indicating simple plant shapes without necessarily identifying the plants.

As you go through this process, remember that all gardens do not have to bloom all the time or include all the colors of the rainbow. A bed of nothing but red tulips and white anemones makes an effective spring planting, for example. After such a bed is finished blooming, you can mulch it for the remainder of the season or transplant some quickly blooming annuals into it for summer color.

Plant a moon garden near the patio. Near a patio, you might want to create an evening garden by planting only white and pale pastel flowers so that they will reflect moonlight and starlight. To add another dimension to this garden, include some plants that release their fragrance in the evening. 'Only the Lonely' flowering tobacco (*Nicotiana alata*), white and yellow four o'clocks (*Mirabilis jalapa*), moonflower vine (*Ipomoea alba*), and 'Colvin's White' sand phlox (*Phlox bifida*) are all good choices for an evening garden. You'll also want to note some practical things about each plant that you are considering. Make columns in your list of plants for height and width, soil requirements, exposure preferences, and general cultural needs. For example, it may be that you can only spend an hour or so each week

THE WHITE PETUNIAS AND FEVERFEW that surround these steps glow in the moonlight they reflect as they lead you through the entryway to this home.

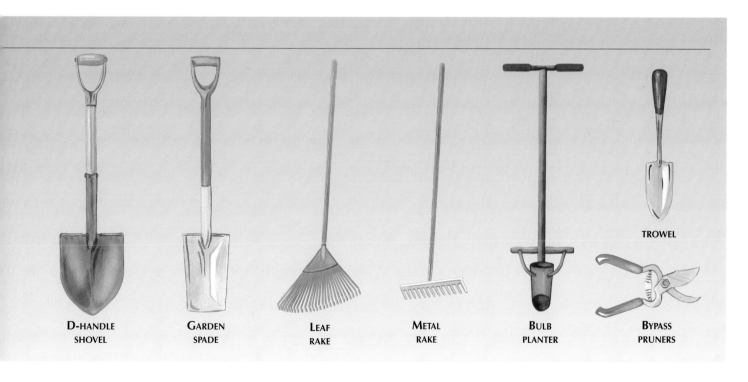

| D-HANDLE | GARDEN | LEAF | METAL | BULB | BYPASS |
| SHOVEL | SPADE | RAKE | RAKE | PLANTER | PRUNERS |

TROWEL

tending the flower bed. In that case, you will want to concentrate on low-maintenance species.

Now that you have a list of possible plants to include in your garden, it's time to get out the graph paper again and start sketching their placement on the map. This part of the design process can be mystifying until you understand that, even in a seemingly random planting, most flower beds are built around at least one focal point.

Find a focal point. A focal point is usually a plant or a plant grouping to which the eye is drawn, but it can also be a structural element such as a birdbath. A prominent size or color generally makes something a focal point, although

a common design trick can also create one. Say that you have decided to make a group of yellow Asiatic lilies the focal point of a summer garden. They are certainly bright enough to draw the eye, but you can emphasize them even more by planting them with a group of daylilies in the same or a complementary color, such as yellow 'Hyperion'. The daylilies can completely surround the lilies, flank them, or be planted as a background. The daylilies will effectively frame the Asiatic lilies, making them even more prominent.

A BRIGHT SPOT OF COLOR can serve as a focal point. Here, the yellows of the *Heliopsis* and *Coreopsis* emphasize the vivid orange 'Enchantment' and foxtail lilies.

SMART TIP

PLANT POSITION DEFINES GARDEN STYLE

Placement of your "frame plants" helps to define the garden's style. If you plant them around the focal point in a symmetrical pattern, you are creating a formal style. But if you group them in an irregularly shaped drift, the planting will appear informal.

FLOWER GARDEN PLANNER

Use the table below to list flowering plants that are appropriate to your garden design. You can photocopy and enlarge this table or use it as a model to create your own. As you consider new plants, add them to your chart, filling in all the columns. You'll have a quick reference to use whenever you want to add to your plantings.

FLOWER NAME	COLOR	HEIGHT	BLOOMING SEASON	NOTES
Bulbs				
Dahlia	All but blue	1' to 6'	Summer to frost	Tender, lift in fall
Perennials				
Astilbe	Pink, red	1' to 2'	Spring to summer	Divide every 3 to 4 years
Annuals				
Centaurea	Pink, red rose,blue	1' to 3'	Summer	Deadhead for continual bloom
Biennials				
Alcea rosea	All but blue	4' to 8'	Midsummer to fall	Easy in the correct location

DAFFODILS NATURALIZE easily in the right location. Here, they are thriving in the bright springtime light under deciduous trees.

BULBS

MOST OF THE PLANTS we call bulbs are extremely easy to grow. They bloom reliably, are rarely bothered by pests or diseases, require very little maintenance, and—with the exception of most tulips—multiply quickly.

Bulbs provide the very first signs of spring throughout most of North America. Shortly after the days have begun to lengthen, the first snowdrops (*Galanthus nivalis*) and winter aconites (*Eranthis*) peek through the melting snow cover. Once these plants bloom, gardeners know that spring is on the way.

Although most people strongly associate bulbs with spring flowers, many bulbs bloom in summer, autumn, and even late winter. Check the bulb directory on pages 67 to 69 for a selection of bulbs and their bloom time.

Plan for multi-season interest. With just a little planning, you can feature color-coordinated bulbs or even bulbs of the same color from early spring to fall. Siberian squill, glory-of-the-snow, species crocus, and species tulips come first, followed by hybrid crocus, hyacinths, and a succession of daffodils, narcissus, and hybrid tulips.

You will most appreciate seeing these harbingers of spring when the calendar says it's still winter. You can guarantee this by planting the very earliest bulbs in a warm,

TRUE BULBS AND OTHER BULB-LIKE STRUCTURES

Despite what we call them, not all of these plants are true bulbs. Instead, many fit into the categories of corms, tubers, tuberous roots, or rhizomes. But all of them share an important characteristic. They evolved in places where the climate was hospitable for only a few months of the year, so they developed the capacity to go dormant for long periods of time. All bulbs grow quickly and store enough nutrients in swollen underground structures to see them through months of high temperatures, droughts, snow, and frozen soil. Where environments roughly match the native locations of bulbs, these plants are among the most dependable you can grow.

Corms. Crocus and gladiolus grow from corms. Although small buds grow on the top of a corm and roots grow from its base, corms are primarily food storage organs, rather than a means of reproduction for the plant. Each year, a new corm forms above the old one. When you dig gladiolus in the fall, discard the old, shrunken corm and keep the new, firm one.

Tubers and tuberous roots. Winter aconite grows from a tuber, an enlarged part of the stem that stores food and contains a bud. Dahlias and tuberous begonias are called tubers, but they grow from tuberous roots.

Rhizomes. Both bearded iris and calla lilies grow from rhizomes. Like tubers, rhizomes are food-storing parts of the stem. But, rhizomes are long, slender, and branched, while tubers are rounded and unbranched. Divide plants with rhizomes by cutting or breaking the rhizome into smaller pieces, each with some leaves and roots growing from it.

sheltered spot, such as tucked between a porch and a wall on the south side of the house.

The weather will still be chilly, so you'll appreciate early bulbs more if you plant them where you can see them from a window. Even though the bulbs are tiny, crocus and species tulips make a huge color impact when massed under deciduous shrubs or in the front of a flower border.

Summer bulbs extend the show. Summer bulbs include both those that are hardy, such as alliums and lilies, as well as tender species such as gladiolus and dahlias. The flowers of summer bulbs are so spectacular that they easily become the focal points in a planting.

When you choose summer bulbs, pay attention to blooming time as well as size and color. Gladiolus bloom eight to ten weeks after you've planted them, so it's possible to keep them blooming from midsummer until frost.

Autumn bulbs are a bonus. In addition to the last of the gladiolus, planted at midsummer, late lilies and dahlias, colchicums (*Colchicum autumnale*), autumn crocus (*Crocus sativus, C. speciosus*), and winter daffodils (*Sternbergia lutea*) all bloom when days get short and temperatures cool. Like spring bulbs, these are best appreciated in spots where you can see them from indoors or as you pass in and out of the house.

Growing Bulbs

Hardy bulbs are planted in the fall. They need time to grow roots and become established before the ground freezes but not enough time, or warmth, to send up shoots. In general, gardeners in Zones 2 and 3 plant in mid-September; Zones 4 and 5, late September to early October; Zones 6 and 7, mid-October to early November; Zone 8, mid-November to early December; and Zone 9, early to mid-December. If in doubt about when to plant, use a soil thermometer. Soil temperature should be 60°F or lower when you plant bulbs.

Planting depth is important for bulbs. The bulb directory, which starts on page 67, gives specific planting depths for individual bulbs, Still, it's also useful to know general planting guidelines. The proper planting depth is two to three times the bulb's length from tip to base. For example, a bulb that measures 3 inches, should be planted 6 to 9 inches deep. If you have sandy soil, plant the bulb the full three-times depth, but if you have heavy soil, use the two-times rule. Many bulbs grow well when they are planted more shallowly than recommended, especially if they are well mulched over the winter months. However, burrowing rodents are less likely to damage bulbs that are more deeply buried. So try to keep to the recommended planting depths. Bulbs should be planted with the base down and the tip up. But bulbs such as windflower (*Anemone*) that don't have an indentifiable top or bottom

which starts on page 67

> **SMART TIP**
>
> **PROTECT BULBS FROM ANIMALS**
>
> If mice, moles, or voles are a problem in your garden, excavate the entire planting area, and line the bottom and sides of the trench with hardware cloth; or place a piece of hardware cloth in each hole over the bulb. Another approach is to plant narcissus and daffodils, which naturally repel rodents.

PLANTING BULBS

Difficulty Level: MODERATE

This cage of ½-inch galvanized wire mesh should prevent tunneling rodents from getting to the bulbs. If you don't have a problem with rodents, skip the cage. But it's a good idea to protect shallow bulbs by covering them with a piece of mesh.

Tools and Materials: **Shovel, trowel, ½-inch galvanized mesh cage or bulb cage, metal rake, tarp, soil amendments.**

1 Add soil with plenty of organic matter to promote drainage. If your soil is sandy or contains a lot of clay, dig in extra leaf mold, or compost.

2 After leveling the soil, set a wire-mesh cage in the excavated area. Bulb-loving rodents will not be able to chew through this cage. Then add an inch of soil.

3 Place bulbs at the depth recommended on the packaging (usually twice as deep as they are long) or as listed in the bulb directory.

4 After placing your bulbs, cover them with soil. For more protection from animals, place a lid of wire mesh over the area before mulching for winter.

CHAPTER 3

DAHLIAS are excellent companions for these lilies. The dahlias keep the lily bulbs and roots cool, and they look good together.

FLOWERS FOR FRAGRANCE

Fragrance gardens are delightful additions to outdoor lounging areas. Choose from plants such as those listed below.

Botanical Name	Common Name
Dianthus plumarius	Cottage pinks (perennial)
Erysimum cheiri, formerly *Cheiranthus cheiri*	Wallflower (biennial)
Lillium 'Stargazer'	Lily (bulb)
Heliotropium arborescens	Heliotrope (annual)
Hyacinthus orientalis	Hyacinth (bulb)
Narcissus poeticus 'Plenus'	Daffodil (bulb)
Nicotiana alata	Flowering tobacco (annual)
Paeonia lactiflora	Peony (perennial)
Petunia x hybrida	Petunia (annual)
Phlox paniculata	Garden phlox (perennial)
Reseda species	Mignonette (annual)

will sprout no matter how they are positioned in the planting hole.

Soil requirements. Bulbs tolerate a great range of soil types and fertility levels, as long as the soil is well drained. If you want to plant bulbs where the soil remains soggy, dig in ample amounts of compost or, if that isn't adequate, some sand. If water still puddles, make a raised bed, and fill it with a light soil mix such as potting soil.

Despite not needing high fertility, bulbs do best in soils with moderate levels of organic matter and high calcium content. Spread about ½ inch of compost over the bulb bed, and dig it in. For the calcium, add 2 to 4 tablespoons of gypsum to each planting hole. In subsequent years, dust the bed lightly with gypsum, and then cover the soil with a ½ inch of finished compost in the very early spring.

Digging and dividing bulbs. If the leaves begin to look crowded and blooms diminish in size or number, the plants are probably running out of space. The best times to dig and divide bulbs are right after the leaves have died back or in the fall; the timing depends on the other plantings in the bed. If the other plants will be disturbed by early summer digging, mark the location of the crowded bulbs, and wait until the fall when the other plants are dying back.

ILLUSTRATED PLANT-BY-PLANT DIRECTORY OF BULBS

Note: To make this directory of plants most valuable, please read "About the Plant Directories," on page 9.

Allium giganteum
Giant Drumstick

Related Species: About 150 of the more than 400 known *Allium* species are domesticated. Favorite members of the family include common chives (*A. schoenoprasum*); the ornamental, 8-to 10-inch-tall, bright yellow lily leek (*A. moly*); and the star of Persia (*A. christophii*) which is used in winter bouquets as well as fresh arrangements because its florets dry in place. *A. giganteum is* the true giant of the group.
Zones: 5 to 10.
Appearance: Leaves are strap-shaped and form a basal mound. Flower scapes rise well above them and the globe-shaped blooms give a tidy, formal look, no matter where they grow.
Size: 3 to 5 feet.
Flower Color: Purple.
Blooming Season: Late spring to early summer.
Exposure: Full sun.
Soil: Prefers sandy soils of moderate fertility but will tolerate heavier soils if they are well-drained.

Planting Depth: Three times the height of the bulb, generally 8 to 10 inches.
Spacing: 8 inches to 1 foot.
Propagation: Divide clumps every three to four years.
Pests and Diseases: Slugs and snails. Thrips occassionally. Botrytis leaf blast, basal rot, and downy mildew.
Notes: Plant in September to October in a well-prepared area. They will be almost trouble-free. The foliage of *A. giganteum* and *A christophii* often withers just before the flower opens.

Chionodoxa luciliae
Glory-of-the-Snow

Related Species: None used in garden.
Zones: 3 to 8.
Appearance: Leaves are strap-shaped and die back early. The 6-petaled, star-shaped 1-inch-wide flowers grow in sprays above the foliage.
Size: 4 to 5 inches high, 3 inches wide.
Flower Color: Blue, pink, and white flowers with white centers.
Blooming Season: Very early spring.
Exposure: Full sun.
Soil: Well-drained, moderate fertility.
Planting Depth: 3 inches deep.
Spacing: 2 inches apart.

Propagation: Self-seeds easily; bulbs divide naturally. Reproduces well in favored locations.
Pests and Diseases: Usually trouble-free, but bulbs may develop fungal rots.
Notes: Use glory-of-the-snow under deciduous shrubs, in the front of a bulb or perennial bed, or near a walkway. It will reproduce to form a large floral carpet but because the foliage dies back so early, is never a nuisance.

Colchicum autumnale
Colchicum, Autumn Crocus

Related Species: *Colchicum speciosum* (meadow saffron) has mauve flowers that can grow as wide as 8 inches.
Zones: 4 to 8.
Appearance: Autumn crocus sends up its somewhat coarse and untidy-looking leaves in spring. They grow and die back by summer, without producing a flower stalk. In the fall, leafless flower stalks appear, bearing chalice-shaped blooms 2 to 4 inches wide.
Size: 6 to 8 inches tall, 2 to 3 inches wide.
Flower Color: Pink, lavender, or white.
Blooming Season: Late summer to early fall.

*Colchicum autumnale/***Colchicum, Autumn Crocus** continued

Exposure: Prefers full sun but tolerates partial shade.

Soil: Moderate fertility, consistently moist and well-drained.

Planting Depth: 3 inches.

Spacing: 8 inches apart.

Propagation: Bulbs divide naturally in favorable locations.

Pests and Diseases: Largely trouble-free, but see Chapter 9, "Preventing Weeds, Pests, and Diseases," pages 266 to 309, if problems occur.

Notes: The leaves can be unattractive, so it's best to plant these bulbs among a groundcover planting or naturalize them in grass. They can also grow along the edge of a woods if they receive adequate light and the soil is well-drained.

Eranthis hyemalis
Winter Aconite

Related Species: *Eranthis hyemalis* is the most popular type, but the lesser known *E. × tubergenii* has the advantage of being less invasive and the flowers are somewhat larger. However, it blooms several weeks later.

Zones: 3 to 8.

Appearance: The cup-shaped flower is surounded by a collar of leaves radiating out around it. This plant can form a carpet of color in favorable locations.

Size: 2 to 3 inches tall, 2 to 3 inches wide.

Flower Color: Brillant yellow.

Blooming Season: Very early spring, usu-

ally with the snowdrops.

Exposure: In northern parts of Zone 7 and northward, prefers full sun but will tolerate patial shade. In warmer parts of Zones 7 and 8, the southern parts of the growing range, plant in partial shade.

Soil: Well-drained, moderate fertility.

Planting Depth: 2 inches deep.

Spacing: 2 to 3 inches apart.

Propagation: Winter aconite can be invasive because it produces a great deal of viable seed. Tubers also reproduce themselves. If you need to divide a crowded clump, dig in early summer and replant immediately.

Pests and Diseases: Largely trouble-free, but see Chapter 9, "Preventing Weeds, Pests, and Diseases," pages 266 to 309, if problems occur.

Notes: Plant in fall and soak tubers for four to eight hours before planting. This plant is very effective in front of foundation shrubs around the house, or in a sheltered spot where snow melts early.

Iris reticulata
Iris, netted

Related Species: Dutch Iris.

Zones: 4 to 8.

Appearance: Leaves are pointed and sword shaped.

Size: 4 to 8 inches tall, 4 to 8 inches wide.

Flower color: Dark violet blue, pale blue, and reddish purple.

Blooming Season: Very early spring.

Exposure: Prefers full sun but will tolerate partial shade.

Soil: Well-drained with high humus levels and moderate fertility.

Planting Depth: Set bulbs 2 inches deep.

Spacing: 4 to 6 inches apart.

Propagation: All irises reproduce easily in favorable locations. In late summer or early fall, lift and divide the clumps of plants every three to four years to keep beds from becoming too crowded.

Pests and Diseases: Iris borers can be a problem in crowded beds. Dig out these maggot-like larvae from leaves and rhizomes. Afterwards, dust rhizomes with powdered sulfur. Slugs, snails, and thrips can also attack. Common diseases include the fungi *Penicillium* species, *Mystrosporium adustum, Sclerotium rolfsii,* and *Didymellina macrospora;* mosaic viruses; and bacterial soft rots in the *Erwinia* and *Pseudomonas* species.

Ixia cultivars
Corn Lily

Related Species: At least 50 species of *Ixia* are known, all of them growing naturally in South Africa. In the U.S., most available corn lilies are hybrids of two or more of these species.

Zones: 8 to 10, in Zones 7 and cooler grow them as tender bulbs.

Appearance: Leaves are narrow and almost grasslike. Young flowers are bell-shaped, then open into six-petaled stars. They cluster at the top of slender stems.

Size: 10 inches to 1½ feet tall, 5 to 7 inches wide.

Flower color: Flowers are bi- or tri-colored, usually with a dark blotch in the center. Colors range from ivory to red, green, yellow, mahogany, and black.

Blooming Season: Midspring to midsummer, depending on planting time.

Exposure: Prefers full sun but tolerates partial shade. Protect from harsh winds.

Soil: Well-drained, average fertility.

Planting Depth: 4 to 6 inches deep.

Spacing: 4 to 6 inches apart.

Propagation: Corms develop cormlets at their base. Remove and plant separately, 2 to 4 inches deep, depending on size.

Pests and Diseases: Largely trouble-free, but see Chapter 9, "Preventing Weeds, Pests, and Diseases," pages 266 to 309, if problems occur.

Notes: In Zones 8 to 10, plant corms in fall. After they are established, the leaves will appear in the autumn and the plant will bloom in spring. Farther north, plant in spring, just after the frost-free date. Blooms will appear in summer. After the leaves have yellowed, lift the corms and store until the following spring. Some gardeners report that the plant is hardy in protected sites in Zone 7.

Leucojum vernum
Snowflake

Related Species: Ten species of *Leucojum are* indigenous to Europe and North Africa. Of these, gardeners in North America are most likely to grow the spring snowflake (*L. vernum*). Summer snowflake (*L. aestivum*) grows 12 to 14 inches tall and blooms in late spring to early summer, while *L. autumnale* is 9 to 12 inches tall and blooms in early fall.

Zones: 3 to 8.

LEUCOJUM AUTUMNALE

Appearance: Leaves are slender and lance-shaped. Flowers resemble snowdrops but are somewhat larger.

Size: 8 to 10 inches tall, 3 to 4 inches wide.

Flower color: White with green or yellow markings.

Blooming Season: Early to midspring, but after snowdrops.

Exposure: Full sun to partial shade.

Soil: Well-drained, moderate fertility, containing humus.

Planting Depth: 3 inches.

Spacing: 4 to 5 inches apart.

Propagation: Bulbs reproduce easily in good conditions but do not become invasive. Lift and divide in early fall.

Pests and Diseases: Largely trouble-free, but see Chapter 9, "Preventing Weeds, Pests, and Diseases," pages 266 to 309, if problems occur.

Notes: Mass in groups in front of foundation plantings or in a woodland planting.

Scilla siberica
Siberian Squill

Related Species: There are more than 90 known squill species, although we grow only a dozen of them in North America. The most commonly grown include *S. autumnalis, S. puschkinioides,* and *S. siberica.*

Zones: 5 to 8.

Appearance: Strap-shaped, erect leaves are generally taller than the flower scapes. The drooping bell-shaped flowers grow singly or in loose clusters.

Size: 3 to 4 inches tall, 3 to 4 inches wide.

Flower color: Intense blue, violet-blue, and white.

Blooming Season: Early spring.

Exposure: Partial shade but will tolerate full sun.

Soil: Moist, humusy soil that is well-drained.

Planting Depth: 3 inches.

Spacing: 3 inches apart.

Propagation: Self-seeds and also reproduces from bulbs.

Pests and Diseases: Largely trouble-free, but see Chapter 9, "Preventing Weeds, Pests, and Diseases," pages 266 to 309, if problems occur.

Notes: Siberian squill will form a carpet of bloom in favorable locations. Don't worry about dividing it unless blooms diminish, showing that it is too crowded.

CHAPTER 3

PERENNIALS such as the yellow *Coreopsis* combine well with annuals, such as cleome and salvia.

where they lie exposed to the cold and drying winds. Soil heaving can also tear the roots. Improve drainage by adding compost to soils with a high percent of sand or clay, and make raised beds in really problematic areas.

Most perennials are deep-rooted and prefer to grow in loose, fertile topsoil a foot deep. Soil that is worked to a depth of 18 inches gives plants an even better start.

Fertilizing

Perennials do not tend to be heavy feeders. Most will thrive in soils of average fertility if you add an inchdeep layer of compost to the bed each spring, just as growth is beginning. But there are some exceptions to this rule. Delphiniums and peonies are both heavy feeders that profit from a second compost application just before midsummer.

If your compost supply is short, you can also use a liquid or bagged fertilizer. A mix of liquid seaweed and fish emulsion is an excellent choice because it generally contains ample phosphorus, the nutrient most needed by flowering plants. Apply this combination once the soil temperature reaches 55° to 60°F and again at midsummer if soil tests indicate that phosphorus levels are low.

PERENNIALS

MOST FLOWERING PERENNIALS ARE tough, sturdy plants that tolerate a wide range of environmental conditions, are resistant to pests and diseases, and require very little coddling. Along with beauty, these are the qualities that people considered when they began to select and breed the wild flowers that have become our favorite ornamentals. The easier a plant was to care for, the more likely it was to become popular. And aside from the often troublesome rose, you can usually be certain that the more "old-fashioned" a plant is, the more reliable and trouble-free it is, particularly if it was widely grown in colonial America.

Soil Preparation

Perennials do not require the same high levels of nutrients as fruits and vegetables, but inasmuch as they will remain in the same spot with the same soil for many years, it's best to take the time to prepare the bed well.

Good drainage is the most important characteristic of soil for perennials. Soggy soil promotes root diseases, and it can contribute to winter damage. The wetter soil is, the more it expands and contracts with freezing and thawing. This continual movement heaves plant roots out of the soil,

ROSES THRIVE in soils rich in organic matter. Sidedress them with compost or aged manure each year to keep supplies high.

Watering

Perennials require less water than fruits or vegetables. However, in dry periods or areas where the soil drains exceptionally quickly, it's often necessary to water perennials. Water perennial plants deeply but infrequently. This guarantees that roots at lower depths have enough water to survive and saves you time and trouble. Set up a rain gauge to measure natural rainfall. If you get less than an inch during an eight- or nine-day period and your soil is average—neither very sandy nor clayey—it's time to water. You'll want to add at least an inch of water, or slightly over 2 gallons for every square foot of garden area. If using a sprinkler, take advantage of your rain gauge by setting it up to measure how much water you add to the soil.

Staking

Staking plants can make an enormous difference to the appearance of the garden. It seems like a lot of extra work and something that couldn't possibly be worth the trouble, but staking is important. First of all, you can do it in the twinkling of an eye and second, it will prevent enough fungal problems to be well worth this tiny expenditure of time.

The need to stake plants with very large or heavy flowers, such as peonies, delphiniums, and lilies, is obvious. But surprisingly, plants with smaller flowers, such as tickseed, ballonflower, and speedwell, may also look better if you stake them.

Set stakes early in the season. Staking is best done in early to midspring, before plants have grown to their full size. Ideally, the stakes should be about two-thirds as tall as the mature plant will be, so they won't be conspicuous. Thick green wire supports and green bamboo stakes are both good choices for tall plants such as delphiniums and peonies. Use green gardener's twine to secure the plants to their supports. Smaller, bushy plants such as tickseed often look best when they are grown against twiggy tree branches. The plants can be tied to the branches or just left to grow through them as they will. Beyond preventing fungal diseases, staking can also improve the look of the plant.

STAKING

Many flowering plants look better if they are staked. Choose stakes to complement the looks of the plant you are supporting.

SMALL BRANCHES can provide support for delicate, thin-stemmed plants such as these cosmos.

MAKE A GRID by enclosing plants with slender stakes and using twine to create the supporting structure.

ADD LAYERS for tall plants as they grow. Add each layer just before plants reach that height.

USE STAKES to support single stems such as this lily.

PINCH OFF all but one or two flower buds to stimulate development of exhibition-size blooms.

Deadheading and Trimming

Some species flower for a longer period of time if they are consistently deadheaded before seeds start to form, while others are just lovelier to look at if you remove spent flowers. When you deadhead, you can just snap or cut off the flower at the top of its stem, or you can remove the whole stem. The choice depends on the growth habit of the plant.

Most of the perennials you will be planting are *herbaceous*, meaning that their stems die back to the ground each fall and regrow each spring. Consequently, they don't need the kind of heavy pruning that woody trees, shrubs, and some vines require. But judicious pinching and trimming of some species can promote bushiness and increase flowering. Asters, chrysanthemums, phlox, and salvias all respond well to having the tips of their stems pinched back in early to mid-spring.

Dividing and Renovating

Perennials vary in the frequency with which they need to be divided. Some, such as peonies, are so slow growing that they almost never need to be divided. But others will die unless they are dug up and divided every few years. In most cases, a little observation will tell you if plants need division.

> ### SMART TIP
> #### WHEN TO DIVIDE PERENNIALS
> Plants are easier to divide successfully at certain points in their growth cycle. Divide spring-blooming perennials a month before the ground freezes in autumn or in very early spring, before new growth has begun. Divide fall-blooming perennials in spring.

The first sign is that the plant is running out of space. In some species, the center of the plant begins to die back while the growth toward the outside of the clump is still vital, and in others, stems and flowers grow smaller than normal.

Bed renovation. Whole beds of perennials require major renovation every six to eight years. In a big bed, it's best to split the area into sections that you work on in sequential seasons. The best time to renovate a bed is in the fall, but early enough so plants can establish new roots before winter. In areas north of Zone 5, renovate in the spring as soon as the soil is workable.

No matter where you live, the first step of bed renovation happens in the spring, when bulbs bloom. Mark their locations, colors, and any other information you want to retain on small plastic or metal tags that you insert beside the plant. If possible, make the stake location consistent, always to the front, rear, or the right or left side of the plant so that it will be easier to know where to dig later on without damaging any bulbs.

When you renovate, dig up the bulbs and each plant in the bed. Take as large a root ball as possible. Dig around plants that resent transplanting, such as peonies and bleeding heart. Place dug out plants on a tarp in the shade and cover any exposed roots with layers of wet newspaper.

Apply a 3- to 4-inch layer of finished compost or aged manure to the bed and till or fork it into the top few inches of soil. Then begin replacing your plants, dividing those that need it.

DIVIDE HOSTAS in early spring when they first appear. Use a shovel to simply dig down and split a plant into sections.

SEASONAL CARE

Each season brings its own routine into the perennial garden. As you gain experience you'll naturally fall into these rhythms. Greet the spring by taking frequent trips to the garden to see what's sprouted, how large it is, and what, if anything, needs to be divided or replaced. As the weather warms, remove the winter mulch from plant crowns because it can promote fungal diseases by retaining too much moisture. If frost is still a possibility, just pull the mulch to the side so that you can easily replace it to protect against a cold night.

Spring. Once the weather has settled and the soil is dry enough to work without compacting it, it's time to add new plants to the garden. You'll also want to cultivate around established plants to get rid of weeds and add needed oxygen to the soil. Compost or other sources of nutrients should be applied as the soil warms to about 50°F.

Mid to late spring is the best time to lay new mulch. Try to wait until the worst of the spring rains have finished, but apply the mulch before the soil begins to get summer-dry.

Summer. Adjust the mulch as necessary to retain soil moisture around the roots, but don't let it touch the stems for fear of encouraging fungal diseases. Staking, trimming, and deadheading are the other chores of summer, with some weeding and watering when necessary. Monitoring for pests and diseases is also a routine job.

Autumn. Autumn is the time for garden clean up. Some plants will need to be divided, and you may want to make some new plantings. If you have been keeping up with deadheading and removing spent flower stalks through the summer, you won't have to do much trimming now. However, as the leaves and stems of herbaceous perennials die back, you may want to move them into the compost pile. Don't add diseased or infested plant material to the compost pile for fear of spreading the problem.

Winter. Winter mulches protect plant roots from damage from freezing/thawing fluctuations; their purpose is to keep the soil consistently frozen. If possible, spread a winter mulch after the top inch or so of the soil surface has frozen. In years when this is impossible, choose the coldest morning you can and apply the mulch before the sun has had a chance to warm the soil surface.

ILLUSTRATED PLANT-BY-PLANT DIRECTORY OF COMMON PERENNIALS

Note: To make this directory of plants most valuable, please read "About the Plant Directories," on page 9.

Achillea millefolium

Common Yarrow

Related Species: Of the 84 other species of *Achillea*, gardeners are most likely to plant *A. filipendulina* and its cultivars, with their tight gold heads that dry so well. 'Moonshine', a hybrid, is particularly popular.

Zones: 3 to 9.

Appearance: The flowers are flat, held on disk-shaped clusters. The gray-green leaves are finely cut and fernlike, sometimes slightly hairy.

Size: 1½ to 3 feet tall, 1 to 2 feet wide.

Flower Color: Best-known cultivars are rich golden yellow, but yarrows display a wide range of colors, including all but true blue, violet, and purple.

Blooming Season: Late spring to late summer.

Exposure: Full sun to light or partial shade.

Soil: Average fertility, well-drained. Established plants tolerate dry conditions.

Spacing: 1 foot apart.

Propagation: Plants form clumps from underground roots. They also self-seed easily.

Pests and Diseases: Trouble-free for pests. Common diseases include powdery mildew and various root-rot diseases in soggy soils.

Notes: Deadhead to prolong bloom and prevent plants from becoming invasive. Divide clumps in very early spring every three to four years. Excellent cut flowers.

Asclepias tuberosa

Butterfly Weed

Related Species: There are more than 100 species in this genus, including the common milkweeds and butterfly weeds.

Zones: 3 to 9.

Appearance: The smooth-margined, slender leaves grow opposite to each other or in whorls. Flowers grow in clusters at the tips of stems.

Size: 1 to 3 feet tall and wide.

Flower Color: Orange, red.

Blooming Season: Summer to early autumn.

Exposure: Full sun.

Soil: Extremely well-drained, slightly acidic, moderately fertile.

Spacing: 1 to 2½ feet apart.

Propagation: Start seeds early indoors for bloom the same year. Light aids germination. Roots resent disturbance, so use peat pots, soil blocks, or plastic pots. Transplant into the garden when all danger of frost is past.

Pests and Diseases: Usually trouble-free. Allow the caterpillars of the monarch butterfly to feed on the plant; they won't destroy it.

Notes: Leaves emerge quite late in the spring. To avoid damaging your butterfly weeds, mark their location with small plastic stakes when you mulch the bed before winter.

Aster species

Michaelmas Daisy, New England Aster, Frikart's Aster

Related Species: Michaelmas daisy or New York aster (*A. novi-belgii*), New England aster (*A. novae-angliae*), and Frikart's aster (A. × *frikartii*) are the best known of the 250 species of asters.

Zones: 2 to 8.

Appearance: With their rangy growth, taller asters can look weedy unless they are placed behind fuller plants. Stems are woody and leaves are lance-shaped. The flowers are daisylike.

Size: 2 to 6 feet tall, 2 to 3 feet wide.

Flower Color: Blue, purple, pink, and white with yellow centers.

Blooming Season: Late summer through fall.

Exposure: Full sun to partial shade.

Soil: Moist, well-drained, humus-rich.

Spacing: Depending on species, 1 to 3 feet apart.

Propagation: Semiripe cuttings, taken in spring and very early summer.

Pests and Diseases: Aphids, Japanese beetles and chrysanthemum lace bugs can attack asters. Control lace bugs with sprays of insecticidal soap or horticultural oil, a highly refined oil sometimes called light oil. Diseases include rust (*Puccinia sorghi* and *Coleosporium asterum*) and leaf spots. Provide high air circulation and pick off any infected leaves.

Notes: To prolong their sometimes short life span, mulch asters for the winter and divide crowded clumps in the early spring every three years or so.

Astilbe × arendsii
Astilbe, False Spirea

Related Species: 12 species and numerous hybrids and cultivars are available, but cultivars of *A. arendsii* are the most common.

Zones: 4 to 8.

Appearance: The always-attractive leaves are fernlike and delicate. Fluffy or plumy spikes of tiny flowers rise above them.

Size: 10 inches to 2½ feet tall, 2 to 2½ feet wide.

Flower Color: White, cream, pink, lilac,

and red.

Blooming Season: Mid-spring through early summer.

Exposure: Full sun in northern areas to partial shade in southern spots.

Soil: Consistently moist, slightly acid, humus-rich, and fertile.

Spacing: 10 inches to 2½ feet apart, depending on species.

Propagation: Start seeds early indoors and plant out the slow-growing plants in mid- to late summer. Divide crowded clumps in very early spring in the North, early fall in the South.

Pests and Diseases: Japanese beetles may attack. Diseases include Fusarium wilt and powdery mildew.

Notes: Astilbes make wonderfully long-lived and dramatic cut flowers.

Baptisia australis
False Indigo

Related Species: Close to 30 species of false indigo grow in North America, but *B. lactea* (white false indigo) and *B. perfoliata* (yellow false indigo) are the only other species grown in gardens.

Zones: 3 to 8.

Appearance: The compound leaves show the family resemblance to clovers and peas. Spikes of pea-like flowers rise above them and are followed by seedpods. The plant looks like a bush, bigger than many typical perennials.

Size: 3 to 4 feet.

Flower Color: Blue.

Blooming Season: Late spring to early

summer.

Exposure: Full sun to partial shade.

Soil: Moist, well-drained, of average fertility.

Spacing: 3 to 4 feet apart.

Propagation: Harvest and plant fresh seed as soon as the pods turn brown in fall and the seeds darken. Take semiripe cuttings after the plant has finished flowering.

Pests and Diseases: Aphids attack when plants are in soils with excess nitrogen. Powdery mildew may develop in areas with poor air circulation.

Notes: These plants resent disturbance, so it's best to space them widely, as recommended above, and leave them in place. If using seeds that have been stored, pour boiling water over them and let them soak for 24 hours before planting.

Boltonia asteroides
False Chamomile

Related Species: Of the eight species of false chamomile, only *Boltonia asteroides* is commonly grown in North American gardens.

Zones: 3 to 8.

Appearance: Leaves small, lance-shaped and entire, forming a mound that is attractive in the spring and early summer, but can look weedy late in the summer. Flowers are daisylike.

Size: 4 to 6 feet tall, 3 to 4 feet wide.

Flower Color: Usually white with yellow centers, although pink, violet, and purple

Boltonia asteroides/**False Camomile** *continued*

cultivars are available.

Blooming Season: Late summer through autumn.

Exposure: Full sun to partial shade.

Soil: Well-drained, moist, and humus-rich.

Spacing: 2 to 4 feet apart.

Propagation: Take semiripe cuttings in early summer. Divide crowded clumps in early spring.

Pests and Diseases: Largely trouble-free.

Notes: Seeds may not produce plants that look like the parent, so be prepared to experiment and perhaps eliminate seed-grown plants. In dry-soil conditions, the flowers are small, but the foliage is still attractive.

Campanula species
Bellflower

Related Species: More than two dozen *Campanula* species are grown in North American gardens. Of these, Carpathian harebell (*C. carpatica*), peach-leaf bell-flower (*C. persicifolia*), and bluebell (*C. rotundifolia*) are the most common.

Zones: 3 to 9.

Appearance: Leaf shape varies with species, but leaves at stem bases are generally broader than those growing higher on the plant. Flowers are bell-shaped and carried on slender stems.

Size: 6 inches to 3 feet tall, 6 inches to 1½ feet wide.

Flower Color: Many shades of blue, also white and pink.

Blooming Season: Late spring through midsummer.

Exposure: Full sun to partial shade. In the South, protect from the hot afternoon sun.

Soil: Moist, humus-rich, average fertility.

Spacing: 1 to 2 feet, depending on species.

Propagation: Start seeds early indoors and plant out seedlings in mid-spring. Divide in early spring or fall. Take semiripe to ripe cuttings after flowering.

Pests and Diseases: Aphids, thrips, and slugs can cause problems. Diseases include crown and stem rot (*Sclerotinia* spp.) as well as several species of rust.

Notes: Campanula plants are lovely in every season, in or out of bloom, and flowers can be cut for arrangements.

Chrysanthemum
Chrysanthemum

Related Species: There are numerous Chrysanthemum species and related plants, including Shasta Daisies (*Leucanthemum* x *superbum*).

Zones:: 4 to 9.

Appearance: Leaves are deeply lobed, bright to dark green, and slightly hairy. There are six divisions of chrysanthemums based solely on the flower form. All are composites, with a central disk surrounded by petals, but they can be single or double and petal shapes vary from division to division.

Size: 1 to 4 feet tall, 1 to 3 feet wide.

Flower Color: Every color but true blue and true crimson.

Blooming Season: Fall.

Exposure: Full sun.

Soil: Well-drained, moist, humus-rich, average fertility.

Spacing: 1 to 2 feet.

Propagation: Stem cuttings, layering, root division, and seeds of some cultivars. Plants may also be purchased. Do not transplant to the garden until the frost-free date.

Pests and Diseases: Aphids, thrips, slugs, leaf miner, earwigs and Chrysanthemum nematode attack. Diseases include botrytis and powdery mildew.

Notes: For bushiness, pinch all stem tips when plants are 4 inches tall and once again, after they have grown another 4 inches. Be sure to stop pinching in July so that plants have time to set buds for fall bloom.

Plants with large blooms must be staked to keep them healthy and looking good. Insert the stakes before planting and secure the stems with a loose, figure-8 tie. It may be necessary to add supplemental stakes just before plants bloom.

IMPROVED MEFO CHRYSANTHEMUM

For exhibition-size blooms, pinch off lateral stems and all buds but one on each stem just after they form.

The stools, or root balls, may be stored in a coldframe that doesn't freeze all winter for early propagation. After frost, cut back the stems to 6 inches. Pack them into boxes and cover with damp compost. Begin watering when new growth begins and take cuttings once they are at least 4 inches long.

Coreopsis species

Tickseed

Related Species: Both annual and perennial species of tickseed are available, but most people grow the perennial lanceleaf (*C. lanceolata*) or threadleaf (*C. verticillata*) species.

Zones: 3 to 9.

Appearance: Depending on species, leaves are narrow and threadlike or lance-shaped. Single or double daisylike flowers are numerous.

Size: 1 to 3 feet tall, 2 to 3 feet wide.

Flower Color: Yellow, orange, pink, and mahogany, sometimes with a maroon or brown splotch around the center.

Blooming Season: Summer to frost.

Exposure: Full sun.

Soil: Well-drained, average to rich fertility. Drought-tolerant once established.

Spacing: 1½ to 2 feet.

Propagation: Start seeds early indoors for blooms the same year, and transplant to the garden once all danger of frost has passed.

Pests and Diseases: Aphids, four-lined plant bugs, and aster leaf hoppers all can attack. Aster yellows, (*Chlorogenus callistephi*) carried by the leaf hoppers, is the only significant disease.

Notes: Coreopsis are long-blooming in the garden and make long-lasting cut flowers. Keep deadheaded to prevent self-seeding. They also help to repel deer from the garden and can be used in a mixed bed bordering wild areas or deer crossings.

Delphinium elatum

Candle Delphinium

Related Species: There are over 200 species of *Delphinium* available to gardeners. Most are perennial, but the annual larkspur (*Consolida ambigua*) is a close relative formerly classified in this genus.

Zones: 3 to 8.

Appearance: Leaves are deeply cut and alternate, generally growing in a mound from which flower spikes rise. Cupped flowers are clustered along the tops of tall stems.

Size: 4 to 6 feet tall, 2 to 3 feet wide.

Flower Color: Blue, purple, white, pink, and lavender.

Blooming Season: Late spring through summer. May rebloom if cut back after first bloom.

Exposure: Full sun in the North; sun to partial shade in southern locations.

Soil: Moist and well-drained, fertile, humus-rich.

Spacing: 1½ to 2½ feet apart.

Propagation: Start seeds early indoors, after freezing for four to six weeks. Cover flats. Seeds germinate in dark. Transplant to the garden a week or so before the frost-free date. Divide crowded clumps in early spring.

Pests and Diseases: Many insects, including slugs, cutworms, aphids, two-spotted spider mites, leaf miners, and stalk borers attack *Delphinium*. Diseases include bacterial leaf spot, bacterial rot, crown rot, aster yellows, Fusarium wilt, and powdery mildew.

Notes: Flower stalks often need to be staked. Plant in a location with good air circulation and quickly draining soil to protect against diseases and pests. Flower spikes make long-lasting and dramatic cut flowers. In southern areas, choose *D. × belladonna* hybrids because they hold up better in heat than other species.

Dianthus plumarius

Cottage Pink

Related Species: There are numerous species of garden pinks. Carnation (*D. caryophyllus*) and sweet William (*D. barbatus*) are two of the more than 300 *Dianthus* species.

Zones: 3 to 9.

Appearance: Leaves are slender and grassy, usually a gray-green color and grow in a mound. Wiry stems emerge from them and the spicy-smelling flowers can appear to form a solid blanket over the stems.

Size: 10 inches to 2 feet tall, 1 to 1½ feet wide.

Flower Color: Pink, white, red, and many bicolors.

Blooming Season: Early to midsummer.

Exposure: Full sun.

Soil: Well-drained, of average fertility, with a pH that is close to neutral.

Spacing: 10 inches to 1¼ feet apart.

Propagation: Start seeds early indoors or take stem cuttings in summer. Transplant to the garden after the frost-free date.

Pests and Diseases: Largely insect-free.

*Dianthus/***Cottage Pink** *continued*

Rust can attack in humid, crowded conditions.

Notes: The foliage is lovely all season, with or without blooms. Grow cultivars in the *Allwoodii* series for taller plants whose fragrant flowers make wonderful additions to bouquets.

Dictamnus albus
Gas Plant, Dittany

Related Species: Although there are several species, *Dictamnus albus* is the only plant in the genus that is commonly grown in gardens.

Zones: 3 to 8.

Appearance: Dittany forms a shrubby clump of erect stems with deep green, lance-shaped leaves. Spidery flowers with long stamens grow on spikes that rise above the leaves.

Size: 1 to 4 feet tall, 1 to 3 feet wide.

Flower Color: White, pink, or purple.

Blooming Season: Late spring and early summer.

Exposure: Full sun to partial shade.

Soil: Moist, well-drained, of average fertility and humus content.

Spacing: 2 to 3½ feet apart.

Propagation: Plant fresh seed outdoors in late summer. This plant transplants poorly, so it should be started in peat pots or soil blocks you don't direct-seed. Transplant to the garden after all danger of frost has past.

Pests and Diseases: Largely pest-free, but can develop root rots in soggy soils.

Notes: Use the clear, white blooms to light up a corner of your yard that receives partial shade in the afternoon.

Echinacea species
Coneflower

Related Species: The roots of *E. angustifolia* are used medicinally to strengthen the immune system, while purple coneflower (*E. purpurea*) and pale coneflower (*E. pallida*) are used in ornamental gardens.

Zones: 3 to 8.

Appearance: The lance-shaped, dark green leaves hug the stems. The erect plant can give a formal or informal look, depending on location and design. The daisylike flowers have cone-shaped centers, and some have reflexed (down-turned) petals.

Size: 2 to 6 feet tall, 1 to 2 feet wide.

Flower Color: Purplish pink, rose, or white petals with shiny orange centers.

Blooming Season: Mid- to late summer.

Exposure: Full sun.

Soil: Well-drained, of average fertility and humus content. Will tolerate dry periods once established.

Spacing: 1½ to 2 feet apart.

Propagation: Start seeds early indoors after refrigerating for a week or two. Seeds need light to germinate. Transplant to the garden after the frost-free date. Roots of crowded clumps can be divided in fall.

Pests and Diseases: Largely pest- and disease-free.

Notes: Deer do not like the odor and will shy away from gardens that are completely surrounded by *Echinacea*. All cultivars make wonderful cut flowers and the seed heads can be dried for winter bouquets.

Eryngium giganteum
Sea Holly

Related Species: There are more than 250 species, many of which are useful in the garden. In cold regions, grow *E. amethystinum* or *E. planum*, which are hardy to Zones 2 and 4, respectively.

Zones: 5 to 8 or 9 to 11 with some shade.

Appearance: The woody stems and erect form make sea holly a versatile landscape plant. Most of the leathery, gray-green toothed leaves grow at the base of the plant, while the flower stalks are nearly leafless. The cone-shaped, bristly flowers are surrounded by a ruff of spiky petals.

Size: 1 to 2 feet tall, 1 to 2 feet wide.

Flower Color: Silvery or steely grayish blue.

Blooming Season: Summer.

Exposure: Full sun in all but the southern-most areas (Zones 9 to 11).

Soil: Well-drained, of average fertility. Drought-resistant once established.

Spacing: 1½ to 2 feet apart.

Propagation: Start seed indoors in very early spring after stratifying in the refrigerator for six weeks. Transplant into garden just before the frost-free date. Fresh seed can also be planted outdoors in fall, where it will naturally stratify over the winter.

Pests and Diseases: Largely trouble-free except for root rots in soggy soils.

Notes: Flowering stems make lovely dried winter bouquets, alone or with other dried flowers. Hang upside down to dry just before the flower opens.

Erysimum species
Wallflower

Related Species: Many of the wallflowers are biennials or, like *E. cheiri,* perennials grown as biennials. The annual species, wormseed mustard, *E. cheiranthoides,* can become a weed in favorable growing conditions. Wallflowers were formerly classified as *Cheiranthus* and are still listed that way in some catalogs.

Zones: 5 to 9.

Appearance: Leaves are narrow and lance-shaped, growing in a mound. Buttercup-shaped flowers cluster on spikes that rise above the basal mound.

Size: 2 to 3 feet tall, 1 to 1½ feet wide.

Flower Color: Yellow, orange, cream, bronze, lilac, and mauve.

Blooming Season: Spring to early summer.

Exposure: Partial shade is best, but will tolerate full sun in moist soil in the North.

Soil: Moist, of average to high fertility.

Spacing: 1 to 1½ feet apart.

Propagation: Start seeds early indoors or in nursery beds once weather is settled. Transplant into final position in early fall.

Pests and Diseases: This member of the cabbage family is prey to the same pests and diseases as its vegetable relatives, but is usually less trouble.

Notes: Wallflowers have an exquisite fragrance, which is strongest at twilight and early evening.

Euphorbia griffithii
Spurge

Related Species: The spurges comprise more than 2,000 species, ranging from small annuals to succulent houseplants to tall trees. Christmas poinsettias are certainly the most commonly grown members of this large genus.

Zones: 5 to 9.

Appearance: Lance-shaped leaves with smooth margins and a prominent central vein are topped by the colorful bracts that surround the small inconspicuous flowers.

Size: 1 to 1½ feet tall and wide.

Flower Color: Bracts are yellow, red, or orange.

Blooming Season: Spring through summer, depending on species.

Exposure: Versatile.

Soil: Well-drained, light, of average fertility.

Spacing: 1 to 1½ feet.

Propagation: Start seed early indoors after freezing it for two weeks and then soaking in water, changed daily, for five days. Alternate soil temperature between 85°F during the day to 70°F at night. Germination may take as long as a month. Divide plants in early spring or fall, or

take stem cuttings in midsummer.

Pests and Diseases: Largely pest-free.

Notes: This plant is said to repel deer and can be used in a mixed bed that borders wild areas or deer crossings.

Gaillardia aristata
Blanket Flower

Related Species: *G.* × *grandiflora* is similar to *aristata* but larger. Try 'Red Plume' for a dark red, long-lasting cut flower. Annual species of this genus also are frequently available.

Zones: 5 to 8.

Appearance: The toothed, hairy leaves grow on sturdy, erect stems that give a fairly open appearance. The flowers are daisylike.

Size: 2 to 3 feet tall, 1½ to 2 feet wide.

Flower Color: Yellow, orange, red, many with a contrasting color on the tips of the petals.

Blooming Season: Throughout the summer.

Exposure: Full sun.

Soil: Extremely well-drained, low to moderate fertility.

Spacing: 2 feet apart.

Propagation: Seeds can be started early indoors. Light aids germination. Transplant to the garden on the frost-free date.

Pests and Diseases: Largely trouble-free.

Notes: Blanket flowers make long-lasting cut flowers and have the added advantage of a long blooming period.

Geranium species
Cranesbill

Related Species: More than 300 species of hardy geranium grow in temperate climates.

Zones: 3 to 8.

Appearance: Plants usually form a loose rosette from which the flower stalks arise. Leaves are divided and may be toothed or lobed. Open-petaled, saucer-shaped flowers range in size from 1 to 2 inches across.

Size: 6 inches to 2 feet tall, 8 inches to 1½ feet wide.

Flower Color: White, pink, blue, and violet.

Blooming Season: Late spring to mid-summer.

Exposure: Full sun to partial shade.

Soil: Humus-rich, consistently moist.

Spacing: 10 inches to 1 foot depending on species and cultivar.

Propagation: Divide in very early spring or fall. Start seeds early indoors or outdoors in late spring to early summer. Transplant to the garden on the frost-free date.

Pests and Diseases: Largely trouble-free.

Notes: Butterflies and songbirds flock to cranesbill plants, for both the nectar and the seeds.

Helenium autumnale
Sneezeweed

Related Species: Though most gardeners grow the perennial sneezeweed, the strongly scented annual, bitterweed (*H. amarum*), is sometimes used in rock gardens.

Zones: 3 to 8.

Appearance: Lance-shaped, hairy, toothed leaves grow on tall stems. Flowers resembling sunflowers top the stems.

Size: 3 to 5 feet tall, 2 to 3 feet wide.

Flower Color: Yellow, orange.

Blooming Season: Late summer to frost.

Exposure: Full sun to partial shade.

Soil: Moist, humus-rich. Will tolerate somewhat soggy soils.

Spacing: 2 to 3 feet.

Propagation: Start seeds early indoors for bloom the same season or outside once spring weather has settled and frost danger is past. Sneezeweed will flower the first summer after planting. Light aids germination, so cover seeds only lightly, with moistened vermiculite, if at all. Transplant to the garden when all danger of frost has past. Divide crowded plants in early spring. Take stem cuttings in early summer.

Pests and Diseases: Largely trouble-free.

Notes: Sneezeweed is a long-lasting cut flower, which attracts butterflies to the garden.

Helleborus niger
Christmas Rose

Related Species: Two of the 15 other *Helleborus* species are generally grown in North American gardens: Lenten rose (*H. orientalis*), which has creamy white blossoms flushed with pink; and stinking hellebore (*H. foetidus*), with pale green to greenish white flowers.

Zones: 3 to 8.

Appearance: The low-growing, leathery leaves may stay green all winter, particularly under a loose, airy mulch. The striking, saucer-shaped blooms rise above the leaves and are erect. The delicate petals surround prominent centers; the flowers are slightly pendant.

Size: 1 to 1⅓ feet tall, 1 to 1½ feet wide.

Flower Color: Pink.

Blooming Season: Late winter through very early spring.

Exposure: Partial shade.

Soil: Humus-rich, moist.

Spacing: 1 to 1½ feet apart.

Propagation: Divide crowns after flowering. Freeze seed for two weeks before planting in flats indoors or sow outside in fall so seeds can freeze and thaw naturally. If direct-seeding stratified seed, plant as soon as soil can be worked in the spring. Transplant to the garden after the frost-free date. Self-seeds in good spots.

Pests and Diseases: Largely trouble-free.

Notes: Deer do not like the odor of hellebores, so they can be used as part of a deer-repellent planting. Flowers are lovely and long-lasting when cut.

Hemerocallis species and cultivars

Daylily

Related Species: With 15 daylily species and so many cultivars, you can find a daylily for any spot.

Zones: 3 to 9.

Appearance: Long, strap-like leaves grow from a central crown arising from underground rhizomes. Branched spikes of trumpet-shaped flowers also grow from the crown.

Size: 1 to 3 feet tall and wide.

Flower Color: Every color and shade except white, blue, and true green.

Blooming Season: Early spring to late summer, depending on species and cultivar.

Exposure: Full sun to partial shade.

Soil: Well-drained, moist, of average fertility.

Spacing: 1 to 3 feet apart.

Propagation: Divide rhizomes almost any time, but early spring is best. Seeds will produce blooming plants in three to five years but will not usually come true to type. If using seeds, freeze for two weeks and then soak for five days, changing water daily. Transplant to the garden after the frost-free date.

Pests and Diseases: Usually trouble-free, although spider mites and thrips can attack.

Notes: Even though individual flowers bloom for only a day, the architecturally interesting branches look beautiful in cut-flower arrangements if you remove the spent blooms each evening. Outdoor plants also look their best if they are deadheaded regularly.

Heuchera cultivars

Coral Bells

Related Species: Numerous species and cultivars are available to North American gardeners. Most of the plants sold and grown today are cultivars of *H.* × *brizoides.*

Zones: 3 to 9.

Appearance: These plants are lovely in or out of bloom with their mounded form. The deep-green or mottled with gray or silver leaves have scalloped edges. The delicate stems covered with tiny bell-shaped blossoms rise in an ethereal mist above the mound of leaves.

Size: 1½ to 2 feet tall and wide.

Flower Color: White, pink, red, and coral.

Blooming Season: Late spring through summer, depending on species and cultivar.

Exposure: Full sun in most areas, partial shade where summers are hot.

Soil: Well-drained, moist, humus-rich.

Spacing: 1½ to 2 feet apart.

Propagation: Start seeds early indoors, covering with a scant layer of vermiculite because light promotes germination. Transplant to the garden after all danger of frost has past. Divide plants in spring or fall.

Pests and Diseases: Largely trouble-free, although strawberry root weevils may attack if you plant coral bells near or following strawberries. Powdery mildew can be a problem in humid conditions.

Notes: While they are in bloom, the tiny flowers of coral bells attract birds and butterflies.

Hibiscus moscheutos

Rose Mallow

Related Species: More than 200 species of *Hibiscus* grow in tropical or semi-tropical areas. In temperate zones, the most commonly grown species include the great rose mallow (*H. grandiflorus*), the cotton rose (*H mutabilis*), the China rose (*H. rosa-sinensis*), and the Japanese hibiscus (*H. schizopetalus*).

Zones: 5 to 9.

Appearance: Plants are large and shrubby. The open flowers have textured petals and prominent stamens.

Size: 3 to 8 feet tall, 3 to 5 feet wide.

Flower Color: Rose, pink, white, and red.

Blooming Season: Midsummer to fall.

Exposure: Full sun to very light shade.

Soil: Well-drained, humus-rich, consistently moist.

Spacing: 4 to 6 feet apart.

Propagation: Take semiripe cuttings in early summer. If you start seeds, before planting, soak them in hot water for 48 hours, changing the water every 12 hours. Cover seed containers because darkness aids germination. Plant out seedlings when danger of frost is past in spring.

Pests and Diseases: Japanese beetles and

Hibiscus moscheutos / **Rose mallow** *continued*

aphids can be troublesome. Viral diseases and leaf spot fungi may attack plants.

Notes: To encourage bushy growth, cut back stem tips after the danger of frost has past in spring. All *Hibiscus* species can be used as focal points in bird and butterfly gardens.

Hosta species and cultivars
Hosta, Plantain Lily

Related Species: 40 species are known, with many more cultivars and hybrids. They range in size from dwarfs a few inches high to big specimens 4 feet across.

Zones: 3 to 9.

Appearance: Large, broad leaves form a mound. In many species and cultivars, leaves are striped or mottled with yellow, silver, and even pink. Trumpet-shaped flowers bloom along tall stems and are fragrant in some species.

Size: 8 inches to 3 feet tall, 8 inches to 4 feet wide.

Flower Color: White, lavender, blue, and purple.

Blooming Season: Summer to late summer, depending on cultivar.

Exposure: Partial to deep shade, depending on cultivar and location.

Soil: Consistently moist, humus-rich.

Spacing: Depending on cultivar 10 inches to 3½ feet.

Propagation: Divide plants in the early spring or fall.

Pests and Diseases: Slugs and snails are

often troublesome. Crown rot attacks if soil remains soggy during the winter months.

Notes: Leaves of many cultivars, particularly those with gold, silver, or other variegated tones, will burn if exposed to hot afternoon sun.

Liatris scariosa
Tall Gayfeather

Related Species: Snakeroot (*L. punctata*) and spike gayfeather (*L. spicata*) are two of the more than 30 members of the genus.

Zones: 2 to 8.

Appearance: The slender, grass-like leaves form basal tufts from which tall, fuzzy spikes of tiny flowers grow. Flower spikes open from top to bottom.

Size: 2 to 5 feet tall, 1 to 2 feet wide.

Flower Color: Purple, pink.

Blooming Season: Midsummer through late summer.

Exposure: Full sun.

Soil: Moist, humus-rich, of average fertility.

Spacing: 1 to 2 feet.

Propagation: Start seeds early indoors after stratifying in the refrigerator for six weeks. Transplant to the garden after the frost-free date. Seeds can also be planted outside in the fall to stratify naturally. Divide clumps, which will have formed tiny cormlets, in spring or fall.

Pests and Diseases: Largely trouble-free in good conditions.

Notes: Full sun is necessary to keep the

plants healthy and erect. In partial shade, they tend to fall over and may develop fungal problems.

Lobelia cardinalis
Cardinal Flower

Related Species: The cultivars of trailing and edging lobelia (*L. erinus*) are often used in the annual garden or in summer containers. Less well known is the blue, or great, lobelia (*L. siphilitica*), which is a lovely, late-blooming blue-flowered species.

Zones: 3 to 8.

Appearance: Narrow, lance-shaped leaves with smooth margins may be green or have a reddish bronze hue. On the tall flower stalks, leaves grasp the stem.

Size: 3 to 6 feet tall, 1 to 2 feet wide.

Flower Color: Clear brilliant red.

Blooming Season: Late summer to fall.

Exposure: Full sun in the North; sun to partial shade in Southern areas.

Soil: Moist, humus-rich, of moderate fertility.

Spacing: 2 to 2½ feet apart.

Propagation: For blooms the same year, start seeds early indoors after stratifying for 10 days in the refrigerator. Seeds must have light to germinate. Transplant to the garden at the frost-free date. Mature plants can be divided in early spring.

Pests and Diseases: Largely trouble-free.

Notes: Perennial lobelias will tolerate damp soil near ponds or at wetland margins. Lobelias attract hummingbirds and butterflies.

Mertensia virginica

Virginia Bluebells

Related Species: Virginia bluebells are members of the borage family, and resemble a more-refined version of this common herb.

Zones: 3 to 9.

Appearance: Leaves are blue-green, oval, and smooth margined. The drooping flowers grow from the tips of the stems.

Size: 1 to 2 feet tall and wide.

Flower Color: Blue.

Blooming Season: Spring.

Exposure: Partial shade, but will tolerate full sun in northern areas.

Soil: Moist but not soggy, humus-rich.

Spacing: 2 to 2½ feet apart.

Propagation: Plant fresh seeds or buy seedlings. Plants resent disturbance and are difficult to divide successfully but will self-sow easily. Transplant volunteer seedlings with a large root ball.

Pests and Diseases: Largely trouble-free.

Notes: Plants will go dormant after they bloom, dying back to the ground. Use ferns or hostas as companions to hide the dying foliage, and avoid planting over them or accidentally digging them up.

Myosotis scorpioides

Forget-Me-Not

Related Species: There are more than 50 species of forget-me-nots, some annuals, some perennials, and some biennials. Of these, *M. sylvatica*, the sometimes biennial forget-me-not, and *M. palustris*, an annual with white as well as blue cultivars, are the most commonly grown.

Zones: 3 to 8.

Appearance: Leaves are lance-shaped and have smooth margins. They generally grow in a tuft close to the ground. Slender, branched stems of dainty, little flowers rise above them.

Size: 8 inches to 1½ feet tall, 10 inches to 1½ feet wide, depending on species.

Flower Color: Blue, pink, and white.

Blooming Season: Spring through early summer.

Exposure: Partial shade, but will tolerate full sun if soil is constantly moist.

Soil: Moist, humus-rich.

Spacing: 6 inches to 1½ feet apart, depending on species.

Propagation: Start seeds indoors, covering only lightly because they need light to germinate. Transplant to the garden after the frost-free date. Will self-sow outdoors in preferred locations.

Pests and Diseases: Usually trouble-free.

Notes: Forget-me-nots are wonderful companions to the spring-flowering bulbs because they bloom simultaneously and keep weeds out of the beds.

Oenothera macrocarpa

Missouri Primrose; Ozark Sundrops

Related Species: Showy primrose (*O. speciosa*), sundrops (*O. tetragona*), evening scented primrose (*O. lamarckiana*) and white evening primrose (*O. pallida*) are some of the more than 80 *Oenothera* species commonly grown.

Zones: 3 to 9.

Appearance: Leaves are narrow with smooth margins. The many-branched plant can look shrubby. Clear, bright yellow flowers are saucer-shaped.

Size: 1 to 1½ feet tall, 2 to 3 feet wide.

Flower Color: Other species can be pink or white.

Blooming Season: Late spring through midsummer.

Exposure: Full sun.

Soil: Well-drained, of moderate fertility.

Spacing: 2 feet.

Propagation: Start seeds early indoors after stratifying in refrigerator for two weeks. Light helps germination. Transplant to the garden after all danger of frost has passed. Mature plants can be divided in early spring and semi-ripe cuttings root easily.

Pests and Diseases: Largely pest-free, but can develop root rot in soggy soil.

Notes: This plant tolerates hot, dry conditions once it is mature. It also attracts butterflies and songbirds to the garden.

CHAPTER 3

Paeonia lactiflora hybrid
Garden Peony

Related Species: Tree peonies (*P. suffruticosa, P. potaninii*) are among the other 30 peony species grown in North American gardens.
Zones: 3 to 8.
Appearance: Bushy peony shrubs have shiny green leaves with smooth margins. Garden peonies die back to the ground each fall and re-emerge in the early spring. The flowers can be single, double, or semidouble and are often fragrant.
Size: 2 to 3 feet tall, 3 to 4 feet wide.
Flower Color: Reds, pinks, maroon, and white.
Blooming Season: Depending on cultivar, from spring through early summer.
Exposure: Full sun to partial shade and best if shielded from morning sun.
Soil: Well-drained, moist, humus-rich.
Spacing: 3 to 5 feet apart.
Propagation: Plants resent disturbance and sometimes die if you try to divide them.
Pests and Diseases: Thrips and Japanese beetles attack peonies. Diseases include botrytis in humid conditions, as well as anthracnose (*Colletotrichum* spp.) and other fungal diseases. Ants are attracted to peonies but do not hurt the blooms.
Notes: Double flowers last longer than singles. To enjoy your plants for at least thirty years, mulch them in spring, stake the flower stems, water when dry, apply ½ inch of compost around stems in late summer, cut stems to the ground in fall,

and don't disturb them. Plant them only a few inches deep. Peonies planted too deeply tend not to flower.

Papaver orientale species
Poppy

Related Species: Nearly 50 poppy species are known. North Americans generally grow annual poppies such as the 'Shirley' poppy (*P. rhoeas*) as well as perennial poppies, including Iceland poppy (*P. nudicaule*) in the garden.
Zones: 3 to 8.
Appearance: Leaves are usually hairy and lobed. Flower stems rise above them. Petals are crinkled like crepe paper and the open blossoms are usually single.
Size: 2 to 3 feet tall, 8 inches to 1 foot wide.
Flower Color: Pink, red, and orange with a dark basal blotch.
Blooming Season: Early summer.
Exposure: Full sun to light shade.
Soil: Well-drained, of moderate fertility.
Spacing: 10 inches to 1½ feet apart.
Propagation: Plant seeds early indoors. Do not cover seeds with media but place a glass panel or plastic wrap over the flats and place in a warm, dark location. Divide plants in fall. Most self-seed easily and you may need to thin them.
Pests and Diseases: Largely trouble-free.
Notes: Poppies do not cut well, but if you try it, singe the bottom of the stem immediately after cutting to prevent sap from leaking and fouling the water in the vase.

Phlox paniculata
Garden Phlox

Related Species: Both annual and perennial species of phlox are grown in North American gardens. Some are upright and shrubby while others are trailing. Almost all have showy clusters of brightly colored flowers. Moss pink (*P. subulata*) is a common addition to rock gardens while the annual phlox (*P. drummondii*) is often used in beds and borders.
Zones: 3 to 9.
Appearance: Smooth-margined leaves grow opposite one another on erect stems topped with pyramidal, fragrant flower clusters.
Size: 3 to 4 feet tall, 2 to 3 feet wide.
Flower Color: White, pink, lavender, and magenta; many have a contrasting central "eye".
Blooming Season: Mid to late summer.
Exposure: Full sun but will tolerate partial or light shade.
Soil: Moist, humus-rich, well-drained.
Spacing: 1½ to 2½ feet apart.
Propagation: Start seeds early indoors after freezing for two weeks; then soaking in warm water, changed daily for seven days. Germinate in darkness. Transplant to the garden after the frost-free date. Stem cuttings taken in summer root easily, and plants can be divided in spring.
Pests and Diseases: Spider mites and phlox plant bugs attack plants. Powdery mildew is common. Thin stems and eliminate surrounding weeds to increase air circulation and minimize both the plant

bugs and the mildew.

Notes: Phlox help to repel deer so they are a good plant to use between the garden and wild areas. Butterflies and hummingbirds are attracted to them, and they make long-lasting cut flowers.

Platycodon grandiflorus
Balloon Flower

Related Species: Balloon flowers are related to Campanula species.

Zones: 3 to 9.

Appearance: Leaves are toothed and lance-shaped. Flower stems rise above the mound they form. Cup-shaped flowers open from buds shaped like tiny hot-air balloons.

Size: 11 inches to 2 feet tall, 1 to 2 feet wide.

Flower Color: Blue, pink, and white.

Blooming Season: Midsummer.

Exposure: Full sun but will tolerate partial or light shade.

Soil: Moist, humus-rich, of average fertility. Established plants tolerate dry periods but not prolonged droughts.

Spacing: 1 to 1½ feet apart.

Propagation: Plant seeds early indoors; do not cover seed because light helps germination. Divide clumps in spring. May self-sow in preferred locations.

Pests and Diseases: Largely trouble-free.

Notes: Plants die back over winter and stems do not reappear until late spring. Mark the location of all balloon flower plants to avoid disturbing them.

Primula marginata
Primrose

Related Species: More than 400 species of *Primula* grow in North American and European gardens. Of these, *P. denticulata*, *P. japonica*, and *P. pruhonicensis* hybrids, or polyanthus hybrids, are garden favorites.

Zones: 3 to 8.

Appearance: Leaves form a rosette from which flower stalks rise. Leaves are serrated, fleshy, and leathery. Flowers form in clusters of up to 20 florets each.

Size: 1 foot tall and wide.

Flower Color: Lilac, lavender, blue violet, pink, or white, often with a contrasting eye.

Blooming Season: Early spring.

Exposure: Partial shade is best, but plants will tolerate full sun if kept constantly moist.

Soil: Moist, humus-rich. Tolerates dry soils after leaves have died back in summer.

Spacing: 8 inches to 1 foot apart.

Propagation: Start seeds early indoors after stratifying in refrigerator for two weeks. Cover seed lightly with vermiculite because it must remain moist; light helps germination. Transplant to the garden after the frost-free date. Divide mature plants in fall.

Pests and Diseases: Red spider mite may attack in dry conditions.

Notes: It's tempting to collect primrose species once you've seen how diverse these lovely flowers can be. *P. villosa* and others with relatively tall, stiff flower stems make good cut flowers.

Pulmonaria saccharata
Bethlehem Sage, Lungwort

Related Species: Lungwort is a relative of borage, as you can easily see from the flowers. *P. angustifolia* is a species with solid green leaves that are not spotted.

Zones: 3 to 8.

Appearance: Leaves are large, oval with a pointed tip, smooth-margined, and spotted with white or silver.

Size: 1 to 1½ feet tall, 1 to 2 feet wide.

Flower Color: Blue, pink, and white.

Blooming Season: Spring.

Exposure: Partial to full shade.

Soil: Moist, well-drained, humus-rich.

Spacing: 2 to 3 feet apart.

Propagation: Plant fresh seed in the fall or buy seedlings. Divide in spring. Plants self-seed easily.

Pests and Diseases: Slugs can be a problem.

Notes: Plants remain lovely all season and can light up a dark corner with their speckled leaves.

Perennial directory continued on page 86

CHAPTER 3

Rudbeckia hirta
Black-eyed Susan

Related Species: *Rudbeckia* species, often called coneflowers, include 15 that are commonly used in North American gardens, among them the popular cultivar 'Goldsturm' and the green-centered *R. laciniata.*
Zones: 3 to 9.
Appearance: Oval, smooth-margined, hairy leaves grow on stiff stems from a central crown. The leafy stalks of daisy-like flowers also grow from the crown.
Size: 1½ to 3 feet tall and wide.
Flower Color: Yellow, orange, some with mahogany streaks. Dark centers.
Blooming Season: Summer to frost.
Exposure: Full sun to partial shade.
Soil: Well-drained, moist, average fertility.
Spacing: 1½ to 3 feet apart.
Propagation: Plants often self-sow. If starting early indoors, freeze seed for a week, refrigerate for another week; then plant in flats kept at 70°F during the day, 60°F at night. Seeds may rot at higher temperatures. Transplant to garden at the frost-free date. Divide three- or four-year old plants in early spring, discarding the older, less vigorous, central portion of the clump.
Pests and Diseases: Usually trouble-free, but will develop root rot in soggy soils.
Notes: These plants are tolerant of heat and dry periods once they are mature. They make long-lasting cut flowers and attract butterflies to the garden.

Salvia × superba
Perennial Sage

Related Species: There are almost 1,000 salvia species. In your garden, you're likely to grow a culinary sage, one of the annual bedding salvias (*S. farinacea, S. splendens*), as well as *S. × superba.*
Zones: 4 to 8.
Appearance: Leaves are oval, with a toothed margin. Plants tend to be bushy with tall, slender flower spikes, which grow above the leaves. Individual trumpet-shaped florets are small and lipped.
Size: 1½ to 3½ feet tall, 2 to 3 feet wide.
Flower Color: Violet-blue.
Blooming Season: Early to mid-summer. Cut back for rebloom in early autumn.
Exposure: Full sun to partial shade.
Soil: Well-drained, moist, of average fertility. Mature plants tolerate dry periods.
Spacing: 2 to 3 feet apart.
Propagation: For bloom the same season, start seeds early indoors after refrigerating for a week. Transplant to the garden after the frost-free date. Divide plants in spring or fall.
Pests and Diseases: Largely trouble-free.
Notes: Salvias make long-lasting cut flowers. Butterflies and hummingbirds are attracted to them, but deer are repelled, so they are a good addition to flower beds that border wild areas or deer crossings.

Sanguisorba canadensis
Canadian Burnet

Related Species: Both the salad plant, garden burnet (*S. minor*), and great burnet (*S. officinalis*) are popular in North American gardens.
Zones: 3 to 8.
Appearance: Leaves are alternate and compound, growing from stiff, erect stems. Flowers grow in cylindrical spikes up to 8 inches long.
Size: 4 to 6 feet tall, 3 to 4 feet wide.
Flower Color: White, cream, rose, and purple.
Blooming Season: Late summer and early fall.
Exposure: Partial shade is best but will tolerate full sun if soil is moist.
Soil: Moist, humus-rich.
Spacing: 3 to 5 feet apart.
Propagation: Plant seeds indoors in early spring after stratifying in refrigerator for six weeks. Transplant seedlings to the garden after all danger of frost has passed. Seeds can also be sown outside in fall. Divide clumps in early spring.
Pests and Diseases: Largely trouble-free.
Notes: These tall plants make good companions for ornamental grasses and late-blooming phlox.

Sedum spectabile (*Hylotelephium spectabile*)
Showy Stonecrop

Related Species: There used to be more than 300 species of Sedum. Botanists have divided the genus into several smaller genera, including *Hylotelephium* and *Rhodiola*. But gardeners and catalogs still call them all sedums. In the home garden, you can choose creeping species such as the white stonecrop (*S. album*), or upright growers, such as *S. maximum*. The hybrid 'Autumn Joy' (now a *Hylotelephium*) is a late-blooming beauty whose flowers slowly change color as they age.
Zones: 3 to 9.
Appearance: Leaves are succulent, opposite, and oval-shaped with small teeth along the margins. Flowers form in clusters on upright stems.
Size: 1 to 2 feet tall and wide.
Flower Color: Red, pink, white, and purple.
Blooming Season: Mid to late summer.
Exposure: Full sun.
Soil: Extremely well-drained, average fertility, tolerates drought.
Spacing: 1½ to 2 feet apart.
Propagation: Divide clumps in spring. Cuttings from non-flowering shoots will root easily; take them in late spring to early summer.
Pests and Diseases: Largely trouble-free.
Notes: Hybrid sedums are often available at local nurseries or through the mail. The seedheads of some, such as 'Autumn Joy', dry to a deep brown that can be attractive in a mixed winter bouquet.

Trollius europaeus
Globeflower

Related Species: Globeflowers are in the buttercup family and look like very fancy versions of them. Numerous hybrids are grown in the U.S. and in Europe.
Zones: 3 to 8.
Appearance: Leaves are dark green, compound, and coarsely toothed. Flowers are buttercup-shaped, but larger and more open.
Size: 1½ to 2½ feet tall, 1½ to 2 feet wide.
Flower Color: Bright yellow. Cultivars with purple, cream, and orange flowers are available.
Blooming Season: Spring through summer.
Exposure: Partial shade is best, though plants will tolerate full sun in northern regions if soil is sufficiently moist.
Soil: Very moist, humusy, and rich. Will tolerate boggy conditions.
Spacing: 1½ to 2 feet apart.
Propagation: Start seeds early indoors after freezing for two weeks, or sow outside in fall. Transplant to the garden after all danger of frost has passed. Divide mature plants in early spring or fall.
Pests and Diseases: Usually trouble-free.
Notes: As cut flowers, *Trollius* are lovely, but short-lived, retaining their petals for only a day or so.

Yucca filamentosa
Adam's Needle

Related Species: Spanish bayonet (*Y. aloifolia*), blue yucca (*Y. baccata*), Joshua tree (*Y. brevifolia*), and soapweed (*Y. glauca*), are also grown in North American gardens.
Zones: 5 to 11.
Appearance: Long, sword-shaped gray-green leaves have curly hairs along their edges. They form a basal rosette from which the tall spike of bell-shaped flowers grows.
Size: 5 to 15 feet tall, 3 to 6 feet wide, depending on cultivar and position.
Flower Color: White, purplish.
Blooming Season: Summer.
Exposure: Full sun.
Soil: Well-drained, average to humus-rich.
Spacing: 3 to 6 feet apart.
Propagation: Odd as it seems for a plant associated with the desert, this seed requires several weeks of freezing before it will germinate. Plant it in a medium that drains quickly, but keep the medium moist. Transplant to the garden after all danger of frost has passed. Plants form side shoots at the base that can be removed in spring or fall and replanted.
Pests and Diseases: Largely pest-free
Notes: Deer do not like *Yucca* plants, so they can be added to a border designed to repel the local herd.

CHAPTER 3

YELLOW AND ORANGE marigolds contrast beautifully with purple heliotrope in this garden. Both provide a long bloom season.

can keep the garden colorful between bursts of bloom from perennials. Annuals make some of the best cut flowers you can grow. Though some annuals look better if you stake them, most get by with almost no care aside from planting and deadheading. Pests and diseases tend to be problems only if you've sited your plants in unsuitable environments.

The diversity of annual flowering plants is astounding. No matter what your design needs or growing environment, you can probably find an annual to suit it. And lastly, these plants are so easy to grow from seed that both the seeds and started plants are inexpensive enough for anyone's budget.

Types of Annuals

Annuals are often categorized as tender, hardy, or half-hardy, and some books and catalogs describe them as "warm-weather" or "cool-weather" plants. For example, Mexican sunflower (*Tithonia rotundifolia*) simply doesn't grow or

ANNUALS

ANNUAL PLANTS COMPLETE THEIR entire life cycle, from germination to seed formation, in a single season. This speed makes them ideal for many garden situations, especially if you want an instant garden. Annuals can also help to fill out a perennial flower bed, giving you color and bloom while you are waiting for the perennials to grow large. You can use annuals to experiment with color and form, too; by planting an annual that is similar in form and color to a perennial you are thinking of buying, you can see if the design choice will work.

Annuals have other advantages as well. Most of them produce scores of flowers over a very long season. They

MEXICAN SUNFLOWER, provides brilliant color and a strong presence in any area where it grows.

flower well in temperatures less than 75° to 80°F, while bachelor's buttons (*Centaurea cyanus*) and blue-eyed African daisies (*Arctotis venusta*) stop blooming in hot weather. The catalog descriptions tell you what the plants can tolerate as well as the conditions that will favor their best development.

Protect tender annuals from frost. Tender annuals cannot tolerate temperatures close to freezing. Plant them out after the frost-free date and either dig them out or be prepared to lose them at the first fall frost. Zinnias, nasturtiums, and impatiens are all in this group.

Hardy annuals survive light frost. Hardy annuals can take some frost. However, frost can sometimes damage seedlings of hardy annuals if they were started indoors, even if you've hardened them off. Try to wait until the danger of hard frost (temperatures of 28°F and below) has passed before setting out these plants, and keep plastic or row cover material handy for covering them on frosty nights.

Hardy annuals have two advantages over their tender cousins. First, direct-seeded and volunteer seedlings of hardy plants will withstand far cooler temperatures than transplants, so they can be planted outside very early in the season, as soon as the soil can be worked. In Zones 7 and warmer, gardeners can plant them for winter bloom. Second, hardy annuals live through the first fall frosts unless it is particularly cold. Take advantage of these qualities by planting annuals such as larkspur, calendula, and bachelor's buttons in the fall if you live in Zone 6 and southward. In Zone 5 and northward, wait until early spring to plant and be certain to add some later plantings to the garden to prolong the bloom season.

Half-hardy annuals succumb to cold before hardies. However they tolerate a few degrees of frost. Petunias and cosmos both fall into this category. If you are transplanting these plants, wait until after the frost-free date to set them out, but you needn't worry that night temperatures in the high 30's will stunt their development. Again, the primary

CUTTING GARDENS are usually composed of rows of selected annuals such as zinnias and marigolds.

advantage comes in fall, when they can live through temperatures that kill the tender annuals.

Perennials and biennials grown as annuals. Some of the plants grown as annuals are actually perennials or biennials that will bloom the first year. The perennials tend to be "warm-weather" plants that will not overwinter outside of their tropical homes. These include geraniums (*Pelargonium* species), impatiens (*Impatiens* species), flowering tobacco (*Nicotiana* species), wax begonias (*Begonia* Semperflorens Cultorum Hybrids), and snapdragons (*Antirrhinum majus*). Biennials that bloom the first season if started early indoors, and usually used as annuals include forget-me-nots (*Myosotis* species), larkspur (*Consolida ambigua*), and pansies (*Viola × wittrockiana*). These are "cool-weather" plants because they perform best in cool temperatures.

Cultural Requirements

Annuals are so diverse that it's impossible to define only one set of cultural requirements for all of them. However, there are some very strong common preferences, even between plants that evolved on different continents.

Soil conditions. Well-drained soil is almost always required. The plants that like bogs and swamps tend to be perennials, not annuals. Pay attention to the drainage qualities of your soil when you first lay out the beds, and improve it if necessary.

Most annuals require slightly acidic soil pH. Those that do not are noted in the directory starting on page 92. When in doubt, always assume that a pH of 6.5 is appropriate for your annual flowers and amend your soil accordingly. A few annuals, such as impatiens and wax begonias, do best

in partial or light shade. But most thrive in full sun. Site gardens where the annuals will receive at least six full hours of sunlight daily.

Keep annuals deadheaded. The whole point of being an annual, from the plant's point of view, is to flower and set seed. Once this is accomplished, it's time to die. The gardener's only way around this lamentable habit is to prevent the plants from forming seeds. Even if you don't cut them for bouquets, pick annual flowers as soon as they begin to wilt, making certain to pluck off the whole flower, not just the petals. If annuals are deprived of the chance to set seeds, they will keep producing flowers.

Most annuals branch well without any help from you,

LEAVE ROOM FOR ANNUALS so they can fill the spaces between the perennials and add color when the perennials aren't in bloom.

but some really benefit from a judicious pinch or two. If you start your own seedlings, pinch the terminal bud on snapdragons, cosmos, petunias, and gaillardia when the seedling is about 4 to 6 inches tall. The resulting branches will carry flower buds and the plant will bloom for a longer period than it would have without pinching.

Give plants room. Correct spacing is important for most plants. If you space them too far apart, for example, you are providing bare ground in which windborne weed seeds can take root. If you grow annuals too close together, you are setting the stage for pest and disease troubles. Most annuals are remarkably resistant to pests and diseases, in the right conditions. But if they suffer from the nutrient deficiencies or high relative humidity levels that are brought on by crowding, pest and disease problems are inevitable.

It's easy to remember to space plants well when you are transplanting. Even if you are setting out tiny plants, it's possible to imagine them as mature specimens and give them enough room to grow. However, when you plant seeds in the soil or have the luxury of a self-seeded crop, it's easy to put off thinning. Do your best to tend to this job as soon as the seedlings have two sets of true leaves. If it is too hard for you to get rid of the tiny extra plants, transplant them to another area of the yard or put them into pots to give away. But thin them to the correct spacing if you want healthy plants that bloom to their full potential.

Clean beds when annuals finish. End-of-the-season work is particularly important with annuals. In mixed beds, where both perennials and annuals have been growing, pull out the annual plants as soon as they begin to die back. In the case of tender annuals, this will be right after frost, though hardy annuals, such as calendula, will keep going until late into the year. But no matter when they die back, remove annuals from the bed and put them in a compost pile that stays at 160°F for at least three days. Throw diseased or insect-ridden material in the trash rather than on a compost pile.

Flower beds composed of only annual plants should be cleared of all plant debris before winter. Work any small debris left on the bed surface into the top inch or so of the soil so that the beneficial organisms will be able to prey on the pathogens or pest eggs.

Choosing Annual Species

The selection of annual species and cultivars at local garden centers and nurseries is often quite limited. If you are

CHAPTER 3

SMART TIP

MULCH BEDS FOR WEED CONTROL

Annual flower beds can be ideal places for weeds to grow if the soil is bare, and thus receptive, early or late in the season. Mulch annual beds to keep weeds from sprouting. You'll avoid injuring plants with deep cultivation and save yourself some work as well. However, if you live in a rainy climate where slugs thrive, don't lay the mulch too close to plant stems. Instead, hand-pull any weeds that sprout and sprinkle a slug deterrent such as dried, crushed eggshells or diatomaceous earth around the plants.

just beginning to garden, it is probably easier to buy established plants, but as you gain experience, you'll probably want to start your own.

Mail order offers variety. For a greater selection of unusual plants, consult mail-order seed catalogs. Seed companies specialize in plants that are rarely found at local nurseries. The seeds are easy to grow and will perform just as well as any of the more common species. Read plant descriptions carefully. Expand your gardening horizons, and choose one or two new annuals to try every year.

Write or call for catalogs in early January. Then sit back, with budget and garden maps by your side, and choose annuals that seem appropriate to your plans. After all, with

ILLUSTRATED PLANT-BY-PLANT DIRECTORY OF ANNUALS

Note: To make this directory of plants most valuable, please read "About the Plant Directories," on page 9.

Unless otherwise noted, most annuals do best in a slightly acidic soil, a pH of about 6.5

Ageratum houstonianum
Flossflower

Related Species: Gardeners in North America primarily grow this annual form.
Appearance: The pointed leaves with smooth margins are highly textured and somewhat hairy. The clustered blooms resemble brightly colored beads.
Size: 6 inches to 2 feet tall, 6 inches to 1 foot wide.
Flower color: Blue, lavender, pink, white, and yellow.
Blooming Season: Early summer to frost.
Exposure Requirements: Full sun.
Soil Requirements: Rich, well-drained, and moist.
Spacing: 6 inches to 1 foot apart.
Propagation: Start seeds early indoors, six to eight weeks before the frost-free date. Light aids germination; do not cover seed with medium but use clear glass or plastic wrap over starting con-

tainers. Remove the covering when seeds sprout. Germinate at 75°F and grow on at 60° to 65°F.
Pests and Diseases: Several species of caterpillar attack flossflowers, but infestations are usually light enough to hand-pick. Whiteflies and diseases caused by *Fusarium* and *Verticillium* wilt fungi can also cause problems.
Notes: Low-growing *Ageratum* cultivars are popular edging plants for the front of the flower border. Taller cultivars such as 'Cut Wonder' and 'Blue Horizon' make long-lasting cut flowers. Cut when flowers are just opening.

Agrostemma githago
Corn Cockle

Related Species: Several cultivars of *Agrostemma githago* are now commercially available but the plant was previously best known as a weed.
Appearance: Leaves are slender, hairy, and somewhat sparse, giving the plant a light, airy appearance. The smooth flowers grow in sprays on slender stems.
Size: 2 to 3 feet tall, 8 to 10 inches wide.
Flower color: White, magenta, lilac.
Blooming Season: Midsummer from a spring planting; successive plantings

produce flowers until frost.
Exposure Requirements: Full sun.
Soil Requirements: Rich, well-drained, moist.
Spacing: 6 to 9 inches.
Propagation: Plant seeds where they are to grow in very early spring. A light frost will aid germination. Inside, plant eight weeks before the frost-free date. Germinate at 65° to 75°F and grow on at 55° to 65°F. Transplant to garden after all danger of frost has passed.
Pests and Diseases: Largely trouble-free.
Notes: *Agrostemma* is an excellent cut flower because the 2-inch-wide blooms are long-lasting and the petals are so lustrous. Cut when two blooms on a spray have opened. The seeds are poisonous.

Ammi majus
False Bishop's Weed

Related Species: The whole plant—compound leaves, flat flower clusters, and roots—declares itself a member of the *Umbelliferae* family.
Appearance: Leaves are finely cut and fernlike. Flat, disk-shaped clusters of tiny flowers top slender stalks and look like a refined version of the roadside weed Queen Anne's lace. Until it blooms, this

lacy, light plant is almost unnoticeable in a mixed bed.

Size: 4 feet tall, 1 foot wide.

Flower color: Most cultivars are white, but 'Green Mist' is a pale green color.

Blooming Season: Midsummer to autumn

Exposure Requirements: Full sun.

Soil Requirements: Average, well-drained. Once established, will tolerate dry periods.

Spacing: 9 inches to 1 foot apart.

Propagation: Success is best guaranteed by sowing where they are to grow once danger of heavy frost has past. For earlier bloom, refrigerate seeds for several weeks before planting. Start in peat pots or soil blocks. Light aids germination. Germinate at 80° to 85°F days, 65° to 70°F nights and grow on at 55° to 66°F. Will self-seed prolifically if not cut.

Pests and Diseases: Largely trouble-free.

Notes: Grow this excellent cut flower at the back of flower beds or in the border. To get straight stems, it is sometimes necessary to support the plants. Use a "grow-through" net, or encircle a group of plants with stakes and use twine to enclose them. Cut when 80 percent of the tiny flowers on the head are open but before pollen shows. Cut or deadhead to prolong bloom.

Antirrhinum majus
Snapdragon

Related Species: Several herbaceous perennials in this genus grow in Europe

and in southern sections of the U.S. However, they are rarely used as garden ornamentals.

Appearance: Leaves are oval, smooth-margined, and somewhat shiny. They form a basal mound from which the flower spikes rise. Leaves grow on the base of the flower stalks. The most common snapdragons have single flowers with upper and lower sections that move apart when the sides of the flower are

ANTIRRHINUM MAJUS 'ROCKET MIX'

pinched. They grow clustered on tall spikes.

Size: 1 to 2 feet tall, 8 inches to 1 foot wide.

Flower color: All but blue and green.

Blooming Season: Early summer through fall.

Exposure Requirements: Prefers full sun but will tolerate partial shade in southern areas.

Soil Requirements: Rich, well-drained, and moist.

Spacing: 8 inches to 1½ feet.

Propagation: Start seeds indoors in mid-February. Do not cover with medium because germination requires light, but use glass or plastic wrap over the starting containers. Germinate at 70° to 80°F daytime, 60°F nights, and grow on at 60°F days, 50° to 55°F nights. Transplant outside into the garden once frost danger has passed.

Pests and Diseases: Aphids, spider mites, and various caterpillars are common pests. Diseases include blight (*Phyl-*

losticta antirrhini), anthracnose (*Colletotrichum antirrhini*), botrytis blight (*Botrytis cinerea*), cercospora blight (*Cercospora antirrhini*), downy mildew (*Peronospora antirrhini*), powdery mildew (*Oidium* spp.), and rust (*Puccinia antirrhini*).

Notes: To encourage plants to grow many flower branches, pinch off the top inch of the stem when seedlings are about 3½ to 4 inches tall. Cut flower spikes when flowers on the lower third of the stem have opened. To prolong bloom, keep flowering stems cut or deadheaded before seeds form. In Zone 7 and southward, seedlings can be started in late summer and wintered over in a cold frame or under protective mulch.

Begonia Semperflorens Cultorum Hybrids
Wax Begonia

Related Species: Hundreds of begonia species are grown in greenhouses, containers, and open gardens all over the world. Tuberous and hardy begonias are both commonly grown in gardens.

Appearance: Leaves are rounded with irregular margins, shiny, and form a mound or rosette. Depending on cultivar, leaves are reddish, bronze or green. The single or double flowers grow only slightly above the leaves but are so colorful that they draw the eye.

Size: 6 to 9 inches tall, 6 to 9 inches wide.

Begonia Semperflorens/**Wax Begonia** *continued*

Flower color: Pink white, red, and bicolors.
Blooming Season: All season.
Exposure Requirements: Partial shade to full sun if soil is moist.
Soil Requirements: Moist, high humus content, moderate to high fertility.
Spacing: 8 inches to 1 foot.
Propagation: Start seeds very early indoors, in January or early February in most locations. Do not cover seed with medium; light and soil temperatures of 80°F aid germination. When seedlings sprout, grow on at 60°F daytime temperature, 50° to 55°F nighttime temperature. Shade leaves from direct sun, even inside. Transplant outside once evening temperatures remain at 50°F or above.
Pests and Diseases: Largely pest-free, although aphids will attack if soil nitrogen is too high. Diseases include pythium rot (*Pythium* spp.), bacterial leaf spot (*Xanthomonas begoniae*), powdery mildew, and botrytis blight (*Botrytis cinerea*).
Notes: Plants do not need deadheading to keep on blooming. Their neat habit, small size, and long blooming season make them ideal for edging. They are also great in window boxes or in the shade.

Brachycome iberidifolia
Swan River Daisy

Related Species: More than 70 members of the genus grow in Australia, New Zealand, and Tasmania, some of them perennial.

Appearance: Bright green leaves are slender and fernlike. The 1-inch, fragrant, daisylike flowers are so numerous they appear to totally cover the plant.
Size: 9 inches to 1 foot high, 8 inches wide.
Flower color: White, blue, lilac, rose.
Blooming Season: Many weeks, but successive sowings will guarantee bloom until frost.
Exposure Requirements: Full sun.
Soil Requirements: Moist, well-drained, of average fertility.
Spacing: 6 to 10 inches.
Propagation: Start seed inside about six weeks before the last frost. Germinate at 70°F and grow on at 60° to 65°F. Transplant after all danger of frost is past.
Pests and Diseases: Largely trouble-free, but can develop fungal root rot diseases in soggy soil.
Notes: This plant looks wonderful in hanging baskets or as an edging plant in the garden. To keep it looking its best, deadhead regularly. Make successive sowings every month until mid- or late July.

Browallia speciosa
Browallia

Related Species: Browallias are members of the nightshade Family, *Solanaceae*, along with potatoes, tomatoes, and petunias. *B. viscosa* is also commonly grown.
Appearance: Plants form a mound. Leaves are smooth-margined and sometimes coated with a sticky sap. Many star-

shaped flowers cover the plant.
Size: 8 inches to 1½ feet tall, 10 inches to 1 foot wide.
Flower color: Blue, violet, white.
Blooming Season: All season.
Exposure Requirements: Partial shade.
Soil Requirements: Well-drained, somewhat low to average fertility.
Spacing: 10 inches to 1 foot.
Propagation: Start seed 10 to 12 weeks before frost-free date. Scatter the tiny seed on the top of moistened soil mix and press into surface without burying. Place plastic wrap over flat to keep moisture in and uncover when the seeds sprout. Do not place in sun while it is covered. Keep medium at 70° to 75°F during germination. Grow on at 60° to 65°F. Seedlings grow slowly but will need to be pinched back when they are 4 to 6 inches tall to promote branching. Transplant to the garden after the danger of frost has past.
Pests and Diseases: Largely trouble-free.
Notes: Do not overwater or overfeed or the plants will produce leaves rather than flowers.

Calendula officinalis
Calendula, Pot Marigold

Related Species: Several species of calendula are available, all are useful in the garden, medicine chest, and at the table.
Appearance: Leaves are narrow, fairly long, a dull green color and somewhat hairy to the touch, with smooth margins. The flowers are daisylike.

Size: 1 to 2 feet tall, 10 inches to 1 foot wide.
Flower color: Yellow, orange, reddish, cream.
Blooming Season: Early summer to beyond the first frosts.
Exposure Requirements: Full sun but will tolerate partial shade, particularly in the South.
Soil Requirements: Well-drained soils of average to below-average fertility.
Spacing: 1 foot.
Propagation: Start seeds early indoors, about six to eight weeks before the frost-free date, in individual peat pots or soil blocks. Bury seeds ¼ inch deep and cover containers with layers of newspaper and black plastic. Germinate at 65° to 70°F and grow on at 55° to 60°F. Then transplant outside after frost-free date.
Pests and Diseases: Slugs, aphids, and caterpillars can attack plants. Root rots may occur in soggy soils and aster yellows (*Mycoplasma* organism) can attack.
Notes: *Calendula* is one of the most useful flowers you can grow. Not only does it make a good cut flower, the edible petals are also pretty additions to mixed salads. Keep cut or deadheaded to prolong bloom through the season.

Callistephus chinensis
China Aster

Related Species: There's only one species, *C. chinensis,* but cultivars differ so much from one another, that it's easy to think that there are lots of China aster species.

Appearance: Leaves are toothed and textured. The plants are multi-branched and each is topped with a brightly colored single or double daisylike bloom.
Size: 9 inches to 1¼ feet tall, 8 inches to 1 foot wide.
Flower color: Wide range including pink, white, lavender, and deep purple.
Blooming Season: Through the season when planted in succession.
Exposure Requirements: Full sun.
Soil Requirements: Well-drained, fertile, humus-rich, and moist.
Spacing: 9 inches to 1 foot.
Propagation: Start seeds indoors about six weeks before last frost. Germinate at 70°F and grow on at 60° to 65°F. Transplant to the garden after all danger of frost has past.
Pests and Diseases: Fungal diseases including fusarium wilt and stem rot, as well as aster yellows. Plant in different parts of the garden each year to avoid problems, and do not put diseased plants in the compost unless you are sure it will be 165°F for at least three days running.
Notes: Be sure to plant a variety of China asters in the cutting garden where the bare plants won't be noticed.

Centaurea cyanus
Bachelor's Button, Cornflower

Related Species: This genus includes more than 450 annuals and perennials, most of them native to the Mediterranean region, but some of which originated on this continent or in Asia.

Appearance: Gray-green leaves are lance-shaped and can be slightly toothed. Stems are wiry with pom-pom shaped flowers.
Size: 1 to 2½ feet high, 10 inches to 1 foot wide.
Flower color: White, pink, rose, purple, red, and blue.
Blooming Season: Midsummer.
Exposure Requirements: Full sun.
Soil Requirements: Well-drained, of average fertility.
Spacing: 9 inches to 1 foot.
Propagation: Plant outside in shallow furrows (¼ inch deep), in late fall or as soon as the soil can be worked in spring. Indoors, plant six weeks before frost-free date. Cover flats with newspaper and black plastic and germinate at 65° to 70°F. Grow on at 55° to 60°F and transplant out at frost-free date.
Pests and Diseases: Largely trouble-free, but aphids, stem rot diseases, and fusarium wilt (*Fusarium* spp.) can attack.
Notes: Plant a succession of bachelor buttons every two weeks until early July for steady blooms. Most cultivars bloom in about 85 days after seeding.

Consolida ambigua
Rocket Larkspur

Related Species: Larkspurs are related to delphiniums. Some seed catalogs list them as *Delphinium ajacis.*
Appearance: Leaves are feathery and plants are well branched. Long flower spikes top the branches.

*Consolida anbigua/***Rocket Larkspur** *continued*

Size: 2 to 3 feet tall, 9 inches wide.
Flower color: Pink, white, and blue.
Blooming Season: Early to midsumme.
Exposure Requirements: Full sun, but will tolerate partial shade.
Soil Requirements: Well-drained, neutral pH, of average fertility.
Spacing: 9 inches to 1 foot.
Propagation: Start seed indoors eight weeks before frost-free date. Freeze seeds and then refrigerate them for a week before planting. Roots dislike disturbance so plant in soil blocks. Cover with newspaper and black plastic. Germinate at 50° to 55°F and grow at the same temperatures. Transplant a week before the frost-free date.
Pests and Diseases: Largely trouble-free, but can contract bacterial leaf spot (*Pseudomonas delphinii*), bacterial rot (*Erwinia atroseptica, E. chrysanthemi*), Phoma crown rot (*Phoma* spp.), aster yellows, Fusarium canker and wilt (*Fusarium oxysporum* f. *delphinii*), and powdery mildew (*Erysiphe polygoni*).
Notes: Seeds are quite poisonous; keep away from animals or children. Stake plants and cut when half of the flowers on a spike have opened.

Cosmos bipinnatus
Cosmos

Related Species: *Cosmos sulphureus* is a small plant with yellow, orange, and reddish blooms.
Appearance: Leaves are feathery and bright green. Plants form many branches, all of which are topped by the brightly colored blooms.
Flower color: White, pink, red, lilac and magenta.
Blooming Season: Early summer to fall
Exposure Requirements: Full sun
Soil Requirements: Moist, well-drained, of average to low fertility.
Spacing: 1 to 1½ feet.
Propagation: Direct-seed once soil is 60°F or higher, or start indoors six weeks before the frost-free date. Inside, germinate at 75°F and grow on at 60° to 65°F. Transplant outdoors once danger of frost has past.
Pests and Diseases: Largely trouble-free, but can contract bacterial wilt (*Pseudomonas solanacearum*), stem blight (*Diaporthe stewartii*), powdery

Cosmos 'sonata'

mildew (*Erysiphe cichoracearum*), and leaf spot diseases (*Cercospora* spp., *Septoria* spp.)
Notes: Pinch young plants to promote branching. Cut flowers often for bouquets or deadhead regularly to prolong bloom. In highly fertile soils, flowering may be delayed until late in the season. For cut flowers, stake plants to promote straight stems and cut when the first flowers on a branch are just beginning to open. Plant successively every three weeks until July for a steady source of cut flowers.

Dahlia, dwarf cultivars
Dahlia

Related Species: Many dahlias that grow from tuberous roots are discussed in the bulb directory, page 67 to 69.
Appearance: Leaves are toothed and clear green. Plants are full with many flowers. Flowers are daisy like.
Size: 1 to 2 feet tall, 1 to 1½ feet wide.
Flower color: All but blue.
Blooming Season: Midsummer to fall.
Exposure Requirements: Full sun.
Soil Requirements: Moist, rich, well-drained.
Spacing: 1 to 1½ feet.
Propagation: Start seeds of bedding types indoors, about eight to ten weeks before frost-free date. Germinate at 70°F and grow on at 60° to 65°F. Plant seedlings or tubers once all danger of frost has past.
Pests and Diseases: Largely pest-free, but can contract bacterial stem rot (*Erwinia cytolytica*), fungal stem rot (*Sclerotinia sclerotiorum*), wilt diseases (*Fusarium* sp., *Verticillium albot-atrum*, or *Pseudomonas solanacearum*), mosaic or ring spot virus, powdery mildew (*Erysiphe cichoracearum*), and Botrytis blight (*Botrytis cinerea*).
Notes: Dahlias are actually perennials in tropical climates, but north of Zone 8, gardeners grow the dwarf cultivars as annuals for cutting or to brighten the flower garden. Keep plants cut or deadheaded to prolong the blooming period. For cut flowers, harvest when flowers have just begun to open.

Emilia species
Tasselflower

Related Species: Both *E. coccinea* and *E. sonchifolia*, which is sometimes called *E. javanica*, are commonly grown to use in mixed arrangements.

Appearance: Leaves are narrow and lance-shaped, and have a winged petiole toward the bottom of the plant but not toward the top. They are usually somewhat hairy. The tassel-shaped flowers are carried on tall, slender stems.

Size: 1½ to 2 feet tall, 6 to 9 inches wide.

Flower color: Red, orange, and yellow.

Blooming Season: Early to mid- to late summer if plants are deadheaded regularly.

Exposure Requirements: Full sun.

Soil Requirements: Well-drained, light, of moderate fertility.

Spacing: 8 inches to 1 foot.

Propagation: Start seeds early indoors, about six to eight weeks before frost-free date. Germinate at 65° to 75°F and grow on at 55° to 60°F. Transplant to garden after danger of frost has past.

Pests and Diseases: Largely trouble-free, but aphids can be a problem.

Notes: Plant a second planting in early June for blooms until frost. But if you keep it cut or deadheaded, the first planting can put out more stems than you can possibly use, even if you're supplying everyone you know with fresh arrangements. Use the red and orange flowers in combination with bishop's weed (*Ammi majus*). The yellow cultivars add lightness

to an arrangement featuring Black-eyed Susan (*Rudbeckia hirta*) or Mexican sunflower (*Tithonia rotundifolia*).

Gaillardia pulchella
Blanket Flower

Related Species: Several other species, including *G. aristata*, *G. × grandiflora*, *G. lanceolata* (all perennials), and *G. amblyodon* (an annual), are grown in North American gardens. Additionally, many types of blanket flowers grow wild in Mexico and the American Southwest.

Appearance: Leaves are long and narrow with coarse teeth. The blanket flower can look untidy if left unstaked, but it grows well when supported with twiggy branches or with horizontal, grow-through supports.

Size: 1 to 2 feet tall, 8 inches to 1 foot wide.

Flower color: Yellow, red, orange, many bicolors; some doubles.

Blooming Season: Midsummer to frost.

Exposure Requirements: Full sun.

Soil Requirements: Well-drained, of average fertility. Will tolerate dry periods once established.

Spacing: 1 foot.

Propagation: Start seed early indoors, about six weeks before frost-free date. Light aids germination, so do not bury the seeds. Germinate at 70°F and grow on at 60°F. Transplant into the garden when frost danger is past.

Pests and Diseases: Largely trouble-free, but aphids can attack and plants may

develop powdery mildew in locations with poor air circulation.

Notes: The cultivar 'Red Plume' was awarded the All America Selections designation a few years ago. Grow this beauty for what seems like an endless supply of 1½-inch wide double blooms of a dark red that can be used in cut flower arrangements with almost any other color. Regular deadheading or cutting is required to keep any of the blanket flowers blooming through the season.

Gazania linearis
African Daisy, Treasure Flower

Related Species: There are sixteen species of this tropical African beauty, some of them annual and some perennial. *G. linearis*, *G rigens*, and the many cultivars and hybrids that we grow are actually perennial, but only as far north as Zone 9.

Appearance: Leaves are elongated, lobed, and hairy. The top surface is a gray-green color and whitish hairs coat the undersides. Flower stems rise above the basal mound or rosette of leaves. Flowers are large and daisylike.

Size: 10 inches to 1 foot tall, 8 inches to 1 foot wide.

Flower color: Cream, yellow, gold, orange, pink, red, many bi-colored.

Blooming Season: Early summer to fall.

Exposure Requirements: Full sun.

Soil Requirements: Well-drained, of moderate fertility. Will tolerate seaside loca-

Gazania/**African Daisy, Treasure Flower** *continued*

tions, even those with a fairly high salt content in the soil.

Spacing: 9 inches to 1 foot.

Propagation: Start seeds indoors in individual peat pots, about six to eight weeks before the frost-free date. Cover pots with layers of newspapers and black plastic because seeds require darkness to sprout. Germinate at 65° to 70°F and grow on at 60° to 65°F. Transplant to the garden after all danger of frost has past.

Pests and Diseases: Largely trouble-free.

Notes: Blooms close at night and on cloudy days. Cut flowers will not last long, but you can extend their life by singing the bottom of the stem with an open flame as soon as you pick it. In good light, gazanias make good winter houseplants. Dig with a good-sized root ball, pot in a 12- to 14-inch container, and place in a sunny window or under full spectrum plant lights. They will continue to bloom for many months. If they remain healthy, cut back in early spring and put them back in the garden.

Gypsophila elegans
Baby's Breath

Related Species: The best known of the hundred or so *Gypsophila* species is perennial baby's breath, *G. paniculata*, commonly used in bouquets.

Appearance: Narrow, lance-shaped leaves are a gray-green color. The plant is bushy and bears numerous sprays of tiny round flowers on slender stems.

Size: 1 to 2 feet tall, 8 to 10 inches wide.

Flower color: White, rose, pink.

Blooming Season: Early to midsummer from first planting.

Exposure Requirements: Full sun.

Soil Requirements: Well-drained, neutral pH, of average fertility.

Spacing: 10 inches to 1 foot.

Propagation: Start seeds outside after danger of frost has past and plant successively every two weeks until three months before your first frost date. For early blooms, start seeds indoors, in peat pots or soil blocks, five weeks before the frost-free date and germinate at 70°F. Grow between 60° to 70°F. Transplant to the garden at the frost-free date.

Pests and Diseases: Largely trouble-free, but seedlings can develop root rot (*Pythium debaryanum, Pellicularia filamentosa*) and mature plants may be attacked by botrytis blight (*Botrytis cinerea*) in areas of poor air circulation.

Notes: Support plants with twiggy branches. Harvest branches when 70 to 80 percent of the tiny flowers have opened. Uncut sprays feed beneficial insects.

Helianthus annuus
Sunflower

Related Species: Seventy species of sunflowers are common in North and South America, including *H. giganteus*, giant sunflower and *H. decapetalus*, thin leaf sunflower. The perennial tuberous vegetable, Jerusalem artichoke (*H. tubero-*

sus), is also a member of this genus.

Appearance: Large, broad leaves are toothed and usually hairy on the upper sides. The stout stems are also hairy. The disc-shaped flowers are somewhat daisy-like, with large, contrasting centers.

Size: 1 to 10 feet tall, 1 to 2½ feet wide.

Flower color: Orange, yellow, white, red; some bicolors and some doubles.

Blooming Season: Midsummer to frost

Exposure Requirements: Full sun.

Soil Requirements: Well-drained, average fertility.

Spacing: 1 to 2 feet.

Propagation: Plant seeds where they are to grow once all danger of frost has past, or start indoors, six weeks before last frost, in large peat pots or smooth plastic pots.

Pests and Diseases: Aphids can be a problem in rich soils. Plants can contract wilt diseases (*Verticillium albo-atrum, Fusarium* spp.) or powdery mildew (*Erysiphe* spp.) in soggy soils.

Notes: Stake tall cultivars or encircle them with twine. Cut flowers or deadhead regularly for maximum flower production. Plant a succession crop two to three weeks after the first.

Heliotropium arborescens
Heliotrope

Related Species: There are over 200 members of this genus, but *H. arborescens* is the only one that is commonly grown in gardens.

Appearance: Stems are almost purple

and leaves are dark green and quite textured. Plants are branched. Tiny flowers grow in clusters at the tips of the stems.
Size: 1 to 1½ feet tall, 10 inches to 1 foot wide.
Flower color: Purple, dark blue, and white.
Blooming Season: Midsummer to frost.
Exposure Requirements: Full sun
Soil Requirements: Well-drained, of average fertility.
Spacing: 1 foot.
Propagation: Start seed early indoors, about ten weeks before frost-free date. Do not bury seeds, cover flats with plastic wrap, and germinate at a soil temperature of 70° to 75°F. Bottom-water if medium becomes dry. Uncover the flats when seedlings appear. Transplant to the garden when night temperatures will no longer dip below 45°F.
Pests and Diseases: Largely trouble-free, but aphids can attack if soil is too rich.
Notes: Check the catalogue description carefully if you want fragrance. Pinch young plants to promote the formation of flower buds. Deadhead regularly.

Iberis amara
Annual Candytuft

Related Species: Most of the cultivated annual candytufts are *I. amara* or the globe candytuft, *I. umbellata*. The low-growing evergreen or perennial candytuft, *I. sempervirens* is quite common.
Appearance: Leaves are lance-shaped and a true green. But the numerous flow-

ers grow so densely that they soon obscure the leaves. The tiny flowers grow in dense, round clusters.
Size: 1 to 1½ feet tall, 6 to 10 inches wide.
Flower color: White, pink, maroon, and rose.
Blooming Season: Summer to fall.
Exposure Requirements: Full sun.
Soil Requirements: Well-drained, average fertility.
Spacing: 9 to 11 inches.
Propagation: Direct seed in the garden in early spring or start early indoors about eight weeks before frost-free date. Light aids germination. Keep soil temperature between 60° and 65°F. In Zones 7 and warmer plant seeds where they are to grow in October.
Pests and Diseases: Largely trouble-free.
Notes: Deadhead to extend blooming. This plant is an excellent choice for city windowboxes because it tolerates smog and adds a light fragrance to the air.

Impatiens walleriana
Impatiens, Busy Lizzie

Related Species: The rose balsam (*I. balsamina*) and the New Guinea impatiens, *I. hawkeri*, are probably the best known ornamental relatives, though increasing numbers of gardeners are also encouraging the wild jewel weed, (*I. capensis*) in their landscapes because it will diminish or eliminate a reaction to poison ivy if immediately rubbed on exposed skin.
Appearance: Leaves are pointed with small teeth along the margins. Stems are

reddish and somewhat succulent. Plants are bushy. Flowers are so numerous that you barely notice the leaves.
Size: 6 inches to 1 foot tall, 6 to 10 inches wide.
Flower color: Wide range, all but blue.

IMPATIENS BALSAMINA

Blooming Season: All season.
Exposure Requirements: Partial to filtered shade, but will tolerate full sun In Zone 5 and cooler if soil is moist.
Soil Requirements: Moist, well-drained, of average fertility.
Spacing: 6 to 10 inches.
Propagation: Start seeds early indoors, about eight to ten weeks before frost-free date. Light aids germination. Use bottom heat if possible and keep soil at an even temperature of 75°F. Grow on at 60° to 65°F. Bottom-water and keep air circulation high because seedlings are prone to damping off diseases. Plant out when all danger of frost is past.
Pests and Diseases: Spider mites, aphids, and whiteflies are all possible pests. Leaf spot fungi (*Stemphylium botryosum, Cercospora fucushiana, Phyllosticta* spp., *Septoria noli-tangeris*) may attack in locations with poor air circulation.
Notes: Impatiens are tender perennials that we grow as annuals. For winter houseplants, take cuttings from garden plants in early fall. Keep them in bright light and feed moderately. They will reward you by flowering all season. In early spring, take more cuttings to grow out as bedding plants for the garden.

Lavatera trimestris
Tree Mallow

Related Species: More than twenty species of *Lavatera* grow in tropical and subtropical areas. Most of these are shrubs or small trees. *Lavatera* belong to the Mallow Family, *Malvaceae*, along with hollyhocks and hibiscus.

Appearance: Leaves are pointed and toothed with a crinkly texture. Plants are naturally bushy and bear numerous flowers at once. The single saucer-shaped blooms have prominent attractive centers.

Size: 2 to 4 feet tall, 1½ to 2 feet wide.

Flower color: Red, white, and pink.

Blooming Season: Midsummer to frost.

Exposure Requirements: Prefers full sun but will tolerate partial shade.

Soil Requirements: Well-drained, moist, and of average to slightly above-average fertility.

Spacing: 2 feet.

Propagation: Plant seeds where they are to grow once danger of frost is past, or start early indoors, about six weeks before the frost-free date. Start in peat pots or soil blocks because roots resent disturbance. Transplant to the garden after all danger of frost has past.

Pests and Diseases: Largely trouble-free, although leaf-rolling caterpillars as well as aphids can be a problem. Adult sphinx moths feed on the flowers without harming them. But since these moths are the mothers of tomato horn worms, don't grow tree mallow near the vegetable garden.

Notes: Tree mallows make wonderful, long-lasting cut flowers. Cut whole branches when 50 percent of the blooms are open. Deadhead or cut flowers regularly to prolong bloom period. If left uncut, plants will self-seed but will not become weedy.

Layia platyglossa
Tidytips

Related Species: Although there are fifteen species of *Layia*, tidytips is the only one that is commonly grown in gardens.

Appearance: Leaves are long and narrow with teeth or lobes. They are generally slightly hairy. The dainty plants are branched and daisy-like.

Size: 1 to 1½ feet tall, 6 to 10 inches wide.

Flower color: Petals are yellow with white margins.

Blooming Season: Early summer to fall

Exposure Requirements: Full sun

Soil Requirements: Well-drained, light, of moderate fertility. Will tolerate dry periods and poor soil when established.

Spacing: 9 to 10 inches.

Propagation: In Zones 7 and southward, sow seeds where plants are to grow as soon as soil can be worked in the spring. In Zone 6 and northward, start seeds early indoors, about six weeks before frost-free date. Germinate at 70°F and grow on at 60°F. Transplant to the garden at the frost free date.

Pests and Diseases: Largely trouble-free, although it will contract root rots in soggy soil.

Notes: Tidytips was popular during Victorian times and into the early part of the 20th century. Once you grow it, you'll probably wonder why it ever went out of fashion. It cuts beautifully and if you keep it deadheaded or cut, rewards you with many, many stems for a long season. Beneficial insects, particularly the parasitic wasps that prey on aphids, love it. Finally, it will grow in dry, sunny spots where many other plants suffer.

Lobelia erinus
Trailing Lobelia, Edging Lobelia

Related Species: The perennial cardinal flower (*L. cardinalis*) is one of the best known lobelias, but there are about 350 other species, both annual and perennial.

Appearance: The small leaves are dark green and slender with smooth margins. Thin stems rise for a few inches and then trail on the ground or out of a container. The tiny flowers are so numerous that they look as if they are swarming over the plant.

Size: 6 to 8 inches tall, 1 to 1¼ feet wide.

Flower color: Blue, pink, and white.

Blooming Season: All season, although they tend to slow down in hot weather.

Exposure Requirements: Full sun but will tolerate partial shade.

Soil Requirements: Well-drained but moist, fertile, high humus content

Spacing: 4 to 6 inches.

Propagation: Start seeds early indoors, six weeks before frost-free date. Light aids germination; cover seed flat or pots with plastic wrap and bottom-water if necessary to keep evenly moist. Germinate at a steady 70°F. and grow on at 60° to 65°F. Remember not to put plastic-covered pots in sun and to remove plastic when the seedlings appear. Transplant to the garden after danger of frost.

Pests and Diseases: Aphids and wireworms can both be problems. Diseases include stem rot (*Rhizoctonia solani)* and various fungal leaf spot diseases (*Cercospora lobeliae, Phyllosticta bridgesii, Septoria lobeliae*) that will attack if air circulation is low and leaves remain wet into the evening.

Notes: To create a full hanging basket, start at least two seeds each in small peat pots or soil blocks. Transplant these containers into the basket when the plants begin to need more root space. Put one pot in the center of a 12-inch basket and place three pots near the perimeter. The plants will be crowded enough so that they will require feeding with a liquid fertilizer through the season, but the basket will be full and beautiful. Lobelia tends to shut down in hot weather, but if you cut the plants back, they will rebloom.

Moluccella laevis
Bells of Ireland

Related Species: Only two species are grown in gardens, *M. laevis* and the very similar *M. spinosa.*
Appearance: Leaves are large, hairy, and smooth margined. Flower spikes rise above the basal mound of leaves. The "flowers" are actually bell-shaped, enlarged calyxes.

Size: 2 to 3 feet tall, 1 to 1½ feet wide.
Flower color: The "bells" are pale green.
Blooming Season: Late summer to early fall.
Exposure Requirements: Full sun but will tolerate partial shade in hot locations.
Soil Requirements: Well-drained, of average fertility
Spacing: 1 to 1½ feet.
Propagation: Start seeds early indoors, about eight weeks before the frost-free date, in peat pots because the plants don't transplant well. Don't bury the seeds, but do cover the pots with clear plastic wrap. Germinate at 70° to 75°F and grow on at 60° to 65°F. Remember to remove the plastic when the seedlings appear. Plant after danger of frost.
Pests and Diseases: Largely trouble-free, but slugs can pose problems in wet soil or if mulch is too close to the plants.
Notes: Use the stems in fresh arrangements or dry for winter bouquets. To dry properly, cut when 90 percent of the caylxes are open but before they start to drop. Set the stems upright in several inches of water and let it evaporate.

Nicotiana alata
Flowering Tobacco

Related Species: Smoking tobacco is in the same genus as all the flowering tobaccos and the entire group is within the Nightshade Family, *Solanaceae.*
Appearance: Leaves are lance-shaped, clear green, sticky, and have smooth margins. Plants branch prolifically. Flowers are tubular with flared petals.
Size: 2 to 3 feet tall, 9 inches to 1 foot wide.
Flower color: White, pink, red, maroon, and pale green.
Blooming Season: Midsummer to frost
Exposure Requirements: Full sun but will tolerate partial shade.
Soil Requirements: Well-drained, of moderate fertility.
Spacing: 10 inches to 1½ feet.
Propagation: Start seeds early indoors, about six weeks before your frost-free date. Germinate at 75°F and grow on at 60° to 65°F. Transplant outdoors at the frost-free date.
Pests and Diseases: Aphids and Colorado potato bugs are the most common pests, but any insect or disease that affects tomatoes or potatoes will also bother *Nicotiana.* Keep the soil well-drained for disease control.
Notes: The old-fashioned white cultivars such as 'Only the Lonely' are the most fragrant. Modern cultivars have lovely colors but lack the wonderful perfume.

Pelargonium × *hortorum*
Geranium, zonal

Related Species: The *Pelargonium* species are what most people refer to as Geraniums. These are the plants that form focal points in window boxes and

Pelargonium/ **Zonal Geranium** *continued*

other containers as well as in bedding designs. Scented geraniums also belong to this genus as do regal (*P. × domesticum*) and ivy-leaved (*P. peltatum*) geraniums.

Appearance: Leaves are a bright green with scalloped margins. In most species, they are slightly hairy and are marked with rings, or zones of contrasting color. Clusters of open flowers top the many branches of the plant.

Size: 1 to 2 feet tall, 1 to 3 feet wide.

Flower color: White, red, pink, and orange.

Blooming Season: All season.

Exposure Requirements: Full sun but will tolerate partial shade or filtered light.

Soil Requirements: Well-drained, moist, of moderate fertility.

Spacing: Depending on cultivar, from 1 to 3 feet.

Propagation: Seeds of many cultivars will not come true to type, so it is best to take softwood cuttings in late winter, as illustrated in Chapter 2 "Gardening Basics" on page 48. Transplant when all danger of frost is gone.

Pests and Diseases: Two-spotted spider mites, whiteflies, slugs, and snails can all be troublesome. Leaf spot diseases include alternaria leaf spot (*Alternaria tenuis*), bacterial blight (*Xanthomonas pelargonii*), and cercospora leaf spot (*Cercospora brunkii*). Rust (*Puccinia pelargonii-zonalis*) and various viruses can also attack.

Notes: Take cuttings from your outside geraniums in August and move them into the house before evening temperatures fall below 50°F. In a bright window, they will reward you with blooms through the winter. The dried leaves and flowers of the scented geraniums make good additions to potpourri and other fragrant mixtures.

Petunia × hybrida
Petunia 'Primetime Blue'

Related Species: Petunias have been hybridized so much that the wild forms are barely recognizable.

Appearance: Leaves are bright green and, in most cultivars, somewhat sticky. Plants branch prolifically if the tips are pinched when stems are 6 inches tall, and flowers are abundant. Trailing types

PETUNIA

of petunias are now widely available. Flowers take many forms—single, double, ruffled—and many sizes.

Size: 8 inches to 1½ feet tall, 2 feet wide.

Flower color: All but green; numerous bicolors.

Blooming Season: All summer.

Exposure Requirements: Prefers full sun, tolerates partial shade in warm climates.

Soil Requirements: Well-drained but moderately moist, fertile.

Spacing: Depending on cultivar, 1 to 2 ½ feet.

Propagation: Start seeds early indoors, about eight to ten weeks before frost-free date. Do not bury seeds but cover seed flat with plastic wrap. Remember not to place plastic-covered flats in sun and to uncover them when the seedlings appear. Germinate at a consistent temperature between 70° to 75°F and grow on at 60° to 65°F. Seeds are tiny and young seedlings grow slowly, but once they have about six leaves, they develop quickly. Plant out after frost is past.

Pests and Diseases: Aphids, slugs, and all the beetles, caterpillars, and true bugs that prey on the tomato family. Diseases include crown rot (*Phytophthora* spp.), alternaria blight (*Alternaria tenuis*), fusarium wilt (*Fusarium* spp.), fasciation (*Corynebacterium fascians*) and various viruses.

Notes: Many people turn up their noses at petunias because they are so common. Many of them have a fragrance that rivals any in the garden and you can usually find whatever color you need for a particular spot. But you may have to search for the perfect petunia in good seed catalogs. Don't depend on the cultivars that the local nursery sells—there are many more choices if you're willing to start your own plants from seed.

Phlox drummondii
Annual Phlox

Related Species: The genus *Phlox* contains annuals and perennials of all sizes and shapes. Some trail along the ground while others form shrubby masses. Annual phloxes add color.

Appearance: Leaves are small, bright green and pointed. But the plants are so full of flowers that you may never notice the leaves. The small, open flowers grow in clusters at the top of the many branches.

Size: 6 inches to 1½ feet tall, 6 to 8 inches wide.

Flower color: Wide range, including red, white, pink, yellow, and many bicolors.

Blooming Season: Midsummer to frost.

Exposure Requirements: Full sun.

Soil Requirements: Well-drained, of moderate fertility.

Spacing: 6 to 10 inches.

Propagation: Start seed early indoors, about seven to eight weeks before your frost-free date. Cover flat with layers of newspaper and black plastic. Germinate at 60° to 65°F and grow on at 50° to 55°F. Transplant at the frost free date.

Pests and Diseases: Aphids, two-spotted spider mites, and slugs can attack. Diseases include cercospora leaf spot, aster yellows and powdery mildew.

Notes: Annual phlox make wonderful cut flowers. Cut when the central florets in a cluster are beginning to open. Cut or deadhead to extending blooming.

Portulaca grandiflora
Portulaca, Rose Moss

Related Species: The purslane plant (*P. oleracea*), which some people consider a weed and other people cherish as one of the best parts of a mixed salad, is the most common *Portulaca* species.

Appearance: Leaves are narrow, fleshy, smooth, shiny, and often slightly reddish. The low-growing plants branch prolifically, even without being pinched. The vividly colored flowers grow at stem ends and open widely in bright light, but close in low light.

Size: 6 inches tall, 8 inches to 1 foot wide

Flower color: Red, pink, orange, yellow, magenta, and many bicolors.

Blooming Season: All summer.

Exposure Requirements: Full sun.

Soil Requirements: Well-drained, of moderate fertility. Established plants tolerate drought well.

Spacing: 6 to 8 inches.

Propagation: Start seeds early indoors, about six to seven weeks before the frost-free date. Germinate at 70° to 75°F and grow on at 65° to 70°F under extremely bright light. Transplant out when danger of frost is past.

Pests and Diseases: Largely trouble-free, but will develop root rots in wet soil.

Notes: Plant portulaca wherever it's too hot and dry to grow anything else. Portulaca makes an excellent plant for hanging baskets. Breeders have been developing cultivars with a more varied color palette during the last few years. Check your seed catalog to find these as well as a new, variegated leaf form too.

Reseda species
Mignonette

Related Species: While there are more than 50 Reseda species, only two are commonly grown in gardens. *R. odorata* has a lovely fragrance, but is best grown in a mixed planting because its flowers are truly nondescript. *R. luteola* also adds a clean, sweet fragrance to the air, but has more visible flowers; spikes of yellow or yellow-green rise above the mound of leaves.

Appearance: Leaves are slender, pointed ovals with smooth margins. Plants branch well, even without pinching, and flower spikes rise above the leaves.

Size: 1 foot tall, 9 inches to 1 foot wide.

Flower color: Whitish green, pale yellow.

Blooming Season: Midsummer to fall.

Exposure Requirements: Full sun.

Soil Requirements: Well-drained, close to neutral pH, moderate fertility and moisture.

Spacing: 9 inches to 1 foot.

Propagation: Plant seeds where they are to grow as soon as the ground can be worked in spring, or start early indoors about six to eight weeks before the frost-free date. Plant seeds in peat pots or soil blocks because roots resent disturbance. Transplant when all danger of frost is past.

Pests and Diseases: Largely trouble-free, but can attract aphids in extremely rich soils.

Notes: Mignonette is grown for fragrance rather than looks. Add the flowers spikes of either species to fresh bouquets for their lovely fragrance. The light-colored flower spikes of *R. luteola* can also add a soft yellow color and can act as a filler. Cut the spikes when slightly fewer than half of the flowers on the spike have opened. Plant new seeds every two weeks until early summer to guarantee a steady supply of flowers for cutting.

Annuals directory continued on page 104

Rudbeckia hirta
Black-eyed Susan

Related Species: Fifteen species of this genus have been identified, all of them indigenous to North America. *R. fulgida*, which includes the cultivars 'Goldsturm' and 'Gloriosa Daisy', and *R. laciniata*, the old-fashioned 'Golden Glow', are the best known other than *R. hirta*.

Appearance: Leaves are narrow and generally hairy with smooth margins. They form a basal rosette or mound from which the daisylike flowers rise on tall stems.

Size: 2 to 3 feet tall, 10 inches to 1¼ feet wide.

Flower color: Orange, mahogany, golden yellow with a dark "eye." Gloriosa daisy is bicolored yellow and red.

Blooming Season: Midsummer to frost.

Exposure Requirements: Full sun but will tolerate partial shade in southern locations.

Soil Requirements: Well-drained, of average fertility.

Spacing: 1 to 1¼ feet.

Propagation: Start seed early indoors, in individual peat pots, about six weeks before frost-free date. Chilling for two to three weeks in the refrigerator before planting can aid germination. Cover seeds with vermiculite and use clear plastic wrap to cover starting containers because light aids germination. Remember not to place plastic-covered flats in sun and to remove the plastic after germination. Germinate at 75°F and grow on

at 60°F. Transplant to the garden at the frost-free day.

Pests and Diseases: Aphids, powdery mildew, and rust can all be problems.

Notes: Black-eyed Susans are wonderful cut flowers but last longer if you plunge the bottom of their stems in boiling water for a few seconds as soon as possible after cutting. In Zones 7 and southward, as well as in some protected sites farther north, these plants may be short-lived perennials.

Salpiglossis sinuata
Painted Tongue

Related Species: There are only two species in this genus but they, like petunias, belong to the Nightshade Family, *Solanaceae*.

Appearance: Leaves are narrow and sometimes toothed or lobed. Foliage is sparse and plants can look untidy if not supported or grown with other, bushier, plants. Flowers are trumpet-shaped and velvety.

Size: 1 to 2½ feet tall, 8 inches to 1 foot wide.

Flower color: The flowers have a base color of yellow, reddish brown, deep red, or purple over which yellow, red, pink, or blue are splashed. Veins are picked out in gold, blue, maroon, or red.

Blooming Season: Midsummer till frost.

Exposure Requirements: Full sun.

Soil Requirements: Well-drained, high fertility, neutral pH.

Spacing: 1 foot.

Propagation: Start seeds early indoors, about eight weeks before frost-free date. Do not bury seeds, but cover starting containers with layers of newspaper and black plastic since darkness aids germination. Germination may take as long as three weeks. Germinate at 70° to 75°F and grow on at 60° to 65°F. Transplant out when danger of frost is past.

Pests and Diseases: Largely trouble-free

Notes: *Salpiglossis* are not as well known as they deserve to be. Stake the plants with twigs to promote straight stems and cut the blooms for arrangements. They are long-lasting and add unusual colors and textures to floral arrangements.

Salvia splendens
Scarlet Sage

Related Species: The huge genus *Salvia* has about 900 species, including the frequently grown mealy cup sage (*S. farinacea*) and culinary sage (*S. officinalis*).

Appearance: Leaves are a gray-green color, highly textured, and smooth margined. Plants send up spikes of tubular flowers. The individual florets of mealy-cup sage are tiny and blue.

Size: 9 inches to 2½ feet tall, 9 inches to 2 feet wide

Flower color: Purple, red, pink, salmon, white, and some bicolors

Blooming Season: Spring to Fall.

Exposure Requirements: Full sun.

Soil Requirements: Well-drained, of moderate fertility.

Spacing: 1 foot.

Propagation: Start seeds early indoors, about eight to ten weeks before frost-free date. Germinate at 60° to 70°F and grow on at 55° to 60°F. Transplant outdoors when danger of frost is past.

Pests and Diseases: Largely trouble-free.

Notes: Sage flowers are favorites for many beneficial wasps that prey on insect pests. Sages such as 'Blue Bedder', a cultivar of *S. farinacea*, make excellent cut flowers. Keep plants deadheaded to prolong bloom.

Scabiosa atropurpurea
Pincushion Flower

Related Species: *S. caucasica*, the perennial *Scabiosa*, is popular as an ornamental as well as a cut flower, and the drumstick or ping-pong *Scabiosa* (*S. stellata*) is a frequent addition to dried bouquets.

Appearance: Leaves form a basal mound and can be entire or deeply lobed or divided. The flowers rise well above them on slender, almost leafless stems. Flowers look like their common name, pincushions, because of the protruding stamens that emerge from the many florets that make up each flower.

Size: 1½ to 2½ feet tall, 8 to 10 inches wide.

Flower color: White, blue, pink, and maroon.

Blooming Season: Midsummer to fall.

Exposure Requirements: Full sun.

Soil Requirements: Well-drained, close to neutral pH, moderate fertility and moisture.

Spacing: 1 foot

Propagation: Start seeds early indoors, five to six weeks before frost-free date. Light aids germination, so press seeds lightly into soil but do not bury them. Germinate at 65° to 70°F and grow on at 50° to 55°F. Transplant after the danger of frost is gone.

Pests and Diseases: Largely trouble-free

Notes: *Scabiosa* make excellent cut flowers. To guarantee a steady supply, plant new seeds every two weeks until midsummer. Butterflies love these flowers, plant some in areas where you want to attract butterflies.

Schizanthus × wisetonensis
Butterfly Flower, Poor Man's Orchid

Related Species: Like petunias, butterfly flowers belong to the *Solanaceae*, with nicotiana, tomatoes, and potatoes.

Appearance: Leaves are clear green and so deeply divided that they resemble fern fronds.

Size: 2 feet tall, 1 foot wide.

Flower color: Red, pink, salmon, lilac, violet, and purple, all with spots, stipples, and stripes.

Blooming Season: Several weeks in early summer from first sowing.

Exposure Requirements: Partial shade

Soil Requirements: Well-drained, rich, and moist.

Spacing: 1 foot.

Propagation: Start seeds early indoors, about eight weeks before the frost-free date. Darkness aids germination, but the seed is too tiny to cover. Instead, place layers of newspapers and black plastic over starting containers. Germinate at 65° to 70°F and grow on at 60° to 65°F. Transplant after danger of frost has past.

Pests and Diseases: Largely trouble-free

Notes: Butterfly flowers dislike hot weather, so try to keep them cool in midsummer by giving them shade in the middle of the day. Rather than cutting the blooms, use decorative pots to plant seeds and let the whole pot be your arrangement. Plant successively every two weeks or so until midseason for continuous bloom.

Tagetes species
Marigold

Related Species: There are 50 species of marigolds, but we tend to grow the tall, large-flowered, African marigold (*T. erecta*), Mexican marigold (*T. lucida*), the small French marigold (*T. patula*), and dainty signet marigold (*T. tenuifolia*). Despite the common names, this genus is native to Mexico and Central America.

Appearance: Leaves are dark green, finely divided, textured, and toothed. Some cultivars and species are slightly hairy and all have a strong scent. Plants are bushy and flowers are round, from single-petaled to many-petaled.

Size: 10 inches to 3 feet tall, 6 inches to 1 foot wide.

Flower color: Yellow, orange, cream,

Tagetes species/**Marigold** *continued*

reddish, mahogany, many bicolors.
Blooming Season: All summer, until the onset of frost.
Exposure Requirements: Full sun.
Soil Requirements: Well-drained, of moderate fertility. Will tolerate a wide range of soil conditions but flower less in rich soils.
Spacing: Depending on cultivar, allow at least 8 inches between dwarfs and 1 foot to 1¼ inches between tall types.
Propagation: Start early indoors, about six to eight weeks before frost-free date. Germinate at 75° to 80°F and grow on at 65° to 70°F. Pinch terminal buds when plants are 4 to 6 inches tall to promote branching. Plant out when frost danger is past.
Pests and Diseases: Largely trouble-free, but stem rot (*Phytophthora cryptogea*) and leaf spot disease (*Septoria tageticola*) can attack in poor conditions.
Notes: Tall types are excellent cut flowers, while smaller plants make excellent edging plants. The petals of the signet marigold 'Lemon Gem' are sometimes used in salad mixes. The roots of African marigolds will repel nematodes in the soil, but they must be left in place for a full year to have any effect.

Tithonia rotundifolia
Mexican Sunflower

Related Species: There are ten species of Mexican sunflower, but gardeners grow *T. rotundifolia* almost exclusively.
Appearance: The plant is bushy and

large, particularly for an annual. Leaves are large, heart-shaped to lobed, and covered with soft, downy hairs. The flowers resemble daisies.
Size: 4 to 9 feet tall, 2 to 4 feet wide.
Flower color: Brilliant orange and yellow.
Blooming Season: Midsummer to frost.
Exposure Requirements: Full sun.
Soil Requirements: Well-drained, of moderate fertility. Will tolerate dry periods once established and flowers better in moderate to low fertility than in rich soil.
Spacing: 2 to 3 feet.
Propagation: Start seeds early indoors, six weeks before frost-free date, in individual 3-inch peat pots. Germinate at 70° to 85°F and grow on at 65° to 70°F. Plant out when danger of frost is past.
Pests and Diseases: Aphids can be troublesome in rich soil.
Notes: These make spectacular back of the border plants for a flower bed filled with hot colors. They are so bright that they steal the show from all but zinnias and other brilliant blooms. If you cut them, singe the bottom of the stem immediately by passing it through an open flame until it seals.

Verbena × hybrida
Garden Verbena

Related Species: More than 200 verbena species grow wild in the tropical and subtropical Americas. They vary from erect, tall plants to spreading mats. Colors range from blue through purples, reds, whites, and mauves.

Appearance: Leaves are dark green and coarsely toothed. Flower stems rise above basal rosettes. Flowers form rounded clusters of five-petaled flowers.
Size: 6 inches to 1 foot tall, 1 foot to 1½ feet wide.
Flower color: Blue, purple, red, pink, lavender, yellow, and white.
Blooming Season: All season.
Exposure Requirements: Full sun.
Soil Requirements: Prefers rich, well-drained but moist soil, but will tolerate sandy soils of average fertility.
Spacing: 10 inches to 1 feet.
Propagation: Start seeds early indoors, about ten weeks before the frost-free date. Bury seeds ⅛ inch deep and cover flats with layers of newspapers and black

VERBENA BONARIENSIS

plastic because darkness is required for germination. Germinate at 65° to 70°F and keep medium only slightly moist because seed rots easily. Germination usually takes three weeks. Grow at 70°F and transplant to the garden at the first frost-free day.
Pests and Diseases: Aphids, spider mites, whiteflies, and leafminers can attack, and powdery mildew is sometimes a problem late in the season.
Notes: Trailing verbenas make really lovely hanging basket plants. Choose cultivars with a white eye and plant them in white pots for a cheery note around the door or outside deck. Verbenas are also good cut flowers for home use, although they don't generally hold up for more than four or five days in the vase.

Zinnia *elegans*

Related Species: There are only about 20 species of this genus, but there are hundreds of hyrids and cultivars. *Z. angustifolia* is one of the most common choices for gardens because of its bright, single flowers. The range of size, flower shape, and color is enormous. Check several seed catalogs to choose those you like best.

Appearance: Leaves are thick, coarse, generally lance-shaped, smooth-margined, and hairy. Stems are stout and also somewhat hairy. Flowers range from single to double to pom-pom shaped.

Size: 6 inches to 2½ feet tall, 6 inches to 1½ feet inches wide.

Flower color: Wide range, all but blue.

Blooming Season: Midsummer to frost.

Exposure Requirements: Full sun.

Soil Requirements: Well-drained, rich, high humus content.

Spacing: The same as the height of the cultivar.

Propagation: Start seeds early indoors, about four to six weeks before frost-free date, in individual peat pots or soil blocks. Alternate germination temperature between 65°F at night and 70°F during the day, and grow on at 60° to 65°F nights and 70°F days. Plant out when frost danger is past.

Pests and Diseases: Spider mites, Japanese beetles, cutworms, alternaria blight, (*Alternaria zinniae*) and powdery mildew (*Erysiphe cichoracearum*) can all be problems.

Notes: Zinnia make wonderful cut flowers, adding rich, vibrant colors to the vase. In the garden, their bright colors usually make them focal points whether they are intended to be or not. Take care with their placement, either setting them in a bed by themselves or surrounding them with other bright blooms.

Tips for Containers and Hanging Baskets

- To keep down the weight of containers filled with soil, fill the lower half of large pots with foam peanuts, perlite, or any other lightweight material that will not compact over time. Put potting mix in the remaining space, and plant as usual.

- To keep up with the heavy feeding most container-grown plants need, add compost to the planting mix or add liquid seaweed or a fish emulsion/liquid seaweed combination to the water every few weeks to ensure a well-balanced supply of all essential micronutrients.

- To remoisten peat moss if it becomes dry, fill a tub with water and add a drop of wetting agent to help the water stick to the peat moss. Set the basket in the water, and leave it for several hours until the peat moss is saturated with water.

- Pinch off dead blossoms regularly to keep container plants bushy and full of flowers.

- Cluster your pots together in a sheltered spot if you will be away for several days. The plants will need watering less frequently, and it will be easier to water if the containers are all in one place.

- To automatically water containers, bury one end of a long wick (such as those sold with oil-fueled lanterns) near the plant's roots. Insert the other end in a bucket of water. The wick will gradually soak up the water and provide a slow, continuous source of water for the plant.

- If a plant is rootbound, prune the roots by cutting back the outer edges of the root ball instead of transplanting it to a larger container. Then repot it in the same container with fresh soil.

- Consider watering many containers with an automatic drip irrigation system; install a line to each container.

- To reduce moisture loss, top the soil in your containers with mulch.

CHAPTER 3

BLOOMING BIENNIALS, such as these holly-hocks, can add a vertical dimension to a planting.

Plants that are transplanted in early fall must have time for their roots to take hold in the new spot before the ground freezes. After the soil is frozen, cover the entire plant with a 6-inch layer of loose straw.

In spring, draw the mulch back from the crown as soon as the ground thaws. Check the biennials directory, pages 110 to 113, for overwintering instructions for plants.

Biennials reward your efforts. Biennial plants are well worth the care you'll give them. The tall spikes of large biennials such as hollyhock (*Alcea rosea*) and foxglove (*Digitalis purpurea*) can provide a necessary focal point in a flower bed or give color and grace to a planting meant to screen an area. Small biennials such as English daisies (*Bellis perennis*) and forget-me-nots (*Myosotis sylvatica*) add color and contrast to beds of early-blooming bulbs such as tulips and daffodils. The seed pods of honesty plants (*Lunaria annua*) are unique and lovely additions to dried arrangements, Johnny-jump-ups (*Viola tricolor*) are as decorative in salads and on cakes as they are in the garden, sweet Williams (*Dianthus barbatus*) add wonderful fragrance to fresh bouquets, and the dramatic spikes of mullein (*Verbascum* species) and Canterbury bells (*Campanula medium*) can define a yard.

Biennials also give you the opportunity to completely transform the look of your garden during the season. For example, once a border of English daisies has stopped blooming, you can remove the plants and transplant a low-growing annual, already in bloom, into the space where the daisies grew. Similarly, you can move Canterbury bells or foxglove into a garden bed shortly before they are to bloom, let them flower, and dig them out in time to put in fall-blooming chrysanthemums or calendula. This flexibility, along with their stunning and sometimes dramatic appearance, is what endears biennials to flower gardeners.

BIENNIALS

BIENNIAL PLANTS COMPLETE THEIR life cycle in two years. They grow leaves, generally in the form of a rosette or mound, during the first season. These leaves overwinter, then early in the following spring, the plant sends up a flower stalk and dies. If the overwintering leaves die, the roots usually die as well. Consequently, the most important thing to learn about growing any biennial is how to overwinter it successfully. (Many biennials can be forced into bloom in Zones 5b and warmer if they are started indoors early and transplanted to the garden).

Overwintering

Keeping biennials alive over the winter is relatively easy in most areas. However, in the North or in spots with a great deal of freezing and thawing action over the winter months, you'll have to pay particular attention to most of the biennials.

Starting Biennials

One-year-old potted biennials are sometimes available at nurseries and garden supply stores in early spring. Buying them at this age practically guarantees success inasmuch as they have already survived the winter. And, one-year old biennials will bloom the year you plant them. However, you'll find that the selection of started biennials is quite limited. If you want a particular color or cultivar, you'll probably have to start your own from seed.

June is the perfect time to start most biennials in Zones 5 and warmer. This schedule allows you time to care for them adequately and also gives them time to grow large enough to live through the winter and respond to spring by forming flowers.

But in Zones 3 and 4, start biennials in early spring, along with the annuals and perennials. Move them to larger containers when they outgrow their starting areas, and put them in an appropriate overwintering site in late summer or early fall.

To refresh your memory about general seed starting techniques, refer back to "Seeds" and "Seeds Outside" in Chapter 2, "Gardening Basics" (pages 50 and 55). If you have a seed starting area set up indoors, take advantage of it for the biennials. Germination is always higher in a controlled, indoor spot far away from the insects and animals that prey on seeds outdoors.

SET BIENNIALS, such as these Canterbury bells, in place in late summer.

Nursery Beds

No matter where you start your biennials, you'll need a place to grow them during the first year. Some biennials, such as felty mullein, have such lovely leaves that they add an ornamental touch to flower beds all through their lives. These plants also decline after disturbance so much that you have to leave them in place after their first transplanting. But other biennials are easily moved around and have such unremarkable leaves that you'll want to grow them in an out-of-the-way spot for the first summer.

Many gardeners develop "nursery beds" where they can grow first-year biennials, young perennials, and plants that they want to move into place late in the season.

Choose the site for a nursery bed carefully. Most biennials, for example, require full sun to develop adequately, so the nursery bed must have excellent exposure. Humus-rich, moderately fertile, rock-free soils that drain well are a second requirement for a place to coddle young plants. If your property does not have the sort of nooks and crannies that will allow hiding this area, set aside a bed or two in the vegetable garden for it.

Plants that are transplanted to garden locations in spring must develop substantial roots quickly. Help them along by transplanting them with as large a root ball as possible when moving them from nursery beds or by growing them in big pots if you have overwintered them in a cold frame.

CHAPTER 3

ILLUSTRATED PLANT-BY-PLANT DIRECTORY OF COMMON BIENNIALS

Note: To make this directory of plants most valuable, please read "About the Plant Directories," on page 9.

Alcea rosea
Hollyhock

Related Species: The majority of the hollyhocks grown in North American gardens are cultivars of the biennial species *A. rosea*, but the single-flowered and more rust-resistant *A. rugosa* is sometimes available.
Zones: 3 to 8.
Appearance: Leaves are large, lobed, highly textured, and somewhat hairy in some cultivars. The leaves form a rosette the first year and send up a tall, straight flower stalk the second. The single or double flowers can be up to 2 inches in diameter and cluster thickly on tall stalks.
Size: 3 to 9 feet tall, 2 to 3 feet wide.
Flower color: Wide range, all but clear blue.
Blooming Season: Midsummer to fall.
Exposure: Full sun.
Soil: Well-drained, moderately fertile, humus-rich.
Spacing: 2 to 3 feet apart.
Propagation: Start seeds in early spring or summer. Light promotes germination. Hold in nursery beds the first summer.
Overwintering: Transplant to the garden in early fall and mulch for winter.
Pests and Diseases: Largely pest-free. Rust can be a problem if plants are grown in the same location for a number of years.
Notes: In windy locations, it may be necessary to stake the flower stalks to keep them upright. Of double cultivars, 'Powder Puffs' has the largest, showiest blooms. Old-fashioned single flowers are becoming more widely available, particularly from seed companies that specialize in heirloom plants.

Bellis perennis
English Daisy

Related Cultivars: Both single and double cultivars are available. Some cultivars, such as 'Aucubifolia', have gold-variegated leaves, while 'Shrewly Gold' has bright yellow, or gold, leaves.
Zones: 4 to 8.
Appearance: Leaves are lance-shaped and smooth, usually forming a basal rosette. Flower stalks rise above them. The many flowers can be single or double; single blooms have bright yellow centers while double blooms look like pom-poms.
Size: 3 to 6 inches tall, 4 to 6 inches wide.
Flower color: White, pink, red.
Blooming Season: Early spring.
Exposure: Full sun to partial shade.
Soil: Moist, of average fertility.
Spacing: 4 to 5 inches apart.
Propagation: Start from seed in a cold frame in early summer.
Overwintering: Set plants in garden locations in early fall and mulch for winter protection.
Pests and Diseases: Largely trouble-free.
Notes: This is actually a perennial plant, but because it is so hard to keep it thriving in cool areas and also because self-seeded plants revert to a small, white form, it is most often grown as a biennial. North of Zone 6, mulch plants for winter protection.

Campanula medium
Canterbury Bells

Related Species: This biennial is a member of the enormous and varied bell-flower genus, *Campanula*. Perennial species are covered in the perennials directory, earlier in this chapter.

Zones: 4 to 9.

Appearance: Leaves are hairy and their edges my be smooth or wavy. Plants form a rosette the first year and in the second send up tall stalks of bell-shaped flowers.

Size: 2 to 3 feet tall, 1 to 1½ feet wide.

Flower color: Blue, white, rose, yellow.

Blooming Season: Spring in Zones 8 and 9, but early summer in more northern areas.

Exposure: Full sun.

Soil: Rich, humus-filled, moist.

Spacing: 1 to 2 feet apart.

Propagation: Start seeds in late spring in flats held in a cold frame or under plastic tunnels in a nursery area. Light aids germination. Growing medium must not be allowed to dry.

Overwintering: In Zones 8 and 9, transpant to the garden in early fall. Elsewhere, overwinter in the cold frame and transplant in early spring.

Pests and Diseases: Largely trouble-free if soil is well-drained.

Notes: Mulching these plants can cause crown rot, so it's best to leave bare soil for an area of a foot around them.

Dianthus barbatus
Sweet William

Related Species: The genus *Dianthus* includes many of the sweetest smelling flowers in our gardens and includes both annuals and perennials. See the Directory of Perennials, earlier in this chapter, for information on perennial *Dianthus*.

Zones: 5 to 8.

Appearance: Rosettes of slender, lance-shaped leaves with smooth margins form the first year. The following spring, clusters of small round flowers rise on tall stems above the leaves. Flower petals have fringed edges, many are striped with a contrasting color.

Size: 1 to 1½ feet tall, 8 to 9 inches wide.

Flower color: White, pink, and red, with many bicolors.

Blooming Season: Spring.

Exposure: Full sun.

Soil: Well-drained with a pH of 6.8 to 7.1, average fertility.

Spacing: 8 to 9 inches.

Propagation: Plant seeds in late spring,

DIANTHUS

either in a nursery bed or flats in a cold frame.

Overwintering: Transpant to the garden in early fall so that plants can become established before winter. North of Zone 7, apply a winter mulch once the ground has frozen.

Pests and Diseases: Largely trouble-free.

Notes: Sweet William is actually a short-lived perennial, but it becomes so ragged looking after it blooms that most people treat it as a biennial. If you allow seeds to set, it will self-sow but subsequent plants are likely to be smaller than their parents.

Digitalis purpurea
Foxglove

Related Species: Most *Digitalis* species are perennial, but we grow the biennial species in our gardens.

Zones: 4 to 8.

Appearance: A basal mound of overlapping, rounded leaves grows in the first year. Slender spikes of tubular flowers rise above them the following spring.

Size: 3 to 6 feet tall, 1 foot wide.

Flower color: White, pink, rose, purple, often speckled.

Blooming Season: Mid to late spring through early summer.

Exposure: Prefers partial shade but will tolerate full sun if soil is moist.

Soil: Moist, well-drained, with high humus and fertility levels.

Spacing: 1 to 2 feet.

Propagation: Plant seeds in midsummer in a fast-draining medium. Grow on in 4-inch pots or widely spaced in a nursery bed.

Overwintering: In Zones 7 and 8, transplant to the garden in early fall. In colder zones, plants may die over the winter, even if they are mulched, so success is better guaranteed by potting them in 4-inch peat pots, overwintering them in a cold frame and moving them into blooming positions in early spring.

Pests and Diseases: Foxglove aphids can be controlled by cutting and destroying all flower spikes as soon as they have finished blooming and covering first-year

Digitalis purpurea/**Foxglove** *continued*

rosettes with row-cover materials. Japanese beetles can also attack. Powdery mildew and crown rot are both common diseases.

Notes: Foxglove will self-sow and form colonies in favorable locations. Simply thin to be certain that volunteer plants have enough space, then stand back to watch the yearly show. These plants are poisonous, so place them where small children cannnot reach them.

Lunaria annua
Honesty, Money Plant

Related Species: The cultivar 'Variegata' has green-and-cream-colored leaves. *L. rediviva* is a perennial form of honesty, but can be difficult to locate.

Zones: 4 to 8.

Appearance: The broad, textured leaves form a rosette the first year from which flower spikes grow the following spring. The four-petaled flowers are delicate and give an airy feeling to a garden or a vase.

Size: 3 feet tall, 1 foot wide.

Flower color: Purple, white.

Blooming Season: Spring.

Exposure: Prefers partial shade, but will tolerate sunnier conditions in moist soil.

Soil: Well-drained, moist, of average fertility.

Spacing: 1 to 1½ feet apart.

Propagation: Plant seeds in late spring to early summer in nursery beds or flats.

Overwintering: Transplant in early fall and mulch for winter protection.

Pests and Diseases: Largely trouble-free.

Notes: This plant is grown for its seed pods, so you must not deadhead or remove stalks after blooms fade. Cut stalks in August, and hang them upside down, in a cool, dark spot to finish drying. Rub off the outer membrane and seeds to expose the translucent "coins." Save the seeds, and replant them the following year. If you don't harvest the seed pods, the plants will self-sow freely.

Myosotis sylvatica
Alpine Forget-Me-Not

Related Species: Most gardeners prefer to grow the biennials *M. sylvatica* and the somewhat shorter *M. alpestris.*

Zones: 3 to 8.

Appearance: Textured, smooth-margined, oblong or pointed leaves with a pronounced central vein form a mound the first year. Little five-petaled flowers with a yellow eye form clusters on thin stems.

Size: 1 to 2 feet tall, 8 to 10 inches wide.

Flower color: Sky blue, white, pink, and lavender.

Blooming Season: Spring.

Exposure: Partial shade to full sun.

Soil: Well-drained, moist, of average fertility.

Spacing: 8 to 10 inches apart.

Propagation: Plant seeds in late spring or early summer for bloom the next year.

Overwintering: Transplant to the garden in early fall and mulch for winter protection. In Zones 3 and 4, overwinter potted plants in cold frames and transplant in early spring.

Pests and Diseases: Largely trouble-free.

Notes: Many people use the smaller *M. alpestris* as an underplanting for spring bulbs because it blooms the same time and likes the shade given by the taller bulb plants. These plants self-sow freely.

Verbascum bombyciferum
Felty Mullein

Related Species: The common mullein (*V. thapsus*), a roadside weed, is a first cousin to this plant, along with about 300 other mullein species.

Zones: 5 to 8.

Appearance: All parts of this plant are covered with lovely white hairs, giving it a "felty" look. Flowers are also covered with fine hairs and cluster thickly along the tall stalks.

Size: 6 to 8 feet tall, 1 to 3 feet wide.

Flower color: Yellow, occasionally white.

Blooming Season: Late summer.

Exposure: Full sun.

Soil: Will tolerate a range but performs best in deep, fertile soils that drain exceptionally well.

Spacing: 2 to 3 feet apart.

Propagation: Plant seeds in pots and transplant to the garden when four true leaves have formed. Leave them in place because the taproot resents disturbance.

Overwintering: Mulch after the top inch of soil has frozen in the fall or early winter. Remove the mulch when the ground begins to thaw.

Pests and Diseases: Largely trouble-free, but will develop root rot in soggy soil.

Notes: To keep flower stems erect, you may want to stake them. This plant will self-seed prolifically; remove flower spikes before seeds form to prevent it.

Viola tricolor
Johnny-jump-up

Related Species: Roughly 500 species of violas, most of them perennials but some annuals, grow in gardens and wild places around the world. Pansies (*V. x wittrockiana*) are the best-known relative because many gardeners use them as bedding plants in spring.

Zones: 4 to 8.

Appearance: Small rosettes of bright green leaves form in the first year and flower stems appear the next spring.

Size: 8 to 15 inches.

Flower color: Usually tri-colored, as indicated from its name, in shades of white, purple, lavender, and yellow.

Blooming Season: Spring to midsummer

Exposure: Versatile, but performs best in full sun in the North, partial shade in the South.

Soil: Moist, rich.

Spacing: 6 to 8 inches.

Propagation: Plant seed in late spring in nursery beds or flats.

Overwintering: Transplant to garden location in early fall.

Pests and Diseases: Largely trouble-free.

V. X WITTROCKIANA

Notes: Violas will self-seed prolifically in favorable locations, but because the flowers are a wonderful addition to salads and a lovely cake decoration, most people can keep up with their spread.

SAVING SEEDS

Because biennials self-seed prolifically, you must deadhead them to keep the planting in bounds. This can be a blessing in a garden of wildflowers or an area where you have the space for naturalized beds. Over the span of only a few years, the planting will grow larger without your having to do much more than thin it every year. However, if you wish to propagate them, you can always save the seeds to plant the following year.

Tools and Materials: **Pruning shears or scissors, paper bag, bowl, storage containers**

1 Cut the seed stalks when the pods are completely dry but before they have opened.

2 Place the seed stalks in a paper bag as soon as you cut them. The bag will catch any seeds that fall.

3 Remove chaff from the seeds before storing them in a tightly covered and labeled container.

CHAPTER 4

SPECIALTY FLOWER GARDENS

*D*eveloping a specialty garden is one of the greatest pleasures of landscaping a property. For many people, these gardens evolve naturally. As you begin to collect plants you love, you discover that you are on your way to building a specialty garden. Other gardeners deliberately set out to create these gardens. For example, if you've always wanted a water feature in the yard, it's likely that you will add the plants to complement it, both in and around the water.

Many specialty gardens grow out of love and fascination with a particular plant genus. Many people love irises, for example, and devote whole gardens to their collections of various species and cultivars. Peony collectors may grow 30 or 40 culti-

ROSES ADD BEAUTY TO ANY GARDEN. Use them as focal points or, as shown here, to climb the trellis that forms the garden entryway.

vars of their favorite plant, just as people who love chrysanthemums, daylilies, or roses may devote considerable time and garden space to their collections. Bulb lovers aren't uncommon either; in spring their properties look like a piece of transplanted Holland.

Don't be surprised if you find yourself drawn to a particular group of plants. Your garden won't lack variety if you give in to the urge to collect them. Instead, plan an area for these plants and take pleasure in developing your first specialty garden. The examples on the following pages can help you get started with four of the most common specialty garden types: rose gardens; bird, bee, and butterfly gardens; rock gardens; and gardens for dried flowers.

One of the best ways to develop a specialty garden is to convert what was a "problem" area into the site of a specialty garden. A rocky slope with thin soil can be transformed into a lovely rock garden. An area with a high water table and consistently wet soils can be an ideal site for exotic bog plants; a shady area can host a collection of ferns, hostas, or caladiums. All it takes to develop such a garden is some imagination applied to a little research about the plants that will thrive in the particular spot you have in mind.

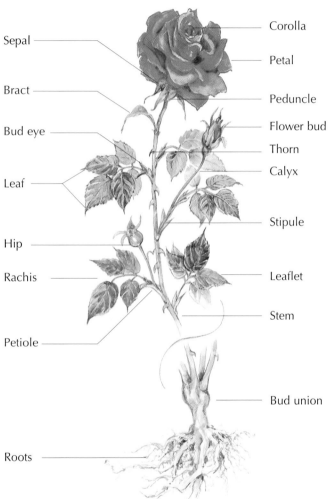

TWO ROSE CULTIVARS, 'Blush Rambler' and 'Excelsa', make this archway a pleasure to walk through. You'll find that you can often grow compatible cultivars together.

LEARNING THE ANATOMY OF A ROSE makes it easier for you to understand specialized information about these plants. Pay particular attention to the location of the bud union.

Sepal

Bract

Bud eye

Leaf

Hip

Rachis

Petiole

Roots

Corolla

Petal

Peduncle

Flower bud

Thorn

Calyx

Stipule

Leaflet

Stem

Bud union

ROSE GARDENS

ROSES HAVE THE REPUTATION of being impossible to grow without huge amounts of labor, time, and pesticides. In some cases, this reputation is deserved—if you try to grow a rose in boggy soil where the air is stagnant or plant one in soil with low humus content, you'll run into trouble. But if you follow some common-sense precautions, roses can be some of the easiest plants you'll grow.

Roses add a touch of elegance to any landscape. While they were once segregated into separate "rose gardens," today they are often used as elements in a mixed landscape. Depending on the species, they can act as a ground cover, an informal hedge, a climbing plant, or a focal point in a bed or border.

Choosing Your Roses

It may be tempting to choose a rose for its color or fragrance, but while these factors are certainly important, you should consider other characteristics, as well. You can minimize problems over the long run by considering the environmental features of the site where the rose will grow, the rose's place and purpose in the overall design of the garden, and particular cultural characteristics such as pruning needs or disease resistance.

TOOLS

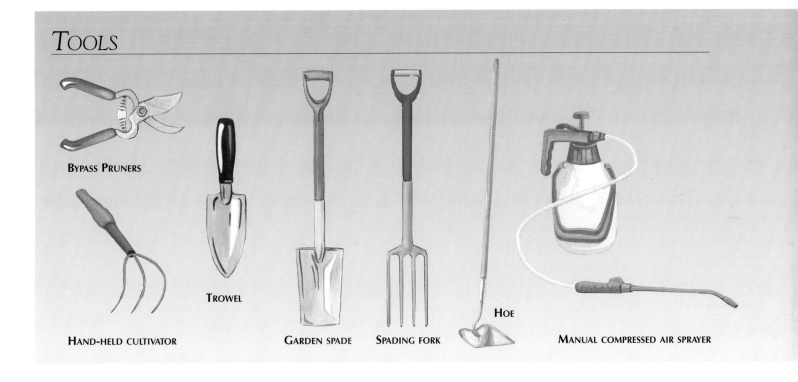

BYPASS PRUNERS

TROWEL

HAND-HELD CULTIVATOR

GARDEN SPADE

SPADING FORK

HOE

MANUAL COMPRESSED AIR SPRAYER

Different roses for different places. If you want to cover an arbor, for instance, look at climbers, a class that includes both "climbing" and "rambling" roses. Both types require the same conditions, but they have slightly different growth patterns. Rambler roses have thin, flexible canes that are easy to train to wrap around a slender support. In contrast, the thicker, more rigid canes of climbers better complement heavier supports such as wooden posts. And ramblers generally bloom once a season in a huge flush that blankets the plant. Some climbers also bloom only once, but many bloom throughout the season. Climbers never bloom with quite the same abandon as the ramblers but produce flowers steadily throughout the season.

You can also choose roses based on their pest and disease resistance. Hybrid teas frequently get black spot and are very attractive to pests. But shrub and rugosa roses, as well as David Austin hybrids are more resistant to problems.

Preplanting Care

Care of a rose begins when you buy it. Most roses you buy will be "budded," meaning that the bud of a desirable cultivar has been grafted to an appropriate rootstock. The rootstock supplies growth characteristics such as hardiness or resistance to pests and diseases, while the bud contributes the leaf and bloom characteristics.

Miniature roses and some classes such as climbers, ramblers, shrubs, and old garden roses are usually grown on their own roots. This can make them grow less quickly and vigorously than budded plants but gives some security in extreme climates. If the top growth dies during a particularly cold winter or hot summer, a rose on its own roots can produce new stems and leaves. If the top growth of a budded plant dies, the new growth would have the characteristics of the rootstock rather than the cultivar you chose.

'REDOUTE', A DAVID AUSTIN HYBRID ROSE, is lovely to look at and resistant to some of the most common rose diseases. Choose pest- and disease-resistant roses whenever you can.

THESE 'PINK BONICA' shrub roses are spaced far enough apart to allow sufficient air circulation even when they are mature.

Give roses room to grow. Spacing depends on the mature size of the plant. Follow the nursery's planting directions, or if none are given, try to plant miniatures and polyanthas 1 foot apart; hybrid teas 2½ to 3 feet apart; shrub roses 3 to 5 feet apart; and climbers and shrubs that are stated to spread 6 feet about 6 to 8 feet apart. Crowding interferes with good air circulation, thus promoting disease. When in doubt, leave more space.

After-planting treatment. If you are planting in the fall, water thoroughly, then mulch with a 6-inch layer of leaves and straw to keep the soil from freezing right away. In the warmer parts of Zones 7 through 11, prune the top growth when you plant. Farther north, wait until spring to prune because pruning stimulates new growth that won't be able to toughen sufficiently for the coming winter.

Pruning

Midsummer pruning is beneficial for many roses. If you see signs of black spot or the plant looks less than flourishing, prune roses in the following classes in late July: all modern once-blooming shrubs, alba, damask, centifolia, gallica moss, species, eglantine hybrids, and rugosa hybrids. Don't prune these plants until they are three years old. Wait until the flowers have faded; then shorten the remaining flower stems to 3 or 4 inches long. Prune off stems on which leaves show signs of black spot. Take old wood from the center of the plant. Prune tea roses as little as possible. Even if you must remove some deadwood, wait until after all danger of frost has passed. Portlands, hybrid perpetuals, Bourbons, ever-

continued on page 120

PRUNING ROSES

PRUNING ROSES IS MANDATORY. It stimulates new growth, opens up the plant to increased air circulation, eliminates some pests, and creates a more attractive, manageable plant. The fine points of pruning depend on the particular species, but fortunately, there are some general rules that make so much sense that you can't forget them.

Remember that ever-blooming roses flower on all the growth produced during a season as well as from the previous year's growth. These species fare best with a very severe, early spring pruning. Remove as much as two-thirds of the plant to stimulate new growth.

Plants that bloom only once produce their best blooms from old wood; don't prune them in the early spring. When pruning, use a light touch and remember these guidelines:

- Make all cuts on an angle, ¼ inch above a bud. The bud should be at the top part of the slant and should point towards the outside of the plant.

- Remove all canes that show unusual discoloration or blotches—this could be a disease.

- Remove all dead canes.

- Remove all weak canes as well as those that cross another cane.

- Remove suckers growing from the rootstock—the leaves will be generally different, so it's easy to identify them.

- Head back all remaining canes, always cutting on an angle with an outside bud at the top of the slant.

PLANTING BARE-ROOT ROSES

Difficulty Level: EASY

Budded roses are generally sold bare-root, while those grown on their own roots are sold in containers. Do not economize when you are buying roses. You'll want to get sturdy container-grown roses that have not become root-bound, or Grade 1 bare-root plants. Grades are deter-mined by the number of canes the plant has, with Grade 1 having three canes.

Tools and Materials: **Spade, bucket, water, soil amendments, stick, watering can.**

1 Unpack your rose as soon as you receive it to inspect it. If you can't plant immediately, repack it and sprinkle the packing matter with water.

2 Eight to twenty-four hours before you plan to transplant your rose, begin soaking it in a bucket containing a thick mud slurry.

3 Dig the planting hole, and amend it with about ¾ cup of rock phosphate to add phosphorus. Scratch the amend-ment into the the soil.

4 Form a firm cone of soil in the planting hole to spread the roots over. Adjust the cone's height until the bud union is at the correct depth.

5 After adding soil around the roots to about the halfway point, fill the hole with water again to settle the soil and remove any air pockets.

6 After you finish planting the rose, water it again. To insulate the plant while it makes new growth, heap soil loosely over the canes.

CHAPTER 4

Continued from page 118

blooming shrubs, climbers, and old roses tend to bloom on lateral growth. As their blooms fade, remove them, cutting back the stem so it has only two leaves. Buds on this stem will give you rebloom later in the season. Ever-blooming roses sometimes experience a midsummer lull. You can often bring them back into bloom by shortening the laterals that have already bloomed or removing some of the older wood. Hybrid Chinas, hybrid Noisettes, and hybrid Bourbons are harmed by midsummer pruning. Unless there is an emergency such as a rampant case of black spot, wait until autumn to prune them.

Winter Care

Winter can be particularly hard on many roses, so it pays to lavish extra attention on your plants in the fall. You can minimize autumn chores by choosing species with the reputation of being reliably hardy in your climate. Even so, you may still need to protect the plants, particularly if you live in an area where snow cover is intermittent throughout the winter months.

No matter where you live, make it a habit to mulch all newly planted roses. Wood chips are an excellent choice for a winter mulch because you'll want to thoroughly cover the bud union. Wait until the soil surface has frozen, and then pile the wood chips about 18 inches high around and into the bush, shaking the canes to make the mulch fall to the center where it will protect the bud union.

SMART TIP

PLANTING ROSES IN COLD CLIMATES

Many rose cultivars are available only in the fall. Autumn planting is generally recommended for roses, as long as the plants have three or four weeks to become established before the ground freezes solid. The best way to determine if you have time to plant is to count backward from the date the ground froze in the previous two years. But in Zones 5 and cooler, this is not always possible, so it's best to heel-in the plants, as described in Chapter 2 on page 45. When you receive your roses, mulch well, and wait until spring to plant them properly. Roses are basically planted the same as any perennial. See Chapter 2 page 55 for instructions on how to plant a container-grown plant.

WINTER PROTECTION

IN WINDY LOCATIONS, windbreaks made from 2x4s and burlap will help to protect your plants. Climbing roses planted in cold climates can be literally buried for the winter. Untie the stems from their supports, bring them down onto the ground, and cover them with a mulch of dry leaves, straw, and wood chips. Shrub roses can be deeply mulched, then covered with burlap sheeting and tied shut. Before you tie the burlap around the stems, stuff dry straw around the enclosed canes to give them even more protection. Remember that *Rosa rugosa* and other roses growing on their own roots will survive almost any winter without extra protection.

Rose Diseases

Inspecting roses for signs of pests and diseases is an important part of routine maintenance. You should be on the lookout for a disease called black spot. This fungal infection can severely weaken and eventually kill roses. Cultivars with yellow blooms seem most susceptible, but almost all roses can develop it. The telltale symptoms are leaves that develop black spots, turn yellow, and drop off. To avoid the disease, space plants so that they receive good air circulation. Water only early in the day, taking care not to splash soil onto the lower leaves.

Baking soda spray (made by mixing 1 tsp. baking soda with 1 quart of water) helps to prevent black spot and powdery mildew if it is used once a week after the leaves unfurl. If your plants do develop black spots, prune off the bottom

BLACK SPOT is notorious in warm humid climates for defoliating rose bushes. Avoid problems by choosing resistant plants, practicing good sanitation, and using preventive techniques.

leaves and any twiggy growth, and spray with antidesiccants, which will form a protective barrier on the leaf. In severe cases, spray with a sulfur-based fungicide every 7 to 10 days, and spray only when the high temperature for the day will be below 85°F. Never use sulfur and horticultural oil on a plant in the same season; the combination will severely burn your plants.

Many of the pests and diseases that attack roses are covered in Chapter 9, "Preventing Weeds, Pests and Diseases," pages 266 to 309. When you see damage, check the table at right as well as the entries for aphids, Japanese beetles, nematodes, and two-spotted spider mites in Chapter 9.

ROSE PESTS

When you see damage, check this table as well as the entries for aphids, Japanese beetles, nematodes, and two-spotted spider mites in Chapter 9, pages 266 to 309.

PEST	DAMAGE	CONTROL
Rose stem girdler	Overwintering larvae cause canes to swell. Cane tips die back as grubs feed on tips	Prune out, cutting below swelling (and grubs)
Rose scale	Feeds on stems, looks like powdery growth on lower canes	Dormant oil spray in late winter
Rose leafhopper	Nymphs feed on young leaf tissue. Not serious in healthy ecosystem	Indigenous leafhopper lacewings prey on leafhoppers, controlling populations
Rose chafer	Beetles skeletonize leaves	Handpick
Rose sawfly	Larvae eat leaves and bore into centers of canes. Adult female lays eggs in leaf tissue	Blast off with water, spray with Neem, or as a last resort, with rotenone
Rose midge	Tips of new growth look burned, shriveled. Peel skin on new growth, and look for creamy or light orange maggots	Beneficial nematodes, particularly *Hydromeris conopophaga*, prey on overwintering pupae
Rose curculio	Bloom is destroyed before it opens. Tiny holes in buds are visible	Spray with Neem oil in spring

TRAINING ROSES

ROSES DO NOT NATURALLY climb. In the wild, rose canes will grow through other plants, but they won't twine, and they don't have tendrils or holdfasts. If you want a rose to climb up a support, you'll have to tie it in place. Use a figure-eight tie to allow some slack, and tie at fairly close intervals. Thin-caned ramblers can be led around a slender support, but climbers with thicker canes won't do this, so you need to tie them in place. Be sure to choose a strong support for climbers because they are usually heavier than ramblers.

GARDENS FOR BEES, BIRDS, AND BUTTERFLIES

GARDENS THAT ATTRACT BEES, birds, and butterflies are thrice beautiful. The plants themselves are lovely, but beyond that, the bright colors and cheerful sounds of creatures flitting through them add an immeasurable dimension to your garden.

While not as visually dramatic as birds and butterflies, bees pollinate flowers that will become fruits and berries. They are an important part of gardens, as well as orchards. Bees are highly sensitive to pesticides, and unfortunately natural bee populations are declining. Many butterfly populations are also declining because of exposure to pesticides and also the scarcity of food plants for them. Even the "benign" control for pest caterpillars, *Bacillus thuringiensis* (BT), kills butterfly larvae—caterpillars.

THIS LOVELY GARDEN DESIGNED TO ATTRACT AND FEED BUTTERFLIES, features scabiosa prominently. In addition to a succession of flowers that butterflies love, this garden also has water for them to drink.

While home gardeners cannot solve these problems by themselves, they can limit their use of BT and other pesticides as much as possible and grow a variety of butterfly food and habitat plants.

Songbirds, too, are in decline over much of North America. Again, home gardeners can make a positive contribution by including plants that offer food and cover for birds in the landscape. It's also helpful to set up a few winter bird feeders as a supplemental food source and to provide a year-round source of clean water. Keep both the food and water out of the reach of cats and squirrels.

Plants to Grow for Wildlife

Creating food sources and habitats for wildlife begins in the early stages of planning your garden. At each step of the design, from deciding how to handle naturally wet areas to choosing plants for the flower beds, take wildlife into consideration. For example, if you are looking for a splash of bright color to anchor the center of an herb garden, consider the brilliantly red bee balm (*Monarda didyma* 'Cambridge Scarlet') because its color and nectar draw both hummingbirds and butterflies.

Birds and butterflies feed on many trees, as well as smaller plants in the landscape. If you watch closely, you'll notice butterflies feeding from dogwoods, willows, and even oaks in the spring. Later in the season, they'll need the nectar from the flowers in your garden. Butterfly larvae (caterpillars) usually eat leaves and stems of plants; thus, it's wise to identify caterpillars before killing them.

BUTTERFLIES need places to rest, as well as food and water. Provide them some shady areas where they can hide, out of the sunshine, during hot afternoons.

BOGGY AREAS are an asset to any landscape; you can grow many interesting plants in them while also supporting wildlife.

SMART TIP
GUIDELINES FOR WILDLIFE-FRIENDLY GARDENS

■ Choose an informal hedgerow over a formal, sheared hedge to mark property boundaries.

■ Choose shrubs that produce fruit.

■ Look for nectar-rich flowers and bright red or scarlet flowers.

■ Keep a fresh source of water near cover, rather than in the open.

■ Place feeders where cats and squirrels can't get to them.

of the animals dependent on wetlands by planting water-loving plants such as marsh marigold (*Caltha palustris*) and cat's tail (*Phleum pratense*) in the boggiest spots and interplanting them with water iris (*Iris ensata*) or blue flag iris (*I. versicolor*). As the ground gets higher and drier, add moisture-loving cultivated plants such as turtlehead (*Chelone glabra*) and yellowroot (*Xanthorhiza simplicissima*).

Remember to welcome frogs into the garden. Frogs and other reptiles may not seem like creatures you want to invite to the garden. However, given that they eat many times their weight in noxious insects, including mosquitoes, keep a boggy spot or prop up a couple of clay pots with stones to give them a home.

Leave a wild area for birds. Many birds are dependent on the seeds and berries that follow flowers. In fall, when you are cleaning up the garden, try to leave a "wild" area where the seedheads of grasses and other plants can remain in place to feed birds over the winter. Also, plant shrubs which produce berries or other fruits.

Birds also eat many of the insects gardeners consider pests. Warblers, flycatchers, thrushes, woodpeckers, mockingbirds, and purple martins are all wonderful insect controls that are attracted to gardens where no pesticides are used.

Wetlands perform so many beneficial roles that it's usually better to leave them undisturbed. However, the area between the wetlands proper and the drier ground where your house and lawn are located is usually too wet to treat as an ordinary garden. You can create a true haven for some

A TINY FROG rests on a squash leaf. Frogs don't eat plants but do consume many bothersome insects.

FLOWERS TO ATTRACT BEES, BIRDS, AND BUTTERFLIES

This table lists some of the best food sources for bees, birds, and butterflies, but it is not all-inclusive. Many other plants provide both food and habitat through the seasons. As you look at other gardens in the area, try to notice whether wildlife comes to feed on the plants that you like. Also learn about plants native to your area that you could incorporate into your garden. Most of the wildlife in your area has evolved to live on these indigenous species. As you expand your gardens, keep adding plants that will provide food and shelter for bees, birds, and butterflies, as well as for frogs and lizards. You'll never regret it.

NAME	COMMON	ZN	HT.	SEASON	COLOR	SOIL	EXPOSURE	COMMENTS
FLOWERS								
Angelica archangelica	**Angelica**	4-8	4'-6'	Midsummer	White	Moist, well-drained	Full sun to partial shade	Attracts beneficial wasps & insects. Pick off flower heads before seeds form
Asclepias curassavica	**Bloodflower**	7-8	2½'	Summer to frost	Red-orange	Moist, well-drained	Full sun	Attracts and feeds many species of butterflies
Asclepias tuberosa	**Butterfly weed**	3-9	3'	Summer	Orange, yellow bicolor	Moist	Full sun	Flowers and seeds feed many birds, insects, and butterflies
Calendula officinalis	**Calendula**	n/a	1'-2'	Summer-fall	Orange, red	Versatile	Full sun to partial shade	Seedheads feed birds in winter
Delphinium elatum	**Delphinium, candle**	3-8	4'-6'	Summer	Blue, pink lavender, white	Rich, moist, humusy, alkaline	Full sun	Feeds butterflies and other flying insects
Gaillardia aristata	**Blanket-flower**	5-8	1'	All summer	Red & yellow	Versatile	Full sun	Butterflies feed from the flowers, birds from the seedheads
Gaillardia pulchella	**Painted gaillardia**	n/a	2'	All summer	Wide range	Versatile	Full sun	Good butterfly flowers; deadhead to prolong bloom
Gentiana asclepiadea	**Willow gentian**	6-8	1½'-2½'	Late summer	Blue	Acid, humusy	Partial shade	Feeds hummingbirds. Group for best effect
Helianthus annuus	**Sunflower**	n/a	1'-12'	Midsummer	Range	Versatile, rich	Full sun	Seedheads feed birds
Hesperis matronalis	**Dame's rocket**	3-8	2'-3'	Late spring	Range	Damp, versatile	Versatile	Feeds birds, particularly goldfinches
Kniphofia uvaria	**Red-hot poker**	6-8	2½'-3½'	Fall	Red	Moist, well-drained	Semi-sun	Feeds hummingbirds
Myosotis spp.	**Garden forget-me-not**	3-8	6"-8"	Spring	Blue	Moist, acid	Partial shade	Feeds birds, beneficial insects
Scabiosa caucasica	**Pincushion flower**	4-8	2'	Midsummer	Blue, white	Moist, neutral pH	Full sun	Feeds birds, butterflies, and insects

ROCK GARDENS

A ROCK GARDEN IS more than just a garden with rocks. It's a special kind of growing environment intended to mimic the look and growing conditions of places where rocks are present naturally, such as mountainsides, boulder-strewn slopes, or screes where gravel collects.

Traditional rock gardens are filled with small alpine plants such as gentian and edelweiss (*Leontopodium alpinum*) set out so that the planting looks natural rather than contrived. Of course, contemporary gardeners often take liberties with the form, grouping almost any plants that will survive in the rock-garden environment. Adherents of each style present good arguments in defense of their approach. Purists note that the alpine plants are so suited to the environment that both their health and appropriate appearance are guaranteed, while people who opt for a more eclectic style argue that the plants they choose are often closer to those found in the native ecosystem of the garden and thus, less artificial looking. But no matter which camp you fall into, you'll want to choose plants that can thrive in a rock garden and design it so that plants and rocks are in scale with each other.

ROCK GARDENS can transform difficult, stony areas on your property into lovely gardens filled with interesting plants.

Choose the Site Carefully

The site for a rock garden must be well chosen. In most climates, an eastern or northern exposure is preferable because it protects plants from radical freezing/thawing action during the late winter and early spring, and also protects them from the high summer temperatures that can build up on south-facing rocky slopes. If you have a naturally rocky spot on your property, use that area for a rock garden without worrying about its orientation.

If you are using a high proportion of alpine plants, remember that they fare best in soil that is moist but extremely well-drained, has average fertility, and is at a neutral to slightly alkaline pH. If possible, site the rock garden where these conditions will be easy to meet. If a soil test shows that your soil is mildly acidic, lime the area well a year before you plant and continue to test and adjust the pH every season.

If your rock garden is on a natural slope, the direction from which people will view it is predetermined. But you'll need to take the background view into consideration too. For example, if your rock garden backs into a natural woodland or the front lawn, you won't want to change a thing. However, if it leads the eye to the neighbors' junk pile, you may want to plant a row of conifers or position a trellis on which you can grow a decorative vine to screen the background view. Even with a natural, rocky slope, you'll probably want to "improve" it slightly by amending the soil and adding well-draining material, such as gravel.

PLANTS FOR ROCK GARDENS

This table lists many good rock garden plants. These plants require about an inch of water a week and soil that drains exceptionally well. Most of them prefer full sun, but some will tolerate partial shade. Begin your rock garden by choosing from this list, but don't be afraid to expand on it. As long as you retain a sense of scale, it's hard to go wrong.

NAME	COMMON	ZONE	HT.	BLOOM	COLOR	NOTES
GRASSES						
Carex humilis	**Blue sedge**	5-9	6"-8"	Late summer	Tawny	Good ground cover in rock gardens, holds soil, forms clumps
Festuca cinerea	**Blue fescue**	4-8	10"	Late summer	Blue foliage	Tufting; fruiting heads reach 2' tall; good with succulents
DWARF CONIFERS						
Chamaecyparis obtusa 'Nana'	**Dwarf Hinoki cypress**	4-8	1.5'	n/a	Dark green	Grows only 20" wide, leaves look like thick moss
Juniperus communis 'Echiniformis'	**Hedgehog juniper**	2-7	2'	n/a	Clear green	The hummock-like shape adds needed contrast to a rock garden
SHRUBS						
Calluna vulgaris	**Heather**	4-7	2.5'	Winter to spring	Range	Choose dwarf heathers. Heather requires acid (6-5.5) pH soil
Erica carnea	**Winter or spring heath**	4-7	1'	Winter to spring	White, pink, red, purple	Many cultivars are available. Heath requires alkaline soil
Rhododendron impeditum	**Yunan rhododendron**	6-8	1.5'	Spring	Purplish-blue	This dwarf shrub has tiny leaves in scale with its size
PERENNIALS						
Achillea clavennae	**Silver alpine yarrow**	3-7	1'	Late spring	White	Requires alkaline (7.5) soil
Aquilegia canadensis	**Rock columbine**	3-8	1'	Late spring	Red, yellow	Requires alkaline to neutral soil. Tolerates light shade
Aquilegia saximontana	**Colorado columbine**	4-6	4"	Spring	Blue, yellow	Requires neutral soil and a sunny location
Arabis spp.	**Rockcress, Wallcress**	4-7	4"-1.5'	Summer	White	Requires alkaline to neutral soil in sunny location. Many species
Armeria caespitosa, A. maritima	**Thrift**	5-8	4"-8"	Early summer	Pink, white	Requires neutral soils in a sunny location. Excellent cut flower too
Gentiana spp.	**Gentian**	3-7	2"-1.5'	Summer to fall	Blue	Several species are available. Prefers sunny location
Leontopodium alpinum	**Edelweiss**	5-7	4"-6"	Late spring-summer	Yellowish-gray/white	This traditional alpine plant requires alkaline soils in sunny locations
Penstemon spp.	**Penstemon**	range	range	Spring to summer	Blue, red pink, white	Wide choice of species, cultivars. Some tolerate acid soils and partial shade
Sedum spp.	**Sedum**	range	range	Summer	Pink, red, yellow	Many species and cultivars are suitable
Thymus spp.	**Thyme**	range	range	Late spring, summer	Pink, purple	Choose creeping species such as *T. serpyllum* & *T. pseudolanuginosus*
Veronica prostrata	**Cliff speedwell**	5-7	6"-8"	Summer	Blue, white	Place in full sun with neutral pH soil
Veronica spicata	**Alpine speedwell**	3-7	6"-8"	Summer	Blue, white	Place in full sun with neutral pH soil

GARDENS FOR DRIED ARRANGEMENTS

DRIED ARRANGEMENTS ALLOW YOU to bring the glory of the blooming garden into the house for the winter. As you'll soon discover, a huge number of plants can be preserved by one method or another. Thin or stiff-petaled flowers and seedpods dry well almost on their own. All you have to do is pick them at the proper time and hang them upside down or stand them upright in a small amount of water to dry in the air. But there are several other ways to preserve flowers. The type of flower usually dictates which method works best. For example, the fleshy petals of a peony dry beautifully in silica gel, but if you want a softer look, preserve peonies in glycerin. Even the microwave oven can be used to dry individual flowers.

Plan to grow some of the easily dried flowers and seedpods listed in the table on pages 130 and 131, but don't confine yourself to working with only those species. As you gain familiarity with preserving methods, you can experiment with other plants.

AIR-DRY FLOWERS in a cool, dark location to retain the most vivid colors.

POSITION plants in a dried flower garden as you do those in a cutting garden. Plant in rows and arrange them by cultural requirements.

CHAPTER 4

Smart Tip

DRYING PLANTS UPRIGHT

If your plants wilt when you try to dry them in an upright position, you'll need to refine the technique. Stretch course netting or wire over the vase top to hold the stems in place, but add an inch of water to the bottom. Set the vase and plants in the drying area and let the water evaporate. The plants will dry more slowly than they would without water, but they will retain a fresher, fuller appearance.

Flossflower (*Ageratum* species), bells of Ireland (*Moluccella laevis*), baby's breath (*Gypsophila paniculata*), cockscomb (*Celosia cristata*) and yarrow (*Achillea filipendulina*) all dry well with this treatment.

Air-drying

Many of the plants we consider "everlasting" dry well in the air. Blooms such as perennial statice (*Limonium* species) and globe amaranth (*Gomphrena globosa*) are usually gathered just before the petals have fully opened, tied into small bunches, and hung upside down in a clean, dark spot with good ventilation. Depending on the species, the flowers will be dry in a few days to a week. There are only a few guidelines to follow with this method:

■ The bunches should be small enough so air can circulate around each bloom.

■ The stems must be bunched so that the blooms are at different heights.

■ The stems should be secured with a rubber band that will automatically tighten as the stems lose water, or a twist tie that can be readjusted.

Some plants air-dry better in an upright position. Grasses, members of the onion family (*Allium* species), and annual statice all do well with this method. Use a tall container and stretch coarse netting or wire over the top. Place the stems through the netting so that the blooms are at different heights. Again, the best location to dry plants is a clean, dark place with good ventilation. (See the Smart Tip above.)

Drying in Silica Gel

Silica gel is a desiccant that dries plants by gradually absorbing their moisture. It's used for such flowers as peonies, daffodils, and iris that lose their petals, color, or shape when they are air-dried. It's always better to have too much rather than too little silica gel, so buy at least 5 pounds from a seed company or crafts supplier. Buy some duct tape, too; you'll need it to seal the lid.

Pick flowers for drying in silica gel when they first open fully and they are dry of rainwater or dew. Wire all flowers you plan to dry with silica gel because it makes the natural stems too brittle to work after they are dry. To save space in the drying container, attach a short wire to the flower, then extend the wire stem after the flowers are dried. Put an inch or so of silica gel in the bottom of the container with a tight-fitting lid, such as a cookie tin or plastic ice cream tub, and set the flowers on top of the material. Place daisy-shaped blooms face-down on the silica. Roses and trumpet-shaped blooms should be set face up. Leave an inch or so of space around each bloom. Gently sift more silica gel onto the flowers, shaking or pushing it down into creases as necessary, until the blooms are covered with about an inch of material. Now put the lid on, and tape it shut.

DRYING FLOWERS IN SILICA

PLACE FLOWERS at least an inch apart; this ensures the correct ratio between the material and the flowers.

ALMOST ANY FLOWER DRIES WELL in silica gel as long as you sift only an inch or so of the heavy material on the top of the bloom. If it is piled too deeply, its weight will distort the shape of the flower.

How Long Does Drying Take?

Drying time varies with species as well as the moisture content of the particular blooms you are drying. Three days in the silica gel should be adequate for quick-drying, thin-petaled flowers like daisies, while fleshy blooms such as peonies and many roses may take as long as two weeks. Check plants by tipping the container so that a few petals are exposed. Touch them. If they feel papery, they are probably dry enough. Even though you want the blooms to be completely dry, you do not want them to become brittle. As with so many other things, experience will be your best teacher. Once you have dried a few batches of flowers, you'll know how they should feel.

Drying wispy stems with multiple florets. The directions above are best for large, single flowers. If you wish to dry flowering stems such as larkspur, wrap florists' wire

continued on page 132

CREATING DRIED FLOWER ARRANGEMENTS

Difficulty Level: MODERATE

Homemade wreaths are one of the greatest pleasures of growing dried material. Though it takes some practice to learn how to make a wreath, it's well worth the effort.

Tools and Materials: **Wire wreath form, florists' wire, small wire clippers, glue.**

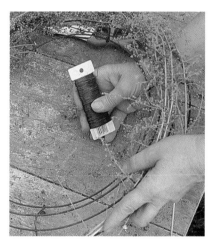

1 Attach the first layer of dried material to the form with florist's wire. Use a grass or leafy material such as `Silver King' *Artemisia*.

2 Use florists' wire to attach individual leaves and flowers to the frame. Work around the frame to keep the design well balanced.

3 If you can't attach a bloom or leaf with wire, use a drop of hot glue to secure it. Place the glue so it is hidden by the dried materials.

4 Hang your wreath in a cool location with indirect light to keep it looking fresh for a long time. You may need to gently dust it occasionally.

CHAPTER 4

EASY-DRY FLOWERS AND SEEDPODS

This table lists many of the most commonly grown plants for drying. The various methods for preserving are described in detail on pages 127-133.

NAME	COMMON	ZN	HT.	SEASON	COLOR	SOIL	EXPOSURE	COMMENTS	PRESERVE
Abelmoschus esculentus	Okra	n/a	2'	Late summer	Brown	Fertile, well-drained	Full sun	Harvest pods before they open but after they have turned brown	Hang-dry
Achillea filipendulina	Yarrow	4-8	2'-4'	Summer	Range	Well-drained	Full sun	Plants bloom from second year. Cut when flowers are fully open. Leave foliage in place	Hang-dry; dry upright
Anethum graveolens	Dill	n/a	1'-3'	Late summer	Brown	Versatile	Full sun	Harvest before seeds drop to avoid volunteers	Hang-dry
Ammobium alatum	Winged everlasting	n/a	2'	Mid-late summer	Silver-white	Light, rich, sandy	Full sun	Cut before centers are visible but after buds begin to open. Cut buds will not open	Wire stems; air-dry
Aquilegia	Columbine	3-9	1'-2'	Late summer	Brown	Versatile, well-drained	Sun to p. shade	Harvest seed pods before seeds drop	Hang-dry
Asclepias	Milkweed	3-9	3'	Late summer	Brown	Versatile	Full sun	Harvest before pods split	Hang-dry
Baptisia australis	Blue false indigo	3-9	6'	Late summer	Dark brown	Fertile, well-drained	Full sun to p. shade	Harvest pods before they open	Hang-dry
Belamcanda chinensis	Blackberry lily	5-9	3'	Summer	Orange, red	Versatile	Full sun	This plant has seed pods that open in autumn to reveal shiny black seeds. Use pods in bouquets	Dries on plant
Carex	Sedge	3-9	2'	Late summer	Brown	Versatile	Full sun	Harvest before seeds drop	Hang-dry
Celosia cristata	Cockscomb	n/a	1'-2'	Summer	Range	Rich, deep well-drained	Full sun	Harvest when almost open. Stand upright in water that you allow to evaporate until dry	Hang-dry
Consolida regalis	Larkspur	n/a	2'-3'	Late summer	Range, brown	Well-drained, fertile	Full sun	Dry flowers when bottom blooms open, use seed pods too	Hang-dry
Cynara cardunculus	Cardoon	5-9	6'	Fall	Gold, bronze	Rich, deep	Full sun	Blanch stems in late summer for 8 weeks to grow as an edible crop. Dry open seedheads	Hang-dry
Dipsacus sativus	Teasel	n/a	4'-5'	Mid-late summer	Brown	Rich, moist	Full sun	Direct seed in place in early summer. The next year, harvest when petals have withered	Dry upright
Echinops ritro	Globe thistle	5-8	3'-4'	Summer	Blue	Heavy, alkaline, well-drained	Full sun	Cut before bracts have fully opened. Remove most of the basal leaves	Hang-dry; silica gel

Name	Common	Zn	Ht.	Season	Color	Soil	Exposure	Comments	Preserve
Eryngium spp.	Sea holly	5-9	1'-4'	Late summer	Blue	Well-drained, alkaline	Full sun	Many different species, all dry well. Check seed catalogues for selections	Dry upright
Gomphrena globosa	Globe amaranth	n/a	1'-1½'	Summer	Range	Moist	Full sun	Use flowers fresh or dried. Harvest when almost fully open	Hang-dry
Gypsophila paniculata	Baby's breath	4-8	3'-4'	Summer	White, pink	Well-drained, neutral pH	Full sun	Cut before flowers are fully open, leaving 1' to regrow. Cut again	Hang-dry
Helichrysum bracteatum	Strawflower	n/a	2'-4'	Summer	Range	Versatile	Full sun	Use flowers fresh or dried. If drying, cut before petals are fully open	Wire stems; dry upright
Helipterum roseum	Acroclinium	n/a	1½'	Summer	Range	Well-drained, high humus, pH 6-6.5	Full sun	Use blooms fresh or dried. If drying, harvest when flowers just begin to open	Hang-dry; glycerin
Iris	Iris	3-9	1'-1½'	Late summer	Brown	Well-drained fertile	Full sun	Harvest seed pods before they split	Hang-dry
Lagurus ovatus	Hare's tail grass	3-9	1'-2'	Late summer	Brown	Versatile	Full sun	Harvest before seeds drop	Hang-dry
Limonium perezii	German statice	5-8	2'	Summer	Blue, white	Versatile, well-drained	Full sun	Germinate in darkness. Harvest when 80% of flowers have opened	Hang-dry
Limonium sinuatum	Statice	n/a	1½'-2'	Summer	Range	Versatile, well-drained	Full sun	Use flowers fresh or dried. If drying, harvest when 80% of florets on a stem are open	Hang-dry
Lunaria annua	Honesty	Bien	2'	Summer	Purple, white	Well-drained	Full sun-p shade	Use flowers fresh and seedpods dry. For seedpods, cut when brown. Rub off skins	Dry on plant; stand upright
Moluccella laevis	Bells-of-Ireland	Bien	1'-1½'	Summer	Green	Well-drained, rich	Full sun	Cut when spike is almost fully open. Stand in 2" of water until evaporated, then dry	Stand upright; glycerin
Nigella damascena	Love-in-a-mist	n/a	1'	Summer	Brown	Versatile	Full sun	Wait until pods are fully formed	Hang-dry
Panicum miliaceum	Broom corn	n/a	3'	Late sum/fall	Brown, red	Moist, rich	Full sun	Harvest when "brooms" are almost fully open	Stand upright
Papaver	Poppy	3-8	1'-2'	Late summer	Brown	Well-drained	Full sun	Harvest before seeds fall	Hang-dry
Physalis alkekengi	Chinese lantern	n/a	1'-2'	Late summer	Orange	Versatile	Full sun	Harvest after seedpods have turned orange	Dries on plant
Ruta graveolens	Rue	4-9	1'-2'	Late summer	Brown	Well-drained	Full sun	Harvest seeds before they open	Hang-dry
Scabiosa stellata	Starflower, Ping-pong	n/a	2½'	Late summer/fall	Pale blue	Versatile	Full sun	Wait until petals have fallen to harvest for dried material but cut before fully brown	Stand upright
Triticum aestivum	Wheat	3-8	1'-2'	Late summer	Brown	Well-drained, fertile	Full sun	Harvest before seeds drop	Hang-dry

CHAPTER 4

Continued from page 129

around the entire stem, and then place it in a tall, narrow plastic container with a lid. Pour in the silica gel very slowly so that the florets are not injured. You can also dry these stems flat if you have a long, shallow container. In either case, cover the container securely, and tape it closed.

Drying in the Microwave

Individual flowers can be dried in the microwave. It's best to do them one at a time, but if you become impatient with this, limit yourself to drying only two or three of the same kinds of flowers together. Prepare single flowers by inserting a wooden toothpick through the calyx. This will give you a hole to thread florists' wire through after the flower has been dried.

Put an inch or so of silica gel in a microwave-safe bowl. Place the flowers or leaves on top of the silica gel, leaving about 1½ inches of space around each flower or leaf if working with more than one. Now sprinkle silica gel over the plant material, covering it to a depth of at least an inch.

Set the microwave at power level 4 if it goes from 1 to 10, or "defrost" if it doesn't. Timing varies with the plant, but if you are drying a single flower in approximately ½ pound of silica gel, (the amount it takes to cover a bloom or two) begin with a setting of 2½ minutes. After the time is up, let the container stand for about 10 minutes for a single thin-petaled flower or leaf, and up to half an hour for

---

SMART TIP

REMOVING FLOWERS FROM SILICA GEL

Silica gel is heavy enough that it can damage your flowers if you yank them out of the containers. Instead, pour off the silica gel, a thin stream at a time, until most of your blooms are exposed. Use a soft brush to push the remaining silica gel away and gently lift out the flowers.

---

a large flower such as a peony. (To prevent the dried material from reabsorbing moisture, put a lid on the container before you let it stand but leave it slightly cracked so that air can escape). After the standing time, gently pour off the silica gel and check to see that the material is dry. If not, recover it with silica gel and reheat it, always using cool silica gel.

As you gain experience with drying in the microwave, you'll learn how long each flower requires. Wait to wire them because if they reabsorb moisture while they are in storage, you may want to reheat them in the microwave.

Preserving with Glycerin

Glycerin is used to preserve whole branches of fairly mature leaves, as well as individual leaves and a few selected flowers. It has the advantages of making preserved plants more pliable than they might otherwise be, gives foliage a waxy look, and also maintains or enhances colors. Some of the flowers that dry well in glycerin are listed on page 131.

Buy glycerin from a pharmacy, or if you are using large quantities, from a chemical supply company. Mix one part glycerin to two parts of simmering water which is just off the boil, stirring to mix thoroughly. Cool the solution to room temperature before using or it will cook your plants.

Whole branches or stems will preserve best if they are harvested in late summer rather than autumn. Cut your material in late morning after a few sunny, dry days.

Dry stems upright. Most stems and branches should be preserved in an upright position. Fill a tall, narrow container with about two inches of glycerin solution. Then stand the freshly cut stems in it, and put the container and stems in a cool, dark place. Check the container every day to make certain that the stems still have a supply of glycerin to draw into themselves. Most plants take from two days to a month to fully absorb the glycerin, but once they have absorbed it, the leaves will feel waxy, their color may have changed or darkened, and their veins will have darkened. Remove them as soon as the appearance has changed.

Preserve baby's breath by standing the stems in glycerin for three or four days, then hanging them upside down for a few days. The flowers will turn a lovely creamy color and the stems will be pliable to use in arrangements. Both Chinese lanterns and statice should stand in a glycerin

---

SMART TIP

DRY SILICA IN THE OVEN FOR REUSE

After you have removed your flowers, you will need to dry out your silica gel so that it can be reused. Some suppliers use a blue dye and some use a pink dye on some of the grains to indicate that the material is dry. You will notice these flecks when you open a new can of the material, but when you remove your blooms from it, the flecks will have disappeared. Dry the gel by putting it in a wide shallow pan in a 250°F oven for about half an hour. Stir it occasionally to expose all of the material to the air. When it is dry, the blue or pink flecks will have returned. Store the material in an airtight container, taped shut, until the next time you want to use it.

solution for two days, then be hung upside down for another two days. Bells-of-Ireland should be completely immersed in a glycerin solution for two or three days, then hung upside down for a day or so to allow the extra solution to drip off.

Arranging Dried Materials

Making winter bouquets and arrangements can fill many a stormy day. Not only can you decorate your own home, you can also make wreaths and bouquets as gifts.

Let your creativity take hold when you arrange your dried flowers. With some florists' wire, florist tape and florist foam, you'll be able to arrange your materials in almost any shape you desire. However, if you are mixing glycerin-preserved branches with air- or silica-dried materials, make certain that the arrangement is loose enough to allow air to circulate through so the flowers don't pick up moisture from one another. You'll also want to check periodically to wipe off any excess moisture. But, aside from this precaution, you can mix and match your dried materials to your heart's content. Enjoy them for a year or two and discard them when they fade.

Storing Dried Materials

If you don't plan to arrange your dried flowers right away, you can store them. They last a year or two depending on the material. Ideal storage containers and conditions vary, depending on how the material was dried.

For air-dried material, large, shallow boxes similar to those florists use for long-stemmed roses, are generally the best containers. Sprinkle silica gel in the bottom and cover it with clean paper towels. Now make small bunches of your dried material and wrap each bunch in tissue paper. Put a single layer in the box, with the bunch tops and bottoms alternating (just the way you keep shoes in the box). Cover the box and put it in a dark, dry spot. Check the mate-

rial every month to determine whether it's reabsorbing moisture. If it is, add more silica gel to the box.

Material that was dried in silica gel must be stored in airtight plastic or tin containers. Sprinkle some silica gel in the bottom of the container; then add your dried material. Seal the lid with duct tape and place it in a cool, dark spot. Store microwave-dried flowers alone or with flowers that have been dried in silica gel.

Glycerin-preserved materials release moisture in storage. Wipe leaves and flowers with an a dish towel; then set them upright in tall cans or jars in a well ventilated area.

WIRING STEMS

Stems of some flowers become so brittle when they are dry that they crack and fall off as soon as you try to arrange them. You can avoid this problem by wiring the flowers. How you wire the stems depends on the weight of the flower. Strawflowers, for example, dry fine with only one wire, while the weight of roses really demands two. For strawflowers, cut a 6-inch length of florists' wire, (thin, green, flexible wire that is available at floral supply or craft shops) for each bloom. Stick one end of the wire through the flower's calyx and bend it around itself to form a new stem. Or, you can pierce the bottom of the center of the flower with one end of the wire, bend it into a hook, and draw it back down into the center of the bloom. For roses and other heavy flowers, stick the two wires through the calyx so they cross each other and then bend the wires around themselves to make the new stem.

Once the bloom has dried, the calyx will have dried around the wire, holding it in place. If you need a longer piece of wire, you can add more wire to the original piece, bending it in place. Use green florists' tape to cover the wire, or to tape several wired blooms together.

USE FLORISTS' WIRE to make a stem for heavy flowers.

WIRE SNIPS or needle-nosed pliers will speed up your work.

CHAPTER 5

VINES

Vines can be one of the most effective elements in your garden. Some flower so lavishly that they steal the whole show while they're in bloom, some attract bevies of hummingbirds and other bright creatures, and the leaves and stems of others can turn any eyesore into an attraction.

In the winter, woody vines contribute structural beauty to the garden, and the bark and berries of many add needed color and texture to the land-scape. With training, vines can add a vertical line, shade an arbor, decorate a wall, and provide a living fence to screen an eyesore.

A vine is usually defined as a long-stemmed plant that needs support to develop. We think of this support as man-made, but in the wild, vines left untended clamber up trees, shrubs, and rock piles. A trip down almost any small road in parts of the

MORNING-GLORY VINES, with their lavish display of blooms, make visitors feel welcome to this lovely garden.

American South affords a good view of the kudzu vine (*Pueraria lobata*) gone wild on telephone poles and power lines. Many vines can grow as well on the ground as they do on supports, as amply demonstrated by the miles and miles of poison ivy growing along road sides and field edges.

Many of the vines we cultivate are woody perennials. Some, such as English Ivy (*Hedera helix*), are evergreen, but most commonly grown vines drop their leaves in the fall. Evergreen or not, gardeners rely on woody vines to decorate outside structures and form permanent screens and garden "walls."

Annual vines grow amazingly fast and large. Although these plants will not provide a permanent garden feature as do woody perennials, they can provide a brightly colored screen around a compost pile or give needed height and color to any garden all summer long.

Both perennial and annual vines share a use-ful trait. They take up little ground space relative to the impact they create, making them ideal for small gardens. The perennials are quite deep-rooted, giv-ing them some resistance to droughts, and the annu-als are ideal for containers, as long as they are watered and fertilized adequately.

How Vines Attach to Supports

AERIAL ROOTLETS grow into crevices in a wall. They are strong enough to pry boards loose but don't hurt bricks.

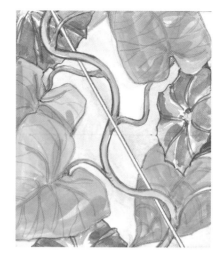

TWINING STEMS simply wrap themselves around a support such as twine or a metal wire.

HOLDFASTS can attach themselves to smooth surfaces because they secrete an adhesive substance.

TENDRILS wrap tightly around their trellises. Give them both vertical and horizontal support structures.

How Vines Climb

VINES CLIMB THEIR SUPPORTS in one of three ways. Their stems may twine around supports, they may have twining tendrils or leaf petioles, or they can have aerial rootlets or disk-shaped "holdfasts."

As shown in the illustrations above, aerial rootlets are dense and bushy and cling by growing into niches. English ivy has adhesive aerial rootlets. Other clinging vines, such as trumpet vine (*Campsis radicans*) and Virginia creeper (*Parthenocissus quinquefolia*), attach themselves to their supports with disk-shaped structures on their stems that secrete an adhesive substance (holdfasts).

Morning-glory (*Ipomoea* species) and honeysuckle (*Lonicera* species) both have tendrils. Clematis vines (*Clematis* species), sweet peas (*Lathyrus odoratus*), and gourd plants grow twining stems or tendrils. Some plants such as climbing roses are scandent, meaning that they send up long stems that lean against other plants or structures unless they are fastened to a support.

Choosing the Best Support

It's important to know how a vine climbs in order to provide a good support for it. In fact, many garden designers start with the support rather than the vine, choosing the look they want and then selecting a vine that can grow against that support. For example, if an outdoor patio is

TOOLS

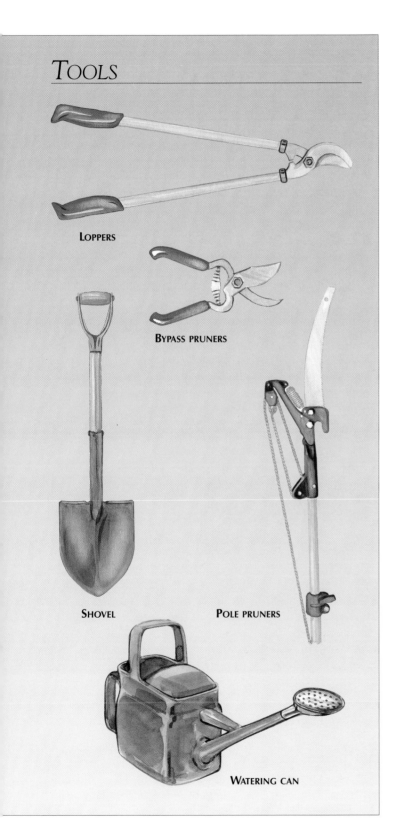

LOPPERS

BYPASS PRUNERS

SHOVEL

POLE PRUNERS

WATERING CAN

WISTERIA VINES are so large and the plants so heavy that they pull down all but the strongest supports.

defined by sturdy posts at the edges and an overhead lattice for shade, a designer is likely to choose a twining vine such as grape (*Vitis* species) or wisteria. In contrast, a wooden screen to hide the garbage pails from view seems to cry out for a layer of chicken wire on which to train a sweet-pea vine (*Lathyrus odoratus*) or the more-delicate sweet autumn clematis (*C. paniculata*) to climb with tendrils. Try Virginia creeper on a stone wall at the edge of the property.

But no matter whether you choose the vine to go with the support or the support to go with the vine, the two must

SMART TIP

LEAVE SPACE BETWEEN VINES AND BUILDINGS

Many vines can cause substantial damage to buildings and other structures or plants against which they grow. But you can prevent structural problems with some simple safeguards. Always plant twining vines at least 10 inches from house walls. This spacing will give them room to grow and still provide a 6-inch space for air to circulate between the wall and the vine itself. Because of the moisture that leaves naturally release, vines planted closer than this can contribute to a rotting problem on wooden walls or, in the case of masonry, a fungus problem on the vine itself.

CHAPTER 5

THIS LUSH JACKMANII CLEMATIS is an excellent choice for a vine to grace a doorway because it blooms for most of the season.

IVY WILL COMPLETELY COVER A STONE WALL. Prune ivy every year to keep it in bounds, especially if it is growing next to a door or window.

match. Herbaceous twining stems grow best when they can twine vertically around supports, while petioles or tendrils climb most easily by wrapping around a horizontal support. Aerial rootlets need a continuous surface with a texture that is rough enough so they can adhere to it. Heavy, woody twining vines such as wisteria require big, strong timbers that are buried below the frost line or reinforced with concrete tube forms. Otherwise, their weight may drag down the support.

Match Vine Habit to Structure

Vines that cling to walls, such as English ivy (*Hedera helix*), should not be planted near wooden buildings because they can grow into cracks and pry apart the wood siding, which can cause rotting. This type of vine is safest growing against stone or brick walls with sound mortar.

Some large vines that climb by tendrils or twining stems

This climbing hydrangea vine fastens itself to the brick with aerial rootlets. The foliage and flowers visually soften the wall.

Use a trellis to support vines. To avoid these problems, don't grow vigorous twining vines near trees or shrubs. Instead, give them a trellis to climb rather than allowing them to grow "wild" on other plants in the garden. This is particularly important with aggressive twiners such as Oriental bittersweet (*Celastrus orbiculatus*).

There are some notable exceptions to this rule. Less aggressive twining vines make good companions for sturdy shrubs. For example, a time-honored design depends on planting a large-flowered clematis species such as *Clematis x jackmanii* at the base of a brawny rose such as *Rosa rugosa*. Not only does the rose provide ideal environmental conditions for the clematis—shaded roots and sunlit top growth—but the flowers of the two plants bring out the best in each other, and the clematis (even when mature) will never strangle the rose.

> ## Smart Tip
> ### Support for Your Vines
> No matter whether you match the vine to the support or the support to the vine, plan so they suit each other. To avoid damaging the vines, set up their supports before you plant. Remember to leave enough space between walls and twining vines so that air can circulate freely around the leaves, removing excess moisture.

can damage trees if they grow into them. Ivy, which climbs by means of adhesive rootlets that can stick to tree bark, will never strangle a tree or branch because it grows upward rather than around. But the more aggressive twining honeysuckle or porcelain berry vines (*Ampelopsis brevipedunculata*) can choke a small tree in just a few years because the vine stems twist tighter and tighter around the trunk as the vines grow thicker with age.

INSTALLING POSTS

The process for installing posts securely is the same for an arbor or a fence. But you must take extra care positioning arbor posts. The corners must be at right angles and the sides parallel. Locating the corners with batter boards and string is the most accurate way to go. Make the batter boards by nailing 1×2 stakes to scraps of 1×3 or 1×4 wood, and position them 1 foot from the approximate location of each post as shown in the boxed drawing below. Locate the exact post positions with string; adjust the string so the diagonal measurements are equal to ensure that the corners will be at right angles.

1 Position the posts with batter boards, taut string, and a plumb bob.

2 Remove the string to dig the holes; then re-attach it and align the outer faces of the posts with the string while you plumb and brace them.

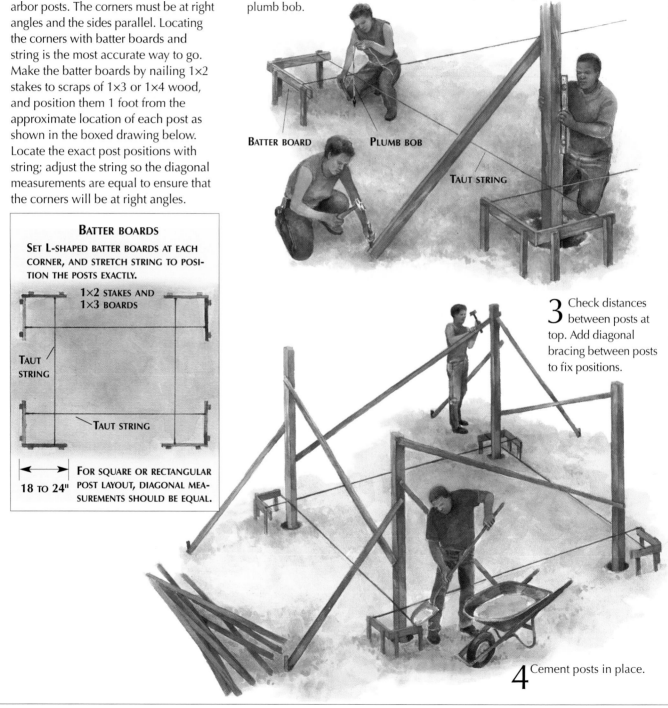

BATTER BOARD   **PLUMB BOB**

TAUT STRING

3 Check distances between posts at top. Add diagonal bracing between posts to fix positions.

4 Cement posts in place.

BATTER BOARDS

SET L-SHAPED BATTER BOARDS AT EACH CORNER, AND STRETCH STRING TO POSITION THE POSTS EXACTLY.

1×2 STAKES AND 1×3 BOARDS

TAUT STRING

TAUT STRING

18 TO 24"   **FOR SQUARE OR RECTANGULAR POST LAYOUT, DIAGONAL MEASUREMENTS SHOULD BE EQUAL.**

BUILDING AN ARBOR

This cozy shelter supports vines and adds a vertical dimension to the garden. Setting the posts (see directions at left) is the most time-consuming and painstaking part of this project. After the posts are in place, this project can be finished in about a weekend. Although nails or screws will hold the double 2×6 joists in place, carriage bolts are far superior. Tack the joists in place with nails. Then bore holes through the post and both joists with an auger bit. Toenailing or installing metal rafter ties will hold the rafters in place. Lattice nailed or screwed to each post provides climbing support for the vines. Sandwich the lattice between 1×2 trim for extra support. If the lattice is stiff enough, you can omit the trim.

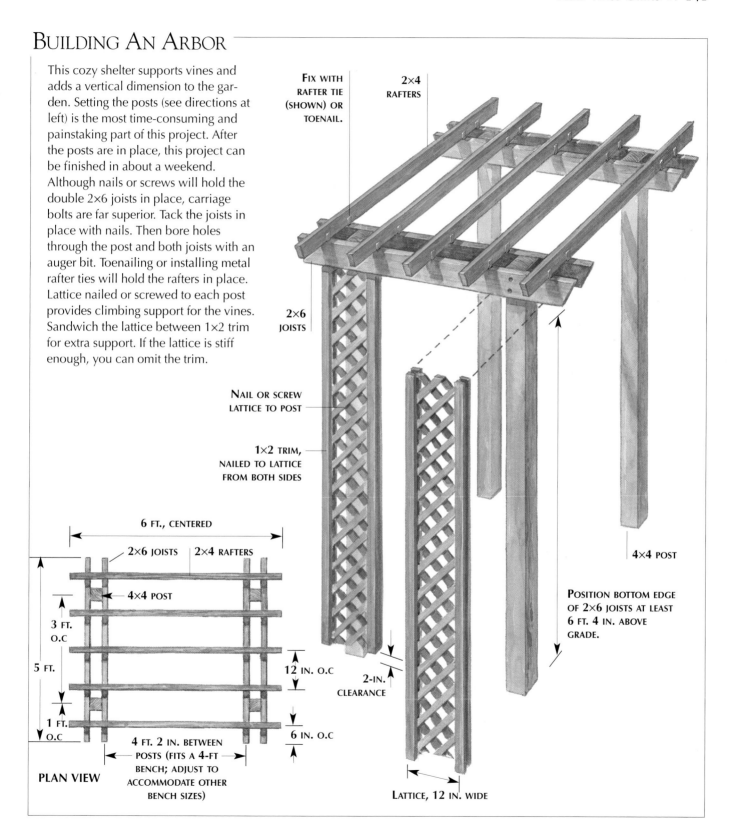

FIX WITH RAFTER TIE (SHOWN) OR TOENAIL.

2×4 RAFTERS

2×6 JOISTS

NAIL OR SCREW LATTICE TO POST

1×2 TRIM, NAILED TO LATTICE FROM BOTH SIDES

4×4 POST

POSITION BOTTOM EDGE OF 2×6 JOISTS AT LEAST 6 FT. 4 IN. ABOVE GRADE.

2-IN. CLEARANCE

LATTICE, 12 IN. WIDE

6 FT., CENTERED

2×6 JOISTS **2×4 RAFTERS**

4×4 POST

3 FT. O.C

5 FT.

1 FT. O.C

12 IN. O.C

6 IN. O.C

4 FT. 2 IN. BETWEEN POSTS (FITS A 4-FT BENCH; ADJUST TO ACCOMMODATE OTHER BENCH SIZES)

PLAN VIEW

CARE FOR VINES as you do your other plants. Water them in dry periods, apply compost yearly and monitor for problems.

TIE AND TRAIN your vines as they grow. If you keep up with the job, they'll be healthier and more attractive.

TRAINING AND PRUNING VINES

PRUNING WOODY VINES IS similar to any other sort of pruning. When you plant, check the vine closely and remove any deadwood or broken stems. If you want to encourage the vine to grow bushy, clip off the terminal growth to encourage branching.

Some vines are sold already trained to a small stake or bamboo pole. If so, remove the support, cutting off a tendril if necessary. If the main stem of the vine is wrapped around the stake, lash the stake and the plant's stem to your support. As the vine grows above the stake it came with, train it to its new support.

Roses and small twining vines must often be given a head start to twine around a trellis. Tie these vines to the support in several places, using a soft plastic or fabric ribbon that won't cut into the stems. Whenever you tie a stem to a support, make a figure eight loop around the stem to prevent it from being constricted. Keep adding more ties for

about a month. By this time, the growth habit of the vine will take over and all you'll have to do is check every so often to see that the plant is staying in bounds.

Vine Maintenance

Yearly pruning is done according to the growth patterns of the vines themselves. As a general rule, vines that flower on the current season's growth, such as trumpet vine, are pruned in late winter, just after the coldest part of the season. Most of these vines bloom in mid-summer to fall. Prune vines that bloom on old wood, such as many types of clematis, after the flowers fade, usually in the spring and early summer. These vines set flower buds after blooming, and pruning later in the season will remove some of next year's flower buds.

To encourage lavish production of flowering wood for the next year, head back the stems that have bloomed. If you need to prune a very vigorous vine

> **SMART TIP**
>
> **GUIDE VINES TOWARD THE SUPPORT**
>
> If you can't plant a vine right next to its support, you can guide its growth by sticking a twig in the ground near the vine for it to grow on. Angle the twig toward the support, and the vine will follow it until it reaches the support.

during the season to keep it in bounds, try to wait until the burst of spring growth has subsided into a more steady, slower pace, but do not wait until fall. Cuts made late in the season heal more slowly because growth has slowed, and any growth that you do stimulate by late pruning will not have time to toughen up for the cold temperatures of winter.

Some plants, such as wisteria, require severe pruning almost every season to limit their growth. You'll also want to encourage horizontal branches. Wisteria, like climbing and rambler roses and many other flowering and fruiting plants, blooms more lavishly on horizontal wood than on vertical wood. However, wisteria also has an unfortunate tendency to strangle itself. Stems will form ropes around each other and cut off the supply of water and nutrients as they grow. Be on the lookout for this, and remove any stems that look as if they are going to strangle their neighbors.

Finish by pruning out dead wood. The final job of pruning vines is routine. Prune out dead, damaged, or weak wood. As much as possible, stick to the recommendations given in the directory starting on page 146. But, if a woody vine breaks at an inconvenient time of year, go ahead and prune the plant down to healthy growth. The vine profiles later in this chapter provide pruning details for many individual vines.

The same rules for pruning roses apply to pruning vines. The cuts are made at the same location with the same angle. See Chapter 4, "Specialty Gardens," page 118 for more specific information on pruning.

GETTING A VINE OFF TO A GOOD START

Difficulty Level: **EASY**

Twining vines can scramble up a trellis. To help vines attach to a trellis with large holes, screw a few eyebolts into the lattice, and stretch wire between them. The vines will cling to the wires and grow across the holes.

Tools and Materials: **Bypass pruners, gloves, eyebolts, floral wire or nylon cord, wire clippers.**

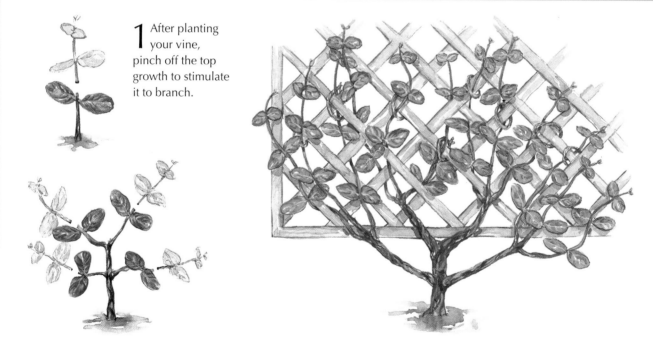

1 After planting your vine, pinch off the top growth to stimulate it to branch.

2 Continue to pinch as the plant grows to encourage more branches to form.

3 Within a year or so, the vine will cover the trellis. Yearly pruning is necessary only to keep it healthy and productive.

THIS LOVELY GOLDEN HONEY-SUCKLE VINE tumbling over a rustic wooden fence gives an informal feeling to the garden.

MORNING-GLORY VINES grow so quickly that you can use them as focal points in the summer garden.

WATERING AND ROUTINE CARE

YOUR VINES WILL GROW well if you give them the same sort of care that you give your other plants.

Most vines require about 1 to 1½ inches of water a week. Drip irrigation systems are usually the best way to water. Many vines are susceptible to fungal diseases, which can be encouraged by overhead watering, especially at night. However, sprinklers are useful for cleaning dust off vines growing near the street, where they can get quite dirty. Dust on the leaves is unattractive and clogs leaf pores, preventing the easy movement of air and moisture into and out of the foliage.

SMART TIP

USING OVERHEAD SPRINKLERS

If you use overhead sprinklers, run them early in the day so that the leaves dry completely by nightfall.

Mulching. Mulches are essential for clematis because it requires cool roots. It is a good practice to mulch other vines as well because it conserves moisture and discourages weeds. In the spring, apply ½ to 1 inch of compost around the plant, water it well, and then apply a 3-inch mulch on top. Reapply the mulch as its level falls during through the season. Be careful not to mulch over the crown during the growing season. In some regions, it may be necessary to cover the crown for winter protection.

Fertilizers. A yearly application of compost will supply needed nutrients for most vines. However, annual vines and large wisteria will grow better if the compost is supplemented by a late

Seasonal care. Fall clean-up tasks include removing all of the dead plant material left behind by annual vines and raking up the leaves of deciduous perennial vines. If the vine is suited to your climate, bare woody stems should weather well over the cold season.

Winter protection for evergreen vines. Evergreen vines can present problems, even in zones where they are supposedly hardy. If they are in a windy place, they may lose too much moisture from their leaves over the winter, when the frozen ground prevents the roots from drawing up more moisture to replace it. To prevent vines from becoming dehydrated, plant them close to north-facing walls so that they will have some protection. If this is impractical or if you are growing some freestanding vines in your landscape, remember that you can wrap them in burlap for the worst of the winter months or spray them with an antidesiccant. Well-watered plants fare better during the winter than those that go into the season with dry soil. Keep the soil moisture evenly high during the fall for all your vines—evergreen and deciduous. After the first hard frost, heap a layer of compost over the crown of each plant, and mulch with 6 inches of loose mulch, 3 inches of a dense one. As with other plants, your goal is to keep the roots consistently frozen during the winter months.

spring or early summer application of liquid seaweed and fish emulsion or a blend containing about 3-4-3 (nitrogen-phosphorus-potassium).

Controlling pests and diseases. Watch for pests and diseases. Most commonly grown vines are not subject to severe pest or disease problems as long as their environmental conditions are appropriate. However, if air circulation is poor, fungal diseases can become troublesome. Spray with compost tea, as recommended in Chapter 9, "Preventing Weeds, Pests, and Diseases," page 297, every 10 to 14 days to prevent problems. Baking soda spray is effective against black spot, a fungal disease that attacks roses. See Chapter 4, "Specialty Gardens," page 120, for information about solving fungal problems with baking soda spray. (And refer to Chapter 9 for other preventive and curative methods.)

Wisteria vines are lovely even in winter. Grow them where they will be visible from a window of the house.

ILLUSTRATED PLANT-BY-PLANT DIRECTORY OF VINES

Ampelopsis brevipedunculata
Porcelain Berry

Life Cycle: Perennial.
Zones: 4 to 8.
Appearance: Leaves are lobed and heart-shaped at the base. Stems and young leaves are slightly hairy.
Climbing Method: Tendrils without adhesive disks.
Size: 10 to 20 feet.
Flower Color: Not showy yellow-green flowers. Plant produces berries that range in colors from amethyst to bright blue.
Blooming Season: Berries form in fall.
Exposure: Prefers light shade to partial shade but will tolerate full sun.
Soil: Versatile but requires good drainage.
Propagation: In early fall, plant seeds where they are to grow. Take softwood cuttings in early summer and hardwood cuttings in late fall or early winter. Keep fall-started cuttings in a protected environment until spring.
Pests and Diseases: Japanese beetles love this plant, and fungal diseases will strike in poor environmental conditions.
Notes: This plant is ideal for the woodland garden because it will perform well in shifting patterns of available sunlight. It will also tolerate a very high pH, so it is a good seaside plant.

Campsis species
Trumpet Vine

Life Cycle: Perennial.
Zones: 4 to 9.
Appearance: Leaves are coarse and compound, consisting of nine to eleven leaflets. The tubular flowers are trumpet-shaped.
Climbing Method: Aerial roots grow from the stem and cling to any support they touch.
Size: 25 to 35 feet.
Flower Color: Shades of orange, red, and yellow.
Blooming Season: Midsummer to fall.
Exposure: Full sun.
Soil: Well-drained, moist, humus-filled but will tolerate a wide range.
Propagation: Hardwood cuttings, taken with a heel from the main stem, root well if taken in early spring. Plants also sucker prolifically from the roots.
Pests and Diseases: Leafhoppers, scales, and citrus whiteflies can all be problems.
Notes: In favorable situations, trumpet vine can become invasive. Prune it back in late winter if it grows out of bounds, thin the stems, and dig and remove unwanted suckers. Hummingbirds love this plant.

Clematis species and cultivars
Clematis

Life Cycle: Perennial.
Zones: 3 to 9.
Appearance: Leaves of most species are a dark glossy green with smooth margins. Flowers may be single or double; the stamens of many cultivars are prominent and decorative.
Climbing Method: Both stems and tendrils twine around thin supports.
Size: 10 to 20 feet.
Flower Color: Depending on species and cultivar, flower colors include white, yellow, pink, red, and purple.
Blooming Season: Depending on species and cultivar, from late spring through fall.
Exposure: Vines must be in full sun but roots prefer to be shaded.
Soil: Moist, well-drained, average to low fertility. Most cultivars grow best at a pH of 7, although some will take more acid conditions.
Propagation: Take softwood cuttings in mid-spring to early summer, or layer stems in late spring through summer. If layering late in the season, wait until the following year to dig and transplant.
Pests and Diseases: Clematis borers, aphids, black blister beetles, tarnished

plant bugs, mites, caterpillars and white-flies prey on clematis. Diseases include bacterial and fungal wilts, as well as fungal leaf spot and stem rot.

Notes: Research the species and cultivars before buying to determine whether they are appropriate to your situation. Some *Clematis* species flower on old wood and some on new. Ask when you buy the plant because this determines pruning time. If the supplier can't tell you, observe the plant for yourself. If it blooms in late spring and early summer, it flowers on old wood, but if it blooms later in the season, it probably blooms on current year's growth. Species such as *C. x jackmanii* bloom on both. Prune species that bloom on old wood by thinning the stems lightly after the bloom period. If the plant blooms on new wood, prune all the stems to the ground after the plant has become dormant in the fall. In the case of species such as *C. x jackmanii,* prune lightly in the late winter or early spring.

Cobaea scandens

Cup-and-Saucer Vine

Life Cycle: Perennial in Zones 9 and 10; grown as annual elsewhere.
Appearance: Leaves are textured, smooth margined and a dark, matte green. Flowers are formed of cup-shaped petals surrounded by saucer-shaped calyx segments.
Climbing Method: Leaf tendrils twine around thin supports.

Size: 10 to 20 feet.
Flower Color: Purple, greenish white.
Blooming Season: Midsummer to frost.
Exposure: Full sun to partial shade.
Soil: Well-drained, average fertility.
Propagation: Start seed early indoors, eight weeks before frost-free date, in individual 3-inch peat pots. Set seeds on edge in the starting medium, and do not bury. Light aids germination. Germinate at 75°F and grow at 60° to 65°F. Pinch stem tips when they are 5 to 6 inches tall and again when you set them out.
Pests and Diseases: Largely trouble-free, but aphids, caterpillars, and Japanese beetles can cause problems. Cup-and-saucer vine will contract fungal diseases such as leaf spot in humid conditions.
Notes: This plant grows so quickly that you can use it as an architectural element in your garden, just as you do perennial vines. Flower buds have an odor that some people find objectionable. However, the fully open flowers smell like honey.

Ipomoea species

Morning-Glory and relatives

Life Cycle: Annual.
Appearance: Leaves vary in size and shape depending on species. Common garden morning-glory (*I. purpurea*) has smooth-margined, heart-shaped leaves while the leaves of cardinal climber, *I. × multifida*, are deeply cut into a number of thin sections and most of cypress vine (*I. quamoclit*) are even more finely

divided. Two cultivars of sweet potato vine (*I. batatas*) 'Blackie' and 'Margarita' are grown for their decorative vines.
Climbing Method: Stems and tendrils twine around thin supports.
Size: 10 to 15 feet.
Flower Color: Wide range, including blue, white, pink, red, purple, and scarlet. Sweet potato vines are not known for their inconspicuous white flowers, but for their lime green or dark foliage.
Blooming Season: Midsummer to frost.
Exposure: Full sun.
Soil: Moist, well-drained, humus-rich.
Propagation: Start seeds early indoors, or outdoors where the plants are to grow. Before planting, nick seed coats with a sharp file or knife, and soak for 12 hours. If starting inside, plant in individual 4-inch peat pots about six weeks before frost-free date. Plant outside when danger of frost has passed.
Pests and Diseases: Largely trouble-free but aphids, mites, thrips, and whiteflies can attack plants. Diseases include fungal leaf spots and wilts.
Notes: Morning-glories are great for screening. This plant is so easy to grow that it is ideal for the children's garden.

Jasminum nudiflorum

Winter Jasmine

Life Cycle: Perennial.
Zones: 6 to 9.
Appearance: Dark green, slightly hairy leaflets form in groups of three. This plant is deciduous, unlike most jasmines

Jasminum/Winter Jasmine *continued*

which have evergreen or semi-evergreen leaves. The solitary flowers are wonderfully fragrant.

Climbing Method: Jasmines are scandent vines, meaning that they lack a means of clinging to their support. In the wild, they lean against trees, but in the garden, you'll need to tie them in place.

Size: 4 to 6 feet long.

Flower Color: Yellow.

Blooming Season: Late winter to early spring, depending on climate.

Exposure: Full sun to filtered shade, depending on climate.

Soil: Well-drained, average fertility.

Propagation: Layer in late spring, leaving the branch in place until late summer, when roots will have formed.

Pests and Diseases: Mealybugs, scale, and whiteflies are common pests; common diseases include leaf spot (various species), blossom blight, and crown gall.

Notes: The berries are poisonous to people, so plant these vines where children and unsuspecting guests cannot reach them. Since winter jasmine is such an early bloomer, it's best to prune it just after it blooms in spring.

Lagenaria siceraria
Bottle Gourd

Life Cycle: Annual.

Appearance: Leaves can be as large as a foot across. They are heart-shaped with smooth margins and distinct veins.

Climbing Method: Tendrils twine around thin supports. These plants can

be so heavy that they will pull down a trellis; instead, grow them on the ground or against a sloped stone wall or hill draped with chicken wire.

Size: 15 to 25 feet.

Flower Color: White.

Blooming Season: Midsummer to fall.

Exposure: Full sun.

Soil: Moist, fertile, humus-rich.

Propagation: Start seeds early indoors in Zones 7 and northward. Plant seeds in individual 4-inch peat pots six to eight weeks before the frost-free date. Soak seed 24 hours before planting and germinate at 65° to 75°F. In Zones 8 and 9, sow outdoors where vines are to grow.

Pests and Diseases: Attracts all pests and diseases common to the squash family.

Notes: The flowers have a lovely fragrance and open in low-light conditions, such as dusk or cloudy days. Like moonflowers, these plants are magical when planted near a terrace where the family eats dinner in the evening.

Lathyrus odoratus
Sweet Pea

Life Cycle: Annual, but some perennial species exist.

Appearance: Leaves are shaped like those of garden peas, with the characteristic clear green leaflets covered with a soft down. The flowers, too, are shaped like those of garden peas, but are fragrant to varying degrees.

Climbing Method: Leaf tendrils and stems twine around thin supports.

Size: 6 to 8 feet.

Flower Color: Wide range including white, pink, purple, red, rose, mauve, blue, cream, pale yellow, and mottled.

Blooming Season: Midsummer to fall.

Exposure: Full sun.

Soil: Moist, well-drained, humus-rich.

Propagation: For earliest flowering, start seeds indoors, about six weeks before frost-free date in soil blocks or 2-inch peat pots. Wait until just before the frost-free date to plant outside. In all cases, soak seeds 12 to 24 hours before planting. Seeds germinate best at 55° to 60°F and in darkness.

Pests and Diseases: Pests include aphids, spotted cucumber beetles, leafminers, mites, and thrips. Diseases include root rots in soggy soil and powdery mildew late in the season.

Notes: Plants perform well at a 6-inch spacing. For the best fragrance, check seed catalogs for the "old-fashioned" cultivars. New types often have showier flowers, but they've lost the "odor" that inspired the "odoratus" part of their name.

Parthenocissus quinquefolia
Virginia Creeper

Parthenocissus tricuspidata
Boston Ivy

Life Cycle: Perennial.

Zones: Virginia creeper, Zones 4 to 8; Boston ivy, 4 to 9.

Appearance: Leaves are glossy and compound, with three lobes. In autumn, they turn a brilliant red.

Climbing Method: Tendrils end in adhesive disks, allowing the vines to cling to rough surfaces as well as twine around supports.

Size: 15 to 30 feet.

Flower Color: Flowers are nondescript, but berries are blue-black.

Blooming Season: Midsummer.

Exposure: Versatile, though Boston ivy performs better in full sun or partial shade than dense shade.

Soil: Well-drained, average fertility.

Propagation: Take softwood cuttings in mid-spring to early summer and semiripe cuttings in late fall to early winter. Layer in mid-spring to late summer, leaving new plants in place until they have a well-developed root system.

Pests and Diseases: Aphids, flea beetles, rose chafers, tomato hornworms, leafhoppers, scales, and weevils can attack plants and fungal diseases are a problem in soggy soil or high humidity.

Notes: Birds love the berries and spread them around lavishly. Consequently, it may be hard to keep up with the volunteers. Nonetheless, these vines are ideal for covering small outbuildings and stone walls.

Schizophragma hydrangeoides
Japanese Hydrangea Vine

Life Cycle: Perennial.

Zones: 5 to 8.

Appearance: The oval leaves are 3 to 4½ inches long, highly textured and coarsely toothed. Flowers form in clusters that look similar to those of lacecap hydrangea (tiny central flowers sur-

rounded by a circle of petal-like bracts.)

Climbing Method: The short roots that grow from the stems are adhesive and will cling to almost any rough-textured support.

Size: 15 to 30 feet.

Flower Color: White.

Blooming Season: Midsummer.

Exposure: Versatile but grows best in full sun to partial shade.

Soil: Moist, fertile, well-drained.

Propagation: Take hardwood cuttings in late fall. Layer in mid-spring through late summer, leaving new plants in place until they have a vigorous root system.

Pests and Diseases: Aphids, caterpillars, scales, mealybugs, and thrips are common pests. Diseases include fungal leaf spots and root rots in soggy soils.

Notes: The showy flowers can be as large as 8 inches across, but even without flowers, the vine is decorative. Prune in late winter, but only if necessary to keep in bounds.

Wisteria species
Wisteria

Life Cycle: Perennial.

Zones: 5 to 8.

Appearance: The shape of the leaves makes it apparent that this vine is in the pea family because of the familiar lobes. Flowers are also pea-shaped but grow in long racemes.

Climbing Method: Thick stems twine around supports.

Size: 10 to 20 feet.

Flower Color: White, purple, pink, and purple-and-white bicolors.

Blooming Season: Early to mid-spring.

Exposure: Full sun.

Soil: Well-drained, somewhat acid, moist, moderate to somewhat low fertility. If nitrogen levels are high, the plants will not bloom.

Propagation: Take hardwood cuttings in late fall, layer or serpentine layer in mid-spring through early summer. Leave the new plants in place until the roots are well-developed.

Pests and Diseases: Pests include aphids, rose chafers, June beetles, leaf rollers, mealybugs, scales, black vine weevils, and fall webworms. Diseases include fungal leaf spots and root rots.

Notes: The fragrant, drooping flower clusters open just as the new foliage emerges in the spring. The Japanese wisteria (*W. floribunda*) twines in a clockwise direction, while Chinese wisteria (*W. sinensis*) twines in a counterclockwise direction. Provide sturdy supports for these heavy plants, and do not let them grow against a building because they will damage it. Pruning is necessary to keep the vines under control; prune in late winter, limiting the old growth to three or four buds.

CHAPTER 6

VEGETABLE GARDENS

*H*ome-grown vegetables never lose their appeal. No matter how wonderful the produce section at the store or how many small farmers set up roadside stands, people still love to grow vegetables. In fact, surveys show that more than half of American families grow some vegetables.

Vegetable gardening is just plain fun. For one thing, with the exception of very few crops, nothing in the vegetable garden is permanent. You can try crazy new crops and cultivars, investigate innovative planting schemes and schedules, test experimental season-extension techniques, and explore the many ways of controlling pests and diseases. You can teach yourself research techniques and set up your own trials, if that's your bent. Or you can create vegetable gardens that are like tapestries in time and space, with new crops and colors coming

HOMEGROWN VEGETABLES are so fresh that they are at their peak for flavor and nutrition.

on through the season. And if you don't like something you've created, you can always deal with it in a very practical way. After all, in the vegetable garden, most of your mistakes taste as good as your successes.

Homegrown vegetables taste far better than anything you can buy. Freshness has something to do with that, of course, but cultivar selection is equally important. If you grow your own vegetables, you can choose cultivars that taste better but are far too delicate to stand up to the treatment that distributors give to produce. You can also grow vegetables that are hard to find. For example, even if you don't particularly care for standard green kale, you may discover the sweet, tender red and wild kales just being introduced to this continent. And if you tend to the health of your soil using compost and amendments, you'll be increasing both the nutritional content and the flavor of the vegetables you grow.

If you don't have much garden space, try using containers. You'll soon discover that many vegetables grow as well, or better, in a large pot as they do in the ground. Use a soil mix that drains well, choose a pot a few inches bigger than the plants will need, and keep them well fertilized.

HEIRLOOM VEGETABLES and edible flowers can enchant even the youngest gardeners.

SMALL VEGETABLE PLOTS are easy to maintain. As you gain experience, add space for more plants.

PLANNING YOUR VEGETABLE GARDEN

PLANNING IS IMPERATIVE IN all types of gardening, but nowhere is it more important than in the vegetable garden. Without some advance figuring, it's entirely possible to end up with 20 heads of cauliflower ready to harvest in the same week, followed by 20 heads of broccoli the next week, dump-truck loads of zucchini for a month, and bitter, inedible lettuces from July onward. That first burst of enthusiasm about vegetable gardening can also lead to plans that are so ambitious that they'd wear you to a snarling frazzle if you actually carried them out.

Scale

Small gardens tend to be neat gardens. Weeds are pulled when they are tiny, and crops are harvested when they are ripe. If a disease or insect threatens a plant, it's easy to notice and control. If you build the soil with compost, mulch to keep down the weeds, and plant intensively, vegetable gardens take less time on a per-square-foot basis than flower gardens. It's impractical to plant so much that you can't keep up with it, but it's perfectly reasonable to plan a garden that's large enough to grow a significant amount of food.

If you are a beginning vegetable gardener, start with a garden that ranges between 15 x 20 feet and 20 x 30 feet. A 15- x 20-foot garden is large enough to grow fresh vegetables to feed a family of four as well as a few extras for preserving or storing for winter use. In a 20- x 30-foot garden, you can grow some of the space hogs such as sweet corn and pumpkins plus summer vegetables and a few preserving crops. As you gain familiarity with each crop's needs, build your soil, and prevent or avoid pest and disease problems, it will be easy to increase the size of the vegetable garden.

Deciding What to Grow

Some people hate brussels sprouts; others would plant a whole garden of them. Growing your own vegetables allows you to be as choosy and idiosyncratic as you want to be—within reason. If you grow exactly the same thing in the same spot every year, certain weeds, pests, and diseases will build up in the area. So if you want to grow nothing but brussels sprouts (or sweet corn), you'll need to find four different places to grow it so that you can "rotate," or change its location, each year for four years. But if you grow a more varied assortment of crops, you can set up a rotation system that puts each crop in a different part of the garden over a four-year cycle.

Begin choosing what to grow by making a list of the vegetables that your family eats most frequently and the approximate number of heads or pounds that you use each

CHOOSING CROPS can be one of the most challenging tasks of vegetable gardening.

week. The table "How Much Should You Plant?" (on page 154) lists approximate amounts of each vegetable that the "average" adult eats each year and the space required to produce that quantity, figured on both a row-foot and a bed-foot basis.

The wonderful world of seed catalogs is the next step

TOOLS

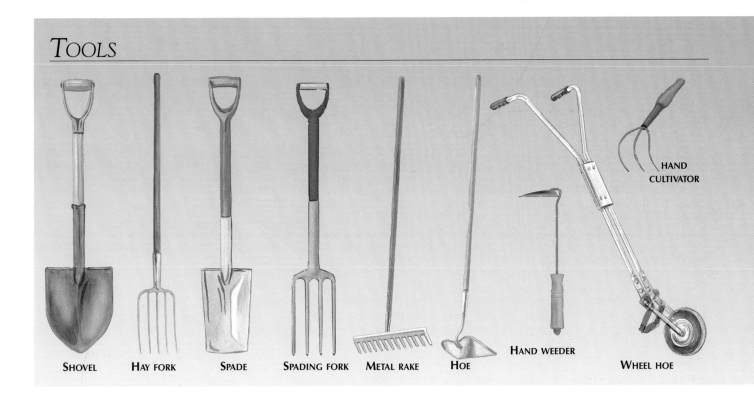

SHOVEL   HAY FORK   SPADE   SPADING FORK   METAL RAKE   HOE   HAND WEEDER   WHEEL HOE   HAND CULTIVATOR

HOW MUCH SHOULD YOU PLANT?

CROP	YIELD LBS. PER ROW FOOT	LBS. NEEDED PER ADULT	ROW FEET PER ADULT	ROWS PER 4' BED	BED FEET PER ADULT
Asparagus	0.33–0.25	7	20	1	20
Beans, bush, snap	0.8	8	6.4	2	3.2
Beans, pole	1.5	10	15	2	7.5
Beet, greens	0.4	4	1.6	4	0.4
Beets	1	10	10	4	2.5
Broccoli	0.75	15	11.25	3	3.75
Brussels sprout	0.6	5	3	3	1
Cabbage	1.5	12	18	3	6
Cantaloupe	1	10	10	1	10
Carrot	1	20	20	4	5
Cauliflower	0.9	10	9	3	3
Chard	0.75	6	4.5	3	1.5
Collard	0.75	6	4.5	3	1.5
Corn	0.96	30	28.8	2	14.4
Cucumber	1.2	10	12	1	12
Eggplant	0.75	10	7.5	2	3.75
Kale	0.75	5	3.75	3	1.25
Leek	1.5	6	9	3	3
Lettuce	0.5	30	15	4	3.75
Onion	1	20	20	4	5
Parsnip	0.75	10	7.5	4	1.88
Pea, English or shell	0.2	5	1	2	0.50
Pea, snow	2	6	12	2	6
Pepper	0.5	10	5	2	2.5
Potato	5	50	250	2	125
Rhubarb	0.8–1.2	8–12	10	1	10
Rutabaga	1.5	5	7.5	3	2.5
Salad greens, misc.	0.5	25	12.5	4	3.13
Spinach	0.75	8	6	4	1.5
Squash, summer	2	8	16	1	16
Squash, winter	2	20	40	1	40
Strawberry	1–3	30 qts	10–20	1 (3)	10–20
Tomato	1.5	20	30	2	15
Turnip	1	8	8	4	2

EVEN IF YOU NEVER READ DIRECTIONS, pay attention to the information given in catalogs and seed packets.

in your planning process. Request several, including at least two that are located in your region. Read catalog descriptions carefully, noting such things as disease resistance and seasonal or cultural recommendations. Try to steer clear of cultivars that are said to "ripen uniformly." This means that the crop has been bred for the convenience of commercial growers; it may taste good, but the flavor is secondary to the harvest characteristics.

You'll soon discover the joys of growing many varieties of the same vegetable. For example, different lettuces and broccoli grow, mature, and taste different, depending on the time that they grow. Similarly, some root vegetable cultivars store well while others don't, and some cultivars of greens stand up better than others under the first frosts and snows of the year. Good seed catalogs guide you by letting you know what cultivars perform best in your area and in the different parts of the season.

After you've made a list of the seeds you want—on a sheet of paper, never directly on the order form—go back

SMART TIP

MAPPING THE GARDEN

Mapping the vegetable garden is similar to mapping the flower garden, except that the dates in the vegetable garden tend to be more complicated and the layout tends to be much simpler.

Place plants that are good companions adjacent to each other, and keep poor companions far apart from each other.

Consider successive plantings of each crop so that you'll have enough space in the right place when you need it.

Change, or rotate, crop locations every year for at least four years.

through to cross off the nonessentials. Even though you can keep the seeds of most crops for a couple of years if you store them in cool, dark, dry conditions, it's best to try to keep your seed purchases to a reasonable quantity. This will make it easier to maintain a planting plan and harvesting schedule.

Companion planting. Plants exert strong influences over each other. They release chemical compounds from their roots and aboveground tissues that affect other plants as well as insects and microorganisms. Some of these effects are directly beneficial, as in the case of a root *exudant* (liquid that is released from the plant) that stimulates the growth or flavor of a nearby plant. Other companion planting effects are indirectly beneficial, as in the case of a flower that serves as a nectar source for an insect that preys on the pest insects of neighboring plants. Still other companion plant effects are negative, as in the case of a root exudant that inhibits the growth or flavor of another plant. Generations of gar-

deners have been noting these reactions. Although not all of these effects have been proved by scientists, gardeners generally find that they work. The table "Companion Plant Influences," on page 156, lists the effects of combining vegetables with each other as well as some weeds, herbs, and flowering plants.

Succession planting. It's important to plan where successive plantings will go right from the beginning. Otherwise, you can find yourself without a good spot to plant fall broccoli or lettuce. Although this extensive planning may seem mind-boggling at first, here are a few tips to make it easier.

Short-season crops, such as lettuce, can follow other short-season crops. If the soil is very fertile, you can get away with simply replanting the area. However, few soils are that rich, especially when you first start to garden. So it's best to apply at least ½ inch of compost, a light dusting of alfalfa or soybean meal, or a balanced organic bagged

continued on page 157

TIME YOUR PLANTINGS so that new crops are maturing as you harvest those planted earlier.

CROP DIVERSITY confuses those pests that depend on odor or appearance to find their hosts.

COMPANION PLANT INFLUENCES

Some plants repel specific pests, and are good companions for plants that are attacked by them. Other plants exude a substance which chemically inhibits the growth of plants.

Species	Attracts	Repels/Inhibits	Common Companion Crops
Allium		Aphids, peas	Roses, daffodils, tulips, aphid hosts in vegetable garden
Beans, bush		Inhibits onions	Carrots, cauliflower, beets, cucumbers, cabbage
Borage		Tomato worm	Strawberry, tomato
Broccoli/cabbage		Tomato	Dill, celery, chamomile, sage, beets, onions, potatoes
Carrots		Dill	Onions, leeks, herbs, lettuce, peas
Catnip	Small beneficials		Catnip tea repels flea beetles
Celery			Leeks, tomatoes, cauliflower, cabbage, bush beans
Chamomile	Small beneficials		Onions, cabbage family
Dill	Small beneficials	Inhibits carrot	Cabbage, beets, lettuce, onion
Eggplant	Potato bugs		Potatoes
Fennel		Inhibits many species	Plant by itself
Garlic		Aphids, Japanese beetles, mites, deer, rabbits	Roses and many vegetables
Hyssop	Bees	Cabbage moth, radish	Grapes, cabbage
Kohlrabi		Potatoes, beans	Onions, beets, cukes, cabbage family crops
Marigold		Nematodes, Mexican bean beetles	Tomatoes, beans, potatoes
Nasturtium	Aphids	Squash bugs	Trap crop with cabbage family
Nicotiana	Potato bugs		Potatoes
Orach		Inhibits potato	
Parsley	Small beneficials		Interplant with carrot, rose
Petunia		Mexican bean beetles	Beans
Potato		Repels Mexican bean beetles/Inhibits tomato, squash, sunflower, raspberry	Beans, corn, cabbage, eggplant, horseradish, marigold
Rue		Japanese beetle	Inhibits many plants
Sage		Cabbage moth, carrot flies	Cabbage family, carrots
Sunflowers		Inhibits nitrogen-fixing bacteria, potatoes	Corn, cukes
Stinging Nettle	Small beneficials		Almost all plants benefit
Summer Savory		Mexican bean beetles	Beans
Thornapple		Deters Japanese beetles	Near grapes, roses, pumpkin
Tidytips	Small beneficials		With aphid hosts
Tomato		Asparagus beetle	Asparagus, gooseberries, roses

Continued from page 155

fertilizer for the second crop. Work the compost or fertilizer into the top couple of inches of soil a week or so before direct-seeding or a few days before transplanting.

If you have lots of space, you can grow a green manure in a planting area until it is time to plant the crop. Green manuring and cover-cropping are discussed in detail in Chapter 1, "Preparing to Garden," on pages 31 and 32. To summarize, plant frost-tolerant annual grasses, grains, or legumes such as oats or fava beans in the area in the early spring. If you are planting later in the summer, use a tender crop such as buckwheat or forage soybeans. Two weeks before you plan to direct-seed or transplant your vegetable crop, till or pull up the green manure, and let it decompose on the soil surface. Water the area lightly if it's dry to promote decomposition. This system not only adds nutrients to the soil, it also prevents weeds from establishing themselves in the garden.

People usually think of crop rotations in terms of where plants grow in successive years. However, if you are double-cropping an area by growing two different crops on it in the same year, that counts as a rotation, too. Refer to the table "Companion Plant Influences," left, to avoid planting a crop where an adversary previously grew. Also, follow the rotation guidelines (right) for the best results.

SUCCESSION PLANTING for continuous harvests is as easy to do in a small garden bed as in a whole garden.

Crop Rotation

There is no doubt that plants affect one another over time (the reason behind rotations) as much as they do through space (the reason for companion planting). Certain crops deplete or replenish particular nutrients in the soil, and some pests and diseases are drawn to and colonize soils where their favorite hosts have recently grown. Consequently, gardeners rotate their crops to vary the soil nutrient requirements as well as minimize potential pests and diseases. Use the following guidelines to develop your own rotation system:

- Leave at least four years between planting members of the same plant family in the same spot.
- Follow heavy feeders, such as corn and squash, with light feeders such as beets, beans, or peas.
- Follow deep-rooted crops, such as broccoli, with shallow-rooted crops such as onion.

A specialized vegetable rotation. Researchers at the University of Rhode Island conducted a 30-year study of crop rotations. Eliot Coleman, an innovative market grower and author, has worked with and fine-tuned this system for more than a decade. After much refining, he has settled on the following rotation as being the most beneficial—and others who have tried it agree. As you make your garden map, try to follow this system:

- Potatoes follow sweet corn,
- Sweet corn follows the cabbage family,
- Cabbage family crops, undersown with legumes, follow peas,
- Peas follow tomatoes,
- Tomatoes, undersown with a non-hardy green oat manure, follow beans,
- Beans follow root crops,
- Root crops follow squash or potatoes,
- Squashes follow potatoes.

4-YEAR VEGETABLE ROTATION

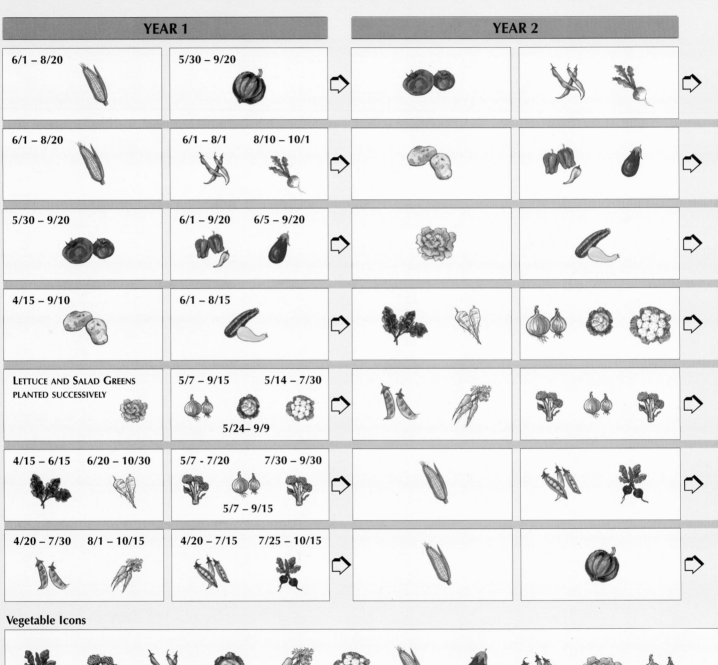

| YEAR 1 | | YEAR 2 | |

Vegetable Icons

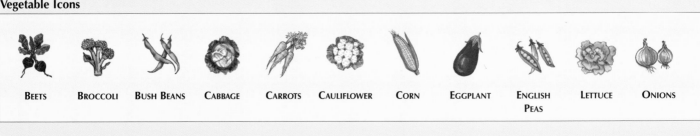

| BEETS | BROCCOLI | BUSH BEANS | CABBAGE | CARROTS | CAULIFLOWER | CORN | EGGPLANT | ENGLISH PEAS | LETTUCE | ONIONS |

CHAPTER 6

Take advantage of the work that crop researchers and farmers have already done to develop the best rotation possible. Although this scheme may seem complicated before you implement it, ultimately it simplifies your garden planning. This rotation can also contribute to the health and vitality of your plants, making them more resistant to many pests and diseases.

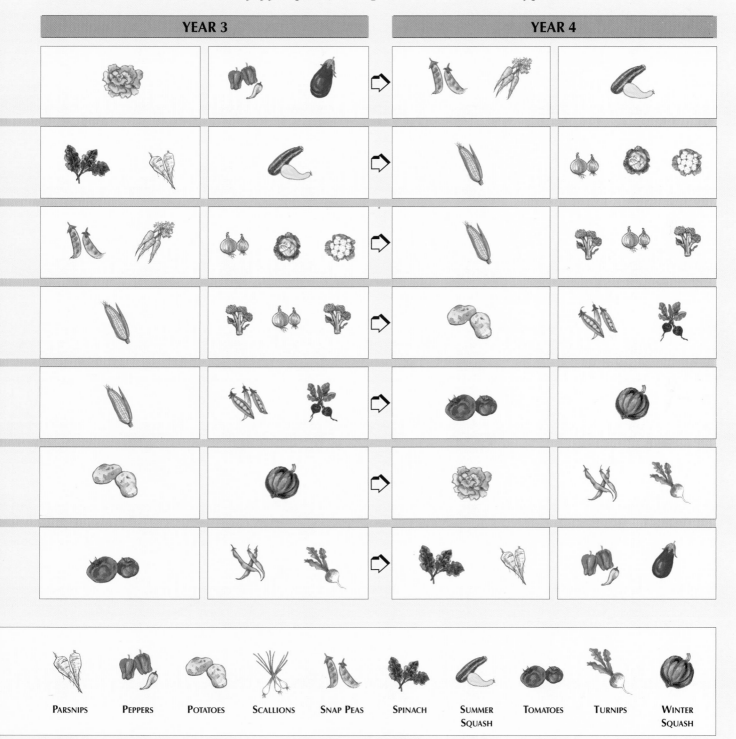

| | | PARSNIPS | PEPPERS | POTATOES | SCALLIONS | SNAP PEAS | SPINACH | SUMMER SQUASH | TOMATOES | TURNIPS | WINTER SQUASH |

Timing

If you plant all of your lettuce in the first week of April, it will all mature between the end of May and the end of June, even if your cultivars have different "Days to Maturity." Good timing solves this problem. Rather than plant everything at once, experienced gardeners plant small amounts of each of the short-season crops all through the season. Most people take a few years to develop a "starting schedule" appropriate to their climate and chosen cultivars.

Using the list of vegetables you'd like to grow, make a chart with the same columns as shown in the table "Typical Starting Schedule—Zone 5," page 162. To customize it for your own use, begin by filling in the "Days to Maturity" (DTM) column. If the crop is one that you direct-seed outdoors, fill in a date when it is safe to plant the seed according to its temperature requirements. Remember not to plant frost-sensitive plants until after the frost-free date in your area. Days to Maturity are listed in the catalog or on the seed packet. Add the DTM to the planting date to learn approximately when the harvest will begin.

Begin by filling in the date that it is safe to transplant to the garden, and then count backward, using the information in the vegetable directory, to learn the date you'll need to plant the seeds indoors. Then count forward, again from the transplanting date, to learn when to expect a harvest. For example, if you know that it's safe to plant cool-loving cauliflower with a DTM of 54 in the garden on May 7th, count backward six weeks to March 26 to learn when to plant the seeds. It ought to be ready by June 30th.

DTM numbers can be confusing if you don't know whether the catalog is referring to days from direct-seeding the crop in the garden or transplanting seedlings. The table at right tells you the usual way of counting for each crop.

USE THE DAYS TO MATURITY on the seed pack to calculate when to plant crops for harvest throughout the season.

The Days to Maturity listed in seed catalogs are fairly accurate for late-spring and early-summer plantings. However, temperature can greatly influence the speed with which vegetables mature. In general, hot weather speeds maturity, and cool weather slows it.

FROM DIRECT-SEEDING DATE	FROM TRANSPLANTING DATE
Beans	Broccoli
Beets	Brussels sprouts
Carrots	Cabbage
Corn	Cauliflower
Cucumbers	Celeriac
Fennel, bulbing	Celery
Greens, salad or cooking	Eggplant
Kohlrabi	Leeks
Lettuce	Melons
Okra	Peppers
Onions	Tomatoes
Parsnips	
Peas	
Pumpkins	
Radishes	
Squashes	
Turnips and rutabagas	

Adjust the DTM for transplants. When you transplant a crop with a DTM date that is counted from *direct seeding*, (seeds that are planted directly into the ground where they will grow), you'll have to adjust your figures. As a general rule, subtract 10 to 14 days from the DTM. (Even though the plant has been growing for 4 to 6 weeks inside, transplanting sets the crop back, so you only gain 10 to 14 days.) If you find yourself direct-seeding a crop that is counted from the transplant date, such as broccoli, add between 14 and 20 days to the DTM. (By direct seeding, you gain 14 to 20 days.)

With experience, you'll learn how long each crop will stand in the garden without losing quality. For example, the earliest spring lettuces and greens stay good for a week or two. But in midsummer, they become tough and bitter very quickly; they will also taste best if picked when slightly young and undersized. Until you know your climate and cultivars, plan so that salad crops slightly overlap each other. If you overplant, you can always give some salad away or add it to the compost pile.

PLANTING LETTUCE IN BEDS

BROADCAST PLANTED SPINACH

DIRECT-SEEDED MESCLUN

RAISED-BED PLANTING

PLANTING YOUR VEGETABLE GARDEN

PLANTING THE VEGETABLE GARDEN is always fun. And the more sophisticated you become as a vegetable gardener, the more planting you will do. Not only will you plant successive crops throughout the summer, you'll also be taking advantage of season-extension technologies to plant earlier and later than normal.

Vegetable gardens were once planted the way farm fields were—in single rows spaced far apart from each other. This system is useful for crops planted in hills, such as potatoes and corn, but many gardeners and small farmers have abandoned it in favor of more practical beds.

There are several advantages to planting vegetables in beds rather than in rows:

- Compost and soil amendments can be concentrated where plants are growing, rather than being wasted on the pathways.
- You can build up the height of the bed, increasing aeration, drainage, and spring heating.
- Plants can be spaced so that they shade out weeds when they are nearly mature, decreasing weeding time.
- Plants grow more quickly and vigorously because their soil has not been compacted by being trod upon.

continued on page 164

TYPICAL STARTING SCHEDULE: ZONE 5

Use this table as a guide to create your own starting schedule. Although this table covers much of the season, you'll notice that you would have to add some crops or plantings, particularly lettuce and salad greens, to be assured of having each type of vegetable at all the possible times during the season. Remember to adjust timing to take into account the low light and cool temperatures in fall.

CROP	DAYS TO MATURITY	STARTING METHOD	SEEDING DATE	TRANSPLANT DATE	HARVEST DATE	NOTES
BEANS, SNAP						
Provider	50	DS*	5/27		7/10	
Rattlesnake (Pole bean)	70	DS*	6/24		9/2	
Jade	56	DS*	7/8		8/7	
BEETS						
Early Wonder Tall Top	48	DS*	5/5		6/22	
Lutz Green Leaf	60	DS*	7/22		9/16	
BROCCOLI						
Green King	65	Inside	4/9	5/19	7/23	Each planting yields for 2–3 weeks
Saga	56	Inside	6/27	8/6	10/1	
Genji	59	Inside	7/22	8/31	10/15	
BRUSSELS SPROUTS						
Prince Marvel	110	Inside	4/24	6/3	9/21	Harvest all fall
CABBAGE						
Hermes	62	Inside	4/5	5/15	7/16	
Storage No. 4	95	Inside	6/9	7/19	10/22	
CARROT						
Kinko	55	DS*	4/23		6/17	Each planting gives 3–4 harvests
Nantes Fancy	68	DS*	6/17		8/24	
Canada Gold	73	DS*	7/14		9/25	
CAULIFLOWER						
Rushmore	54	Inside	3/29	5/8/	7/1	
Snow Crown	50	Inside	6/12	7/22	9/10	
CUCUMBER						
Lemon	51	Inside	5/14	6/11	8/1	
Marketmore 76	44	Inside	5/16	6/13	7/27	
EGGPLANT						
All Cultivars	55–68	Inside	3/30	6/6	7/25 on	Harvest until frost
KALE						
Wild Garden Kale Mix	55	DS*	7/16		9/9	
LEEKS						
King Richard	75	Inside	4/19	6/28	9/11	

CROP	DAYS TO MATURITY	STARTING METHOD	SEEDING DATE	TRANSPLANT DATE	HARVEST DATE	NOTES
LETTUCE						
Buttercrunch Bibb	40	Inside	3/22	5/1	6/10	DTM is from transplanting and reflects seasonal changes
Crispino	44	Inside	4/10	5/20	7/3	
Cerise	48	Inside	5/11	6/20	8/7	
Parris Island Cos	48	Inside	6/8	7/18	9/4	
Carmona	64	Inside	6/13	7/23	9/25	
ONIONS						
Ailsa Craig	110	Inside	3/15	5/24	9/1	
Redman	101	Inside	3/11	5/20	8/29	
PARSNIP						
Andover	120	DS*	6/10		10/8	
PEAS						
All cultivars	56–70	DS*	4/20		6/14–7/10	
PEPPERS, SWEET						
All Cultivars	59–75	Inside	4/2	6/3	8/5 on	
PEPPER, HOT						
All cultivars	55–75	Inside	3/31	6/6	8/12 on	
POTATOES						
All cultivars		DS*	4/16		8/1 on	
RADISH						
Cherry Belle	28	DS*	5/7		6/4	
Daikon	50	DS*	7/22		9/21	
Miyashige	50	DS*	7/23		9/1	
RUTABAGA						
Pike	100	DS*	6/12		9/20	
SCALLIONS						
Evergreen White Hardy	65	DS*	5/10		7/14	
SPINACH						
Denali	36	DS*	4/22		5/28	
Denali	36	DS*	8/6		9/11	
SQUASH, SUMMER						
Condor	48	Inside	5/12	6/2	7/20	
Seneca Prolific	51	DS*	6/11		8/1	
SQUASH, WINTER						
All Winter Cultivars	85–110	Inside	5/5	5/26	8/18 on	
TOMATOES						
All Cultivars	60–80	Inside	4/26	6/4	8/2	
TURNIP						
Purple Top Globe White	50	DS*	8/11		9/30	

*DS–Direct seed

Continued from page 161

Planting Designs

Many gardeners make their beds 4 feet wide. This width allows you to grow four rows of a small crop such as lettuce, three rows of a larger crop such as Chinese cabbage, two rows of big crops such as corn or tomatoes, and a single row for members of the space-hogging squash family in a single bed. If you look back to the table "How Much Should You Plant?" on page 154, you'll see a column giving the numbers of rows per 4-foot bed for every vegetable listed. These figures assume that the soil is adequately supplied with both nutrients and moisture for the particular crop. If the fertility is still a little lean, plant two rows of either broccoli, cabbage, or cauliflower instead of three.

Row planting. Planting in rows makes weeding quick and efficient. You can simply move a hoe down the bed between the rows to uproot the weeds. You will have to do some hand-weeding in the row, of course, but the major part of the job can be done in only a few minutes. However, rows are not the only way to plant in beds.

Broadcast seeding. Small crops like carrots and baby lettuce can be broadcast-seeded in a bed. A broadcast pattern is scattershot. You plant by holding the seed loosely in your hand and releasing small amounts as you flick your wrist over the area. After the plants are up and have their second set of leaves, thin them to the recommended in-row spacing.

The advantage to a broadcast planting is that the plant density and yields per square foot are much greater than they are in a row system. But to work well, the soil must be largely free of weeds. If it isn't, you'll have to do so much hand-weeding that the crop will end up costing you lots of extra time, or you'll abandon it and turn it all under. Once your garden is well established and weeds are under control, it's certainly worth experimenting with broadcast seeding to see how you like it. Carrots, beets, scallions, radishes, salad greens, baby turnips, and spinach are appropriate for broadcast seeding.

STAKES AND STRINGS

Prepare some stakes and strings by wrapping slightly more string than the length of your bed around one stake and tying it to another. Set up the stakes and strings each time you plant, measuring at both ends of the bed. Make your furrows directly under each string. Planting in straight rows saves time in the long run. You'll be able to hoe and cultivate between the rows very quickly if you don't have to adjust for inconsistencies.

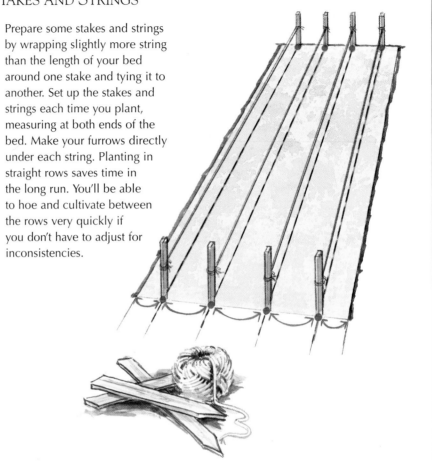

Planting Techniques

Whether you are planting in single rows or rows in a bed, begin by marking the row locations. You may feel that the stake and twine system (shown above) is overly complicated, but this technique saves time and trouble by making weeding easier and assuring that plants have adequate growing space. Make shallow furrows just under the strings—no deeper than three times the width of the seed.

In drought conditions, it's sometimes best to plant in deep furrows. This works best if the soil along the sides of the furrow, will not fall in and bury the seed too deeply. To make the most of this technique, create a deeper-than-normal furrow, and water it well. Then plant in the bottom as usual. Cover the seed with an appropriately thin layer of soil, and water again, using a misting nozzle or water-breaker on your hose to avoid displacing the soil.

Proper seed practices. Space seeds carefully. Most seed packets list a spacing distance, but in many cases this recommendation will require that you thin. Reliable spacing distances are given for each vegetable in the vegetable directory, on pages 172 to 193. If you follow these suggestions, you won't have to bother with the chore of thinning.

It's easy to handle large seeds such as beets, peas, and corn. Even the smaller broccoli and cabbage seed won't cause you problems. But tiny seeds, such as carrot, can be hard to space well. If you have difficulty getting a sparse enough seeding, use an old trick. Mix the carrot seed with equal portions of dry sand. Take up pinches of this mixture, and sprinkle them along the furrow. The tiny seed should be spaced well with this method.

Seeds must be consistently moist to germinate. In the spring, when the soil is wet and rains are frequent, this is rarely a problem. Water just after you plant, using a fine misting nozzle or rose. Check the soil each morning and evening until the seeds germinate to see whether you need to water again. But if you're planting seeds in hot weather or in a drought, you'll have to cover the soil with something that will hold moisture. See the smart tip below for details.

Seeds that require light to germinate often dry out if you leave them on the soil surface. Avoid this problem by making the furrow as described on page 164 and filling it with vermiculite. Plant the seeds on the surface of the vermiculite and then water with a misting nozzle or fine rose. The water will work the seeds into niches in the vermiculite so that they will remain wet, but enough light will penetrate the vermiculite so that they can germinate.

PLANT LETTUCE so that the crown is just level with the soil surface. If you bury the crown, or leave the roots exposed, the plant will die.

Transplanting

Many vegetable seedlings are transplanted directly into the garden. (See Chapter 2, "Gardening Basics", page 54 for hardening-off and transplanting instructions.) Most vegetables are set into the soil at the same depth they grew in their starting containers, but there are exceptions. Large portions of the stems of tomato plants are routinely buried. Roots will grow from the stem, further stabilizing the plant and increasing its ability to obtain food and water.

Seedlings that have grown top-heavy and tall as a consequence of low light levels can be planted deeper as long as they grow from the top, as broccoli does. However, deep planting will kill plants such as lettuce, which grow from the crown. (See photo above for proper depth.)

Vegetable seedlings require immediately available supplies of phosphorous, especially in cold soil. Soak the flats or root balls of your transplants in a solution of liquid seaweed and fish emulsion, diluted as recommended on the bottle, for at least 15 minutes before planting. Later in the season, when the soil is warm, this root drench will keep the root ball wet while the plant is adjusting to its new environment.

SMART TIP

KEEPING SEEDS MOIST

Keeping the soil moist in summer or during periods of drought can be a challenge. You can either plant in a deep furrow, as described in "Planting Techniques," on page 164, or plant in a furrow of normal depth and cover your rows with row-cover material or untreated burlap. Saturate the covering with water several times a day. If the seeds germinate in the dark, you can even cover them with a layer of wet newspapers, as long as you check for germination every morning and evening.

Chapter 2, "Gardening Basics," pages 50 to 55 contains more detailed information on starting plants from seeds.

SQUARE CAGE

FLOATING ROW COVER

POLY ROW COVER

GLASS CLOCHE

COLD FRAME

EXTENDING THE SEASONS

SEASON EXTENDERS ENABLE YOU to grow plants outside earlier and later in the season than normal, and they also give a certain amount of security against sudden cold snaps. Unless you live in a frost free area, it's well worth investing in a roll of row-cover material at the very least. As your vegetable gardening horizons expand, you'll probably want to add other season extenders to your tool kit.

Although a number of devices are classified as "season extenders," they vary tremendously in both effectiveness and cost. Some are most useful for covering large areas when a light frost threatens, while others can actually protect plants from temperatures in the low 20s. Most experienced vegetable gardeners have several extenders to use for whatever situation arises.

Once you get used to using season-extension devices, you can plan your spring gardening schedule around them. In the fall, most gardeners depend on floating row covers to keep their plants producing through the first frosts. Row covers can be put up quickly and, because they "breathe," do not have to be removed unless the succeeding days are bright and hot. Use two layers of row cover material whenever temperatures threaten to fall below 28°F. You'll be getting at least 6°F and possibly as much as 8°F of protection, meaning that your plants will not only survive, they will also suffer less than those that just make it through the low temperatures.

Keeping Soil and Plants Healthy

Healthy soils make healthy gardens. But knowing that your soil should be healthy and knowing how to help it become that way are two different things.

Basic soil science is covered in Chapter 1, "Preparing to Garden," pages 18 to 30. That information is essential for all kinds of gardening, from roses to tomatoes. But you'll need to add to that information to grow many other vegetables.

Feed the Soil

Vegetables absorb huge amounts of nutrients from the soil. Some, like corn and spinach, are nitrogen hogs, while others, such as onions and peppers, use and store more phosphorus, potassium, and minor nutrients such as magnesium. But no matter what the vegetable, you can be sure that you will need to replenish the nutrients frequently.

Compost is the best way to maintain soil health. Compost is the first line of defense, of course. Vegetable gardens need an average application of ½ to 2 inches each spring. The ½-inch application simply replenishes what the crop has removed from the soil during the past growing season, while 2-inch application helps build up soil that is deficient in organic matter and/or nutrients.

Getting Vines off the Ground

Training tomatoes up a trellis instead of letting them sprawl has a huge impact on the plant's health. Trellising improves air circulation, keeps animal and soil-dwelling pests away from the crops, and decreases soil-borne diseases.

Tomatoes can be "determinate," meaning that they are bred to grow to a certain height, or "indeterminate," meaning that they will continue to grow for as long as they are alive. Catalogs indicate which is which.

Knowing how a tomato plant grows is important. Determinate tomatoes form fruit on the branches (or suckers) that grow between the main stem and first branches. If you remove these suckers, you will be removing the fruit-production sites.

In contrast, removing suckers is a good way to prune indeterminate plants. Because the plants continue to grow from the top of the stem, they continue to produce blossom- and fruit-bearing branches. This pruning technique is referred to as "suckering."

Bean tepees are easy to make and lots of fun. You can pick the beans from inside or outside.

Gourds, like other cucurbit crops, are healthier when the vines are supported and off the ground.

HEIRLOOM cultivars such as these 'Clear Pink' tomatoes and assortment to the left tend to have superior flavor.

HYBRIDS such as these 'Black Bell' eggplants are uniform in appearance and may have disease resistance.

SAVING YOUR OWN SEED

UNTIL THE 1940s all gardeners and farmers saved their own seeds. People often had specialties that they shared with friends and relatives. Certain families became known for their superior varieties of this tomato or that bean.

All of these seeds were open-pollinated (OP) varieties or cultivars, meaning that the parents of the seed were genetically similar, but not identical, to each other. The plants that grew from these seeds were similar to their parents, and the seeds they produced were "true to type" because they carried the characteristic traits of their parents. These plants are called *heirlooms*.

Hybrid seeds result from crossing two or more plants of the same species that are quite different genetically. A hybrid seed produces a plant that is different from each of its parents but almost identical to every other plant grown from the same cross. If you grow a hybrid crop and save seed from it, the resulting plants will not come "true to type." Instead, they can resemble any plant, or combination of plants, in their heritage. Examples of OP tomatoes include 'Arkansas Traveler' and 'Brandywine', while hybrids include cultivars such as 'Celebrity' and 'Big Beef'. See page 170 for instructions on saving seeds.

Ironically, open-pollinated plants of the same variety or cultivar usually have more genetic diversity between individual plants than do hybrids. This makes qualities such as their days to maturity, size, color, and pest- and disease-resistance variable but also provides a certain security for the gardener. If a disease strikes an open-pollinated crop, for example, it is likely that some of the plants will be resistant to it, and the gardener can then save and propagate seeds from these plants.

But hybrids make life much more convenient. Knowing that all the broccoli heads will mature within a few days of each other makes it possible to schedule the harvest as well as streamline freezing operations.

Benefits of Hybrids vs. Open-Pollinated Plants

Most of the seeds you find in catalogs are hybrids that have been bred for certain characteristics. In some cases, these plants are superior to any open-pollinated crop you can grow, but in others, delicacy and flavor have been inadvertently bred out of the plant while hybridizers were working on good shipping or processing qualities. Many hybrids used by commercial farmers have another limitation. Seeds are being bred that will not grow unless they are treated with specific fertilizers and pesticides.

Shrinking gene pool creates problems. Gardeners and small farmers all over the continent have become concerned by the shrinking gene pool of our most common crops. Not only are thousands of wonderful varieties being lost in favor of the hybrids that are replacing them, the genetic similarity of many crops is making them more vulnerable to catastrophe. In 1970, for example, more than half of the U.S. corn crop in the South was stricken with a fungal disease; overall, more than a billion bushels were lost. All of the affected corn shared parentage, even though they had different cultivar names. This disaster, as well as the loss of 40 percent of the Soviet wheat crop in 1971, which was also due to genetic uniformity, alerted farmers and gardeners alike to these serious problems.

In response, people all over this continent began to save seeds, just as their grandparents and great grandparents once did. Seed-saving groups are now selling open-pollinated seeds as well as trading them between members. The Seed Starters Association, based in Decorah, IA, is the pioneering group.

Getting Started with Seed Saving

You'll discover how exciting it is to carefully protect a plant from crossing with other members of the species, save its seed, and then grow it out again for the seed. Before too many years have passed, you'll see some tangible benefits, too. Crops for which you save seed will become healthier and stronger as they become more and more adapted to the conditions in your backyard.

Some plants are easier to save seed from than others. Many people begin with tomatoes, partially because the seeds are easy to save and because some of the old-fashioned open-pollinated varieties are more flavorful than the new hybrids. But hybrid tomato cultivars are often more resistant to diseases than open-pollinated tomatoes. So even if you are totally committed to saving seed, grow a few hybrids along with the heirloom types until you learn how the open-pollinated cul-

SMART TIP

MALE AND FEMALE PLANTS

Spinach is one of the few vegetables with male and female flowers on different plants. You can't tell the difference before the plants flower, so it is best to enclose an entire bed with row-cover material and let the wind pollinate them.

Male plant   Female plant

Ovule

tivars respond to the diseases in your environment.

Pepper and lettuce are also good choices for beginning seed savers. But no matter what crop you begin with, start by buying open-pollinated seed. Seed catalogs indicate whether a plant is a hybrid by describing it that way or putting a small F1 or F2 beside the cultivar name. Without such a designation, you can be pretty sure it's open-pollinated.

How pollination works. Seeds are formed when the ovule at the base of the flower is fertilized by pollen from the same or another flower. "Perfect" flowers are those that contain both pollen and ovules. Many of these flowers can fertilize themselves if the wind or an insect pushes the pollen from the anthers to the stigma. Tomatoes, peppers, beans, and peas are all self-pollinating.

A few perfect flowers are "self-incompatible," meaning that they contain all the parts but can only be fertilized by pollen from another flower. Wind rarely achieves the necessary transfer, so these plants are dependent on insects for pollination. Radishes, broccoli, and cabbage all fit into this category.

Other plants have flowers that are either "male," producing only pollen, or "female," with ovules. Usually, insects move the pollen from one to another bloom, but sometimes, as in the case of corn, wind accomplishes the task. In some cases, such as squash and corn, male and female flowers grow on the same plant, but in others, such as spinach, entire plants are either male or female.

Commercial breeders keep lines pure by "isolating" plants, or growing them miles away from any others in the same species. In the home garden, this degree of isolation is virtually impossible. Even if you were to grow only one type of squash, for example, foraging bees traveling from neighboring gardens could fertilize the squash growing in your garden with pollen from a different type of squash.

Instead, gardeners can use barriers to protect flowers from this sort of stray crossing. Flower clusters may be bagged with floating row-cover material, (Photos 2 and 3 below), or plants may be grown in cages covered with row-cover material or fine-mesh screening or kept under row covers for the season.

Effecting pollination. To pollinate flowers that are normally wind-pollinated, such as tomatoes, enclose the flower clusters before the blooms open. Check them daily after the morning dew has dried. Once they do open, jiggle the stem gently to release the pollen from the male flower to the female flower. Remove the floating row cover pouch after the petals from all the flowers have dropped or dried up. Then mark the branch by tying a piece of string or ribbon on it to show that the fruits should be saved for seed rather than eaten.

Insect-pollinated flowers, such as squashes, must also be protected. The normal procedure is to check plants every evening for both male and female flowers that will open the following day. Tape the tips of male and female flowers closed with masking tape. In the morning, remove the tape from a male flower, cut it off the plant with a few inches of its petiole, and pull off the petals. Now gently remove the tape from the female flower and rub pollen from the male into each section of the stigma on the female plant. Success will be best guaranteed if you use several male flowers for each female flower.

After pollinating a female flower, tape it shut again to exclude insects. Tie a plastic strap around the flower stem so that you'll know which ones have been hand-pollinated.

To breed for a particular characteristic of a plant, choose male and female flowers only from that plant, but to ensure genetic vigor, choose flowers from several different plants. If possible, work with the first and second batches of flowers that form on the plant because later blooms may be aborted if the plant is under any stress.

SAVING TOMATO SEEDS

Difficulty Level: MODERATE

Tomatoes are one of the many plants that have perfect flowers that contain both male and female organs and fertilize themselves.

Tools and Materials: **Row-cover material, scissors, twist-tie**

1 Tomatoes often fertilize themselves before they open, but you can still protect them from cross-fertilization.

2 Cover the unopened flower clusters with a square of floating row-cover material.

3 Leave the row-cover material in place until all the petals in the cluster drop.

4 Tie a ribbon around the stem of the flower cluster so that you remember to save the seed.

HAND POLLINATING SQUASH   *Difficulty Level:* MODERATE

Summer squash, like all cucurbits, bears male and female flowers on the same plant. You can identify the female flowers by the fruit behind them.

Tools and Materials: **Masking tape, scissors**

1 Check your plants nightly so you can identify the female flowers that are going to open the next day. Tape them shut to keep them closed.

2 Tape the male flowers shut too. Even though they can't be fertilized, an insect could transfer pollen from another cultivar onto them.

3 Remove petals from the male flower, and rub it against the inside of the female flower.

4 To ensure plant vigor, use several male flowers to pollinate each female flower.

5 Retape the female flower closed so that insects don't add new pollen to the already fertilized flower.

Melon and cucumber flowers, which are much smaller than squash blossoms, are sometimes hard to retape closed. Instead, just enclose the bloom in a sack of row-cover material after you have fertilized it and leave the material in place until the fruit starts to grow.

Directions for saving seed of each of the vegetables covered in this book are included in the listings in the vegetable directory beginning on page 172. Even if seed-saving seems complicated to you, try saving seed of only one or two vegetables, such as a favorite pepper or tomato. It won't take long to discover that seed-saving is a simple way to increase your gardening pleasure.

ILLUSTRATED PLANT-BY-PLANT DIRECTORY OF VEGETABLES

Alliums

GARLIC

ONIONS

ONION FLOWERS

ONION TOPS BENT OVER

Temperatures: Moderate. Onion bulbs may be watery if temperatures rise above 85°F when they are forming. Garlic cloves must be chilled to freezing or below to form bulbs. Leeks tolerate frosts when mature and can overwinter with protection.

Soil: Moist, humus-rich, fertile, well-drained, pH of 6.0 to 7.0.

Propagation: *Onion* seeds can be planted indoors, 8 to 10 weeks before the frost-free date and transplanted to the garden a week or so before that time. Keep soil temperatures at 70° to 75°F during germination. In Zones 5 and warmer, direct-seeded onions will have time to form bulbs. Sets can also be used, but the resulting onions will not keep well through the winter. *Leeks and scallions* are planted from seed, either early indoors or directly in the garden. *Garlic* cloves are planted in autumn when you plant tulips—mid-October in Zones 4 to 5, early October in Zones 3 and 4, and late October in Zones 7, 8, and 9. Plant several inches below the soil surface, and mulch with 6 to 12 inches of straw or rotted leaves once the top surface of the soil

has frozen. To plant in spring, pre-chill the cloves for a month in the refrigerator and plant as soon as you can dig a hole in the ground.

Spacing: *Onions,* 6 to 8 inches between large Spanish onions and 4 to 6 inches between storage onions. *Scallions,* ½ inch apart in double rows a foot apart. *Garlic,* 6 to 8 inches in rows at least 1 foot apart. *Shallots,* 6 inches in rows 1 foot apart.

Culture: In soils with moderate fertility, drench rows of all alliums with compost

tea or a seaweed/fish emulsion once a month until late summer. Cultivate shallowly because roots, particularly those of leeks, are near the surface.

Onions and Leeks: Trim leaves if they threaten to fall over in their starting containers and again when you transplant them to the garden, cutting so top growth is no more than 6 inches tall. Hill leeks to increase the length of the white stem. To avoid damaging the roots, take the soil for hilling from the walkways or another section of the garden rather than from between the rows.

Garlic and Shallots: In early spring, pull back the mulch to see if shoots are appearing, but leave the mulch along the row so you can re-cover the plants if frost threatens. Plants may die if the leaves are heavily frosted. Similarly, they rot easily if too wet, so pull mulches back whenever possible.

Days to Maturity: *Onions:* 90 to 120. *Scallions:* 60 to 70. *Leeks:* 50 to 120. *Garlic:* 270 days for fall-planted garlic, 120 for spring-planted garlic. *Shallots:* 80 to 90 for set-grown bulbs, 100 to 110 for direct-seeded crops.

Average Yields: *Onions:* One pound a row foot. *Scallions:* ½ pound a row foot. *Leeks:* 1½ pounds a row foot. *Garlic:* ¼ to ½ pound a row foot.

Harvest: *Onions:* For fresh use, harvest as soon as they are usable. For storage onions, check to see that all the tops have fallen over in late summer, and knock over any that haven't. Wait until the tops dry and the bulbs have formed a tight neck. Then pull and place in a single layer in a warm, dry area with good air circulation. Wait until the skins rustle before storing.

Scallions: Pull as soon as they reach a harvestable size. If you have planted thickly, pull alternate plants to let the remaining ones size up.

Garlic: Harvest fall-planted bulbs in mid-July in most regions. Count leaves to be certain that there are (or have been) at least seven, meaning that the bulb is covered with seven layers of skin. If harvesting for seed, wait until the end of the month to harvest. Dig the bulbs only after several days of dry weather. Wait until fall to dig spring-planted garlic.

Shallots: Handle fall-planted sets as you do fall-planted garlic and direct-seeded crops as you do spring-planted garlic.

Storage: *Onions:* store in mesh bags in low humidity conditions at temperatures ranging from 33° to 45°F.

Leeks: Store in refrigerator for a month or so, in a cooler at near-freezing temperatures for several months, or place roots in damp sand or peat moss, and store in the root cellar at temperatures just above freezing for most of the winter. To overwinter leeks in the ground, mulch deeply once the ground is frozen.

Garlic and Shallots: Cut stems back to 8 inches and let the bulbs dry in a dark, airy place until the skins rustle and the stalk is thoroughly dry. Trim the stalks, and put the bulbs in paper or net bags. Store over the winter at 65 percent humidity at 35°F.

Pests: Onion maggots and thrips attack all members of the family.

Diseases: *Onions* are attacked by smudge (*Colletotrichum circinans*), smut (*Urocystis cepulae*), pink root (*Pyrenochaeta terrestris*), white rot (*Sclerotium cepivorum*), downy mildew (*Peronospora destructor, Botrytis* spp.), purple blotch (*Alternaria porri*), and basal rot (*Fusarium* spp.). High populations of soil organisms and proper spacing usually discourage diseases.

Leeks have problems with neck rot (*Botrytis* spp.), a mold that appears during storage. Blue mold (*Penicillium* spp.) attacks plants in spring and white rot (*Sclerotium cepivorum*) infects plants in cool, soggy soil conditions. Most of the other onion diseases also attack leeks.

Seed-Saving: All onions, including shallots and walking onions, can cross pollinate. Though they have perfect flowers, they are self-infertile and need to be hand-pollinated. Surround plants grown for seeds with cages covered with row-cover material, or bag at least 10 individual flowers. Every morning, between 10 AM and noon, move pollen from one flower head to the next with a small brush.

Onions are biennial and must be overwintered at 33° to 40°F, 50 to 70 percent humidity, and then planted if you wish to produce seeds. The seeds shatter easily once dry. Avoid this by encasing seed heads in bags secured with rubber bands around the stem.

Leeks are also biennials with perfect flowers, but they do not cross with onions, chives, or shallots. They can cross with other leeks, including 'Elephant Garlic'. Overwinter them under a mulch in Zones 7 and warmer. In Zones 6 and cooler, dig the plants and hold them for the winter in a root cellar kept at 32°F, 70 to 90 percent humidity. Isolate cultivars by growing 10 to 20 plants under a cage covered with row-cover material. Hand pollinate as described for onions. To save 'Elephant Garlic', plant the bulbils that form around the basal plate.

Shallots grown for seed need to be covered with row-cover material so they don't cross pollinate with other alliums. You can also save bulbs that display the characteristics you prefer and plant them the following year.

Notes: All allium seeds have a very limited viability. If stored at temperatures of 40° to 45°F and kept in the dark, up to 80 percent of the seeds will germinate the first year, but only 50 percent will germinate the second year.

All alliums inhibit the growth of legumes, so do not plant them near peas or beans.

If necks of onions, shallots, or garlic do not dry properly during curing, check for a potassium deficiency in the soil.

Bulbing onions are one of the few vegetable crops that really care how far from the equator they're growing. Although we call cultivars "long-day" or "short-day" types, they form bulbs only when exposed to the correct hours of darkness each night. Northerners, who live where day-length is well over 12 hours all summer long, should choose "long-day" types. But if you live where average day-length is about 12 hours, plant the "short-day" cultivars. Fortunately, you'll find the seeds and sets in your local gardening stores and through regional catalogs. Cultivar descriptions also tell you the preferences of particular plants.

Scallions are both spring and fall crops. In most areas of the U.S., spring temperatures are cool enough so you can make several plantings, starting three weeks before the frost-free date and continuing every week to ten days later. Plant the fall crop about two months before the first expected frost. Fall-grown plants take longer to mature and hold until early winter, so rather than making successive sowings, plant enough to take you through the early winter.

Leeks will form long white stems without hilling if you plant them in a 6-inch-deep trench and fill it with soil. Choose cultivars such as 'Laura', 'Elefant', and 'Winter Giant' to overwinter. The largest leeks come from the largest transplants, grown with adequate moisture, organic matter, and nutrients.

Garlic grows in one of two forms—soft neck (*A. sativum* subsp. *sativum*) or hard neck (*A. sativum* subsp.

subsp. *ophioscorodon*). Soft-neck types are said to store the longest but some of the hard-neck types are the most hardy and thus the most reliable in Zones 3, 4, and 5. Cut off flower stalks of all types before flowers open. ▪

Helianthus tuberosus
Artichoke, Jerusalem

Temperatures: This perennial grows in Zones 3 to 9.
Soil: Well-drained, of average fertility, with a pH of 6.0 to 6.5.
Planting: Buy tubers to plant in spring or fall. Plant each tuber 4 inches deep.
Spacing: Allow 1 to 2 feet between plants in rows 2 to 3 feet apart.
Culture: These plants tend to take care of themselves. Mulch to keep the soil evenly moist and discourage weed competition, water in drought conditions, and top-dress with ½ inch of fully finished compost every year or two.
Days to Maturity: Perennial.
Average Yields: 5 to 8 lbs. per row-foot.
Harvest: A small harvest can be taken the first fall, but it is best to allow plants a full year and a half before harvesting heavily. Dig tubers with a spading fork. It's unlikely that you will find all of the tubers, but it's best to intentionally leave some in place for the following year.
Storage: Washed tubers will store in the refrigerator for a week or so, but lose quality if kept longer than that. For prolonged harvests, dig as necessary in the fall. Store tubers in sand or peat moss in

the root cellar.
Pests: Largely trouble-free.
Diseases: Largely trouble-free.
Seed-Saving: Simply replant tubers to produce more plants, or leave some tubers in place.
Notes: Think carefully about the location of this plant,—more than one gardener has discovered that it is nearly impossible to eradicate once it is established. Plant it in an out-of-the-way corner where the rangy growth won't be noticed and the bright yellow flowers can add a cheerful note. You'll love it forever. ▪

Asparagus officinalis
Asparagus

Temperatures: Versatile, grows in Zones 2 to 9.
Soil: Deep, well-drained, fertile, and humusy, with a pH of 6.5 to 6.8. Add 2 inches of fully finished compost to the growing area before planting.
Planting: Buy one-year-old crowns or start seeds outdoors as soon as the soil temperature is 50°F and evening lows are in the high 30s or low 40s. Plants naturally enlarge from the crown each year, giving you more spears.
Spacing: Space crowns 2 inches apart in rows 4 to 6 inches apart.
Culture: Soak roots in compost tea for several hours before planting. Plant in early spring, as soon as the soil temperature is 50°F. If your soil is soggy, heavy, or compacted, make raised beds. Dig a

trench, about 8 to 10 inches deep, and make mounds of compost-enriched soil every 2 feet along its length. Drape the roots of the crowns over the mound, spreading them like an octopus. Cover them with 2 to 4 inches of soil. Every two to three weeks during the first season, add another couple of inches of soil to the trench until it is slightly raised above the surrounding soil surface. Let the ferns grow undisturbed the first year.

Keep asparagus beds well weeded. Every fall, cut the dried ferns off at the soil surface and heap 2 inches of compost over the bed. Mulch deeply as soon as the ground freezes. In spring, pull back the mulch when spears begin to appear.
Days to Maturity: Asparagus begins to yield slightly in the second and third years.
Average Yields: 3 to 4 lbs. per 10 foot row. Plant at least 20 feet per person.
Harvest: Do not harvest the first year. Harvest lightly during the second year. During the fourth year, you can count on a harvest season of three to four weeks and eventually build to six to eight weeks. To harvest, snap off the spears at or just below ground level when they are 6 to 10 inches high and the tips are still closed. Best storage results when spears are harvested in very early morning.
Storage: Cool immediately in water. Then stand upright in a tray filled with an inch of water in the refrigerator. Asparagus freezes well.
Pests: Asparagus miners, asparagus beetles, beet armyworms, cutworms, onion thrips, asparagus aphids.
Diseases: Rust (*Puccinia asparagi*), fusarium wilt (*Fusarium* spp.), white rot (*Sclerotinia* spp.), and needle blight (*Cercospora asparagi*).
Seed-Saving: You can save seeds if you have both male and female plants. The female plants produce red berries that contain the seeds. Gather the berries before the first frost. Crush them and place seeds and pulp in a bowl of water. Pour off the water, saving the seeds that are heavy enough to drop to the bottom of the bowl. Dry the seeds for at least a week before storing.

Notes: Male plants yield significantly more spears than female plants. Buy an "all-male" hybrid or, if you grow your own plants, weed out the females in the seedling stage. Female flowers have a distinct three-lobed pistil, visible with a hand-lens, while male flowers are bigger and lack a pistil. If you buy crowns, try to locate one-year-olds; older than that, they are difficult to establish. If spears are weak and spindly, suspect low nutrient content and sprinkle 1 to 2 lbs. of alfalfa meal on the soil surface before adding the compost in the fall. Remember that frost will injure aboveground spears, so re-cover plants with mulch when frost is predicted. ■

Beans

POLE BEAN

LIMA BEAN

SOY BEAN

Temperatures: Warm; minimum night temperatures of 40°F and minimum day temperatures of 50°F are required, but plants perform better in warmer conditions. Frost kills both seedlings and mature plants.

Soil: Well-drained, humusy, moderate fertility, with a pH of 5.5 to 6.8.

Planting: Plant seeds where they are to grow in late spring or early summer, after danger of frost has passed and soil temperature is 60°F. For a continuous harvest, plant short-season cultivars every two to three weeks until midseason. Yields will be higher if you dust the seeds with a "bean and pea" inoculant powder (available at garden centers) before planting.

Spacing: Plant seeds 4 to 6 inches apart in rows 1½ to 2½ feet apart. In 4-foot-wide beds, plant two rows.

Culture: Bacteria on the roots fix nitrogen for beans, so they can thrive in low nitrogen soils. However, they do require high levels of potassium and phosphorus, supplied by greensand and rock phosphate, respectively. Test and adjust soils if necessary. Keep soil moist but not soggy. If diseases have been a problem, water only the soil, not the foliage. Never walk near the beans when foliage is wet. In areas where pests have been troublesome, cover plants with row-cover material until they are ready to harvest.

Days to Maturity: 50 to 120.

Average Yields: Bush beans yield about 8 lbs. per 10-foot row, pole beans yield about 15 lbs. per 10-foot row, and dry beans yield about 8 lbs. per 100-foot row.

Harvest: Keep beans picked to prolong flowering and fruiting. Pick beans with the petiole to lengthen storage time.

Storage: Snap beans will keep for as long as a week in the refrigerator. To avoid fungal problems, use vented plastic bags. Dry beans will keep for as long as a year in dark, dry conditions. Snap beans freeze and pickle well.

Pests: Bean weevils, Mexican bean beetles, tarnished plant bugs, bean aphids, spider mites, and bean leaf beetles.

Diseases: Halo blight (*Pseudomonas phaseolicola*), rust (*Uromyces* species), botrytis blight (*Botrytis cinerea*), anthracnose (*Colletotrichum lindemuthianum*), and bean mosaic viruses.

Seed-Saving: Bean flowers are perfect and self-pollinating but nonetheless, to prevent insects from crossing one type of bean with another, keep seed-saving bush beans under tunnels made of row-cover material, or bag the blossoms of pole beans. Leave seed-saving plants in place until the pods are brown and dry. Pull the whole vine, bring it indoors, and hang it to let it finish drying. Put old sheets under the drying vines to catch any seeds that may fall. Once pods are dry, split any that haven't already opened to collect the seeds. To check that seeds are dry, place a few on a hard surface and hit them hard with a hammer. If they shatter, they are dry; if they mush, they aren't. Once they are thoroughly dry, freeze them for five days to kill bean weevils. Remove from the freezer but do not open the container for 24 hours. After this, you can pack the seeds in plastic or paper bags and store them in a dark, cool location for up to five years.

Beans continued

Notes: *Green and pole beans:* In hot climates where the soil may be too warm for bean germination during midsummer, cover planted seeds with vermiculite rather than soil, and water deeply. The vermiculite will reflect light, keeping the soil cooler.

Favas are the only beans that can withstand cool temperatures. Plant them where they are to grow four to five weeks before the last expected fall frost. In addition to making a very tasty shell bean, favas are also excellent cover crops. Plant them in the spring; then mow them and incorporate them into the top few inches of the soil two weeks before planting the area with a fall crop such as spinach, lettuce, or transplanted broccoli. Because they are a legume, they add a great deal of nitrogen and their large size contributes plenty of food for nutrient-releasing microorganisms.

Lima bean cultivars are available as both bush or vining types. For maximum production, choose the vines and trellis them as you do vining string beans. Bush types mature somewhat more quickly than the vining cultivars and are more appropriate to Zones 3 to 5.

Soybeans are one of the most gratifying beans to grow for yourself, primarily because you can let them dry or eat them as shell beans. Fresh soybeans for shell beans are unavailable commercially but are delicious, particularly when served with a tomato sauce. Home-grown dried soybeans taste superior to those you can buy, primarily because they are fresher. Choose a cultivar that is appropriate to your climate, paying particular attention to the days to maturity. ■

Beta vulgaris
Beet

Temperatures: Moderate; but prefer nights of 55° to 60°F and days of 65° to 75°F, but will tolerate temperatures of 55° to 85°F. Mulch in warmer temperatures.

Soil: Well-drained, moist, high fertility, and friable with a pH of 6.0 to 6.8. Beets do not tolerate boron deficiencies. If soil is slightly deficient, spray plants with liquid seaweed every two weeks.

Planting: Direct-seed when soil temperatures are at least 45°F and air temperatures are 50°F or above. For successive harvests, plant every three weeks until midsummer. Plant storage beets about 60 to 70 days before your first expected fall frost.

Spacing: Plant seeds 3 to 4 inches apart in rows 1 foot apart. Because several seeds are enclosed in each "seed," you will need to thin seedlings to stand 4 to 6 inches apart in the row. Wait to thin until the thinnings can be used in salads or cooked as baby greens.

Culture: Beets require steady supplies of moisture and nutrients. In lean soils, water them with a compost tea or a solution of liquid seaweed and fish emulsion every two weeks.

Days to Maturity: 45 to 60.

Average Yields: For moderately sized beets, about 1 lb. for every row-foot.

Harvest: Thin plants successively to harvest baby beet greens, then baby beets, and finally mature beets. Cut tops from beets, about 2 inches above the beet

itself, as soon as you harvest, and store separately. Beets that will go straight to the table can be allowed to stand in moderate frosts. However, for the best-quality storage roots, pull them several days before your first expected frost.

Storage: Store beets in the refrigerator for as long as a month or two. Bury storage beets, such as 'Lutz Green Leaf' in dry sand or peat moss to keep in the root cellar. Beets freeze and pickle well.

Pests: Aphids, leaf miners, flea beetles, and beet armyworms.

Diseases: Downy mildew (*Peronospora farinosa*), rust (*Uromyces betae*), scab (*Streptomyces scabies*), cercospora leaf spot (*Cercospora beticola*), curly top virus.

Seed-Saving: These biennial plants form seeds only in their second year. Overwinter them in a cold cellar (36° to 33°F) or, in warm climates, in the garden. Beets have very light pollen that can travel for miles, so it is necessary to enclose a group of plants to ensure that the resulting seed is true. Cover a group of seed stalks with a large plastic bag. At the base, stuff cotton batting around the stems before tying the bag shut. Leave the bag in place for several weeks. Cut the seed stalks when they are almost dry. Let them finish drying inside, hung over an old sheet to catch any seeds that might drop. Remove the seeds (which are actually dried up fruits containing several seeds) from the stalks by enclosing them in an old pillowcase and jumping up and down on them.

Notes: Swiss chard has the same cultural requirements as beets. Thinnings can be used in salad mixes or, when slightly larger, steamed. If you cover fall crops with two or three layers of row-cover material, you can harvest Swiss chard until you have to climb through the snow to get to it. ■

Brassicas

BROCCOLI

BRUSSEL SPROUT

CABBAGE

CAULIFLOWER

KALE

Temperatures: Cool. 50 to 60°F nights, 60 to 75°F days. *Broccoli:* May "button," or form small heads at lower temperatures or form small, loose heads prematurely at warmer temperatures. *Cauliflower* is more temperature-sensitive than other members of the family. Germinate seeds at a soil temperature of 70 to 75°F and keep seedlings at night temperatures of 50°F and day temperatures of 60°F to avoid problems with premature bolting. *Kale and Brussels Sprouts* stand well in freezing temperatures. Use row covers to harvest kale until midwinter.

Soil: Nutrient- and humus-rich, well-drained, high calcium, with a pH between 6.7 to 7.2.

Planting: *Broccoli, Cauliflower, and Cabbage:* For first crop, start seeds indoors about two months before last spring frost, keeping them in their ideal temperature range. Harden off and transplant five to six week old seedlings about two to three weeks before last frost, under row cover material. Successive crops can be started in containers and transplanted or started in nursery beds and transplanted. Plant fall crops to mature just at the time of the first expected frost. They require about two weeks longer to mature in the fall but keep their quality in the field much longer than they do in the spring.

Brussels Sprouts: Plant or transplant this long-season crop only once a season, timing it to mature just at the first expected frost date.

Kale: Direct-seed four to six weeks before last spring frost. Plant fall crops two months before the first expected fall frost. To transplant, start in peat pots or soil blocks six weeks before the frost-free date and transplant at that date.

Spacing: *Broccoli, Brussels Sprouts, Cauliflower, and Cabbage:* 1½ to 2 feet apart in rows 1½ to 2 feet apart.

Kale: Plant seeds about 3 to 4 inches apart. Thin plants to stand 12 to 15 inches apart. As long as plants do not become crowded, thinning can wait until plants are large enough to eat.

Culture: Many pest problems can be avoided by covering newly transplanted or seeded crops with row-cover material and leaving it in place as long as temperatures are 75°F or below. Keep soil evenly moist and weeds under control. Keep nutrients high; in moderately fertile soils, drench the soil with a seaweed/fish emulsion every three weeks, applying about a cup per row foot or foliar feed once every three weeks with compost tea or a seaweed/fish emulsion early in the morning.

Brussels Sprouts: When sprouts begin to develop, snap off the leaf petioles just under those that have begun to grow. Continue to do this every two weeks throughout the season. The plant will look like a very strange sort of palm tree by late summer, with knobs all along the

Brassicas continued

stem and a tuft of leaves at the top. About two weeks before frost, pinch off the central growing tip of the plant to encourage it to put energy into maturing the sprouts.

Cauliflower: Cauliflower heads turn yellow if the sun hits them. Avoid this by "banding" them. As soon as the developing head is the size of a silver dollar, pull the leaves together over it and secure them with a rubber band. Peek inside the leaves every couple of days to determine when to cut the heads. Some cultivars are said to be "self-wrapping," meaning that they don't need this treatment. However, leaves don't always protect these heads so it's best to band them too.

Days to Maturity (from transplanting): *Broccoli:* 55 to 75. *Brussels Sprouts:* 90 to 130. *Cabbage:* 60 to 85. *Cauliflower:* 50 to 60. *Kale:* 30 to 60 from direct-seeding. Subtract 14 days if transplanting.

Average Yields: *Broccoli:* 7½ lbs. for every 10 row-feet or one main head and 6 to 8 small side shoots per plant. *Brussels Sprouts:* ¾ lb. for every row-foot. *Cauliflower:* 1 head per plant. *Cabbage:* 1 head per plant. *Kale:* ¾ to 1 lb. per row-foot.

Harvest: *Broccoli:* Cut main head when it looks fully formed and while buds are still tight. Best quality is assured by cutting in early morning, before plants have warmed. For maximum side-shoot production, cut the main head with a short stalk. Cut side-shoots as they develop. In most cultivars, they will continue to develop for up to six weeks beyond the time you cut the main head.

Brussels Sprouts: Light frost improves the flavor, but if sprouts are left on the plant too long, they loosen and open. Avoid this by harvesting the bottom sprouts as they become large enough, frost or not. To harvest, push the sprout to one side with your thumb, holding the plant steady with your other hand.

Cauliflower: Cut cauliflower when the heads have fully expanded, while the

curds are still tightly bunched together. Even though this may seem difficult to determine, a little experience with various cultivars will make this easy. Cauliflower will not make side-shoots. Once you've cut the head, the leaves and roots are ready to be composted.

Cabbage: Cut whole heads when they feel tightly packed when you gently squeeze them. If you cut above the crown, up to four smaller heads will form.

Kale: Pick early in the morning when plants are cool. Pick whole plants while thinning the rows. After that, harvest bottom leaves by pulling down sharply on their petioles. The break will be clean and callous quickly, preventing fungal spores from entering.

Storage: *Broccoli and Cauliflower:* Cool broccoli heads in water as soon as you cut them. Shake off and store in the refrigerator for up to five days. Broccoli freezes very well.

Brussels Sprouts: Sprouts will remain good through very heavy frosts but to protect quality, dig whole plants, shake the soil off the roots, and hang them upside down in the root cellar. Brussels sprouts also freeze quite well.

Cabbage: Keeps good quality for several months in the refrigerator. Young plants that are still actively growing store the longest in a root cellar.

Kale: Immediately after picking, cool leaves or plants in cold water. Shake dry and store for a few days in the refrigerator. Kale freezes beautifully.

Pests: Imported cabbage worm, cabbage loppers, aphids, flea beetles, cabbage root fly maggots, thrips, cutworms, root-knot nematodes, and tarnished plant bugs.

Diseases: White rot (*Sclerotinia sclerotiorum*), head rot (*Rhizoctonia solani*), black rot (*Xanthomonas campestris*), club root

(*Plasmodiophora brassicae*), blackleg (*Phoma lingam*), Alternaria leaf spot (*Alternaria brassicae*), downy mildew (*Peronospora parasitica*), powdery mildew (*Erysiphe cruciferarum*), and yellows (*Fusarium oxysporum f. conglutinans*).

Seed-Saving: *Broccoli:* Broccoli crosses with other members of the *Oleracea* species, making it necessary to cage it. However, flowers must be insect-pollinated because the pollen is self-incompatible—unable to fertilize flowers on the same plant. The best way to ensure that seeds will come true is to cage a group of plants and hand-pollinate them with a brush, moving the pollen from one flower to another. Leave the cage in place until the plant stops flowering. Seedpods must dry on the plant for seeds to be viable, but because the seeds shatter easily, its best to cover the seed stalk with row-cover material, secured at the bottom with a rubber band around cotton batting. Cut the seed stalk when most of the seedpods are dry. Store seeds in a dark, dry location.

Brussels Sprouts and Cauliflower: Seed production is hard in Zones 7 and cooler because it is difficult to keep plants living over the winter either in the root cellar or garden. In Zones 8 and warmer, mulch plants to protect them over the winter. Cage them in the spring to prevent crossing, but allow insects to pollinate the self-incompatible flowers or do it by hand.

Cabbage and Kale: Store whole plants in a root cellar between 32° and 45°F or in the garden in Zones 8 and warmer. Plants must experience a few weeks at temperatures close to freezing before they can bloom. Cage and introduce insects to pollinate.

Notes: *Broccoli:* Choose cultivars according to the season when they will grow. In general, fall broccoli is the easiest to grow but some cultivars do well in spring and a few grow well in summer. To prevent broccoli from buttoning, cover plants with row-cover material if temperatures fall to 30°F nights and 50°F days. Boron deficiency is responsible for stems with a hollow center and calcium deficiency causes the leaf tips to turn brown and die. Foliar feeding with seaweed/fish emulsion corrects both problems. Broccoli tastes best when mature heads are lightly touched by frost; grow your freezer crop to mature just as frost is expected, remembering to plan for the extra 14 days that broccoli usually takes to mature in fall conditions.

Brussels Sprouts: If late-season aphids are a problem, direct-seed a tall cultivar of dill between the plants about two months before the expected frost date. The dill will feed the many aphid predators, keeping the pests' populations in check.

Cauliflower is more difficult to grow in the spring than in the fall, primarily because night temperatures can be too low during the early part of their growth and day temperatures can be too high while heads are forming. Minimize problems by choosing early-maturing cultivars meant for spring, covering plants with row-cover material until it is warm, and maintaining high soil moisture and nutrient levels. In Zones 5 and northward, certain cultivars can make good heads in the summer. Check seed catalogs to learn which types are recommended for warm temperatures.

Cabbage: Choose several cabbage cultivars because they vary so much from one another. If splitting after a rain is a problem, harvest large heads, or retard their growth by slicing through half the root system with a sharp hoe.

Kale: Try 'Red Russian' or 'Wild Garden' kale if you think you don't like this vegetable. All species of kale have the finest flavor after frost and also stand up to repeated freeze/thaw cycles without losing quality. Where deer are a problem, cover the plants with row-cover material. If the roots and crown overwinter, they will send up new leaves in the spring before they flower and go to seed. ■

Zea mays var. *rugosa*
Corn, Sweet corn, Table corn

Temperatures: Warm; corn grows best in night temperatures of 60°F or above and day temperatures of 75°F and above.
Soil: High fertility, deep, with high organic matter, pH of 6.0 to 6.8.
Planting: Plant where it is to grow, once danger of frost has passed. Seed germinates poorly at soil temperatures below 65°F, but plastic laid over the soil surface for a few weeks or so just before the frost-free date, will raise temperatures sufficiently. (Check the temperature with a soil thermometer before planting). In Zones 5 and cooler, earlier planting is possible if you plant seeds in a 6-inch furrow, cover them with only an inch of soil, and then cover the furrow with clear plastic. Let seedling plants grow under the plastic, venting it if necessary during the day to prevent fungal diseases. Remove the plastic when temperatures stabilize. In Zones 5 south, plant a succession of cultivars to prolong harvest.
Spacing: Plant 8 inches to 1 foot apart in rows 2 feet apart. Plant in blocks of at least 4 rows to ensure proper wind pollination.
Culture: Corn is an extremely heavy feeder. If soil nitrogen is low, side-dress with compost every month or drench the soil with 1 cup of compost tea or liquid seaweed/fish emulsion solution per row-foot. Make certain soil moisture is steady once plants tassel.
Days to Maturity: 65 to 90.
Average Yields: An average of 1 ear per row-foot.

Harvest: When silks have dried and ears feel full, peel back a few husks and puncture a kernel with your thumbnail. A milky-colored liquid should spurt out. Pull ears downward to harvest.
Storage: Try to pick corn less than half an hour before you cook it. If a huge harvest comes in at once, cut kernels off the cobs, bag and freeze them, without blanching. Whole cobs can also be frozen.
Pests: Animals, particularly raccoons and birds. Insect pests include corn earworm, European corn borers, earwigs, corn rootworms, stalk borers, wireworms, corn root aphids, and Japanese beetles.
Diseases: Various leaf spot diseases, bacterial wilt, rust, corn smut, crazy top, and various viral diseases.
Seed-Saving: To prevent cultivars from weakening, breeders grow at least 200 plants and save seed from the choicest 100 of these. On a small garden scale, you can save seed from as few as 25 plants as long as they are fertilized with pollen from 25 other plants. To avoid natural pollination, place special shoot and tassel bags over the ears and tassels (available from seed-saving groups). Bag the ears just before the silks start to emerge and the tassels before they open. Every day, between 10 AM and 1 PM in dry weather, shake the tassel bags to collect pollen. Then open several ear bags and shake the pollen over the silks. If you do this every day for a week, you're sure to get pollination. Leave the bag over the ear until the silks die back, and mark those ears that you have fertilized so you can save the kernels for planting.
Notes: When possible, orient rows in a north-south direction to maximize sun exposure. Super-sweet cultivars must be isolated from regular corn cultivars by at least 100 feet to prevent the tough kernels that cross-pollination creates. Where this is impossible, time plantings so that there will be at least ten days between the varieties tasseling. For example, you could plant a 75-day super-sweet ten days before you plant a 75-day standard corn, or at the same time that you plant an 85-day or 65-day standard cultivar. ■

Crucifers

CHINESE CABBAGE

COLLARDS

PAC CHOI

RADISH

RUTABAGA

TURNIP

Temperatures: Cool. Nights of 40° to 50°F and days of 55° to 70°F are ideal although plants will tolerate light frosts and temperatures as high as 80°F.

Soil: Moderate fertility with steady moisture, high humus, and a pH of 5.5 to 6.8. *Rutabagas and turnips* require balanced amounts of potassium, phosphorus, and boron, and a pH of 6.0 to 7.0.

Planting: *Radish, table:* Plant small numbers of seeds where they are to grow, beginning about three to four weeks before the last expected spring frost and continuing each week until about two weeks after the frost-free date. Plant fall crops two months before first expected fall frost, and continue until a week before.

Radish, daikon: Plant two months before first expected fall frost.

Pac Choi, Collards, and Chinese Cabbage: Start indoors, four weeks before the frost-free date, in peat pots or soil blocks. Direct seed two weeks before the frost-free date. Plant fall crops two months before the first expected frost.

Turnip: Direct seed three to four weeks before the last expected frost and every week after until temperatures are too warm. For fall crop, plant two months before the first expected frost.

Rutabaga: Plant in mid- to late July.

Spacing: *Radish, table:* ½ inch apart in triple rows 1 foot apart. Thin to allow 1 inch per plant. *Radish, daikon:* 4 inch, *Pac Choi, Collards, and Chinese Cab-*

bage: 6 inches apart and harvest to leave 1 to 1½ feet between plants.

Turnip and Rutabaga: 4 inches and harvest to 6 to 8 inches between storage cultivars.

Culture: If leaves look yellow, drench the soil with a cup of compost tea per row foot or spray foliage with a seaweed/fish emulsion. Cover plants with row-cover material in the spring to prevent cabbage root fly maggot and flea beetle damage.

Days to Maturity: *Radish, table:* 20 to 50, *Radish, daikon:* 50 to 60. *Pac Choi, Collards, and Chinese Cabbage:* 45 to 60. *Turnip:* 35 to 50. *Rutabaga:* 95 to 100.

Average Yields (per row-foot): *Radish, table:* 1 to 2 bunches. *Radish, daikon:* 2

roots. *Pac Choi, Collards, and Chinese Cabbage:* 1 to 3 lbs. *Turnip:* ½ to 1 lb. *Rutabaga:* 1½ lbs.

Harvest: *Radish, table:* Pull before roots are so large that they split. Cool radishes in water immediately after harvesting, and remove the leaves if you plan to store them for more than a day.

Radish, daikon: Pull and cut tops, leaving 1" of stems. If you are storing, do not wash but let the soil dry and brush off excess. If eating fresh, wash immediately.

Pac Choi, Collards, and Chinese Cabbage: Cut entire plant at the crown or, for prolonged harvest, pick outside leaves as needed.

Turnip: Handle as table radishes.

Rutabaga: Tastes better after a frost. Pull them on a dry day. If you are storing, do not wash but let the soil dry and brush off excess.

Storage: *Radish, table:* Keep in the refrigerator for a week but the best quality is assured by eating them within two days of harvest.

Radish, daikon: Keep for one to two months in a root cellar held just above freezing with 85 to 90 percent humidity.

Pac Choi, Collards, and Chinese Cabbage: Immediately after picking, cool leaves or plants in cold water. Shake dry and store for a few days in the refrigerator. Keep for a week in the refrigerator. They freeze beautifully.

Turnip: Keep for a month or more in the refrigerator.

Rutabaga: Rutabagas store in the refrigerator for months. They also store in a root cellar, held just above freezing at 80 to 90 percent humidity. Prevent the rutabagas from losing moisture by packing them in damp sand or peat moss. Check weekly to remove any that are getting soft.

Pests: Aphid, cabbage root fly maggot, fall armyworm, flea beetle, imported cabbage worm.

Diseases: *Radishes:* Club root (*Plasmodiophora brassicae*), yellows (*Fusarium oxysporum, F. conglutinans*), downy mildew (*Peronospora parasitica*), and scab (*Streptomyces scabies*).

Pac Choi, Collards, and Chinese Cabbage: Downy mildew (*Peronospora parasitica*), powdery mildew (*Erysiphe cruciferarum*).

Turnip and Rutabaga: Black leg (*Phoma lingam*), black rot (*Xanthomonas campestris*), Alternaria leaf spot (*Alternaria brassicae*), and downy mildew (*Peronospora parasitica*).

Seed-Saving: *Radishes:* They will cross between groups and cultivars but will not cross with other members of the cabbage family. Most require insect pollination from one plant to another because the flowers on a particular plant are self-incompatible. Grow only one cultivar for seed at a time. Allow the seed stalks to form, insects to pollinate them, and the seedpods to dry. Cut the seed stalks once the pods are dry. Split the pods to remove the seeds, using a rubber mallet to pound the pods, if necessary. Store the seeds in a cool, dark place for as long as five years.

Pac Choi, Collards, and Chinese Cabbage: Can cross with other *Brassica rapa* plants, including turnips and broccoli rabe. In areas with short growing seasons, overwinter Chinese cabbage and plant it out in spring. Pac choi and collards will flower the same year as they are planted. Cage at least ten plants and allow insects in to pollinate them, or do it by hand.

Turnip: Can cross with other turnips, Chinese cabbage, mustards, and broccoli rabe. Overwinter roots of long-season cultivars. Short-season turnips flower the same season they are planted. Insects fertilize the self-incompatible flowers. Cage at least 20 plants, and let insects in to pollinate, or do it by hand.

Rutabaga: Store the roots over the winter in a root cellar or under deep mulch in the garden because they are biennial. Plant stored roots out in the garden in early spring. The perfect flowers can pollinate themselves and are usually wind-pollinated. However, insects can also pollinate them and will produce crosses of rutabaga, rapeseed, and some types of turnips. Avoid this by caging the plants. Allow the seedpods to dry on the plant but cut when the pods lowest on the stalk begin to open. Hang the stalks in a dark, cool area, over an old sheet or other material to catch falling seeds. Store in dark, cool conditions for as long as five years.

Notes: *Radishes:* The common table radish belongs to the radiculata group of *Raphanus sativus* but the foot-long white daikon radish belongs to the *R. longipinnatus* group. Table radishes develop more bite in warm temperatures, particularly if the soil is somewhat dry. To keep them edible toward midseason, plant them to the east of a tall crop or cover them with shade cloth or burlap. Most daikon radish cultivars bolt prematurely when planted in the spring. Plan to harvest these early, when they are only 8 to 10" long.

Collards: Their taste is better after a frost but collards have the benefit of being one of the few greens that grows well through the heat of the summer as long as the soil is moist. Best quality through the season is guaranteed by making both spring and midsummer plantings. Harvest by pulling down on bottom leaves—they will snap cleanly off the main stalk.

Chinese Cabbage: Two major forms are available: Napa, or barrel-shaped Chinese cabbages, and the taller, open-headed or "lettucy" types. The lettucy types have thinner leaves and slightly less "cabbage" taste. If you start Chinese cabbage early, use peat pots or soil blocks because plants bolt early if the taproot is injured in any way, as can happen when transplanting.

Pac Choi: Read catalog descriptions carefully to discover which stand best in hot or cold temperatures. If plants bolt early, use them in stir-fries and other cooked dishes. Like Chinese cabbage, the taproot must be undisturbed during transplanting.

Turnips and Rutabagas: Turnips have a sharp taste, but rutabagas are sweet and mellow. Try the heirloom 'Gilfeather' turnip for a large, fall storage turnip that tastes like a cross between a rutabaga and a turnip. ◼

Cucurbits

BUTTERNUT SQUASH

HYBRID CANTALOUPE

CUCUMBER

GREEN SQUASH

WATERMELON

WINTER SQUASH

Temperatures: Warm. Night temperatures of 55 to 65°F and day temperatures of 75° to 85°F are ideal, although plants thrive in much warmer conditions.

Soil: Rich fertility, well-drained, moisture-retentive, with high humus levels and a pH of 6.0 to 6.8.

Planting: *Cucumbers, Summer, and Winter Squash:* In Zones 7 southward, start seed where plants are to grow once the soil is 55° to 60°F. In Zones 6 northward, plants may be started early indoors. Plant three seeds in each 4-inch plastic or peat pot about three to four weeks before the frost-free date. Thin to the best two seedlings, and transplant a week after the frost-free date, taking care not to disturb the plant's roots. If disease is a problem,

plant a second crop in late June or early July to carry you through the season.

Melons: Start seeds indoors, no more than three weeks before your frost-free date, in 4-inch peat or plastic pots. If possible, set seedlings under artificial lights, and give them a 16 hour day-length. Transplant to the garden once all danger of frost has passed. If nights are cooler than 55°F, immediately cover with row-covers or slitted plastic tunnels. Melons may also be direct-seeded once the soil is 60°F.

Spacing: *Cucumbers, Summer, and Winter Squash:* Grow two plants in each hill. Space hills 3 to 4 feet apart in rows 4 to 6 feet apart, depending on size of mature plant.

Cucumbers may also be planted 6 inches apart and thinned to 1 foot apart in rows 4 feet apart.

Melons: Plant two to three seedlings or 3 to 5 seeds in hills spaced 6 feet apart in all directions.

Cultural Care: Cover plants with row-cover material until they begin to bloom to prevent the striped cucumber beetle from transmitting cucumber blight to the plants.

In Zones 6a and cooler, black paper or plastic mulch will increase yields. Both black and IRT, (infra-red transmissive), plastics are effective, with the IRT giving slightly better yields in northern areas. Tunnels made of slitted poly or row-cover

PUMPKIN

STRIPED SQUASH

material also increase yields in the North by increasing temperatures. Remove the tunnels once flowering begins to allow insect pollination. Keep plants consistently moist, but avoid watering foliage to keep diseases down. If nutrition is low and to help prevent powdery mildew, particularly on the second crop, spray compost tea on the leaves every two to three weeks after removing the covers.

Days to Maturity: *Cucumbers:* 48 to 68. *Summer Squash:* 48 to 60. *Melons:* 70 to 85. *Winter Squash:* 85 to 10.

Average Yields: *Cucumbers:* About 12 lbs. per 10-foot row. *Summer Squash:* 2 lbs. per row foot at a minimum. *Melons:* About 1 lb. per row foot.

Winter Squash: 2 lbs. per row-foot.

Harvesting Guidelines: *Cucumbers:* Pick cucumbers while they are still slender and completely green; do not let the spot where they rest on the soil surface become yellow or they will be seedy. Cut with the petiole for longest storage life.

Summer Squash: Cut squash from plants, taking at least an inch of stem. Pick daily, taking young fruit that is no longer than 8 inches or, in the case of round cultivars, 4 to 6 inches in diameter. Do not cool squash in water if you plan to store it because this might promote fungal diseases. Instead, wipe it off with a damp cloth.

Melons: Some cantaloupes "slip" from their stems when they are ripe. Test them by gently pushing against the stem every day or so once they look mature. The pale spot on the bottom of other melons, including watermelons, will be distinctly yellow when the melon is ripe and the tendril just above the fruit's stem will have withered and died back. Cut melons that do not slip, taking the stem. Watermelons will continue to ripen after they are cut but muskmelons will not.

Winter Squash: Check for maturity by noting the size, skin toughness, and color, particularly the yellow of the patch on the bottom of the fruit. Cut squash from plants, taking at least an inch of stem. To cure winter squash for long storage, set them on racks or screens, elevated several feet above the ground, where they will receive full sun for a week to ten days. Turn the fruits every few days to expose all parts of the skin to the light. If a light frost threatens, cover the squash, but if the frost will be heavy, take them indoors until the temperature moderates again.

Storage Techniques: *Cucumbers and Summer Squash:* Use within a day of harvest, or place in a plastic bag and store it in the refrigerator for as long as a week. Summer squash freezes well when mixed with a liquid such as chopped, cooked tomatoes but does not fare well when

steamed and patted dry before being packed. Many fine pickles and relishes can be made with summer squash.

Cantaloupe, Muskmelon: Store at room temperature in a dark area. Depending on ripeness, they will last for a week or more.

Watermelons: These melons continue to ripen slightly after they are picked. Store at room temperature; they will keep for a week or two if picked when just ripe.

Winter Squash: After they are cured, store at 55° to 60°F. Many types will keep until spring.

Pests: Cucumber beetles (striped and spotted), squash bugs, aphids, pickleworms, whiteflies, and spider mites.

Diseases: Choanephora wet-rot (*Choanephora cucurbitarum*), black rot (*Didymella bryoniae*), bacterial wilt (*Erwinia tracheiphila*), powdery mildew (*Erysiphe cichoracearum*), downy mildew (*Pseudoperonospora cubensis*) and various viruses including mosaics and shoestrings.

Seed-Saving: Members of the same species in this huge family can easily cross with each other, meaning that gardeners will have to check the species of the plants they are growing and isolate, cage plants, or tape the flowers and hand pollinate as described on page 170.

Best results come during midsummer when plants are setting fruit vigorously. Set aside several plants for your seed-saving efforts; fruits will have to fully mature, so production will decline dramatically. After the fruit is fully mature and has begun to soften, cut it from the vine. Scoop out the seeds, with their encasing gel, and let them ferment for a day or two in a darkened area. Stir the seeds a couple of times a day. Mold will form on the surface and fermentation is finished when most of the seeds have settled to the bottom of the container. Add water to the bowl while stirring to remove empty seed cases and the mold. Strain the seeds and let them dry on a cookie sheet until they are dry. Store them in plastic bags.

Notes: *Cucumbers:* They yield more fruit, have greater resistance to fungal leaf diseases, and have a better chance of being straight when grown on a trellis. Deformed fruit may be caused by water stress or contact with the soil or another obstruction. If cucumbers are bitter, suspect irregular watering or nutrient deficiencies. Compost tea, sprayed on leaves once a month, not only protects plants against some fungal leaf diseases but also supplies the nutrients needed to keep them sweet-tasting. Many pest and disease problems can be minimized by keeping plants covered with row-cover material until they bloom. In the North, production can be increased by combining the covers with black paper, plastic, or IRT mulch.

Melons: If you have had trouble getting melons to mature in your climate, try growing short-season cultivars of muskmelons and "ice-box" watermelons, using IRT plastic mulch and slitted poly tunnels.

Summer Squash: This category includes zucchini, yellow straight-neck or crookneck, patty pan or scallop squash, and Lebanon squash. In all cases, they are eaten before they have matured. Plant about 10 radish seeds in every squash hill when you plant or transplant summer squash on bare ground. The radish helps to repel squash bugs and squash vine borers. If squash vine borers continue to be a problem, wrap the stems with panty hose or other light, stretchy fabric to prevent their burrowing into the tissue.

Winter Squash: Pumpkins are one of the many winter squash and are grown, harvested, and cured in the same manner as the others. Butternut is the only cultivar that does not tolerate light frost. Harvest at the first frost warning. Heavy frost can damage the skin and interfere with storage qualities of all other winter squashes. ▪

Lactuca sativa
Lettuce

Temperatures: Cool; day temperatures of 60° to 65°F and night temperatures of 50° to 55°F are ideal, although plants can tolerate temperatures close to freezing and as high as 80°F without losing quality.

Soil: Well-drained, high fertility with good nitrogen levels and humus content, pH of 5.8 to 6.8.

Planting: For very earliest crops, start seeds early indoors, about six weeks before the frost-free date. Place seeds on top of soil mix because light aids germination. Germinate at 55° to 65°F soil temperature. At soil temperatures above 68°F, seeds of many cultivars will become dormant. Grow plants at air temperatures of 45° to 50°F nights and 55° to 60°F days. Transplant to the garden when plants are six-weeks-old or have four fully developed leaves, covering them with row-cover material or poly tunnels until the spring weather has settled.

Spacing: Allow 10 inches to 1 foot between plants in rows 1 foot apart when growing plants for heads. Leaf lettuces grown for baby salad mixes can grow as close together as 1½ inches in rows 4 to 6 inches apart.

Culture: Keep young lettuce plants well weeded. Steady moisture is necessary for best growth. If fungal problems develop, thin plants to reduce humidity levels and improve air circulation.

Days to Maturity: 40 to 70.

Average Yields: One head or ½ to ¾ lb. per row-foot.

Harvesting: For whole heads, cut when plants are full size. If the cultivar is a true head lettuce, gently squeeze it to feel whether it is somewhat solid on the inside. Heads of leaf lettuces should simply be dense and close to the size listed in the cultivar description. For "cut and come again" harvests, cut off leaves about 1½ to 2 inches above the crown. Immediately after cutting heads or leaves, plunge them into very cold water and let them cool for at least half an hour. Shake or spin dry before storing. Refrigerate in vented plastic bags.

Storage: Cooled and dried lettuces store in the refrigerator for at least a week, but the best quality is guaranteed by eating them within a few days of harvest.

Pests: Aphids, cutworms, thrips, tarnished plant bugs, armyworms, slugs, and snails.

Diseases: Bottom rot, big vein, wet rot, corky root, downy mildew, powdery mildew, Botrytis gray mold, aster yellows, lettuce mosaic virus.

Seed-Saving: Lettuce cultivars can cross with each other as well as with wild lettuce (*Lactuca serriola*). Lettuce flowers are usually self-pollinating, but insects can transfer pollen from one flower to another, making crosses. If you are growing more than one type for seed-saving, cage the plants to ensure seed purity. To save seed, allow lettuces to flower. If the seed stalk is having trouble pushing through the wrapper leaves, cut an "✕" into the top of the head. Lettuce seeds do not ripen all at once. To capture the maximum number of mature seeds, shake the seed stalk into a paper bag every day, starting two weeks after they flower and continuing for three weeks. To separate the seeds from chaff, rub them in your hands, and then strain them through a fine-mesh sieve or screen.

Notes: Try a variety of lettuce cultivars to liven up both the look and taste of salads throughout the year. Plant lettuce every three weeks for continual harvests. In midsummer, shade the plants with burlap-covered tunnels or shade cloth. If these techniques are not effective on their own, cut and use baby lettuce for "salad mixes." ▪

Mescluns

ARUGULA

ENDIVE

MACHE

MIZUNA

NEW ZEALAND SPINACH

CHICORY

MALABAR

SWISS CHARD

Temperatures: Cool, with the exception of purslane, malabar spinach, and New Zealand spinach.

Soil: Fertile, moist, well-drained.
Planting: Start seeds in flats, even after weather is warm. Plant each cultivar in a separate container or row in a channel flat. Transplant to the garden, again in separate rows for different cultivars, when seedlings are three- to four-weeks old. Plant every ten to fourteen days throughout the season, changing cultivars to match environmental conditions.
Spacing: ½ inch to ¾ inch apart in the starting container. Break into 2-inch to 3- inch-long blocks at transplanting time and set these 4 inches apart in rows at least 8 inches apart.
Culture: Keep consistently moist. If you are growing successive crops on the same soil, add compost or a blended organic fertilizer between plantings.
Days to Maturity: 30 to 40 for most.
Average Yields: ½ lb. per row-foot.
Harvest: Cut leafy crops with scissors

when they are 6 inches high, leaving about 2 inches of growth above the crown. Most crops can be cut two times. In the fall or early spring, many hold their quality for a third cutting. Pick bottom leaves of malabar spinach and stem tips of New Zealand spinach. Immediately plunge leaves into cold water, drain when they are cool, and spin dry.

Storage: Keeps up to one week in the refrigerator.

Pests: Aphids, flea beetles.

Diseases: Rare because harvest is so fast.

Seed-Saving: See entries of related crops for information about seed-saving.

Notes: *Arugula:* Grows well in spring and fall but tastes bitter if grown in high temperatures. Responds well to growing under plastic shade cloth.

Curly cress, garden cress: Cress germinates quickly and grows to harvestable size in as little as ten days.

Edible chrysanthemum: Cut very small to avoid bitterness. Stands well in fall.

Endive, Escarole: Blanch by setting a flower pot over the plant when it is almost mature.

Lettuce: Make a mix of at least five cultivars of different colors and textures. 'Cocarde', 'Summer Bibb', 'Two Star', 'Red Fire', and 'Parris Island Cos' is a mix that works well in moderate temperatures. Experiment to find mixes for each season.

Mache: Grows in extremely cold conditions and thrives in compacted soil.

Malabar Spinach: In Zone 6 and colder, start plants early indoors, about four weeks before the last expected frost, in 3" peat pots or soil blocks, and transplant to the garden once the danger of frost has passed. Plants require staking. Harvest by picking leaves throughout the summer. This beautiful East Indian crop is good raw in salads or cooked in curries or with sauces.

Miner's Lettuce, Claytonia: Grows well

in early spring and late fall in Zones 6 and northward. In many locations in Zones 7 to 9, it will grow all winter long. Cold frames and poly tunnels prolong the harvest deep into the winter and also allow very early spring planting.

Mizuna: Grows well in cool conditions but tolerates summer temperatures in most of the U.S. when it is harvested young. If plants get ahead of you and become too large for salads, cut them under the crown and lightly braise or steam them. A dash of lemon or lightly flavored sauce makes mizuna an excellent cooked vegetable.

Mustard: Grows well in spring or late summer and early fall. With protection or in warm climates, it stands through the fall and winter. Space salad crops only an inch or so apart in the row. To get double duty from them, thin them as you harvest, leaving a plant every 8 to 10 inches in rows 12 inches apart. Let these crops grow to braising size—from 8 to 10 inches tall—before cutting leaves or whole plants. High temperatures increase the "heat" in the taste. If leaves become too strongly flavored, remember that cooking reduces the bite and turns mustard into a somewhat mild-flavored green. For a visual treat, grow both red and green cultivars.

New Zealand Spinach: New Zealand spinach is used for a green in warm areas where spinach and other greens have trouble. This plant is amazingly resilient and survives both wet and dry periods. Few pests and diseases are attracted to it though slugs and root rots can be a problem. Begin by planting only a few plants because yields are high if you harvest by picking off stem tips and leaves rather than whole plants. This crop has very different culinary qualities depending on how it is used, so try it both raw and cooked before you make a final decision about it.

Orach: Germination can be erratic for this lovely salad crop. Increase your chances of success by freezing the seed

for two to four weeks before planting it. This crop grows well as either a spring or fall crop. Spring crops will yield for several months if you keep the soil moist, provide afternoon shade in hot climates, and pick leaves rather than the whole plant. When planting in midsummer for a fall crop, use the ice cube trick. Place one seed in each cell of an ice-cube tray, add some water, and freeze. Plant the ice cubes 4 inches apart in a 1-inch deep furrow, covering each cube with no more than ½ inch of soil.

Purslane: Cultivated purslane has much larger leaves than the common weed you probably remove from your garden. Some cultivars are also 'golden,' adding a lovely color contrast to salads. But cultivated or not, purslane is delicious and very nutritious. This succulent green has a high amount of the omega-3 oils that have been found to be so important for the health of your heart and arteries. Exercise patience, and wait to plant purslane until the soil has warmed to 60°F or above since it, like its weedy cousin, is a warm-weather plant that does not tolerate frost.

Radiccio: Grow radicchio just as you grow lettuce. Although great advances have been made recently in breeding more uniform cultivars that tolerate heat as well as head up well, this plant is still close enough to its wild relations to give some variation. For a home gardener however, this poses no problem because the leaves of this plant taste the same no matter whether they have formed a head or not. Choose cultivars of radiccio based on the season when you'll grow them, spring or fall. ■

LETTUCE PLANTED IN A BED

Abelmoschus esculentus

Okra

Temperatures: Warm; minimum of 50°F nights, 75° to 85°F days, although plants will tolerate warmer conditions.

Soil: Minimum temperature of 70°F; moderate to high fertility, high humus content, moderately moist, very good drainage; pH of 6.3 to 7.0.

Planting: In Zones 7 and northward, start seeds early indoors, about four weeks before the frost-free date. If you have fluorescent lights, give seedlings a 14-to 16-hour day. Start in individual peat pots or soil blocks. Germinate at 80°F and grow at 65° to 70°F. Transplant to the garden about a week after your frost-free date. In Zones 8 to 11 sow okra directly in the garden.

Spacing: In Zones 6 and north, allow 1 foot between plants in all directions; in Zones 7 and south, allow 1½ feet.

Culture: Plants require at least 1 inch of water a week and profit from midseason side-dressing or foliar feeding, even in good soils. If fertility is low, foliar feed with weak compost tea every two weeks.

Days to Maturity: 50 to 65 from transplanting.

Average Yields: 1 to 2 lbs. per plant in average conditions.

Harvest: Cut off pods when they are only 3 to 4 inches long for best flavor.

Storage: Store in plastic bags in the refrigerator for three to four days. Okra freezes well and makes a good pickle.

Pests: Corn earworms and other caterpillars, stink bugs, and root-knot nematodes. Aphids generally indicate that the plant is water-stressed.

Diseases: Fusarium wilt (*Fusarium* spp.), powdery mildew (S*phaerotheca fuliginea*), and a flower and pod rot called (*Choanephora cucurbitarum*) that causes black spots on tissue before it browns and rots. Compost tea sprays may prevent this disease and sulfur spray kills it.

Seed-Saving: The perfect flowers of this annual are self-pollinating, but insects often cross-pollinate okra. Bag the flowers the night before flowers open, and leave the bag in place for two days. Let pods dry on the plant. Wear gloves to harvest and remove the seeds from the pods.

Notes: In Zones 3 to 5, a black plastic mulch on the soil surface usually improves yields by raising the soil temperature. Use slitted poly tunnels over the plants to increase the air temperature. In Zone 7 and warmer, cut back the top 2 feet of each plant in midsummer to encourage flowering and fruiting sideshoots. The edible flowers resemble those of the related hibiscus. ∎

Pisum sativum

Peas

Temperatures: Cool; 45° to 50°F nights, 55° to 75°F days.

Soil: Very deep, high levels of phosphorus and potassium. If soil is high in nitrogen, plants will produce luxuriant foliage and fewer pods than normal. Conversion of atmospheric nitrogen will also drop. Keep the soil evenly moist and provide good drainage to prevent root rots. Maintain pH levels between 6.0 to 7.0.

Planting: Plant seeds outdoors where plants are to grow as soon as the soil can be worked in spring, generally about four to six weeks before the last expected frost. Plant fall crops about eight to ten weeks before first expected frost date.

Spacing: Plant 2 to 3 inches apart in rows 1 foot apart.

Culture: Tall cultivars must be supported on trellises or nets, but even dwarf types yield better if vines are kept off the ground. Push 3-foot-tall twiggy brush into the soil about 6 inches away from the pea row to provide support for these smaller plants. Depending on the characteristics of taller types, they may need supports as high as 5 feet tall.

Days to Maturity: 52 to 80.

Average Yields: 2 lbs. per 10 row-feet of English, or shell, peas; 2 lbs. per row-foot for snap or snow peas.

Harvesting: Pick snow peas when pods are a few inches long, before they have begun to toughen. Pick snap peas when pods are plump and either before or after peas have begun to fill out, depending on which you prefer. Pick English peas when peas have expanded to fill the pod but before they are so large that they create bulges. When in doubt, hold the pod up to the sunlight to see the peas inside.

Storage: Peas store well in the refrigerator for up to five days but taste best if eaten within only ½ hour of picking.

Pests: Aphids in high-nitrogen soils, pea weevils, thrips, pea moths, and leafminers.

Diseases: Root rots, Fusarium wilt (*Fusarium oxysporum, F. pisi*), blight (*Ascochyta* spp., *Pseudomonas pisi*), powdery mildew (*Erysiphe polygoni*), mosaic virus.

Seed-Saving: The perfect flowers are primarily wind-pollinated but can be crossed by insects. To be absolutely sure that you aren't getting crossing, cage dwarf plants or cover them with light row-cover material. Flowers of taller, trellised types can be individually cloaked, or a whole group can be wrapped in row-cover material. Leave the pods on the plant until they are dry. Toward the end of the period, check the pods daily. If pods look in danger of opening, pick them off. Remove the seeds from the pods and let them dry for a few more days. To check if they are dry, place a few on a hard surface and hit them with a hammer. Dry seeds will shatter, but wet ones will dent or mush. Once they are dry, pack them in airtight containers, label them, and store them in the freezer. Freezing is necessary to kill pea weevils. Leave the seeds in the freezer until time to plant them the following year.

Notes: Fall crops often develop fungal diseases. To prevent problems, spray plants with weak compost tea every seven to ten days once they are a month old. If they still develop fungus, use a mixture of baking powder and fine horticultural oil, as directed in Chapter 9 page 296, "Preventing Weeds, Pests, and Diseases," to kill the fungus.

Avoid problems in the spring with fungal diseases by planting only in well-drained soil and choosing disease-resistant cultivars. ■

Rheum rhabarbarum
Rhubarb

Temperatures: Hardy from Zones 3 to 8.
Soil: Deep, rich, moist, high humus content, well-drained, with a pH of 5.0 to 6.5.

Add at least 2 gallons of fully finished compost to each planting hole.
Planting: Plant roots about six weeks before last expected frost in deeply prepared holes. Cover the crown and buds with 2 inches of soil. Once plants are established, roots can be divided as soon as the spring soil can be worked.
Spacing: A minimum of 3 feet apart in rows 6 feet apart.
Culture: Keep plants well-supplied with moisture, irrigating in dry periods. In spring and early summer, flower stalks will form. Snap these off before the buds open to allow the plant to conserve energy. In cold climates, mulch the plants for winter with 8 inches to 1 foot of straw after the top of the soil has frozen.
Days to Maturity: A full year before first small harvest.
Average Yields: Varies with the age of the plant; fully established plants give 4 to 5 lbs. of stems each year.
Harvesting: As soon as stems are large enough, cut them an inch or so above the crown. Always leave at least four to six stems on each plant. Cut off all the green leaf material and compost it. It contains a chemical that is poisonous if eaten but which breaks down in the compost pile.
Storage: Stems keep in the refrigerator for up to a week but quality is best when they are eaten within a few days of harvest. Cooked rhubarb freezes well.
Pests: Rhubarb curculios and Japanese beetles.
Diseases: Fusarium wilt (*Fusarium* spp), Verticium wilt (*Verticillium* spp.), southern blight (*Sclerotium rolfsii*), crown rot (*Phytophthora cactorum, P. parasitica*).
Seed-Saving: Simply divide plants to enlarge your planting.
Notes: Rhubarb plants can thrive for many years, but productivity will decline if they become overcrowded or the soil fertility is not adequate. Prevent nutrient deficiencies by pulling back the mulch each spring and top-dressing with at least 1 inch of fully finished compost over the entire root zone. Lift and divide plants every five years, using the root divisions to increase your planting; or to give to friends. ■

Solanaceae

EGGPLANT

Temperatures: *Eggplant, Pepper, and Tomato:* Warm. Night temperatures of 55° to 65°F and days of 75° to 85°F, though eggplants and peppers tolerate warmer days. *Potato:* Moderate. Night temperatures of 50° to 60°F and day temperatures of 70° to 80°F.
Soil: Well-drained, moderately fertile, humus-rich, with a pH of 5.5 to 6.8. *Potato:* pH of 5.2 to 5.8 is ideal but will tolerate a pH of 6.0 to 6.5.
Planting: *Eggplant, Pepper, and Tomato:* Best started indoors in almost all locations. Start peppers and eggplants eight to ten weeks before the last expected frost and tomatoes six to eight weeks before the last expected frost. Germinate seeds at a soil temperature of 80°F and grow the seedlings at night tempatures of 50°F or above and days of 65° to 75°F. If using artificial lights, keep them on a 12-hour day-length.

Potato: The potato itself is the "seed" of the plant. The tuber is actually an enlarged stem and the eyes are buds from which new stems, roots, and potatoes will grow. Cut seed potatoes into pieces about the size of an egg, each with at least one, but preferably two, eyes. Let the cut portion callus over for a day or two to prevent rotting. Many people plant as much as a month before the last spring frost, but this early planting can lead to fungal diseases, and growth

PEPPER

TOMATO

is slow until spring temperatures settle. If fungal diseases have been a problem, wait to plant until the soil is at least 50°F.

Spacing: *Eggplant, Pepper, and Tomato:* 2 to 2½ feet apart in rows 2 to 2½ feet apart, depending on size of cultivar. *Potato:* Plant pieces about 1 foot apart in rows 2 to 3 feet apart. Plant only 3 to 4 inches deep to avoid rotting.

Culture: *Eggplant, Pepper, and Tomato:* Transplant seedlings to the garden when night temperatures are consistently 50°F or above, although tomatoes can tolerate night temperatures of 45°F. If this is impossible, use plastic, IRT, or black paper mulch with poly tunnels, row covers, or Wall-o-waters™ to increase soil temperatures. Supply steady moisture levels while fruits are forming to keep the flavor mild and sweet. Do not over-fertilize, particularly with nitrogen-bearing materials, or plants may produce more leaves than fruit. Monitor for pests and diseases every few days, checking under leaves and on growing tips.

Tomato: Once plants are established and summer has come, keep soil temperatures cool by covering soil or black mulches with a layer of straw. Remove suckers on indeterminate plants every three to four days, also tying them to supports as necessary.

Potato: Tubers form only above the seed potato, so it's important to provide

lots of space for them to develop. As the plants grow, heap soil from the pathways over them, covering all but a few inches of the top of the plant. Continue to hill the plants this way every week to ten days until midseason. Straw mulches can be used in place of the soil as long as they really cover the tubers. Tubers that are exposed to light will develop the green-colored solanine, a chemical that can make you sick. Steady moisture is important to potatoes; irrigate in dry periods. To maintain the high fertility levels potatoes require, drench the soil around each plant with compost tea or a seaweed/fish emulsion in late June and again in mid-July. Foliar sprays every two to three weeks with a weak compost tea help to prevent some of the worst fungal diseases and also give needed nutrition.

Days to Maturity: (from transplanting): *Eggplant:* 55 to 70. *Pepper:* 60 to 90. *Tomato:* 60 to 80. *Potato:* 60 to 120 from planting.

Average Yields: *Eggplant:* ¾ to 1 lb. per row foot. *Pepper:* five to seven fruit per plant for bell peppers, variable for hots. *Potato:* 4 to 6 lbs. per plant. *Tomato:* 1½ lbs. per row foot at a minimum.

Harvest: *Eggplant:* Cut when they look full size and still have shiny skin. Once the gloss begins to dull, seeds are forming, and the meat is becoming bitter-tasting. Cut with at least an inch of petiole to

guarantee good storage.

Pepper: Pick the first pepper on each plant just a bit early to promote more flowering and fruit set. Cut peppers, taking some stem, to prevent harming the somewhat brittle plants. To get high yields of red or other colored bell peppers, allow the fruit on half your plants to begin to mature once a few green peppers have been harvested from them. Avoid some rots by picking these fruits when they are 50 to 75 percent colored. They will finish coloring if you hold them in dark conditions at 45° to 50°F.

Potato: When plants bloom, tubers are forming. If you are careful not to greatly disturb the plant, you can dig directly under it two weeks after it has flowered and pull out a couple of small new potatoes. Wait to harvest the balance until the foliage dies back in the late summer or fall. To avoid some fungal diseases that develop in storage, dig the potatoes when the soil is moderately dry, before the first frost. Do not wash the potatoes but set them in a dark spot to let the soil on the skin dry before storing.

Tomato: Pick fruit when it is at least half-colored for a vine-ripened flavor. Many cultivars split if left to ripen fully on the vine, particularly if it rains during their last day or two of coloring. Set fruit in a dark, warm place to finish ripening. Avoid leaving overripe or rotting fruit on the vine or ground because disease spores will travel through your planting.

Storage: *Eggplant:* Wipe off muddy fruit with a damp towel if necessary, but do not submerge in water. Store in a vented plastic bag in the refrigerator for as long as a week. Eggplant is difficult to freeze well but can be dried in a dehydrator.

Pepper: Wipe peppers with a damp cloth, and store at 45° to 55°F in dark conditions. They will keep for a week or more. Peppers freeze well. Do not blanch. Simply remove the core and slice, dice, or pack whole in airtight bags.

Potato: Keep well in a root cellar or basement held at about 40°F with 85 percent humidity. Store in paper bags that allow some air circulation, and check often to remove any soft ones.

Solanaceae continued

Tomato: Store tomatoes in dark, warm conditions, at temperatures between 45° and 70°F. Do not place them in the refrigerator because cell membranes burst at temperatures of 40°F and below. Tomatoes can be preserved by canning, freezing, or drying.

Pests: Colorado potato beetles, flea beetles, striped cucumber beetles, aphids, russet mites, spider mites, blister beetles, root-knot nematodes, leafhoppers, cutworms, and whiteflies. *Pepper:* Corn earworms, European corn borers, pepper weevils. *Potato:* Potato tuberworms. *Tomato:* Tomato fruitworms, tomato pinworms, tomato hornworms, and leaf miners.

Diseases: Verticillium wilt (*Verticillium* spp.), Fusarium wilt (*Fusarium oxysporum, F. lycopersicae*), Phomopsis blight (Phomopsis vexans), anthracnose (*Colletotrichum* spp.), alternaria blight (*Alternaria solani*), southern blight (*Sclerotium rolfsii*), tobacco mosaic and cucumber mosaic (viruses), late blight (*Phytophthora infestans*), leaf curl (viruses).

Potato: Scab (*Streptomyces scabies*), Scurf (*Pellicularia filamentosa*).

Seed-Saving: *Eggplant, Pepper, and Tomato:* The perfect flowers are usually self- or wind-pollinated, but shaking the blossoms helps to ensure fertilization. Enclose blossoms in row-cover material to avoid insect pollination. Save seed from at least six to ten plants. Pick tomatoes when almost mature, peppers and eggplant when completely mature. Squeeze or scrape the seeds into a bowl. Include the surrounding gel of tomato seeds, and add water to the others. Let tomato seeds form a white mold on the surface of the bowl. When it completely covers the seeds, add water and let the good seeds sink to the bottom. Pour seeds of all species through a strainer and dry on a ceramic plate. Stir several times a day to prevent seeds from sticking together.

Potato: Save tubers from plants you like and replant them the following year.

Notes: Flowers will abort in cool temperatures or when plants are water-stressed. ■

Rumex scutatus
Sorrel

Temperatures: Cool; hardy in Zones 3 to 8. Best flavor is guaranteed when leaves grow at night temperatures of 40° to 50°F, and daytime temperatures are no warmer than 75°F.

Soil: Moderate fertility, well-drained, high humus content, pH of 5.5 to 6.5.

Planting: Start seeds early indoors, about six weeks before the last expected spring frost for harvest the first fall. Otherwise, direct-seed where plants are to grow after the frost-free date.

Spacing: Plant seeds only 4 inches apart in rows 1 to 1½ feet apart, and thin seedlings to 8 inches apart in the row.

Culture: This easy-care perennial doesn't require much work. Weed, irrigate in dry periods, and top-dress with ½ inch of fully finished compost each year in late winter or early spring. Prevent sorrel from becoming a weed in the garden by snapping off all the developing flower stalks before the blooms open.

Days to Maturity: 100 days from seed for first small harvest, a full year for more-substantial harvests.

Average Yields: About ½ lb. per row-foot per year.

Harvest: Snip off largest bottom leaves in the fall of the first year for transplanted crops. If you planted seeds directly outdoors, wait until the following spring. Always remove the largest leaves, but let four to seven young ones stay on the plant to continue photosynthesis. Wash

and cool leaves immediately after picking.

Storage: Sorrel only keeps for a couple of days in the refrigerator. It's best to pick on the morning or evening you plan to use it.

Pests: Leaf miners, slugs, aphids, and flea beetles.

Diseases: Rarely bothered but can develop root rots in soggy soils.

Seed-Saving: Rather than saving seed, most gardeners divide the roots of three-year-old plants. However, if you do want to save seeds, put a cage around at least ten plants to prevent them from crossing with the weedy sorrels that may grow around the perimeter of the garden. Let insects into the cage to carry pollen from the male to the female flowers. When the seeds begin to look brown and dry, bag them with row-cover material so they don't drop onto the soil.

Notes: The earliest spring leaves, picked young and tiny, are a great addition to salad mixes. As the weather warms, the plant becomes more pungent and lemony. Use larger leaves picked later in the season for a traditional sorrel soup or as an addition to cooked dishes. They can also be cut into a thin chiffonade and sprinkled over cold tuna, egg, or potato salad for a burst of wonderful lemon taste. ■

Spinacia oleracea
Spinach

Temperatures: Cool; night temperatures of 45° to 50°F and day temperatures of 60° to 65°F are ideal. Bolting occurs when plants are exposed to long days and temperatures of 75°F and above, or conversely, when temperatures are consistently 40°F and below.

Soil: High in nitrogen, well-drained but moist, with a pH of 6.5 to 7.5.

Planting: Start seeds outdoors in very early spring where plants are to grow as soon as the soil can be worked. Use row- covers to protect plants from freezing temperatures and any late snows. Plant every seven to ten days, scheduling so that plants will mature before temperatures are consistently above 75°F. Fall crops can be planted 6 weeks before the first expected fall frost.

Spacing: Plant seeds 1 to 2 inches apart in rows 1 to 1½ feet apart. Thin plants as they grow, removing alternate plants until remaining plants stand 8 to 10 inches apart.

Culture: Weed young plants early and regularly, and keep the soil consistently moist. If leaves look yellow, foliar-feed with compost tea or a solution of liquid seaweed/fish emulsion. Keep plants thinned so that leaves of adjacent plants do not touch, because crowding also promotes early bolting.

Days to Maturity: 36 to 45 from seed.

Average Yields: 2 lbs. per row-foot.

Harvesting: Thin alternate plants until the remainder stand 8 to 10 inches apart. To harvest whole plants, cut the main stem just below the crown so that leaves stay intact on the plant. To prolong the harvest of fall crops, break off bottom leaves as you need them. Immediately cool plants or leaves in very cold water for ½ hour and shake dry before refrigerating.

Storage: Store in the refrigerator in vented plastic bags for up to five days. Spinach freezes beautifully.

Pests: Leaf miners, flea beetles, slugs, and aphids.

Diseases: Downy mildew, rust, fusarium wilt, and cucumber mosaic virus.

Seed-Saving: Spinach plants are either male or female. Pollen from the male plant is carried to the female plants by the wind. To avoid crossing, grow only one cultivar for seed saving unless you enclose the whole planting in a cage or row covers. Let seeds dry on the plant; then remove them from the seed stalk.

Notes: If you haven't yet tried some of the new smooth-leafed types of spinach, make it a point to grow them. They have the same taste as the savoyed (wrinkled) types but are far easier to clean.

Spinach plants can be overwintered for extra-early spring harvests. Plant seeds only three to four weeks before the first expected fall frost, and let them grow without harvesting, other than picking to thin the row. After the top inch of the soil surface has frozen, mulch the plants with at least 8 inches of straw. In spring, pull back the mulch as soon as night temperatures are likely to fall no lower than 20°F Should they dip below this, replace the mulch until the weather warms again. The overwintered plants will bolt quickly because of the temperature fluctuations they have experienced, but with a large enough planting, you can be assured of fresh spinach for several weeks very early in the season. ■

Ipomoea batatas

Sweet Potato

Temperatures: Warm; night temperatures no lower than 55°F and day temperatures between 80° to 90°F are ideal. Plants do not tolerate freezing temperatures and grow slowly in cool conditions.

Soil: Average fertility, high humus levels, moist but well-drained, with a pH of 5.5 to 6.0. Calcium, magnesium, and boron should all be in balance. If not, foliar-spray with seaweed/fish emulsion and liq-

uid seaweed every four weeks throughout the season.

Planting: Sweet potatoes are started from "slips." Purchase them in the spring from seed companies. You can grow your own slips indoors six to eight weeks before the frost-free date by simply laying the tubers on good garden soil and covering them with straw. Choose a reliably warm cold frame, greenhouse, or even a windowsill. When the slips are about 6 to 8 inches long, break them off and root them in a flat of fresh potting soil. In about a week, when they have roots, plant them outdoors, making certain that all danger of frost has past.

Spacing: In Zones 6 and colder, plant slips 1 to 1½ feet apart in rows 2 to 3 feet apart. In Zones 7 to 11, allow 3 feet in all directions. Sweet potatoes can be trained up trellises in all climates. A-frame trellises with nylon netting give excellent sun exposure and support.

Culture: In Zones 4, 5, and, colder, black plastic mulch and row-covers or slitted poly tunnels increase yields dramatically by raising temperatures. In all climates, keep plants weed-free when they are young. Once they become established, the plants will shade out all possible competition.

Days to Maturity: 95 to 120 from transplanting.

Average Yields: 15 to 30 tubers per plant in optimum conditions; 5 to 10 tubers in cool climates.

Harvest: Dig by hand to avoid bruising the tubers. Choose a warm, dry day a week or so before you expect the first frost. Brush the soil off the tubers and cure them in 60° to 75°F, 80 percent humidity.

Storage Techniques: Sweet potatoes keep well for several months at 60°F and 80 to 90 percent humidity. Do not expose them to cool root-cellar conditions.

Pests: Sweet potato weevils, root-knot nematodes, sweet potato flea beetles.

Diseases: Black rot, scurf, pox, and fusarium wilt.

Seed-Saving: Propagate sweet potatoes from the tubers you save over the winter.

Notes: In Asia, the vines are cooked and eaten as often as the tubers. ■

Umbelliferae

CARROT

CELERY

SALSIFY

CELERIAC

PARSNIP

Temperatures: Moderate. Night temperatures of 50 to 55°F and day temperatures of 65 to 80°F. *Carrots and Parsnips:* Grow slowly in temperatures as low as 45°F; mature roots withstand freezing. *Celery:* Temperatures above 80°F make plants stringy.

Soil: Deep, sandy or loose, well-drained, fertile, moist, and rock-free, with a pH of 5.5 to 6.8. Boron deficiencies cause hollow heart; spray foliage with liquid seaweed to prevent. *Carrots and Parsnips:* High nitrogen levels can make roots fork.

Planting: *Carrot:* Wait until the threat of severe frost has passed, and seed where plants are to grow. Plant successively, every three or four weeks until three

months before expected fall frost date. Seeds require as long as three weeks to germinate.

Celery and Celeriac: Start seed early indoors, about ten to twelve weeks before the frost free date. Seeds may take several weeks to germinate, even at ideal soil temperatures of 75° to 80°F. Grow on at night temperatures of 55° to 60°F, day temperatures of 65° to 70°F, if possible. Plants are slow-starting but must not be allowed to dry out or get too cool during their seedling phase. Transplant to the garden once all danger of frost has passed. If nights threaten to dip below 55°F, use row covers or other season extension devices to protect plants.

Parsnip, Salsify, and Scorzonera: Use

only fresh seed since it loses viability quickly. Soak seed overnight in weak compost tea or liquid seaweed, diluted to half the strength recommended on the bottle. Direct-seed in spring or early summer, once the soil is 55°F or above. Cover seed furrows with vermiculite and row-cover material. Seed will take three to four weeks to germinate. In Zones 4 and northward, seeds can be started indoors in 3-inch peat pots, about six weeks before the frost-free date. Slit the bottom of the peat pot when you transplant to the garden after all danger of frost has passed.

Spacing: *Carrot, Parsnip, Salsify, and Scorzonera:* Plant seeds ½ inch apart in rows 12 inches apart. Thin to 2 inches apart as you weed. *Celery and celeriac:* 8 inches to 1 foot between plants in rows 1½ to 2 feet apart.

Culture: All umbelliferae must be kept as weed-free as possible, but this is particularly true for the root crops. Begin by flame weeding the beds shortly before seeds sprout. Then weed, thinning as necessary, as soon as second leaves are fully expanded. Weed and thin at least twice more through the season. All species perform best with steady moisture levels and high nutrient levels. Keep rows well watered all through the season and beginning in midseason, side-dress with compost, drench with a cup of compost tea for every row foot of growing area, or foliar feed with a seaweed/fish emulsion, every month.

Days to Maturity: *Carrot:* 55 to 80. *Celery and Celeriac:* 80 to 110. *Parsnip, Salsify, and Scorzonera:* 110 to 120.

Average Yields: *Carrot:* 1 to 1½ lbs. per row-foot. *Celery and Celeriac:* 2 to 3½ lbs. per row-foot. *Parsnip, Salsify, and Scorzonera:* ¾ lb. per row foot.

Harvest: *Carrot:* Crops develop their sugar content during the last three weeks before they are mature. Pull and taste-test a carrot or two to determine whether they are ready to be harvested. To avoid pulling off the tops, loosen soil with a spading fork before pulling.

Celery: Cut celery just below the soil surface. Cool in cold water immediately. To prolong the harvest of individual plants, snap off one or two outer stems as needed. Mature celery can stand a light frost. Prolong fall harvests by piling mulch around the plants and covering with row-cover material.

Celeriac: Pull after the first few frosts. Use a spading fork to loosen the soil around the roots and pull them free. If you are planning to eat it within a week or so, use a sharp knife to trim off the stringy roots coming from the central "knob." It will keep well in the refrigerator. Always peel celeriac before using it raw in salads or adding to stews, soups, and stir-fries.

Celery: Cut just below the soil surface. Cool in cold water immediately. To prolong the harvest of individual plants, snap off one or two outer stems as needed. Mature celery can stand a light frost. Prolong fall harvests by piling mulch around the plants and covering with row-cover material.

Parsnip, Salsify, and Scorzonera: These roots taste best after hard frosts. Wait to dig until there have been at least two frosts, one of which has been heavy. Use a spading fork to loosen the soil along the sides of the row, and then grasp the top of the root and pull. You can also leave these in the ground over the winter. To do this, mulch plants heavily (1 to 2 feet) after the tops have died back in the fall and the top surface of the ground has frozen. Dig the following spring before top growth begins.

Storage Techniques: *Carrot, Parsnip, Salsify, and Scorzonera:* For immediate use, wash right away and twist off the tops. They will keep in the refrigerator for several weeks. If harvesting for long term root-cellar storage, cut off the stems about an inch above the root and do not wash them. Instead, set them in a cool, dark spot and let the soil dry. Then layer them in boxes or bury in moist sand or sawdust, and store at temperatures close to freezing. They will keep until spring. Carrots also freeze, dry, pickle, and pressure-can well.

Celeriac: For long-term storage, let the soil dry on the knob. Place it in peat moss or sand in the root cellar. It will keep for a minimum of three months.

Celery: Drain cooled plants, and store in the refrigerator for at least a week. To store in the root cellar, pull plants, taking some root, and pack in dry leaves or straw.

Pests: Aphids, slugs, caterpillars, carrot rust flies, carrot weevils, root-knot nematode, and wireworm.

Diseases: *Carrot:* Black rot (*Alternaria radicinia*), leaf blight (*Alternaria dauci*), leaf spot (*Septoria apiicola, Cercospora carotae, Xanthomonas carotae*), and aster yellows.

Celery and Celeriac: Also pink rot (*Sclerotinia sclerotiorum*), bacterial soft rot (*Erwinia carotovora*), and celery and cucumber mosaics (viruses).

Parsnip, Salsify, and Scorzonera: Canker and leaf spot (*Itersonilia perplexans*).

Seed-Saving: *Carrot, Parsnip, Salsify, and Scorzonera:* These biennials must be overwintered. Mulch them deeply in the garden or keep roots in the root cellar and replant in spring. The flowers are self-infertile. Bag them with row-cover material before they open. Secure the bottom of the cloaking material with a twist-tie so you can easily open it. Each morning, for at least two weeks, but preferably three or four weeks, open a few bags at a time, and use a brush to move the pollen from one flower to others. Rebag the flowers to prevent insects from pollinating.

Celery and celeriac: These biennials will cross with wild celery. Grow seed-saving crops under row covers if wild celery grows in your area or you allow more than one type of celery or celeriac to flower; otherwise, don't worry about crossing. In Zones 6 and southward, mulch plants heavily to overwinter in the garden. In Zones 5 and northward, overwinter plants in the root cellar. To do this, dig the roots, cut back the top growth and "plant" the celery or celeriac in damp sand with the crowns exposed. Leave in the cold, dark root cellar at temperatures just above freezing for the winter. In spring, set out overwintered plants or uncover mulched ones. Allow insects to pollinate the flowers. Cut the umbels before seeds shatter to the ground, and finish drying inside.

Notes: *Carrot, Parsnip, Salsify, and Scorzonera:* To keep seeds evenly moist while they are germinating, make furrows as usual, but fill them with vermiculite. Seed on the surface, water thoroughly, and cover the rows with a row-cover or untreated burlap. Water every day in warm sunny conditions, less frequently in cloudy moist weather. Keep roots covered with soil while they are growing; green shoulders are not only unattractive, they also taste bitter. If wireworms or nematodes are a problem, apply beneficial nematodes to the soil as directed on the package. With high enough populations, they may also prey on rust fly larvae and weevils.

Celery: Blanching is not commonplace anymore, primarily because new cultivars have a milder taste than old-fashioned types. However, if you hanker after some blanched celery, pile mulch around the stems several weeks before you plan to harvest. If your celery develops black heart, a condition that makes the center leaf-tips turn brown and rot, the soil may be low in calcium, high in potassium, and too dry. Test and amend the soil to balance calcium and potassium, and keep plants moist. ■

CHAPTER 7

HERB GARDENS

*H*erb gardens are satisfying to create and tend. Unlike those plantings that depend on blooms to make them beautiful, well-designed herb gardens look spectacular at any time of the year. Herbs are so easy to grow and have so few pest and disease problems that they rarely create extra work.

Many people grow herbs among vegetables or mixed into flower beds rather than in separate herb gardens. This method allows you to take advantage of herbs' benefits in places where they are most needed. For example, a mixture of garlic chives (*Allium tuberosum*) and lavender (*Lavandula),* used as an underplanting for roses, discourages Japanese beetles from attacking roses, while flowering dill (*Anethum graveolens*) and chervil (*Anthriscus cereifolium*) attract other beneficial insects.

Herbs make ideal container plants, too. If

A COLLECTION OF SAGE plants is as decorative as it is useful for cooking, hair-rinses, and dried herbal wreaths.

your outdoor space is limited, you may want to plant your herbs in pots. Containers can complement the looks of the herbs and give you maximum flexibility for location.

Most herbs have a long period of usefulness. Unlike many vegetables and fruits, many perennial herbs can be picked at any time during the growing season and some are generally picked before or after they bloom, but even they can be used while they are flowering. Annual herbs taste strongest before they bloom. Experienced gardeners work around this by picking consistently to prolong the life of the herbs as well as making second and sometimes third plantings of the fastest-maturing species.

When you plan an herb garden, you may think first of the many ways you can use herbs in cooking. But once you start growing them, you'll have a large enough supply to begin experimenting with other uses. Herbal preparations are amazingly easy to make. From herbal vinegars to potpourris, infused oils, salves, and skin creams, all it takes to create these treasures is a little time and a few simple ingredients and kitchen tools. In this chapter, you will be introduced to many herbal preparations, and given basic instructions.

VARYING FOLIAGE COLORS of herbs give this formal garden a distinct look.

Sometimes this will spur your creativity, and you'll be inspired to dry a collection of thymes for everyone on your gift list. But if you don't react this way to overwhelming abundance, you may want to consider creating an informal herb garden where you can grow only as much as you need of each species.

Guidelines for Design

Formal gardens are generally based on geometric shapes. For example, the perimeter of the garden may be a square or rectangle, while the interior space is divided into smaller rectangles, squares, or triangles. Circular designs are also common, with either pie-shaped or curved divisions inside the outline. In some cases, the pathways of the garden form the structure of the design, while in others, the

DESIGNING HERB GARDENS

SAY THE WORDS "HERB GARDEN," and many people conjure up a picture of a formal stylized design, such as a knot garden or a geometrically patterned bed. Most herbs are ideal subjects for formal designs because all it takes is a little pruning every year to coax them into the tidy forms that make up the structure of formal gardens. And the wide range of green tones displayed by herbs makes it easy to create a garden built around a subtle tapestry of hues.

Herb gardens certainly do not have to be formal. Increasingly, gardeners are creating informal designs or using herbs as elements in other gardens. In a formal design, simply for appearances' sake, you usually have to grow much more of particular herbs than you may plan to use.

INFORMAL HERB GARDENS can be planned according to the herbs you'll actually use and the quantities you'll need rather than the amount required in the design of a formal herb garden.

KITCHEN HERB GARDENS needn't be all work and no play. Here, marigolds liven up a collection of culinary herbs.

herbs themselves create it. In either case, for the best results, keep the lines simple. Formal gardens look good only if they are well maintained. You'll have to keep up with weeding, pruning, and edging if you want the garden to continue to look its best. Fortunately, these gardens are often easier to maintain than informal ones because the spaces are so clearly delineated, but again, routine maintenance is always easiest if the lines of the design are simple.

You can build informal herb gardens in any shape that is convenient. Although they are designed more for function than for aesthetics, you'll probably enjoy informal herb gardens more and take better care of them if you give careful thought to the design. Refer back to the guidelines in Chapter 1, "Preparing to Garden," page 12, for useful tips.

Kitchen herb gardens. Whether you live in a city apartment or a house with a yard, you'll want to grow the herbs you use most frequently. It's a treat to have parsley (*Petroselinum crispum*), dill (*Anethum graveolens*), basil (*Ocimum basilicum*), tarragon (*Artemisia dracunculus*), and chervil (*Anthriscus cereifolium*) just outside the door. So whether it's a container garden, or a bed in the ground, be

sure to plant some kitchen herbs to use in your cooking.

Kitchen herb gardens are ideal places to mix perennial and annual plants. It's usually best to site the perennial herbs first, leaving ample space between them so that you can tuck in annuals during the season. Tarragon (*Artemisia dracunculus*), oregano (*Origanum vulgare*), some of the thymes (*Thymus* spp.), mints (*Mentha* spp.), chives, and sage (*Salvia officinalis*) usually form the perennial backbone of the kitchen garden. Oregano and the thymes make good edging plants, while sage, chives, and tarragon grow large

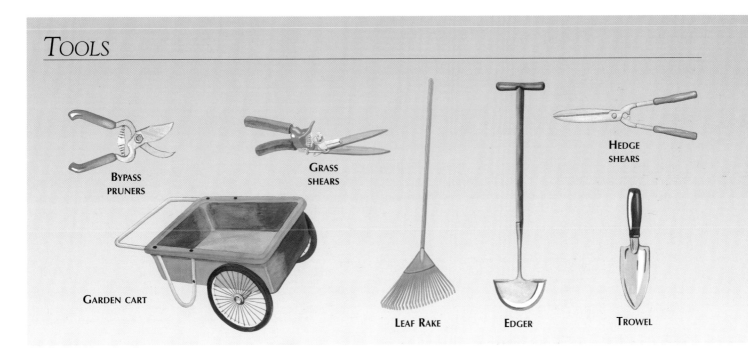

TOOLS

BYPASS PRUNERS

GRASS SHEARS

HEDGE SHEARS

GARDEN CART

LEAF RAKE

EDGER

TROWEL

MANY HERBS ARE SO VERSATILE that they can be used in teas and cooking as well as in medicines and cosmetics.

enough to be used in the middle or back of the bed. As always, confine mints to pots or a garden all their own.

Successive plantings are the best way to maintain steady supplies of many annual herbs. Chervil and coriander (*Coriandrum sativum*), for example, can be picked for only a few weeks to a month before they flower and die. Midseason plantings of chervil will only thrive in a cool shady spot, generally under a taller plant such as bee balm (*Monarda didyma*). However, the last chervil planting of the year, which usually matures a week or so before the first frost, can tolerate brighter conditions. In contrast, cilantro and basil grow well in summer heat and full sun. But unlike basil, which is easy to transplant into the garden and generally gives good yields from only two plantings per year, cilantro must be direct-seeded or carefully transplanted every month to provide continuous harvests. Check the herb directory, starting on page 205, for more tips on successive planting.

Tea gardens. Herbal teas have become a mainstay in most homes. Many of us routinely buy colorful boxes of exotic combinations with wonderful names. Many basic tea ingredients—the mints, chamomile (*Matricaria recutita*), rosehips, and berry leaves—are easy to grow and dry at home. And even though you might not harvest hibiscus flowers or citrus peel, you can buy these ingredients and mix them into your homegrown tea combinations.

Many of the best tea ingredients are members of the invasive mint family, so it's wise to give the tea garden several beds of its own, far away from the ornamental flowers or vegetables.

Or you can simply plant mint in pots. You can sink them in the soil or not, depending on the look you want, but if you sink them, you'll have to keep stems from taking root in the surrounding soil.

Chamomile is another ingredient often used in herbal tea. The first planting usually blooms in early to midsummer and dies shortly after you harvest its flowers. To keep the garden looking tidy, pull out the dead plants, and mulch the area or transplant a second crop in its place. If you don't want a second crop of chamomile, try an edible flower such as dwarf nasturtium (*Tropaeolum minus*), Johnny-jump-ups (*Viola tricolor*), or sweet alyssum (*Lobularia maritima*), which feeds beneficial insects.

SMART TIP

MANAGING INVASIVE MINT PLANTS

Divide the area into squares that measure at least 2 feet on each side. Plant one mint in the center of each of these areas, and mulch the space with straw or another nonweedy material. At monthly intervals during the summer, pull back the mulch, and use a sharp spade to cut into the soil at the divisions of the squares. By the second year, you'll have to prune off traveling stems, which, along with underground rhizomes, will be trying to move into their neighbors' areas.

CONTAINERS

HERBS ARE WONDERFUL CONTAINER plants. The qualities that make container gardening a bit more demanding than growing in the soil are often inconsequential or even beneficial for many herbs. For example, the soil in containers dries out quite quickly. Depending on conditions, many pots must be watered at least once, if not twice, a day. Fast-growing annual herbs, such as basil and chervil, require as much water as vegetable plants. But the heat-loving Mediterranean herbs—oregano, thyme, and rosemary—all welcome a bit of drying between watering.

Vegetables in containers normally require fertilization every week to ten days. Again, this will be true for some of the fast-growing annual herbs, but perennials such as tarragon, rosemary, thyme, oregano, and sage are less demanding. They require supplemental feeding, but less frequently. Use a mixture of liquid seaweed and fish emulsion once a month. If the leaves begin to yellow, fertilize container-grown herbs once every two weeks.

Containers have the virtue of being adaptable, too. You

> ### SMART TIP
> #### USE SMALL CONTAINERS TO CONTROL GROWTH
>
> Small containers can stunt plants. When plants become rootbound, they slow their top growth accordingly. In the case of vegetables or flowers, this is rarely desirable. However, given that a rosemary (*Rosmarinus officinalis*) can grow into a shrub within two or three years, a single sprig of lemon grass (*Cymbopogon citratus*) can become a 3-foot-wide thicket in a single summer, and oregano and thyme can take over an area several feet in all directions, some dwarfing isn't all bad.

can move them to areas where they are needed most or where the environment suits them best. For example, when you're serving iced tea, set a pot of lemon verbena (*Aloysia triphylla*) on the table to use as a garnish, or set out a pot of basil when you have a pizza party.

A WINDOW BOX OF FRESH HERBS is delightful outside a kitchen window where it can be tended regularly.

CONTAINERS make an ideal growing environment for many herbs and offer more flexibility because they can be moved.

HERBAL VINEGARS, honeys, and jams make wonderful gifts from your garden that friends will treasure.

of shade or filtered sun a day; the soil should be well drained. If you don't have such a spot, split the herb garden into two areas: one in full sun and one with shade or filtered sun. As in the kitchen herb garden, use the perennials to form the backbone structure of the garden, and leave enough space between them to plant annuals.

Drying and Freezing Herbs

Once you start growing herbs successfully, you may want to preserve some for winter use. With a broad enough selection, you can make numerous combinations of both dried and frozen herbs. But begin by simply preserving the herbs

A GARDEN OF TREASURES

HERBAL PRODUCTS ARE ANOTHER luxury that herb growers can give themselves, as well as to their friends and family. In the following pages, you'll learn how to make some of the most basic items such as potpourris, infusions (very strong teas covered while steeped), and skin lotions. But the first step is growing as many ingredients as possible.

Begin your "Treasures Garden" by listing all of the herbs you'll want to use in various preparations. You'll quickly see that most herbs can play several roles. Mint and chamomile, for example, are as important as tea herbs as they are for beauty preparations. Calendula flowers are as useful in a salad or fresh bouquet as in a skin salve, and lavender can be used in everything from baked goods to teas, dried arrangements, potpourris, and antiseptic skin lotions.

For maximum flexibility, site this garden where part of it will receive full sun and part of it will receive several hours

SMART TIP

HARVESTING HERBS FOR PRESERVING

In most cases, it's best to harvest herbs for preserving in the morning, after the dew has dried. Rinse them quickly and shake off the extra water. If you intend to dry them, try not to bruise or bend the leaves. Lay the herbs on absorbent cloth or paper towels to soak up additional moisture. When their surfaces are dry, you can continue with the preserving process.

you use most frequently. Individual entries in the herb directory, pages 205 to 217, give the best harvesting and preserving methods for each species.

Drying herbs. Drying is the easiest way to preserve herbs. Most herbs are dried the same way as flowers, hung upside down in a dark dry area with good air circulation, as described in "Air-drying," page 126. If dust can get into the drying area, drape cheesecloth or floating row cover material over the herbs to keep them clean during the drying process. When you are drying plants for their seeds, enclose the ripe flower heads in small paper bags before you hang them. As the seeds dry, they'll drop into the bag.

Delicate herbs such as chamomile dry best on screens. As shown in the drawing below, it's important to allow for good air circulation under as well as over the screens. If you are using old window screens, keep your herbs clean by covering the screening with

SMART TIP

FREEZING HERB STEMS

Freezing retains even more flavor and color and is the only way to maintain the quality of delicate herbs such as coriander and chervil. If you are freezing whole stems of plants such as parsley, simply lay them on cookie sheets in the freezer. When they have frozen, pack them into reusable plastic bags or tubs, label and store until you need to remove a stem or two.

cheesecloth or row cover material. Use upturned glasses to hold a second layer of material above the herbs. This layer protects against dust and stray insects.

Making herbal products seems like a big undertaking until you actually do it. But once you get into the habit of routinely drying and preserving various herbs and flowers when they are at their peak, you'll discover how easy it is to put a few gifts together on a rainy fall day.

Dried arrangements, as described in Chapter 4, "Specialty Gardens," page 125 are lovely mementos of the previous summer. Dry flowers for them, of course, but don't neglect the herb garden when you are looking for materials for these bouquets. Bee balm (*Monarda didyma*), lavender cotton (*Santolina chamaecyparissus*), lavender, rue (*Ruta graveolens*), sage (*Salvia officinalis*), and tansy (*Tanacetum vulgare* var. *crispum*) all make wonderful additions to winter bouquets.

DRYING CHAMOMILE

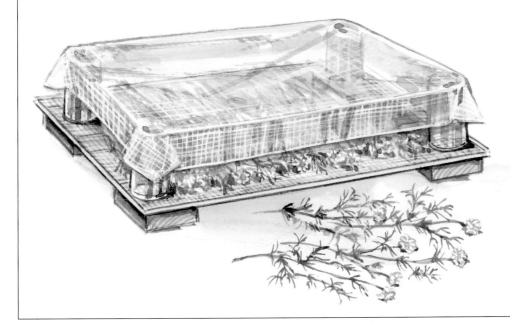

USE SCREENS TO DRY your most delicate herbs, such as chamomile. Use coated or nylon screening rather than aluminum, which could give an off-flavor to the herbs. Rinse it after every use with a 10 percent bleach solution; then with clear water. If insects fly under the top covering, cut it so that it is large enough to fold under the boards used as feet.

MAKING HERBAL POTPOURRIS

Potpourris can be made of almost any combination of fragrant herbs and flowers. For lasting fragrance, add two purchased ingredients to your herbal mixtures: a commercially prepared essential oil and a fixative such as orrisroot or oakmoss. You can also add store-bought materials such as bayberries, cinnamon sticks, and star anise.

■ Choose four to eight ingredients that go well together. For a clean, fresh scent, combine lavender leaves and florets, lemon verbena leaves, mint leaves, chamomile flowers, rosemary leaves, and lemon-scented geranium leaves with oil of lavender and oakmoss fixative. Rosebuds, lavender florets, mint leaves, rose-scented geranium (*P. capitatum*) leaves, cinnamon sticks, cloves, oil of rose and orrisroot create a sweeter, spicier scent.

■ Decide how you want the mix to smell, then combine 1 to 2 cups of each major ingredient and add ¼ to ½ cup of the secondary ingredients. To every 6 to 8 cups of potpourri material, add 6 to 10 tablespoons of the fixative and 10 to 20 drops of an essential oil.

■ Place the mix in a plastic storage container with a tight-fitting lid. Tape the lid shut with duct tape and set it in a dark, warm place such as the linen closet. Shake the tub at least once a day. After six weeks, open it up and pour it into a decorative bowl. The potpourri will retain its fragrance for months.

■ When the fragrance fades, put it back in the tub with more fixative and essential oil and shake daily for another six weeks.

■ To make sachets, crush the finished potpourri and stuff small, homemade pillows with it. Sachets can be sweetly scented for the linen closet and dresser drawers or filled with materials that repel moths and other pests. The best insect-repellent herbs are lavender cotton, lavender, rosemary, and tansy. Use essential oil of lavender for fragrance and oakmoss as a fixative for this mixture. Insect-repellent sachets can be used among stored clothing or in your pet's bed.

HERBAL ICE CUBES give a summer-fresh flavor to winter stews and soups. Transfer the cubes to a plastic bag, which takes up less freezer space than the tray. Be sure to label the bag.

PREPARE HERBS FOR FREEZING as you would for cooking, but leave those you will dry intact so that you can crush them as you need them throughout the winter.

Follow the drying and preserving instructions in the herbal directory for best results.

Drying herbs for culinary purposes. Some herbs do not retain their quality if they dry slowly. To keep them green and flavorful, you'll have to dry them quickly in an electric or solar dehydrator, or freeze them. If you are using an electric dehydrator, be sure to check the herbs every few hours. When they are sufficiently dry, you will be able to crumble a leaf between your fingers. Don't dry the leaves beyond this point or you'll risk losing some flavor and color. Once you can crumble the leaves, pour them into a glass, screw-top canning jar. Every day for three or four days, pour the herbs from one jar to another. This process, known as *conditioning*, allows the herbs to dry completely by giving them plenty of air circulation. Store them in amber glass jars or in clear containers kept in a dark spot.

Herbal ice cubes are easy to make and give you the flexibility of using small amounts. If you are putting the herb in a sauce where the water won't be noticed, simply drop in the ice cubes. But if you are adding them to an oily mixture, remove most of the water first by letting the herbal ice cubes thaw in a strainer.

Herbs can also be made into an oil-based paste and frozen. Check the listings in the herb directory, pages 205 to 217, to learn which oils to mix with the various herbs that preserve well this way. Small dabs of these herbal pastes can be frozen in ice-cube trays and used as needed. If you are freezing a more complicated mixture, such as a fully completed basil and parsley pesto, pack it into a plastic tub and dribble a layer of olive oil over it before covering and freezing it.

HOMEMADE HERBAL COSMETICS are so much nicer than those you can buy that once you make some, you'll continue to do so.

Infusions are very strong teas, made by pouring boiling water over fresh herbs and steeping in a container with a tight lid for at least 20 minutes. You can keep an infusion for up to three days in the refrigerator.

Decoctions are made from fresh roots. You can use both infusions and decoctions to rinse your hair after shampooing. The qualities of each herb used in hair care are listed in the herb directory starting on page 205.

Herbal oils can soothe irritated skin. Calendula, listed in the annual directory, page 94, is one of the most effective. Using just the flowers, make an oil, as described below. Extra-virgin olive oil gives the greatest medicinal benefit, but it can make you smell like a salad. If you want to go out after applying this oil, use almond or avocado oil.

HERBS FOR BEAUTY

A QUICK TRIP DOWN the cosmetics aisle shows you the popularity of herbal beauty products. However, even though the various shampoos and skin creams advertise themselves as being "herbal," the list of ingredients indicates how many preservatives and other non-herbal elements have been added. It's tempting to think that all of these extras increase the effectiveness of the various products, but this isn't always true. In some cases, they do boost the effectiveness, but in others, the extra ingredients simply provide fragrance or lathering qualities.

You can make effective, truly natural cosmetics quite easily. Most herbal cosmetics are made from infusions, decoctions, or oils.

Preparing herbal oils. To make herbal oil, fill a clear glass jar with the herb, crush the plant tissue with a wooden spoon, and then pour in enough top-quality oil such as extra-virgin olive, grapeseed, almond, or avocado to cover the herbs. Cap the jar and set it on a sunny windowsill. Every day, shake the mixture. After three or four weeks, strain out the herbs, squeezing them against the jar so that every last bit of their essential oil is released into the herbal oil. You can store this oil for up to a year in a dark dry spot.

TO KEEP YOUR HERBAL OILS clear and clean, wash all leaves and flowers extremely well and allow their surfaces to dry thoroughly before you add them to the jar.

ILLUSTRATED PLANT-BY-PLANT DIRECTORY OF COMMON HERBS

Note: To make the best use of this directory, please read "About the Plant Directories," on page 9.

Ocimum basilicum
Basil, sweet

Life Cycle: Annual.
Size: 1 to 2 feet tall, 8 inches to 1 foot wide.
Appearance: Depending on cultivar, the opposite leaves may be smooth-margined or toothed, deep green, light green, or purple. Small white or pink florets grow in terminal spikes.
Uses: Culinary—use fresh or dry leaves as a seasoning in composed dishes, the primary ingredient in pesto, or to infuse vinegars or oils. Florets can be added to salads or used as a garnish. Medicinal—use to sooth stomach upsets and ease digestion, can reduce fevers. Aromapathic—use for stimulating qualities. Insect repellent. Wildlife—bees love basil. Ornamental—use ruffled and purple cultivars in mixed arrangements.
Exposure: Full sun.
Soil: Well-drained, moist, nutrient-rich.
Propagation: Start seeds early indoors, about 5 weeks before the frost-free date, or seed directly in garden after all danger of frost has passed.
Spacing: 1 to 1½ feet apart.
Harvesting Guidelines: Begin pinching off branch tips when plants are 6 to 8 inches tall. Always leave a pair of leaves on the stem because new leaves will grow from the buds in the leaf axils. If flowers do form, pinch them off to prolong the usefulness of the plant. Harvest only when plants are dry. If storing for a day or so, stand the stems in an inch or so of water, and keep cool and dark.
Preserving Techniques: Dry by hanging or in electric dehydrator. Blanch and freeze in ice cubes or on cookie sheet. Freeze raw in butter or oil.
Pests: Aphids, rose chafers, Japanese beetles, slugs.
Diseases: Fusarium wilt (*Fusarium* spp.), many leaf spot fungi, viruses.
Notes: Transplant or direct-seed a second crop in early to mid-July to ensure a continuous supply of leaves throughout the season.

Monarda didyma
Bee Balm

Life Cycle: Perennial.
Size: 3 to 5 feet tall, 1 to 2 feet wide.
Appearance: Plant has a light, open appearance. Opposite leaves are dark green with toothed margins. Flowers can be red, white, pink, or purple and form in tiered whorls at stem tips in midsummer. Plants die back in fall.
Uses: Culinary—leaves make an excellent tea and the edible flowers can be sprinkled on salads or used as a garnish. Wildlife—bees and hummingbirds love bee balm. Ornamental—use fresh flowers in mixed arrangements and dry by hanging for use in winter bouquets.
Exposure: Prefers partial shade but will tolerate full sun.
Soil: Well-drained, moist, nutrient-rich.
Propagation: Start seeds early, eight weeks before the frost-free date. Transplant to garden just before all danger of frost has passed. Mature plants can be divided in early spring. Layer stems in spring through summer.
Spacing: Allow 2 square feet between plants in all directions.
Harvesting Guidelines: Harvest leaves any time after plants are 8 inches tall or flower stems when plants are dry. To cut for dried flowers, harvest just before flowers are fully open, taking a foot of stem below the flower whorls. To harvest for drying for tea, cut whole stems, an inch or two above the soil surface, just before bloom and then again in early fall. To harvest small amounts for a pot of tea, pinch off a few leaves.
Preserving Techniques: For flowers, hang whole stems to dry. For tea, strip leaves from plants and dry in an electric dehydrator or on window screens.
Pests: Largely pest-free.
Diseases: Rust (*Puccinia menthae*), powdery mildew (*Erysiphe* spp.).
Notes: The central stems of bee balm plants tend to die out after a few years. Keep the plants healthy by digging and dividing them every three years, replanting only the outside portions of the clump.

Matricaria recutita
Chamomile, German

Life Cycle: Annual.
Size: 2 to 3 feet tall, 8 inches to 1 foot wide.
Appearance: The bushy plants give a light and airy feeling. The plants are erect with feathery-looking leaves. Flowers have a large raised central disk surrounded by white petals.
Uses: Culinary—the central disks of chamomile flowers make an excellent tea. Medicinal—chamomile tea is calming and can promote sleepiness. Cosmetic—strong infusions of chamomile tea can be used as a hair rinse to brighten blonde highlights, help to prevent dandruff, and condition dry hair. Aromapathic—use chamomile in potpourris to add a clean, soothing fragrance.
Exposure: Prefers full sun but will tolerate partial shade.
Soil: Well-drained with moderate fertility and moisture levels. Sandy soils are best but plants will grow well in heavy soils if given a raised bed.
Propagation: Plant outside when the soil temperature has reached 55°F.
Spacing: Allow 6 to 8 inches between plants in all directions.
Harvesting Guidelines: When flowers are fully open, pinch them off or cut whole stems. A specialized chamomile rake can also be used to collect the flowers. Pick only when plants are completely dry.

Preserving Techniques: Dry flowers on screens covered with cheesecloth or in an electric dehydrator. When fully dry, store in glass jars or sealed plastic bags.
Pests: Largely pest-free.
Diseases: Largely disease-free.
Notes: If you are allergic to ragweed, you may also be allergic to chamomile. Test yourself by sniffing fresh tea before you commit to a patch of it in your yard.

Anthriscus cereifolium
Chervil

Life Cycle: Annual.
Size: 1 to 1½ feet tall, 6 to 8 inches wide.
Appearance: The plant resembles a delicate form of carrot. The leaves look like ferns and the tiny white flowers grow in umbels.
Uses: Culinary—add this lightly licorice-flavored leaf to soups, salads, casseroles, and peas immediately before serving. In France, it is often used in preference to parsley. Wildlife—many beneficial insects feed on the flowers.
Exposure: Prefers partial shade but will tolerate full sun in the North.
Soil: Moist, rich soil with high levels of organic matter.
Propagation: Plant seeds where they are to grow a week or two before the last expected frost. If plants set seed, they give a volunteer crop late in the season or the following year.
Spacing: Allow 6 to 8 inches between plants.

Harvesting Guidelines: Pinch leaves when plants are 6 to 8 inches tall. Crop can be extended if stems are picked before the plant forms blooms. Harvest only when plants are dry.
Preserving Techniques: Chervil can be frozen in ice cubes or butter but loses flavor if dried.
Pests: Aphids, carrot weevils.
Diseases: Fungal leaf spot and root rot diseases in high moisture conditions.
Notes: Plant chervil every two to three weeks during the season to have a steady supply. For midseason plantings, choose a location that is shaded during the heat of the day.

Allium schoenoprasum; Allium tuberosum
Chives, standard; Chinese or Garlic chives

Life Cycle: Perennial.
Size: Both plants grow 1 to 1½ inches tall and eventually form clumps measuring 8 inches to 1 foot wide.
Appearance: Standard chives have round, hollow leaves with pointed tips, while garlic chives have flat leaves. The flowers of standard chives form bright purple balls in late spring or early summer. Garlic chive flowers form flat, open heads in late summer and early fall.
Uses: Culinary—use both types of chives in salads, soups or any other dish where a mild oniony or garlicy flavor is needed. Flowers of both kinds of chives are good

nishes—bees love chive flowers.

Exposure: Prefers full sun but will tolerate partial shade.

Soil: Well-drained, moderate fertility with high humus content.

Propagation: Start seeds early indoors, eight to ten weeks before frost-free date, and transplant to garden a week before that date. Seeds can also be directly sown, but plants can be mistaken for grassy weeds.

Spacing: Plant about ten seeds in each pot or cell of the starting flat. Space clumps of plants about a foot apart in the row. Plants will enlarge to fill in the row.

Harvesting Guidelines: When plants are 5 inches tall, cut leaves 2 or 3 inches above the soil surface. Cut flowers just after they open. Harvest only when plants are dry.

Preserving Techniques: Snip chives into small pieces, and freeze in ice cubes. Drying is rarely successful.

Pests: Largely trouble-free.

Diseases: Fungal root rots can strike, but plants usually stay healthy.

Notes: Garlic chives are particularly offensive to Japanese beetles, so many people grow them with roses and other plants that are plagued by these insects.

Coriandrum sativum
Coriander

Life Cycle: Annual.

Size: 2 to 3 feet tall, 6 to 8 inches wide.

Appearance: Coriander has a light, airy feeling. Leaves resemble flat-leaf parsley and the white flowers immediately declare these plants as a member of the *Umbelliferae* family.

Uses: Culinary—salsa, chili, and many curry dishes rely on coriander. Crushed seeds give excellent flavor to safflower or canola oil. Wildlife—many beneficial insects feed on the flowers.

Exposure: Prefers full sun in the North and partial shade in the South.

Soil: Well-drained, moderate fertility with good moisture levels.

Propagation: Plant seeds in early spring where plants are to grow, or use peat pots or soil blocks to avoid disturbing roots when you transplant.

Spacing: 8 to 10 inches apart in the row.

Harvesting Guidelines: Begin cutting leaves when plants are 6 to 8 inches tall and continue for as long as possible. To prolong the harvest of leaves, cut flower stalk as soon as it forms. To harvest seeds, allow flower stalks to form and insects to pollinate. As the umbels begin to dry, watch them carefully. When they appear almost dry, place a paper sack over them and secure it at the bottom with a twist-tie. Bend the seed head over and shake. When you can hear the seeds drop into the bag, cut the stalk and finish drying the seed head inside.

Preserving Techniques: Coriander does not dry well. Freeze leaves in ice cubes or use to flavor oils.

Pests: Largely pest-free.

Diseases: Root rots can strike in soggy soils but plants usually remain healthy.

Notes: Plant a new crop every 2 to 3 weeks through the season to have a steady supply. If you allow seeds to drop to the ground, volunteer plants will appear late in the season or the next year.

Anethum graveolens
Dill

Life Cycle: Annual.

Size: 1½ to 5 feet tall, depending on cultivar; 8 inches to 1 foot wide.

Appearance: Upright, light and airy. The blue-green leaves are threadlike with a satiny sheen. Flowers are yellow-green and form umbels similar to those of Queen Anne's lace.

Uses: Culinary—leaves and seeds are used to flavor soups, cheeses, and a variety of mixed dishes as well as dill pickles. Both seeds and leaves can flavor vinegars or oils. Wildlife—many beneficial insects feed on the flowers.

Exposure: Full sun.

Soil: Well-drained, moist and fertile but will tolerate leaner soils.

Propagation: If starting seeds early indoors, plant groups of four or five seeds in peat pots or soil blocks and space these clumps a foot apart when you transplant. Otherwise, in early spring, plant seeds where the plants are to grow.

Spacing: 6 inches between plants unless they are grown in clumps, as described above.

Harvesting Guidelines: Clip off individual leaves beginning when plants are 8 inches tall. If cutting to dry, allow plants to reach close to full height and then cut, before flowers form. To harvest seeds, allow plants to flower and set seed. Enclose seed heads in plastic bags once they're nearly dry. Shake the seed head every day or so, and when you hear the seeds rattling around, cut off the seed head and bring it inside to finish drying.

Preserving Techniques: Hang stems to dry leaves or cut leaves from stems and dry on the fruit leather insert of an electric dehydrator. Leaves can be frozen in ice cubes. Dried seeds will keep for a year in plastic bags or glass jars.

Pests: Largely pest-free, though the occasional caterpillar may feed on plants. (Share with the caterpillars since they do so little damage.)

Diseases: Largely disease-free.

Notes: Make a second planting in early July to keep supplies steady and to feed beneficial insects.

Foeniculum vulgare
Fennel

Life Cycle: Perennial grown as annual throughout most of the U.S. and Canada.

Size: 2 to 5 feet tall, 1 foot wide.

Appearance: The plant grows erect. The threadlike leaves resemble those of dill and the flowers look like dill blooms.

Uses: Culinary—the mildly licorice-flavored seeds and leaves are used in raw and cooked dishes. Make flavored oils with canola or safflower oil. Medicinal—use a strong fennel tea to alleviate colic in infants and flatulence in children and adults. Cosmetic—crushed fennel seeds will exfoliate dead skin cells. Wildlife—many beneficials feed on the flowers. Slugs and snails are repelled by the odor.

Exposure: Full sun but will tolerate partial shade in southern locations.

Soil: Well-drained, moderately fertile, and consistently moist.

Propagation: Plant seeds where plants are to grow about a week before your last expected spring frost or, in Zones 6 southward, in the fall.

Spacing: 6 inches apart in the row.

Harvesting Guidelines: Snip off leaves from the time the plant is 8 inches tall until just before it blooms. Enclose seed heads as you do with those of dill.

Preserving Techniques: Hang stems to dry leaves. Finish drying seed heads by hanging upside down in paper bags. Leaves retain more flavor when frozen in ice cubes.

Pests: Largely pest-free.

Diseases: Develops fungal root rots easily in soggy soils.

Notes: Plant two or three times for a steady supply of leaves. Wear gloves to protect yourself from oil in the seeds.

Pelargonium spp.
Scented Geraniums

Life Cycle: Annual in most zones.

Size: Depending on species and cultivar, plants can range from 1 to 3 feet tall and 1 to 6 feet wide.

Appearance: Varies with species and cultivar, but all have beautiful leaves and flowers.

Uses: Ornamental—scented geraniums make lovely container plants and also grow well in the border. Dried leaves and flowers are good additions to potpourri mixtures and fresh stems are

PELARGONIUM CAPITATUM

lovely in arrangements. Culinary—use fresh leaves to make jams, jellies , baked goods, and beverages. Flowers can be used as garnishes on the plate. Wildlife—beneficial insects feed on the flowers.

Exposure: Full sun but will tolerate partial shade or south windowsills in winter.

Soil: Well-drained, moderately fertile, high humus levels, and consistently moist.

Propagation: Take softwood or semi-ripe cuttings from established plants from late winter to midsummer.

Spacing: 1 foot apart in all directions.

Harvesting Guidelines: Cut individual leaves and flower clusters as needed. Leaves have highest fragrance before the plant blooms.

Preserving Techniques: Dry on screens covered with cheesecloth or in an electric dehydrator.

Pests: Whiteflies.

Diseases: Bacterial wilt (*Pseudomonas* spp., *Erwinia* spp.), botrytis blight (*Botrytis cinerea*), various fungal root rots.

Notes: If you live in an area with frost, dig scented geraniums several weeks before first expected frost, pot up, and bring inside for the winter. Move blooming plants to areas where you'd like to attract beneficial insects.

Laurus nobilis
Laurel, Bay Laurel, Grecian

Life Cycle: Perennial in Zones 8 to 10.
Size: 5 to 60 feet tall, depending on location; 3 to 15 feet wide.
Appearance: Bay trees have evergreen, smooth-margined glossy dark green leaves. Flowers are inconspicuous. The bark is shiny and gray.
Uses: Culinary—use bay leaves in a variety of cooked dishes. Medicinal—an infusion of bay leaves is said to calm the stomach. Ornamental—plant a bay tree in a container if you live in Zones 7 and north, and enjoy it indoors.
Exposure: Full sun.
Soil: Well-drained, moderately rich, consistently moist but not soggy.
Propagation: Buy established plants, and propagate by taking stem cuttings in the fall. Seeds usually rot.
Spacing: At least 15 feet between trees.
Harvesting Guidelines: Pick off leaves or whole stems when the plant is a foot tall.
Preserving Techniques: Hang upside down to dry. Weigh leaves with heavy objects to keep them from curling.
Pests: Largely trouble-free but can host spider mites.
Diseases: Largely trouble-free but can develop root rots in soggy soil.
Notes: In northern areas, move your potted bay tree in and out, taking care to bring it back inside a few weeks before the first fall frost.

Santolina chamaecyparissus
Lavender Cotton, Santolina

Life Cycle: Perennial in Zones 6 to 8.
Size: 2 feet tall.
Appearance: The plant has a delicate, upright appearance. Leaves are gray-green or silvery, narrow, and grow in an alternate pattern along the stems. Flowers are tight buttons of bright yellow.
Uses: Ornamental—use the branches as a base for fresh herbal wreaths, and dry the flowers for winter bouquets and potpourris. Wildlife—both fresh and dried santolina repels most insects.
Exposure: Full sun.
Soil: Well-drained, low to moderate fertility and a pH of 6.5 to 7.5.
Propagation: Plant seeds early indoors, about eight weeks before the frost-free date. Transplant to the garden after all danger of frost has passed. Established plants can be divided in early spring.
Spacing: 1 to 2 feet between plants.
Harvesting Guidelines: Cut branches for their leaves in early summer before plant has bloomed. If cutting for flowers, wait until blooms begin to open. Cut stems about 3 inches above the soil.
Preserving Techniques: Hang stems upside down to dry.
Pests: Largely pest-free.
Diseases: Largely disease-free.
Notes: Wrap stems in tissue paper and set them in the linen and clothes closets to repel moths.

Lavandula angustifolia, Lavandula dentata
Lavender, English; Lavender, French

Life Cycle: Perennial, Zones 5 to 8.
Size: 2 to 3 feet tall, depending on species and cultivar.
Appearance: Leaves are opposite, narrow and smooth edged. In most cultivars, they are gray-green or silvery and slightly hairy. Flowers form in whorls of tall spikes and depending on species, range from purple-blue through lavender, pink and white.
Uses: Culinary—lavender flowers are often added to black tea for fragrance. They may also be added to baked goods and preserves. Medicinal—lavender tea is calming. Soak a washcloth in an infusion and lay it on your forehead and eyes to relieve headaches. Cosmetic—lavender oil makes a good conditioner for oily hair. Ornamental—lavender adds a lovely note to any herb or flower garden. Add dried flowers and leaves to potpourris and sachets.
Exposure: Full sun but tolerates partial shade.
Soil: Well-drained, moderately fertile, somewhat alkaline soil.
Propagation: Start seeds early indoors, eight to ten weeks before last expected spring frost. Transplant to the garden after all danger of frost has passed. Take stem cuttings from established plants in late spring or early summer.

CHAPTER 7

Lavandula angustifolia/ **Lavender, English** *continued*

Spacing: Allow 1 to 3 feet between plants, depending on species and cultivar.

Harvesting Guidelines: Cut stems for leaves just above the node where green growth begins, leaving that node to form new branches. To harvest flowers for arrangements, cut the stems several inches below the blooms.

Preserving Techniques: Dry lavender on screens or hang upside down.

Pests: Largely pest-free.

Diseases: Fungal root rots attack if plants are grown in soggy soil.

Notes: Let the top inch of the soil dry between waterings to keep plants healthy. If plants develop diseases, dig them up and transplant them into a raised bed where drainage will be improved. In spring before plants have begun to leaf out, trim branches back to a neat shape.

Melissa officinalis
Lemon Balm

Life Cycle: Perennial, Zones 4 to 9.

Size: 1 to 2 feet tall.

Appearance: Plants tend to form neat, compact mounds of clear green, opposite leaves with clearly marked veins and toothed edges. In midsummer, small white flowers form in leaf axils. Plants die back over the winter.

Uses: Culinary—lemon balm is one of the best tea herbs. Also, leaves can be minced and used fresh or cooked in a variety of dishes. Cosmetic—a strong infusion conditions oily hair. Ornamental—blooming plants are lovely in the flower border, and stems add a pleasing fragrant note to mixed bouquets.

Exposure: Full sun in the North; filtered shade in the South.

Soil: Moist, well-drained, with average fertility.

Propagation: Start seeds early indoors, approximately eight weeks before the last expected frost. Transplant outside after all danger of frost has passed. Or you can plant seeds where they are to grow, about two weeks before the frost-free date. Stem cuttings can be taken from established plants at any time during the growing season.

Spacing: Allow approximately 2 feet between plants.

Harvesting Guidelines: Cut off stem tips as needed. When cutting lemon balm for drying, cut stems about 4 inches above the soil surface.

Preserving Techniques: Strip leaves from the stems, and dry them on the fruit leather insert of a food dehydrator. Freeze whole leaves in ice cubes to use in iced teas and other cold beverages.

Pests: Largely pest-free.

Diseases: Powdery mildew.

Notes: Lemon balm won't invade the garden as the other mints do.

Cymbopogon citratus
Lemongrass

Life Cycle: Perennial, Zones 9 to 10; grown in containers elsewhere.

Size: 3 to 5 feet tall; 1 to 3 feet wide.

Appearance: Lemongrass looks like a grass. The leaf bases are enlarged and whitish.

Uses: Culinary—leaves and bulbous stems are commonly part of the Asian diet and are used in a huge number of Thai and Vietnamese dishes. Dried leaves make an excellent addition to an herbal tea mixture. Ornamental—dried leaves add a pleasant lemony fragrance to potpourri.

Exposure: Full sun.

Soil: Moist, rich soil with a pH of 6.5. In containers, fertilize once a month during the season.

Propagation: Start seeds in early spring, and transplant them to your garden or a larger container after all danger of frost has passed. Clumps enlarge naturally and quickly, so divide plants every year or so. When dividing the plants, cut back the leaves to between 3 and 4 inches above the soil surface.

Spacing: Allow 2 to 4 feet between plants in Zones 9 to 10. Elsewhere, grow plants in 5-gallon nursery pots through the winter.

Harvesting Guidelines: Once the diameter of the base is about 2 inches wide, pull off older outside bulbous stems from the base. In this way you'll be taking the leaves too. You can also cut the leaves from the plant for use in a tea without having to take the bulb.

Preserving Techniques: Use fresh because the plant does not retain full flavor when dried.

Pests: Cats occasionally eat the leaves and dig up the plants.

Diseases: Largely disease-free.

Notes: If you live in the North, you can grow lemongrass in the ground during the summer. Remember to dig it out and pot it so that you can bring it back inside several weeks before your first expected frost and before you turn on the heat. This will give the plant ample time to adjust to the warmer, drier conditions in the house.

Aloysia triphylla
Lemon Verbena

Life Cycle: Perennial, Zones 9 to 10; container plant elsewhere.

Size: 2 feet tall by 2 feet wide.

Appearance: Narrow, smooth-margined leaves are pointed and grow in whorls of three or four. In some cultivars the leaves are hairy, but most have smooth, almost shiny leaves. Stems become woody as the plant matures. In late summer, spikes of tiny pink or lavender flowers grow from the leaf axils, as well as branch tips.

Uses: Culinary—use the leaves in salads, deserts, sauces and dressings. Lemon verbena makes an excellent tea, alone or in combination with other herbs. Ornamental—grow lemon verbena in hanging baskets or containers near the outdoor living area.

Exposure: Full sun.

Soil: Well-drained, nutrient-rich soil with high humus content.

Propagation: Buy established plants. In late spring or early summer, take softwood cuttings and keep them in a high humidity area while they are rooting.

Spacing: Outdoors, allow 2 feet between plants. Plant in 12-inch pots.

Harvesting Guidelines: Snip leaves as needed. When plant begins to look scraggly, cut all the branches back to 4 inches and let them regrow.

Preserving Techniques: Dry on screens or in an electric dehydrator.

Pests: Whiteflies, spider mites.

Diseases: Largely disease-free.

Notes: Pinch a leaf of lemon verbena for an instant air freshener. Indoors grow the plant under a wide-spectrum plant light to keep it healthy.

Levisticum officinale
Lovage

Life Cycle: Perennial, Zones 4 to 8.

Size: 6 feet tall, 2 to 3 feet wide.

Appearance: Clear green, compound leaves with toothed margins resemble celery leaves. The tiny white flowers form in umbels similar to those of Queen Anne's lace. Plants die back in winter.

Uses: Culinary—the celery-flavored leaves and seeds are used in soups and stews as well as anywhere else that you would use celery or celery seeds. Medicinal—a strong infusion is antiseptic and will help wounds heal. The tea stimulates digestion.

Exposure: Partial shade but will tolerate full sun, particularly in the North.

Soil: Well-drained, moist, high fertility.

Propagation: Plant fresh seed in late summer, either in peat pots or where plants are to grow. Established plants can be divided in spring.

Spacing: Allow 2 feet between plants.

Harvesting Guidelines: Beginning in spring, snip off leaves from established plants as you need them. Harvest stems for drying by cutting to within 8 inches of the soil surface. For best flavor, cut before flowers form. If harvesting for seeds, enclose seed heads in paper bags closed with twist-ties to prevent seeds from falling to the ground.

Preserving Techniques: Strip leaves and dry in a dehydrator. If freezing, blanch leaves for 60 seconds first.

Pests: Leaf miners.

Diseases: Largely disease-free

Notes: This huge plant grows on you. Plant it in a shady spot where the height will be an asset.

Mentha spp.
Mint

Life Cycle: Perennial, Zones 5 to 9.

Size: 1½ to 2 feet tall, 1 to 3 feet wide.

Appearance: Stems in this family are always square, and the opposite leaves are usually toothed with highly visible veins. Depending on species, flowers may be pink, purple, or white. They grow in tall spikes that rise above the leaves and appear in mid- to late summer.

Uses: Culinary—use mint in salads and with stews, fish, grains, and peas. Most mints make excellent tea. Medicinal—mint tea settles the stomach and relieves flatulence. Spearmint and peppermint are calming and can promote sleepiness. Cosmetic—mint infusions condition oily hair. Ornamental—dried mint leaves make a nice addition to potpourris. Wildlife—many beneficial insects feed on the tiny mint flowers when they are in bloom.

Mentha spp./**Mint** *continued*

Exposure: Partial shade but will tolerate anything from full sun to shade.

Soil: Moist, moderate fertility. Do not plant in high-nitrogen soils.

Propagation: Most cultivars do not come true from seed and must be propagated from cuttings or divided. Take cuttings before the plants bloom. Divide plants in early spring or early fall. If you do plant seeds, expect to get mint plants that are fine for tea but which contain less mint flavor than the named cultivars.

Spacing: Allow 1 foot in each direction.

Harvesting Guidelines: Pinch off stems tips or individual leaves from dry plants as needed. If harvesting to dry, cut stems

MENTHA SPICATA

before the plant blooms and then again in the fall. Cut 4 to 6 inches above the soil surface for the first cutting and only an inch above it in the fall.

Preserving Techniques: Hang stems upside down to air dry or strip leaves from stems and dry in an electric dehydrator. Pack dried leaves in glass jars or resealable plastic bags for storage. Freeze leaves in ice cubes or chopped in butter or oil.

Pests: Aphids, spider mites, mint flea beetles, cutworms.

Diseases: Rust (*Puccinia menthae*), verticillium wilt (*Verticillium albo-atrum*), anthracnose (*Colletotrichum* spp.)

Notes: Mints deserve their reputation for being invasive. Do not plant them in a mixed bed or they will take it over within

only a couple of years. Instead, plant one or more species in a bed or area by themselves. Even so, you'll have to watch to see that one or another type doesn't become dominant.

Tropaeolum majus
Nasturtium

Life Cycle: Annual.

Size: 1 to 1½ feet tall, from 1 to 6 feet wide, depending on cultivar.

Appearance: Leaves are marked with prominent veins and wavy or slightly lobed margins. Flowers are an ornamental treat. Funnel-shaped with a spur at the rear, they range in color from cream to reds, oranges, yellows and bicolors.

Uses: Ornamental—bush cultivars add a cheerful note to flower beds, hanging baskets and window boxes and vining cultivars will give quick coverage on a 5-foot fence or screen. Culinary—use both flowers and leaves in salads and as edible garnishes. Pickle seedpods in heated vinegar to use as you do capers.

Exposure: Full sun.

Soil: Moderate fertility, well-drained.

Propagation: Start seeds early indoors in 3- to 4-inch peat pots, about 4 to 5 weeks before the last expected frost. Transplant to the garden or move outdoors after all danger of frost has passed. Seeds can also be planted where they will grow after all danger of frost has passed.

Spacing: 1 foot apart in all directions.

Harvesting Guidelines: Once plants are 8 to 10 inches tall, pinch off leaves and

flowers as needed through the season.

Preserving Techniques: Nasturtium leaves and flowers do not preserve well; use fresh.

Pests: Aphids, leaf miners.

Diseases: Bacterial wilt (*Pseudomonas solanacearum*), Heterosporium disease (*Heterosporium tropaeoli*), verticillium wilt (*Verticillium* spp.).

Notes: Nasturtiums will indicate how much nitrogen is in your soil. If leaves are only 1 to 2 inches across, the soil is nitrogen deficient. If they are 3 to 4 inches across, nitrogen is low for most vegetables but will support light-feeding herbs and flowers. Leaves that are 6 inches across indicate that nitrogen-loving vegetables can grow well.

Origanum vulgare
Oregano

Life Cycle: Perennial, Zones 5 to 9.

Size: 1 to 2 feet tall, 1 to 2 feet wide; stems are usually recumbent so plant appears only a few inches tall.

Appearance: Leaves are opposite and have toothed or smooth margins. Like all mints, the stems are square. Tiny white flowers grow on spikes in midsummer.

Uses: Culinary—use in sauces, pizza, and other cooked dishes.

Exposure: Full sun.

Soil: Well-drained, average fertility.

Propagation: Start seeds early indoors, about eight to ten weeks before the frost-free date. Plant seeds in groups of two or three. Transplant to the garden just before the frost-free date. Plants may also be layered by covering stems with soil and allowing them to form roots. Plants will propagate themselves after the first year and the plot will need thinning.

Spacing: Allow a foot between groups, 6 inches between individual plants.

Harvesting Guidelines: Pinch off stem tips as needed once the stems are at least 6 inches long. If harvesting for drying, cut whole stems just before the plant flowers. A second cutting may be made in late August. When you take stems, cut 2 to 3 inches above the soil.

Preserving Techniques: Strip leaves from stems and dry on the leather insert of an electric dehydrator or hang stems upside down, over a clean piece of material.

Pests: Aphids, leaf miners, spider mites.

Diseases: Fungal leaf spot (*Cercospora* spp., *Septoria* spp.), fungal root rots.

Notes: Oregano plants vary in flavor. If you have one you like, propagate it by layering. If you are starting from scratch, look for 'Greek' oregano with white flowers. Pink flowers signal that the flavor and holding quality is inferior.

Petroselinum crispum
Parsley

Life Cycle: Biennial but usually treated as an annual.

Size: 10 inches to 1¼ feet tall, 8 inches to 1 foot wide.

Appearance: Parsley can be "curled leaf," meaning that the leaflets are frilled and ruffled, or "flat leaf," meaning that the toothed leaflets are smooth and flat. Parsley grows from a central crown and the stiff petioles hold the stems in a spray formation.

Uses: Culinary—parsley is used as a garnish, an ingredient in many cooked dishes and as a primary component of some pestos. Wildlife—the parsley caterpillar is the larvae of a swallowtail butterfly. Cosmetic—add a strong parsley infusion to your hair conditioner to help prevent dandruff and condition dry hair.

Exposure: Full sun in the North, partial shade in the South.

Soil: Well-drained, moist, high fertility.

Propagation: Start seeds early indoors, about eight to ten weeks before the frost-free date. Germination can take as long as three weeks. To speed it up, soak seeds for 24 to 30 hours. Drain them in a tight-meshed strainer. Every few hours for the next two to three days, run tepid water over the seeds in the strainer to wash off the compound that inhibits germination. At night, put the seeds back in a jar or sealed plastic bag, along with a wet cotton ball, to keep them from drying out. Seeds will usually germinate in five days after this treatment.

Spacing: 1 foot in each direction.

Harvesting Guidelines: Cut outside stems first, about 1 inch above the soil surface.

Preserving Techniques: For the best flavor, freeze stems on cookie sheets and then pack them in plastic bags, or mince and freeze in ice cubes. Air-dried parsley loses flavor and color but it will hold both if you dry it in an electric dehydrator.

Pests: Aphids, carrot weevils.

Diseases: Crown rot (*Phytophthora* spp.)

Notes: Plants that overwinter in the garden will bloom in late spring of their second year. The flowers feed many beneficials but signal the end of the plants' culinary usefulness because they lose quality and then die shortly after blooming. Nonetheless, mulch to overwinter a few plants so that you can enjoy early parsley and feed the early beneficials. To bring in for the winter, pot up in a container 1 to 1½ feet deep and supplement light from a south window with a grow light.

Rosmarinus officinalis
Rosemary

Life Cycle: Perennial, Zones 8 to 10, grow in container elsewhere.

Size: 2 to 6 feet tall, 1 to 4 feet wide.

Appearance: The inch-long evergreen leaves are needle-like and leathery and grow opposite from each other on branches that become woody as they mature. Old plants develop woody, gnarled trunks. The tiny flowers are pink to purple and grow in leaf axils along the stem. They appear in late winter or early spring.

Uses: Culinary—poultry seasoning wouldn't be the same without rosemary, nor would many other dishes. Cosmetic—rosemary is used in hair rinses to condition oily hair, help prevent dandruff, give hair body, and add highlights to dark hair. Aromapathic—rosemary acts as a stimulant in the bath or in skin lotions. Ornamental—add rosemary to sachets and potpourris for a clean, piney scent.

Exposure: Full sun.

Soil: Well-drained, moderately fertile soil. Do not overwater.

Propagation: Rosemary can be started from seed, but most people take softwood cuttings from established plants in early spring or late summer. Stems may also be layered in late spring or early summer.

Spacing: Allow 1 to 3 feet between plants, depending on size.

CHAPTER 7

Rosmarinus officinalis/ **Rosemary** *continued*

Harvesting Guidelines: Once plant is 6 to 8 inches tall, snip off branch tips as needed. If harvesting to dry, cut green stems to within a node or two of the previous year's woody stems.

Preserving Techniques: Dry flat on screens or in an electric dehydrator.

Pests: Scale, mealy bugs, spider mites, whiteflies.

Diseases: Fungal root rots, botrytis blight (*Botrytis cinerea*).

Notes: North of Zone 8, plant rosemary outside once all danger of frost has passed. Several weeks before the first expected fall frost, dig it up and pot it in a deep nursery container for the winter. Overwinter it in a south window or under plant lights. Plants will live for many years, eventually becoming too large to transplant each year. Instead, grow them in 10-gallon nursery tubs on wheels so you can move them.

Ruta graveolens
Rue

Life Cycle: Perennial, Zones 4 to 9.
Size: 2 to 3 feet tall, 1 to 2 feet wide.
Appearance: This blue-green plant has an erect, ferny look. The evergreen leaves grow in alternate leaflets with smooth margins and are often covered with a whitish powder similar to the bloom on a grape. Flowers are yellow and bloom at stem tips in midsummer.

Uses: Ornamental—rue is a lovely plant to add to a border because the leaves add year-round interest and the color complements so many other plants. Dried stems and seedpods are often added to winter arrangements. Wildlife—the odor is offensive to many insects, including fleas. Add some dried rue to your pet's cushions.

Exposure: Full sun but will tolerate partial shade.

Soil: Well-drained, low fertility.

Propagation: Start seeds indoors eight to ten weeks before frost-free date. Take softwood cuttings or layer established plants in late spring or early summer.

Spacing: 1½ to 2 feet apart.

Harvesting Guidelines: Harvest only in dry conditions. If harvesting leafy stems,

RUTA GRAVEOLENS

cut before the plant flowers. If cutting for seedpods, wait until they have fully enlarged, but cut before they turn brown.

Preserving Techniques: Hang stems upside down to air-dry.

Pests: None.

Diseases: Root rots in soggy soils.

Notes: Many people are allergic to an oil contained in fresh rue stems. Wear gloves and long sleeves to minimize your exposure. Rue inhibits the growth of many plants, particularly those in the cabbage family, mints, and sages. Plant it far from these plants and do not rotate any of these plants into an area where rue was grown during the previous four years.

Crocus sativus
Saffron Crocus

Life Cycle: Perennial, Zones 6 to 9.
Size: 8 inches to 1 foot tall, 3 to 6 inches wide.
Appearance: Grasslike leaves, sometimes with a white stripe, appear in the spring and then die back in summer. The lavender, white, or purple flowers bloom in fall and look just like spring crocuses.

Uses: Culinary—saffron threads add a spicy, slightly bitter flavor and vivid yellow coloring to cooked dishes.

Exposure: Partial shade but will tolerate full sun.

Soil: Well-drained, average fertility.

Propagation: Bulbs multiply. Dig and divide when plantings look crowded.

Spacing: 6 inches between bulbs.

Harvesting Guidelines: Use tweezers to pull out the yellow-orange stigmas once flowers are fully open.

Preserving Techniques: Dry the stigmas by putting them between sheets of brown paper and in an airy location. Saffron dries easily.

Pests: Pest-free.

Diseases: Root rot in soggy conditions.

Notes: Each crocus produces only three saffron threads and it takes about 100,000 plants to produce a pound. If you plant a dozen bulbs, you'll probably get enough saffron for two recipes. If you want more, plan to develop a large patch of this lovely flower that adds real charm to autumn flower beds.

Salvia officinalis
Sage

Life Cycle: Perennial, Zones 4 to 8.
Size: 2½ to 3 feet tall, 1 to 2 feet wide.
Appearance: The gray-green, opposite leaves can be hairy, velvety, or pebbly, depending on species and cultivar. But whatever they are, they have a striking appearance. Stems on the previous year's growth are woody, but those of the current year are soft. Tall spikes of tubular flowers rise above the leaves in late spring and early summer. Depending on cultivar, flowers are white, pink, purple, or blue.
Uses: Culinary—fresh and dried leaves are used in many cooked dishes. Cosmetic—sage infusions are used to condition and add body to dry hair. A tub of sage infusion will also soften, deodorize, and soothe tired feet. Ornamental—sage stems make a good base for herbal wreaths.
Exposure: Full sun.
Soil: Well-drained, average fertility.
Propagation: Start seeds early indoors, about eight weeks before the frost-free date. Freeze seeds for a week before planting. Cover seedling flats with newspaper; they require darkness to germinate. Transplant to the garden a week before or after the frost-free date. Or take softwood cuttings in spring or early summer.
Spacing: 2 feet apart in all directions.
Harvesting Guidelines: Snip branch tips as needed. When harvesting stems, cut a node or two above the woody growth, preferably in late summer or early fall.
Preserving Techniques: Hang stems upside down to air-dry.
Pests: Spider mites, spittlebugs, slugs, and snails.
Diseases: Bacterial wilt (*Pseudomonas* spp.), verticillium wilt (*Verticillium* spp.), fungal root rots in soggy soil.
Notes: Sage plants loose their good looks sometime in the third or fourth year. If you want them to do double-duty in your garden, providing beauty as well as flavor, make new plantings every third year and remove the old plants. Change the location of the new plants to avoid any root diseases that may have built up in the area.

Origanum majorana
Sweet Marjoram

Life Cycle: Perennial grown as annual.
Size: 1 foot tall, 10 inches wide.
Appearance: The somewhat fuzzy leaves are oval, smooth margined and opposite. Flower buds look like knots before they open. The tiny flowers are white or pink.
Uses: Culinary—sweet marjoram tastes like a sweet oregano. Use it raw or cooked whenever you want a mild oregano flavor. Medicinal—tea can settle the stomach or be used as a gargle to sooth a sore throat. Aromapathic—use a strong infusion in the bath for energizing qualities. Ornamental—dried leaves add fragrance to potpourris and sachets.
Exposure: Full sun but tolerates partial shade.
Soil: Well-drained, sandy, low to moderate fertility. Do not overwater.
Propagation: Start seeds early indoors about eight to ten weeks before the frost-free date. Plant several seeds in a pot. Transplant this slow-growing herb to the garden once all danger of frost has passed.
Spacing: Space plants 6 to 8 inches apart.
Harvesting Guidelines: Snip off stem tips as needed. When harvesting for drying, cut whole stems, a few inches above the soil surface. Pick only when plants are dry, and harvest for preserving before plants flower.
Preserving Techniques: Hang upside down to dry or strip stems and dry in an electric dehydrator. Freeze leaves in ice cubes or minced in oil or butter.
Pests: Generally pest-free.
Diseases: Generally disease-free but can develop fungal root rots or leaf spot diseases in wet soils or high humidity conditions. Plant in containers or raised beds if this is a problem.
Notes: Plant a second crop in early July for a steady supply during the season.

Galium odoratum
Sweet Woodruff

Life Cycle: Perennial, Zones 3 to 9.
Size: 8 inches to 1 foot tall, 6 to 8 inches wide.
Appearance: Six to eight bright green

leaves grow in whorls. Leaf margins are smooth and leaves are oval to lance-shaped with pointed tips. Clear white flowers grow in clusters above the mounded leaves in early to midspring.
Uses: Ornamental—use the clean-smelling dried leaves and flowers in potpourri but do not place these pot-pourris where children or pets can reach them because this plant can cause liver damage if ingested. Plants make excellent ground covers in wooded or shaded areas.
Exposure: Shade but will tolerate partial sun.
Soil: Moist and humus-rich with a pH of 5.0 to 5.5. Mulch with leaves from hard-wood trees or apply ½ inch of finished compost to the area in very early spring.
Propagation: Seeds are difficult to germinate, so it's best to buy plants. If using seeds, plant in the fall where they are to grow, and let them freeze and thaw over the winter months. Germination can take 6 to 18 months. Sweet

GALIUM ODORATUM

woodruff self-sows easily in favorable locations.
Spacing: 8 to 10 inches apart in all directions.
Harvesting Guidelines: From late spring until midsummer, snip topmost leaves and stems from established plants when plants are dry.
Preserving Techniques: Hang upside down to air-dry.
Pests: Generally pest-free.
Diseases: Generally disease-free.

Notes: Sweet woodruff is often used to give a vanilla flavor to commercially-available wines and alcoholic beverages. According to the FDA, this use poses no danger. However, on a home level, it's best not to ingest it in any form.

Tanacetum vulgare var. *crispum*
Tansy, Fern-leaf Tansy

Life Cycle: Perennial, Zones 4 to 8.
Size: 3 to 4 feet tall, 1 foot to 1½ feet wide.
Appearance: Leaves are finely divided into about a dozen leaflets with toothed edges. They have a ferny look, not only in shape but also in texture. Leaves die back in winter and grow from the crown in very early spring. Flowers grow in flat clusters at stem tips. Individual blooms are yellow, and formed of many tightly packed petals. Blooming begins in mid-summer and continues until fall.
Uses: Medicinal—soak tansy leaves and flowers in heated oil to make a lotion to control mild acne. Wildlife—tansy plants repel many insects, including ants and fleas. Dry it to use in pet cushions and use oil extractions in insect-repelling lotions. Ornamental—fresh tansy stems are wonderful in bouquets. Dried flower stems keep their color.
Exposure: Partial shade but tolerates full sun if soil is consistently moist.
Soil: Moist, well-drained, average fertility. Add ½ inch of compost in early spring.
Propagation: Start seeds early indoors,

TANACETUM VULGARE

about six to eight weeks before the frost-free date. Transplant seedlings to garden after all danger of frost has passed. Divide established plants in early spring or fall.
Spacing: Allow 2 feet between plants.
Harvesting Guidelines: Cut when plants are 8 inches tall and after the plants are dry in the morning. Wait until afternoon to cut flowers, and cut when almost all the flowers on a stem are fully open.
Preserving Techniques: Hang dry.
Pests: Aphids.
Diseases: Usually disease-free.
Notes: Tansy self-sows huge numbers of plants. Avoid this by deadheading. If you don't get to it, they are easy to pull.

Artemisia dracunculus var. *sativa*
Tarragon, French Tarragon

Life Cycle: Perennial, Zones 4 to 8.
Size: 1½ to 2 feet tall, 1 to 1½ feet wide.
Appearance: Leaves are slender with smooth margins and a prominent central vein. At the base of the plant, they

grow in groups of three but at the top, they grow alone. The flowers are inconspicuous, but if you look closely, you might see tiny round flowers at the ends of the stems in midsummer. Plants die back in fall and appear again in early spring.

Uses: Culinary—tarragon is essential in some cooked dishes, such as chicken with 40 cloves of garlic. It also makes a good addition to salad dressings and many sauces. Add at the end of the cooking period. Make tarragon vinegar with high quality white wine vinegar.

Exposure: Full sun but will tolerate filtered shade.

Soil: Well-drained, fertile, and humus-rich. Add ½ inch compost to growing area each spring.

Propagation: Tarragon does not come true from seed; buy plants and propagate them by stem cuttings in the fall. Root and overwinter the stem cuttings indoors and plant out the following spring. Divide three- to four-year old plants in early spring.

Spacing: Allow 2 feet in all directions.

Harvesting Guidelines: Once plants are 8 to 10 inches tall, cut stem tips in the morning, after the dew has dried. When harvesting for drying or preserving, cut stems to within a few inches of the soil surface in late June. Stems may also be cut back in fall before frost.

Preserving Techniques: Dry in an electric dehydrator to keep flavor and color. Freeze for the best results, either in ice cubes or a butter or oil mixture. Tarragon preserved in white wine vinegar can be used in dishes where the vinegar is an asset.

Pests: Usually pest-free.

Diseases: Disease-free in good conditions but can develop root rots, downy mildew, or powdery mildew (many fungal species) in soggy soils.

Notes: The seeds you may see for "Tarragon" are for Russian tarragon, a plant that looks something like French Tarragon but lacks the flavor.

Thymus spp.
Thyme

Life Cycle: Perennial, Zones 5 to 9.

Size: 6 inches to 1¼ feet tall, 6 inches to 1¼ feet wide, depending on cultivar.

Appearance: Leaves are tiny and narrow with smooth margins. The leaves of many cultivars have pale hairy undersides. Stems become woody after the first year and retain leaves in all but the coldest locations. Blooming begins in midsummer and lasts for a month or so. Flowers of most cultivars grow in clusters and are pink.

Uses: Culinary—thyme is used in a huge variety of cooked and raw foods. Medicinal—a strong infusion settles an upset stomach. Cosmetic—strong infusions help prevent dandruff when used as a hair rinse and also have antiseptic qualities that help to heal rough, raw skin. Wildlife—many beneficial insects are attracted to thyme flowers but the dried leaves can act as an insect repellent. Aromatherapy—thyme infusions added to the bath have a stimulating effect. Ornamental—thyme adds a piney scent to potpourris.

Exposure: Full sun but tolerates partial shade.

Soil: Well-drained, sandy soil with low to moderate fertility. Do not overfertilize or overwater.

Propagation: Some cultivars can be grown from seed but others cannot. If planting seeds, start them indoors, about 8 to 10 weeks before the last expected frost. Plant five to eight seeds to a pot or cell. Transplant to the garden a week before or after the frost-free date. Stems can be layered in late spring to early summer. Take cuttings in spring and divide plants in spring or fall.

Spacing: 1 foot between plants.

Harvesting Guidelines: Harvest before or after plants are in bloom. Cut stem

THYMUS × CITRIODORUS

tips or whole stems before the plant blooms, leaving at least 2 inches of stem above the soil surface. After bloom, take only stem tips to let the plant build resources for the coming winter.

Preserving Techniques: Bunch stems with a rubber band and cover with a paper bag. Hang the bag upside down to air-dry. Leaves will fall into the bag as they dry.

Pests: Spider mites.

Diseases: Usually disease-free but will contract fungal root rots in soggy soils.

Notes: Check a good catalog to see how many wonderful species of thyme are available. To have a steady supply of non-flowering, harvestable plants all through the season, grow a few plants each of 'silver', 'lemon', 'English,' and 'German' thyme.

CHAPTER 8

FRUITS

*F*ruits add a new dimension to your gardening, not only in skills and the types of food you can produce but also in appearance. Most fruiting plants are lovely additions to the landscape throughout the year. And many fruiting plants make ideal focal points in the landscape.

For example, a pair of apple trees can mark the entryway to the backyard; a nicely trellised row of raspberries can define one side of the vegetable garden; blueberries can make a double-duty foundation planting; and kiwis can add interest to a garage wall. Good planning ensures both blooms and fruits for a long stretch, and as you'll quickly discover, yields of fruiting plants are generally high.

The flavor of homegrown fruit is a revelation for most people. Even experienced vegetable gardeners who expect the difference in taste between winter grocery store tomatoes and their own summer tomatoes are surprised to find that the difference in fruit is just as extreme. Homegrown fruit is picked when it is naturally ripe, and as with vegetables, home gardeners can choose cultivars for flavor or preserving qualities rather than shipping characteristics.

On a large scale, fruiting plants can be difficult to grow because of pest and disease problems. But in a small planting, the major fruit pests and diseases are relatively easy to manage. Unless you live next door to a commercial orchard, it is unlikely that you will lose a plant or a crop to a pest or disease. However, this doesn't mean that you can neglect your fruiting plants. To keep them healthy, you'll need to follow the guidelines in this chapter for selecting, planting, pruning, general cultural care, and pest and disease management.

All the attention you give to fruiting plants is worth it. Before long, you'll be looking forward to clear days in February when you can prune the apple trees, early mornings in May when you foliar-feed the berries, crisp days in September when you prepare plants for winter, and harvesting throughout the season. But the only way to discover this is to take courage in hand and plant some fruit.

BACKYARD TREES and other fruit plants contribute as much beauty as they do good things to eat.

CITRUS TREES are easy to grow in the right climate but can be disappointing in areas that occasionally get frost.

Hardiness ratings do not tell the full story. Fruit cultivars are given hardiness ratings, just as other perennials. However, the hardiness rating doesn't tell the whole story. No matter where you live, try to buy plants that have been raised in your region. This is particularly important in Zones 3, 4, and 5a, because conditions within in these zones can vary so much as a consequence of location. In the Northeast, temperatures fluctuate widely during the winter and early spring, but in the Midwest and prairie provinces of Canada, they are much more stable. Because alternating thaws and freezes are much harder on plants than a period of steady cold, trees grown in the Midwest sometimes have difficulty adjusting to New England conditions. In western Massachusetts for example, January thaws are common, while they're rare in northern Michigan.

FRUIT TREES

WHEN YOU THINK OF GROWING FRUIT, you may visualize a bowl of strawberries covered with a dollop of sweet whipped cream. If you preserve food, jars of brandied peaches may pass in front of your mind's eye. Bakers tend to plan for treats such as apple pies or blueberry muffins. But whatever your tastes, your first task as a fruit grower is to learn whether the fruits you want to grow will thrive in your area, and if so, which cultivars are the best choice to plant.

Environmental Considerations

Climate determines whether or not you can grow a particular fruit. For example, though few Vermonters expect to be able to grow oranges or bananas in their backyards, they are usually surprised to learn that sweet cherries are beyond their climatic reach. Similarly, it is a rare apple that can survive and produce in Zones 8b, 9, and 10. Two factors are responsible for plants' climatic preferences—their tolerance to temperature extremes and their requirements for certain numbers of "chilling" or "heating" hours. (See the box, "Heating and Chilling Hours," right.)

Trees and shrubs are similar to other plants in their ability to stand extreme cold or heat. A prolonged period of below-freezing temperatures is as certain to kill a lemon tree as it is to kill a tomato plant. But just as some tomato cultivars can stand cooler temperatures than others, certain fruit cultivars have been bred to tolerate warmer or colder conditions where January thaws are common.

HEATING AND CHILLING HOURS

Fruiting plants require sustained cold or warm temperatures. "Heating hours" are the number of hours above 65°F to which a plant is exposed. If the heating requirements are not met, the plant will decline, and in some cases, fruit will not develop or mature.

"Chilling hours" are the number of hours below 45°F that a plant experiences. If a plant is not exposed to adequate chilling hours, it will not be able to break dormancy in the spring. Because the plant cannot leaf out, it dies. The lack of an appropriate number of chilling hours is usually the culprit when a proven northern cultivar fails to grow in a southern location.

Various cultivars of the same species have different chilling-hour requirements. When you buy a plant, ask how many chilling hours the cultivar requires. If the nursery lists them as low, moderate, or high, translate these terms to mean 300 to 400 hours for a low rating, 400 to 700 for a moderate rating, and 700 to 1,000 for a high requirement. To learn the average chilling hours in your area, check with the Cooperative Extension Service or local horticultural societies.

Pollinators

The flowers of most apples, pears, blueberries, and sweet cherry cultivars are "self-infertile," meaning they cannot pollinate themselves. Instead, insects must fertilize them with pollen from an entirely different cultivar. To make this even more complicated, certain cultivars can pollinate one another, but others can't.

Check for compatibility. When you buy fruit plants, check with the nursery or mail-order distributor to learn which plants and trees to pair with which, and be sure to buy those pollinators at the same time. Some growers also graft, or attach, selected scion (or top growth) branches of different cultivars to the top of their trees. However, grafting is not always reliable, and it is a difficult process with which to obtain predictable results. For inexperienced fruit growers, it is usually recommended to begin by growing compatible trees, then move on to grafted trees.

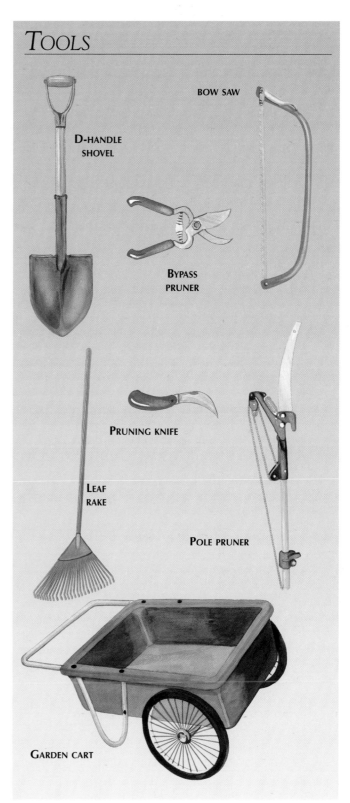

TOOLS

D-HANDLE
SHOVEL

BOW SAW

BYPASS
PRUNER

PRUNING KNIFE

LEAF
RAKE

POLE PRUNER

GARDEN CART

CHAPTER 8

CHOOSE A DWARF or semidwarf tree if working on a ladder bothers you. Harvesting safety will never be a concern again.

Maintenance Requirements

Some tree species are harder to successfully grow than others. In Zone 5, for example, many peaches are prone to frost damage at either end of the season. If you choose to grow peaches in Zone 5 anyway, plan from the beginning to take the steps necessary to protect them from frost.

Similarly, some apple cultivars are relatively pest- and disease-free while others are more susceptible. If you know the characteristics of a cultivar before you buy, you can choose to prepare well for potential problems or sidestep them by selecting a more resistant plant.

Research your choices before you purchase any fruiting plant. Begin this process by searching out other fruit growers through local gardeners' associations. Growers in your own area will be able to tell you specifics about the performance of various trees in your climate.

Other considerations. Ripe soft fruits such as peaches and nectarines attract yellow jackets, so try to pick up all of the fallen fruit as soon as possible. You may also want to plant the trees in an out-of-the-way place in the yard so that the children will be less likely to play in the area and not be bothered by the bees. Even if you have to stretch your imagination, try to think of all the possible annoyances your fruit can give you; then develop strategies to avoid these problems.

Big or Small?

Think carefully about the mature size of the trees you select. In most parts of the country, you can choose between dwarf, semidwarf, and standard trees. This choice will not only affect the design of your yard, it will also affect the number of years before the tree bears fruit, and in many cases, the type and amount of care it requires.

Tree sizes can vary naturally, without any help from breeders. The smallest naturally growing fruit trees, which are called "genetic dwarfs," grow only 10 to 15 feet high, making them easy to maintain. However, the flavor of their fruit usually leaves much to be desired, and they tend to be quite susceptible to diseases.

In the early 1900s, horticulturists at the East Malling Research Station in England discovered that when they grafted top growth from a standard tree (with good flavor) onto the roots of a genetic dwarf, the fruit remained the same size, but the tree grew only as large as the dwarf. In some cases, resistance to diseases increased too. Since then, breeders have developed several different dwarf rootstocks and have worked with combinations of rootstocks and scions. Each combination produces a different result, but growers can tell you what to expect.

Dwarf trees have several advantages. Because they are so small, it is easy to give them adequate attention. Their yields per tree are lower, but a well-tended orchard of dwarf

trees gives as much or more fruit per square foot as an orchard of standard trees. Picking is easier and safer too. With a small stepladder, you can reach the fruit on every tree.

But there are some disadvantages to dwarf trees. Most dwarf trees have a shorter life expectancy than standards of the same cultivar, and almost all of them are shallow rooted. Consequently, they don't survive harsh winters well. Their roots are also brittle; a strong windstorm can knock over a mature dwarf tree. To counteract this, commercial orchardists support their dwarf trees with post-and-cable-trellises.

Growers have simply adapted to the shorter life span by planting new orchards more frequently. And in the North, where dwarfs really don't survive well, gardeners and orchardists use semidwarf rootstocks or work with dwarfing interstems. To create a tree with a dwarfing interstem, breeders begin by growing a standard, long-lived, hardy rootstock. They graft a genetic dwarf scion onto this rootstock and let it grow for a year or two. The next step is to prune off all of the branches and the top of the genetic dwarf and graft a scion of the selected cultivar onto the top of the interstem. The resulting tree is usually the size of a semidwarf.

While dwarf trees typically grow anywhere from 20 to 60 percent the size of a standard of the same cultivar, semidwarf trees usually grow to about 75 percent of that size. If you live in Zones 3 to 5a, the extra size is worth it when compared with losing a tree to bad weather.

THE VERSATILITY OF DWARF TREES. Shown from left to right: training an apple tree on a dwarf rootstock; a tabletop apple tree, 'Red Grieve'; and a stepover apple tree, 'Pixie'.

THESE 'RED PIXIE' APPLES are one of the many cultivars that grow well in containers and give a small yield.

Trees in Containers

Many dwarf fruit trees grow well in containers. Ask your nursery or supplier for cultivar and rootstock combinations that thrive with a restricted root space.

Both plastic and wooden containers are appropriate choices. Because container soils dry so quickly, look for containers with the thickest walls possible. Most dwarf trees will grow in a pot that is 2 feet wide by 3 feet deep, although more room never hurts. Because fruit-bearing trees can be top-heavy, the best containers are wide enough at the bottom that they won't tip over in the wind.

Soil drainage is essential. If you are planting in an old barrel or other container, drill several ¾-inch holes in the bottom. Add a layer of nylon window screening, and then fill the container with a nutrient-rich and quickly draining soil mix.

SMART TIP
PROTECT CONTAINER-GROWN PLANTS FROM FROST

Protect the roots of your trees over the winter if you live in an area where temperatures go below freezing. Sink the pots in soil during the late fall to give the best protection. If you have an unheated area such as a garage where temperatures remain above 32°F, move the container there once the plant is dormant. If neither of these options is possible, move the container to a somewhat protected niche and pile plastic bags filled with autumn leaves under, over, and all around the container. Tie a strong plastic tarp around this construction to hold it in place. In the spring, wait until heavy frosts have subsided to bring the container out in the open again.

PLANTING FRUIT TREES

CHOOSING WHERE YOUR FRUIT trees will grow is the first step in planting them. Although this might seem straightforward, determining the location of a tree is as important as deciding what species and cultivars to grow. If possible, take a year to make this decision. During that time, you'll be able to observe various locations closely. You will know where frost comes first and last, where puddles form in heavy rainstorms, and where winds are strong, moderated, or stagnant. In cases where you simply do not have this much time to learn about the site, try to take the following characteristics into consideration.

Exposure. Most fruiting plants require full sun to bear well. But the topic certainly doesn't end there. Full sun on a south-

CHOOSE LOCATIONS for each of your fruit trees carefully to minimize the chance of environmental damage.

ern slope is far different than full sun on a northern one, and your plants will respond accordingly. If you live in an area with late spring frosts (which can damage the blooms of a tree), plant on a northern slope if at all possible. Because it is cooler there than on a southern slope or on level ground, trees will be a little later in blooming. As a result, there will be fewer years when you need to protect the trees from late spring frosts.

Space. Adequate space is essential for fruiting plants. Plan to space trees as far apart from each other as they will be tall when they are mature. If trees of different heights are planted next to each other, use the taller one as your guide.

THE HEDGE EFFECT

Hedges make excellent windbreaks because they trap some of the air coming through them but, unlike walls, do not create a turbulent area on the far side.

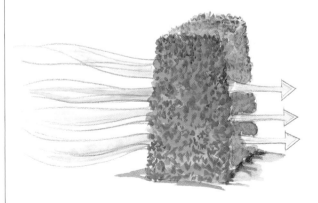

PLANT your fruits far enough away from the hedge so they still get good light exposure.

AIR DRAINAGE

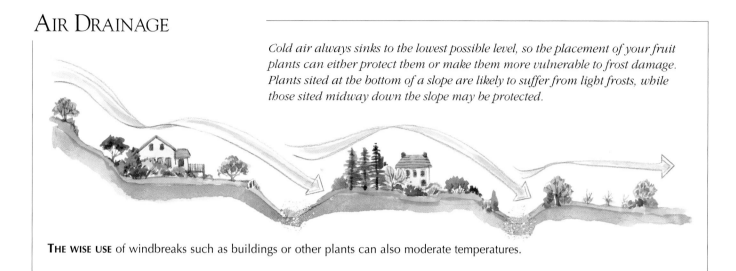

Cold air always sinks to the lowest possible level, so the placement of your fruit plants can either protect them or make them more vulnerable to frost damage. Plants sited at the bottom of a slope are likely to suffer from light frosts, while those sited midway down the slope may be protected.

THE WISE USE of windbreaks such as buildings or other plants can also moderate temperatures.

Soil characteristics. Fruit trees grow in the same location, with the same soil, for anywhere from 15 to 50 years. You won't be able to do much to improve the soil once the trees are planted, so choose the site with the best possible soil in the beginning.

Look for soil that has good drainage, a pH of 6.0 to 6.8, and moderate to high fertility levels with a high concentration of organic matter content. Because so few garden soils are totally ideal, you'll probably have to do some soil improvement, as discussed Chapter One, "Preparing to Garden," pages 18 to 30, before planting. Only two circumstances should prevent you from planting fruit in an area: one is a pH that is more than one point away from ideal, and the other is extremely poor drainage. Both of these problems will be so difficult to manage over the long term that they may seem like a losing battle not worth waging.

Air drainage. Many fungal diseases become more troublesome on plants growing where the air is stagnant. Fruit trees are especially susceptible to fungi, so try to site them where the prevailing breeze will rustle through their leaves each day.

Planting considerations. For decades, common knowledge asserted that the best way to plant a tree was to dig a big hole with straight sides and then amend the soil from the hole with compost, peat moss, or sand before using it to backfill around the roots. Today, however, researchers report that many trees planted this way may have difficulty establishing themselves because their roots tend to stay in the area where the soil has been modified. Because there is plenty of nourishment right there, the roots do not spread out in search of food and water. As a result, the best contemporary advice contradicts the old knowledge.

Do not dig the hole too deep, and remember that trees often sink a bit after they are planted. Try to plant your trees at the same depth that they were growing at the nursery. This level will be easy to determine if the tree is balled and burlapped or in a container, but even if it is bare-root, you should be able to see the soil mark on the trunk. Proper planting depth is particularly important in the case of grafts and interstems.

Always plant so that the graft union is 2 to 3 inches above the soil surface, and never cover the graft with mulch. Ask the nursery how deep to plant the rootstock because it can vary depending on cultivar, interstem, and rootstock.

SMART TIP

HOW TO PLANT FRUIT TREES

Make a hole with sloping sides, as deep as the depth of the root ball and twice that width at the top. To help the roots penetrate the surrounding soil, use a handheld claw to roughen up the sides of the hole. After the tree is in position, backfill with the soil from the hole without amending it in any way. Form a mound of soil 12 to 18 inches from the trunk to create a 6-inch deep basin for watering. As always, water deeply when the hole is half to three-quarters filled and again when the backfilling is complete.

CHAPTER 8

PRUNING FRUIT TREES

PRUNING INTIMIDATES MOST NEW gardeners, primarily because it seems so irrevocable. Many people worry that they will cut off a necessary branch, leaving their tree without a proper framework. But the fearful should take heart. If you pay attention to what you are doing, it is unlikely that you will cut off an important branch and even if you did, trees have the capacity to grow more than one limb in roughly the same area. Remember, too, that if pruning required the IQ of a genius or a sixth sense about plants, there would be far fewer apples in the world. Pruning, despite its importance to the tree, is not difficult to learn to do successfully. But pruning does require some thought. Before you begin, think about the purposes of your pruning task, the ways that the tree will react to various cuts, and the best timing for your pruning operation.

Purposes of pruning. Good pruning strengthens the tree and makes it more productive. When the tree is young, you prune to give it a strong framework of scaffold branches that are positioned to allow both light and air into the center of the tree.

As the tree matures, you prune to keep the tree from growing too large, to maintain a balance between shoot and fruit production, to remove weak, damaged, or diseased growth, to allow air and light to reach all parts of the tree, and to stimulate new growth where you want it.

WINTER IS THE PERFECT TIME TO STUDY THE FORM of your trees and decide how best to prune them.

The consequences of pruning. Plant growth is regulated by chemical compounds called *auxins*. They promote growth at the tip of the stem but inhibit the development of buds lower down on that stem. This effect, known as apical dominance, is what prevents a tree from growing a new limb at every bud. When you prune off the tip of a stem, you remove the site where the auxin is produced and stimulate once-dormant buds to develop. By choosing how much of a branch to remove, you can direct the plant's response. For example, pinching off the very tip of the

TREE ANATOMY

Pruning is much easier once you can identify the various parts of a tree. Though each tree is different, you'll see many of these structures on your own tree.

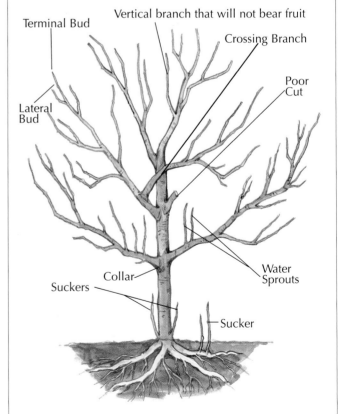

Terminal Bud

Vertical branch that will not bear fruit

Crossing Branch

Poor Cut

Lateral Bud

Water Sprouts

Collar

Suckers

Sucker

PRUNE TO BRING OUT THE BEST characteristics of each of your trees and minimize their weak points.

TREE SHAPES

The shape of your tree will be determined in large part by the type of tree it is. In general, dwarf and semidwarf trees are best pruned as vase or modified central leader trees, while standard trees can be pruned as central leader or modified central leader trees.

CENTRAL LEADER PRUNING depends on well-placed scaffold branches to allow light into the center.

MODIFIED CENTRAL LEADER PRUNING requires you to cut out the central leader after the fourth or fifth scaffold branch grows.

VASE, OR OPEN, PRUNING is done by cutting back the leader to form a completely open center.

branch encourages branching just below the pinched area. When you shorten a stem by cutting back by a third, several of the buds just below the cut will begin to grow. To promote even more vigorous growth of a bud very low on the branch, prune off two-thirds of the stem. In general, the buds nearest the cut make the most vigorous upright growth, while those that grow lower down on the stem make wider angles. The bud that develops nearest the tip of the stem will eventually become a dominant branch and produce auxins to inhibit the growth of buds below it. All pruning cuts used to cut back stems are referred to as heading cuts.

Thinning cuts are those that totally remove growth. Use thinning cuts to prune off weak or poorly positioned branches, water sprouts, and sprouts from the rootstock. When you remove a branch along a stem, the tip of the stem grows even more vigorously and latent buds are less likely to develop. If you want the stem to form a branch in

> ### SMART TIP
> #### ENCOURAGING BRANCHING
> Sometimes, despite the best possible pruning cuts, a bud stubbornly refuses to develop. If you really need that branch to balance the tree, you can often stimulate growth by making a small notch in the stem about an inch above the bud.

a different spot than the branch that you pruned, remove the site of auxin production by heading back the stem an appropriate distance, as discussed at left.

Fruit seeds also produce auxins that affect subsequent growth. If too many auxins are present, such as when the tree has produced a large crop, far fewer flower buds will sprout for the next year's crop. This is why some trees bear heavily only in alternate years.

Thinning, or pruning off, the developing fruit not only evens out production from one year to the next, but it also increases the size of the remaining fruit. It is best to thin the fruit twice, once just after the blossoms have dropped and again just after the June fruit drop. As a general rule, allow a space two to three times the size of the mature fruit between the fruit you leave on the tree.

Timing. Most heading-cut pruning on apples, pears, and quinces is done in late winter or very early spring, while the plant is still dormant. When the tree comes out of dormancy, the lack of auxin production at the headed-back stem tips causes lateral buds to grow vigorously.

In contrast, very little to no dormant pruning is done on peaches and nectarines because it promotes early blooming. The first defense against frost damage to these trees is to wait until the tree is already in bloom to make heading cuts. If done at this time, the tree still responds by producing new growth along branches that have been headed back.

Pruning in summer reduces rather than stimulates regrowth. You can use this to your advantage when you are making thinning cuts to bring light into the center of the tree or to remove unwanted growth. Heading cuts done in midsummer can have the effect of stimulating the formation of flower buds rather than those that will grow into shoots. Growers use this method to promote maximum fruiting on espalier-trained trees, as discussed on page 231.

BEFORE PRUNING. The branches of this peach tree are too closely spaced and prevent light from reaching the center of the tree.

AFTER PRUNING. The same peach tree has been opened up so light can reach the center, eliminating weak or misplaced growth.

Preparing for pruning. Before taking so much as the first cut on your tree, learn about its natural growth habits and the shape that most growers give it. As illustrated on page 227, the three most common ways to prune and train fruit trees are central leader, modified central leader, and vase, or open, shape. In general, dwarf and semidwarf trees are pruned to a vase or modified central leader, while standards are frequently pruned to a modified central leader or central leader. Specific pruning instructions for each fruit tree are given in the directory on pages 235 to 241.

Once gardeners were advised to prune off all the branches of a young tree when they planted it to allow roots to grow before leaves did. However, current knowledge about plant growth means that growers now give very different instructions.

If the tree is "feathered," meaning that it already has some branches, plant it and then look carefully at it. Your goal is to retain any well-positioned branches. Pruning, even if done when the tree is dormant, stimulates growth near the cuts but sets back the tree's overall growth. Ideally, the bottom branch will be about 2 feet above the soil surface and will be growing at an angle of at least 40 degrees from the trunk. If as many as two other branches are spaced 6 to 8 inches apart on the trunk, grow or can be trained to

SMART TIP

PRUNING WHIPS

If your tree is a "whip" (all of the branches have already been pruned off), plant it and then head back the stem to about two to three feet above the soil surface. By heading back the central stem, you will encourage the growth of buds lower down. The topmost bud that develops will eventually become the central leader and exert apical dominance over lower buds. However, the tree will develop branches that can become scaffold limbs before the top bud exerts apical dominance over the lower buds. (See page 226.)

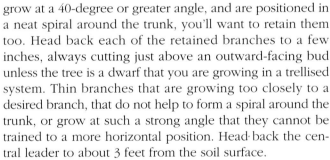

USE A SMALL PRUNING saw to cut branches that are no thicker than ½ inch thick.

DORMANT PRUNING on a warm winter day can be a highlight of the gardening season.

grow at a 40-degree or greater angle, and are positioned in a neat spiral around the trunk, you'll want to retain them too. Head back each of the retained branches to a few inches, always cutting just above an outward-facing bud unless the tree is a dwarf that you are growing in a trellised system. Thin branches that are growing too closely to a desired branch, that do not help to form a spiral around the trunk, or grow at such a strong angle that they cannot be trained to a more horizontal position. Head back the central leader to about 3 feet from the soil surface.

In the second year, pruning is dictated by the tree's form. If you are growing a central-leader tree, head back the leader again so that a new tier of scaffold branches will develop, thin out undesirable growth, and head back the branches. Cut back about a third of the previous year's growth from the central leader.

With a modified central-leader tree, cut back the central leader to just above the fourth scaffold branch. If the tree lacks this branch, head back the central leader. By the third season, there will be enough branches for you to cut back the central leader. Head back the branches you have

decided to keep, and then thin out any undesirable growth.

With trees with open centers, the central leader is usually removed during the second year. By this time, the trees usually have grown the three branches that form the vase shape. Thin undesirable growth.

You can widen branch angles in several ways. Insert a wooden toothpick between a developing branch and the leader to force the branch into a more horizontal form, or weight the branch with wooden clothespins. You can hang weights from larger branches or tie these branches to weights on the ground.

Pruning mature trees. Trees require pruning at all growth-stages. Good pruning helps to maintain the health of the tree, keeps it a manageable size, and promotes top-quality fruit every year. Make it a habit to cut out diseased branches while the tree is dormant, unless it is a peach or nectarine. (See page 238, "Peach Pruning," for specific instructions.) As the tree ages, you'll make most of your thinning cuts, many of which can be done in summer, toward the top of the tree and most of the heading cuts toward the bottom.

PRUNING GUIDELINES

■ Prune only as much as necessary to create the desired shape, to allow light into the center, and to keep the tree healthy and bearing well.

■ When pruning a dormant tree, wait to prune until the wood has thawed in the morning sun.

■ Use only appropriate tools, and sharpen them before every use. Sterilize tools with a 10 percent laundry bleach solution after every cut on a diseased tree.

■ When pruning off diseased or insect-infested growth, cut back the branch at least 6 inches beyond the site of the problem.

■ Remove and destroy all diseased and insect-infested wood. Do not leave it near the tree or compost it.

■ Cut all branches just below the collar. (See illustration on page 226.) When pruning branches back, make the cut above an outward-facing bud.

■ Do not use tree paint to protect wounds.

■ Make clean cuts with sharp tools.

■ Angle all cuts so excess moisture drips off, discouraging organisms that thrive in high-moisture conditions.

■ Prune peaches and nectarines only when they are actively growing, not when they are dormant. With your finger, rub off undesirable buds during the growing season so you won't have to prune them off the following year.

■ Prune off diseased growth immediately. If you wait until the tree is dormant, the problem can worsen.

SPURS FORM best on lateral branches pruned back to the top flower bud.

FRUIT GROWS FROM the buds left on the branch. A spur will remain after harvesting.

ADDITIONAL SPURS will form each year. They will be just below the fruits that grow.

AFTER A FEW years spurs will become too crowded. Prune out older ones.

THIN THE SPURS as necessary in late winter or early spring every year.

ESPALIERED TREES add a note of elegance to any yard.

ESPALIERED FRUIT TREES

AN ESPALIERED FRUIT TREE can be the centerpiece of your yard. These formal designs also have the advantage of ensuring that trees are extremely well maintained and that the fruits are large and healthy.

The most appropriate trees for espaliers are cultivars that bear on spurs. Espalier designs dictate that you remove many stem tips and some lateral branches, the sites where trees without spurs flower and fruit. Because spurs grow all along the branches, espalier training does not cut the yields of spur-bearers. Experienced growers recommend that you espalier dwarfs or small semidwarf trees because their less vigorous growth means less pruning and training.

The first step toward establishing an espaliered tree is choosing where to grow it. Many of these trees are planted and trained against walls. A wall gives excellent support for the training wires and can protect the plant from harsh winds. Stone or masonry walls store enough heat to moderate temperatures, as well. As long as you remember to protect blooms from late hard frosts, this temperature moderating quality can work in your favor for marginally hardy cultivars.

Some commercial orchardists have begun to put in acres of intensively grown dwarf or semidwarf cultivars that are trained on wires in an espalier fashion. A series of trees is grown on long rows of the trellis system, spaced far enough apart to allow air to circulate between trees. Even though this training system is more labor-intensive than growing normal modified central leader trees, the increased yields and consistent fruit quality make it economically practical.

How to prune espaliers. Pruning for espalier systems differs from other types of pruning in two important ways. First, the only branches you retain are those you can train along the horizontal supports, and second, late summer or early fall pruning is as intense as dormant pruning.

During the first season, allow three or four branches to grow along the supports, tying them into place as they grow. Small shoots will grow from these branches during the summer. In the late summer or early fall, after the bark on these shoots has turned brown and the bases of the shoots have become woody, cut them back to retain three leaves beyond the basal cluster of leaves. In future years, when you will prune some stubs that you created the year before, prune to one leaf above the basal cluster.

When the tree is dormant, prune the fruiting spurs so that the fruit will be well spaced. If any of the shoots you pruned the previous fall or late summer have regrown, prune them back again. Use this time to head back the horizontal branches as well.

THIS APPLE CORDON has been trained along a fence to form a simple espalier.

FRUIT TREES provide shade, fruit, and a handsome focal point.

CARE OF YOUR FRUIT TREES

THE FIRST THREE TO FIVE years a fruit tree grows are the most influential and the most demanding. As with children and puppies, early care determines adult health. Be scrupulous about pruning, watering, mulching, protecting against animals, monitoring and controlling pests and diseases, keeping the area around the tree clean, and preparing it for winter. Once the tree is mature, which will happen within 5 to 6 years for dwarfs and 10 to 12 for standards, maintenance needs decrease as long as you take care of the basics—routine pruning, monitoring and controlling pests and diseases, harvesting, and winter preparation.

Watering. Adequate water supplies are mandatory for getting a new tree off to a good start. As described earlier, water the planting hole deeply when you plant. Unless you live in a dry climate or your soil is unusually dry, do not water again until you see new growth. Because the tree's roots are not actively growing yet, soggy soils can invite rot. But once the buds begin to plump out, put the tree on a regular watering schedule.

Set up a rain gauge near the tree. Watch it and record all rainfalls. Your tree will require between 1 to 2 inches a week. If rainfall is less than this, you will need to irrigate. Check the fruit trees directory, pages 235 to 241, for the required quantities of water.

When you plant, make a 3- to 4-inch mound around the tree about 1 to 1½ feet from the trunk. The mound creates a basin to hold water. Soak this area thoroughly, reapplying water as necessary to add an equivalent of at least 2 gallons per square foot of root area. The basin and mound arrangement is particularly important when you are watering balled-and-burlapped trees. Because it takes the roots a season to grow into the adjoining soil, they do not absorb water well on the edges of their root zone for at least the first year.

As the tree grows each year, expand the area of the basin so that it extends just beyond the branch tips. When you calculate watering requirements, remember that the roots actually extend into the soil about one and a half times the diameter of the top growth.

Trees growing in lawns require more water than the lawn. Set up a rain gauge near the tree to track rain, and supplement it as necessary.

Fertilizing. Nutritional requirements vary according to the needs of the particular tree and the reserves in the soil. In good soil, an application of 5 to 10 pounds of compost per tree every spring maintains an adequate nutrient supply. However, because this application simply replaces the nutrients that were lost during the year, you may need to supplement with greater quantities and other nutrient sources.

Get into the habit of testing the leaves for nutrient content every two to three years. Laboratories that provide this service can be found on the Internet by searching under plant and tissue testing. Using the recommendations of the lab, apply needed nutrients in slow-release forms to prevent burning the roots. For example, alfalfa or soybean meal will add nitrogen, rock phosphate and kelp supply phosphorus, and greensand provides potassium. Please refer to the table, "Nutrient Contributions of Common Soil Amendments and Fertilizers," in Chapter 1, "Preparing to Garden," page 29, for a list of slow-release nutrient sources.

Mulching. Use organic mulch around your fruit trees. Mulch supplies food for nutrient-supplying microorganisms, holds soil moisture, and prevents weed growth. But it can also provide a cozy habitat for rodents and other tree pests unless you use it carefully.

When you plant, apply a layer of mulch outside the mound area. This placement guarantees that there will be at least a foot of bare soil surrounding the trunk. Although this distance may not seem like much, most mice will think twice about nibbling on something that far from cover.

Apply a deep enough layer of mulch to ensure that it will keep weeds down and slow evaporation from the soil. Depending on your climate and the biological activity in your soil, up to 6 inches of straw or 2 inches of shredded bark mulch will disappear over the season. Prepare for this by stockpiling extra material at the beginning of the season so that you can replace it as it degrades.

Sanitation. Good sanitation helps to keep pests and diseases from building up significant populations near your garden plants. But nowhere is it more important than around fruiting plants. Even if you occasionally let the rest of the garden get sloppy, save yourself misery by staying on top of housekeeping chores near the fruit.

DROPPED FRUIT can harbor pests and diseases. Pick it up before problems multiply.

Sanitation begins when you prune. As you remove growth, no matter how small, put it into a cart so that you can wheel it away at the end of the pruning session. If you have a chipper, put the pruned branches through it before adding them to a hot compost pile. If you don't have a chipper, dispose of the branches far away from the trees, or if your town allows, burn them. As a last recourse, you can bury the pruning debris at least 6 inches deep and as far as possible from the fruit plants. This fastidious care is warranted because many pests and diseases overwinter in the bark. If you simply leave the pruning waste hanging around the edge of the property, the pest organisms will move back into your trees in the spring.

Small fruits may drop to the ground in early June if they are infested with plum cucurlio (*Conotrachelus nenuphar*) or codling moth (*Cydia pomonella*) larvae. It is imperative to interrupt the pest life cycle by picking up the fruit and destroying it. Do not put June drops in a compost pile or bury them. Instead, put them in a plastic bag destined for the landfill, or burn them.

At the end of season, when you are preparing your trees for winter, remember to rake off all the old mulch around the trees along with the fallen leaves. Use this material to build or add to a hot fall compost pile. If your supply of nitrogen-rich green material is low, add alfalfa pellets to boost the nitrogen level.

ORGANIC MULCHES can contribute nutrients, minimize weeding chores, and hold soil moisture.

PEACHES CAN FINISH RIPENING inside without losing any of their flavor or nutritional qualities.

Preparing for winter. Fall is one of the busiest seasons for the fruit grower. Use this time to be sure that trees go into the winter with the best possible sanitation. In addition to raking up old mulches and debris, remove all the shriveled fruit that is still on the tree and destroy it. Add new mulch around the tree, 12 inches from the trunk. Protect the trunk from winter sunscald by wrapping it with a tree guard or painting it with white latex. Enclose painted trees with fine-mesh wire to keep rodents away.

In some areas, deer can destroy young trees over the winter. If you live where the deer population is high, think about enclosing entire saplings in a cage made of chicken wire. Although this might seem like an extreme response, it is often the only thing that works. Remember that rodents can squeeze through the wire, so you'll still need to protect stems with a tree guard or fine-mesh wire.

Winterkill is actually a response to drought. Even though it usually happens in midwinter, it may not be apparent until spring when you suddenly notice dead tissue. Winterkill occurs during winter warm spells when twigs and small branches thaw enough so that water transpires from the bark. Since the ground is still frozen, roots can't take up water to replace transpirational losses, and the moisture-deficient tissues die. Protect against this by watering deeply in the fall. And site the trees on northern slopes and other areas that are slow to thaw in midwinter sunshine.

Monitoring for pests and diseases. Many of the most damaging pests and diseases start so slowly that is easy not to notice them until they have inflicted major damage. The only way to protect your trees is by careful observation. Once a week, take the time to really look at your plants. Check the top and bottom surfaces of the leaves, examine the bark, and check all new growth to be certain it is clean and healthy. After you have grown each type of fruit plant for a while, you will know which pests and diseases are most likely to strike and how to manage them so that they inflict the least possible damage. But before then, rely on the information in Chapter 9, "Preventing Weeds, Pests and Diseases," pages 266 to 303, to identify and control problems. Compare the pests and diseases listed in the fruit trees directory, starting on the next page, with the directory listings for those pests and diseases in Chapter 9. Remember, it's important to properly identify the pest or disease first before treating the symptoms.

Harvesting. The first harvests of your fruit trees are among the most exciting times in the garden. But to make certain that the fruit is the best possible quality, it's important to harvest and eat it at the correct stage. For example, peaches will taste best if they are picked before they are fully ripe. Refer to the entries in the fruit trees directory, starting on the next page, to learn when and how to harvest each type of fruit you are growing.

SMART TIP

WHEN IS A PEACH PERFECTLY RIPE?

Pick peaches when they are fully colored and slightly soft around the stem, and then let them finish ripening in a dry spot indoors. Check the fruit trees directory, page 238 for general harvesting information, and remember to ask the nursery for tips on your particular cultivars.

ILLUSTRATED PLANT-BY-PLANT DIRECTORY OF FRUIT TREES

Malus

Apple

Zones: 3 to 9.
Size: 8 to 30 feet tall, 8 to 40 feet wide.
Flowers: In early spring, white or pink, 1-inch, star-shaped flowers with five petals grow in clusters.
Leaves: Shiny, dark green leaves have pointed tips and serrated leaf margins. Veins are prominent. In autumn, leaves turn a drab yellow or brown before falling.

PLANTING

Exposure: Full sun, preferably on a north-facing slope.
Soil: Well-drained, moderately fertile, pH of 6.5 to 6.8. In early spring each year, apply 5 to 10 lbs. of compost to the soil surface, from about 6 inches from the trunk to just beyond the drip line. Send the leaves to a lab to tissue test for nutrient content every 3 years, and amend the soil or foliar feed accordingly.
Spacing: Plant trees as far apart from each other as they will grow tall.
Pollinators: Check with the nursery or supplier to learn which of the cultivars that bloom at the same time are compatible. Try to buy pollinating cultivars at the same time to be assured of getting them.

CULTURAL CARE

Watering: Apply approximately 2 gallons per square foot of root area every week.
Mulching: After planting, leave an 8- to 12-inch-diameter area around the trunk weed-free and clear of mulch. Beyond this, mulch with 4 to 6 inches of straw or 3 to 4 inches of a denser material. In a lawn, mulch a minimum of 4 square feet around each tree.
Pests: Codling moths, plum curculios, apple maggot flies, aphids, leaf rollers, European red mites, two-spotted spider mites, scale, leafhoppers, tarnished plant bug, and round-headed apple tree borer.
Diseases: Apple scab (*Venturia inaequalis)*, fire blight (*Erwinia amylovera*), apple rust (*Gymnosporangium juniperivirginianae*), black rot (*Sphaeria malorum*), sooty blotch (*Gloeodes pomigena*), fly speck (*Microthyriello rubi)*, phoma fruit spot (*Mycosphaerella pomi*), and powdery mildew (*Podosphaera leucotricha*).

PRUNING

After Planting: Choose future scaffold branches and thin the others. Head back the leader and branch tips.
Routine Pruning: Prune to modified central leader, central leader or open-center form, depending on size of tree. Make heading cuts while the tree is dormant, and thin as much as possible in summer.
Mature Plants: Thin spurs and fruits as necessary, prune out damaged or infested growth, thin to allow light and air into the center of the tree.

HARVESTING, STORING, AND PRESERVING

Fruiting: Depending on cultivar, plants fruit on 1- to 10-year old wood, on spurs or tips of branches.

Years to Bearing: 3 to 8, depending on rootstock and cultivar.
Harvest Season: Late summer to late fall.
Yields: 10 to 30 bushels for standards and semidwarfs, less for dwarfs.
Notes: Apples suffer from several storage disorders and diseases but proper storage temperatures minimize damage. Keep them in a root cellar at a temperature close to freezing. Do not store near potatoes because they hasten ripening and spoilage of each other.

Young spur-bearing apple trees grow about 6 to 12 inches each year, while non-spur-bearing trees grow anywhere from 1 to 2 feet. Once trees are mature, growth slows to about 6 to 10 inches a year for both types.

Prunus armeniaca, P. armeniaca var. *mandschurica, P. armeniaca* var. *sibirica*

European apricot, Manchurian apricot, Siberian apricot

Zones: European, 5 to 9; Manchurian and Siberian, 3 to 8.
Size: 4 to 25 feet tall, 6 to 25 feet wide.
Flowers: White and/or pink, five-petaled, 1-inch wide, fragrant. Flowers appear in

Prunus species/**Apricot** *continued*

very early spring.

Leaves: Oval, 1 to 2 inches long with finely serrated margins, deep green with reddish undertones when young, turning bright yellow in the fall.

PLANTING

Exposure: Full sun in an area protected from winds and early and late frosts.
Soil: Well-drained, sandy loam soils, moderate to high fertility.
Spacing: As far away from other trees as the tree's mature height.
Pollinators: Apricots, even the self-fruitful European cultivars, bear best with pollinators. Buy several compatible trees. 'Nanking' cherry is a good pollinator.

CULTURAL CARE

Watering: At least 2 gallons per square foot of root area every week or an inch of rainfall.
Mulching: After planting, leave an 8- to 12-inch diameter area around the trunk weed-free and clear of mulch. Beyond this, mulch at least a 4-foot- square area with 4 to 6 inches of straw or 3 to 4 inches of a denser material.
Pests: Codling moth, plum curculio, aphids, spider mites.
Diseases: Bacterial canker, brown rot.

PRUNING

After Planting: Retain any branches that will make good scaffold limbs, and head them back unless you are training the tree as an espalier.
Routine Pruning: Prune to a modified central leader or open-center form. Head back branches in spring, and make as many thinning cuts as possible in summer. Thin fruit to at least 2 inches apart.
Mature Plants: Stimulate new growth by thinning small branches after they are three years old and keeping all branch tips headed back.

HARVESTING

Fruiting: Apricots fruit on 1-year-old spurs and branch tips.
Years to Bearing: 3 to 5.
Harvest Season: July and August. Fruit will not ripen after being harvested, so pick when it has softened but before it drops.

Yields: 1 to 2 bushels for dwarfs, 3 to 4 bushels for standard-size European cultivars.
Notes: Apricots make ideal espalier or cordon trees.

Prunus avium
Cherry, sweet

Zones: 5 to 9.
Size: 6 to 35 feet tall, 8 to 40 feet wide, depending on rootstock and cultivar.
Flowers: Showy white clusters in early spring.
Leaves: Dark green, pointed leaves are 3 to 6 inches long with serrated margins. They turn yellow in the fall.

PLANTING

Exposure: Full sun.
Soil: Well-drained, deep, and moderately fertile, pH of 6.0 to 6.8. Maintain fertility with 5 to 10 lbs. of compost around each tree in very early spring.
Spacing: As far apart as the mature tree will grow.
Pollinators: Almost all sweet cherries require pollinators and the few that are self-fruitful yield better if they have a pollinator. Check with your nursery to buy the correct pollinator because not all sweet cherries are compatible.

CULTURAL CARE

Watering: A minimum of an inch of rainfall or 2 gallons per square foot of root area every week. Keep soil moisture consistent when fruit is ripening, and do not overwater for fear of promoting cracking.

Mulching: Leave between 8 and 12 inches of soil bare around the trunk. Beyond that, apply 3 to 4 inches of a dense mulch, such as shredded hardwood bark, or 6 to 8 inches of a loose mulch such as straw.
Pests: Cherrry fruit fly maggot, pear slug (larvae of pear sawfly), plum curculio, black cherry aphids, green fruit worms, and birds.
Diseases: Cherry leaf spot (*Xanthomonas pruni, Coccomyces* spp.), verticillium wilt (*Verticillium* spp.), brown rot (*Monilinia fructicola, M. laxa*), little cherry, X-disease, and small-bitter Cherry (various viruses), powdery mildew (*Erysiphe* spp.), canker (*Valsa leucostoma).*

PRUNING

Fruiting: Fruit forms on 1- to 10-year-old spurs.
After Planting: Choose which scaffold limbs you will retain, and thin the other branches out. Head back the retained limbs to stimulate branching.
Routine Pruning: Prune and train to an open center form whenever possible. Keep up with training branches to spread because the natural growth habit is quite upright. Remove scaffold branches that form opposite each other because their weight may eventually spit the trunk. Do not thin fruit.
Mature Plants: Cherries need minimal annual pruning. Remove all diseased or damaged growth, and thin out branches that prevent light from entering the center of the tree.

HARVESTING

Years to Bearing: 4 to 5.
Harvest Season: July to August.
Yields: ¾ bushel for dwarfs, 1 bushel for semidwarfs, 2 bushels for standards.
Notes: Sweet cherries require a minimum of 1,000 chilling hours but will not fruit well where summer temperatures regularly exceed 90°F. If fruit appears hard, shriveled, and blotchy, have the leaves tissue-tested. Boron deficiencies, quite common in the eastern United States, are the usual cause. Because excess boron is lethal, follow the lab's recommendations to the letter.

Prunus cerasus
Cherry, sour

Zones: 4 to 8.
Size: 8 to 20 feet tall, 10 to 25 feet wide.
Flowers: Clusters of white, ¾- to 1-inch-wide flowers bloom in early spring.
Leaves: Oval, with a pointed tip, serrated margins; leaves turn yellow in the fall.

PLANTING
Exposure: Full sun but trees can tolerate a bit of light shade in the afternoon. In Zones 4 and 5, a protected niche on a north-facing slope is ideal.
Soil: Well-drained with moderate fertility levels and a pH of 6.0 to 6.8. Maintain fertility by applying 5 to 10 lbs. of compost around each tree in early spring.
Spacing: As far apart as mature tree height.
Pollinators: None required.

CULTURAL CARE
Watering: A minimum of 1 inch of rainfall or 2 gallons per square foot of root area every week. Keep soil moisture consistent when fruit is ripening, and do not overwater to prevent cracking.
Mulching: Leave 8 to 12 inches of soil bare around the trunk. Beyond that, apply 3 to 4 inches of a dense mulch such as shredded hardwood bark or 6 to 8 inches of a loose mulch such as straw.
Pests: Cherry fruit fly maggot, pear slug (larvae of pear sawfly), plum curculio, black cherry aphids, green fruit worms, and a variety of fruit-eating birds.
Diseases: Cherry leaf spot (*Xanthomonas*

pruni, Coccomyces spp.), verticillium wilt, brown rot (*Monilinia fructicola, M. laxa*), little cherry, X-disease, and small-bitter cherry (various viruses), powdery mildew (*Erysiphe* spp.), canker (*Valsa leucostoma* and *V. cincta*).

PRUNING
After Planting: Choose well-positioned scaffold branches and thin others. Head back leader and branches.
Routine Pruning: Prune to an open-center form or a modified central leader. Thin branches to allow light and air into the center of the tree. Train branches to form wide angles.
Mature Plants: Thin poorly positioned or diseased branches.

HARVESTING
Fruiting: Fruit forms on 1- to 10-year-old spurs.
Years to Bearing: 4 to 5.
Harvest Season: Mid-July to early August.
Yields: 1 bushel, dwarf trees; 2 bushels standard trees.
Notes: Sour cherries can be trained as espaliers. If you live in the North, choose a sour cherry such as 'Evans' that is known for its hardiness.

Citrus spp.
Citrus trees, including grapefruit, lemon, lime, and oranges

Zones: 9 to 10.
Size: 5 to 35 feet tall, 8 to 35 feet wide, depending on species and type.

Flowers: Fragrant, white, waxy, 1-inch-wide flowers bloom throughout the year.
Leaves: Glossy, dark green leaves are 3 to 5 inches long. Citrus trees are evergreen.

PLANTING
Exposure: Full sun, although some limes and lemons will tolerate afternoon shade in extremely hot locations.
Soil: Well-drained, high fertility and good moisture-holding capacity with a pH of 6.0 to 6.5. Nitrogen demands are relatively high, so it may be necessary to apply a cup of alfalfa pellets under compost applications. Unless the soil is unusually fertile, spread 10 to 20 lbs. of compost under the tree every six weeks to two months.
Spacing: As far apart as trees are tall.
Pollinators: None required.

CULTURAL CARE
Watering: Generally about 1½ to 2 inches a week or about 3 gallons per square foot of root area.
Mulching: Use a nitrogen-rich mulch such as grass clippings or alfalfa hay to add nitrogen to the soil. If weeds become a problem, apply several sheets of newspaper under the mulch.
Pests: Aphids, mealybugs, mites, navel orange worms, and scales.
Diseases: Collar rot (*Phytophthora citrophthora*), citrus scab (*Sphaceloma fawcettii*), brown rot (*Phytophthora* spp.), and various viral diseases.

PRUNING
After Planting: Head back branches.
Routine Pruning: Citrus trees do not require specialized pruning because they naturally form the most productive forms. After harvesting, prune to remove dead, weak or poorly positioned branches. On oranges, remove all suckers. On lime bushes, thin old stalks periodically.
Mature Plants: Thin to allow light and air into the center of the plant. Remove old wood that no longer bears well.

HARVESTING
Fruiting: Plants bear on the current year's growth.

Citrus species/**Citrus Trees** continued

Years to Bearing: 2 to 4.
Harvest Season: Varies with fruit type and location. Check with your supplier. If frost threatens, protect trees with blankets or other heavy covers.
Yields: Varies depending on fruit type and tree size. Again, your supplier can give you details.
Notes: Refer to local references and growers associations to learn more about growing citrus trees. Citrus must almost always be purchased locally since rootstocks are chosen to suit particular locations. In the North, you may want to grow containerized dwarf cultivars. If so, keep the tree in a protected spot during the summmer, and move it indoors long before frost. Indoors, they must receive full sun from a south-facing window. Mist the leaves twice a day to maintain good humidity levels.

Prunus persica var. *nucipersica*
Nectarine

Prunus persica
Peach

Zones: 5 to 9.
Size: 4 to 20 feet tall, 6 to 25 feet wide.
Flowers: Pink, sometimes double, 1- to 2-inch-wide flowers bloom in early spring.
Leaves: Lovely, glossy medium green leaves 6 to 8 inches long grow in drooping clusters and turn yellow in the fall.

PLANTING
Exposure: Full sun in a protected area on a north-facing slope.
Soil: High fertility, sandy, and well-drained with a pH of 6.5 to 6.8. After petal drop, supplement fertility by spreading a cup of alfalfa meal, 1 cup of gypsum, and 1 cup of rock phosphate over the root area before applying 10 to 20 lbs. of fully finished compost.
Spacing: As far apart as the mature height of trees.
Pollinators: None required for most cultivars; check with supplier to be certain.

CULTURAL CARE
Watering: Trees require a minimum of an inch of moisture a week. Supplement rain with irrigation if necessary, using 2 gallons per square foot of root area.
Mulching: Keep 8 to 12 inches of soil around trunk bare to discourage rodents. Mulch beyond this with 6 to 12 inches of straw or 3 to 6 inches of shredded hardwood bark. In the North, apply at least a foot of new mulch before snowfall to protect the roots over the winter.
Pests: Aphids, Oriental fruit moths, peach twig borers, European red mites, peach-tree borers, and tarnished plant bugs.
Diseases: Brown rot (*Monilinia [Sclerotinia] laxa, M. [Sclerotinia] fructicola*), peach scab (*Cladosporium carpophilum*), peach leaf curl (*Taphrina deformans*), peach yellows (viruses), and peach mosaic (viruses).

PRUNING
After Planting: Choose well-positioned scaffold branches and thin the others. Head back the leader and branches to stimulate branching.
Routine Pruning: Prune to an open-center or modified central leader. Nectarines require a great deal of pruning to remain productive and healthy. Wait to prune until tree is in bloom. Each year, cut back the longest branches, including the leader.
Mature Plants: Continue to cut back branches and the leader. Thin fruit to 6 to 8 inches apart. Thin weak, dead, and crossing branches. Thin to allow light and air into the center of the tree.

HARVESTING
Fruiting: Fruits form on 1-year-old wood.
Years to Bearing: 3 to 5.

Harvest Season: Late July, August, and early September, depending on cultivar. Pick early if frost threatens because fruit continues to ripen off the tree.
Yields: 3 to 5 bushels for standard trees, 1 to 3 bushels for dwarfs.
Notes: Chilling requirements for nectarines range between 800 to 1,200 hours. Choose a cultivar with an appropriate requirement. Where nectarines are marginal, grow a dwarf tree in a container so that you can protect the tree from frost damage and winterkill. Chilling reqirements for peaches range from 200 to 1,200 hours. Check with your supplier to learn the requirements of any tree you are interested in buying.

Pyrus communis
Pear

Pyrus pyrifolia, P. ussuriensis, P. bretschneideri
Pear, Asian

Zones: 4 to 9.
Size: 8 to 40 feet tall, 10 to 25 feet wide, depending on rootstock and cultivar.
Flowers: Lovely 1- to 1½-inch-wide white flowers bloom in clusters in spring.
Leaves: Shiny, dark green, 1 to 2½-inch-long leaves with slightly toothed margins. The leaves turn yellow before dropping in fall.

PLANTING
Exposure: Full sun, high air circulation.

Soil: Moderate fertility and well-drained. Pears can tolerate clay soils if humus content is high to promote drainage and pH is between 6.0 and 6.5. Do not over-fertilize, particularly with high nitrogen sources because excesses promote fire-blight, a troublesome disease.

Spacing: As far apart as the mature trees are tall.

Pollinators: Not all pears are compatible, check with your supplier to choose the best pollinators.

PYRUS CALLERYANA 'BRADFORD'

CULTURAL CARE

Watering: Trees require an inch to 1½ inches of moisture a week. Apply 3 gallons of water per square foot of root area.

Mulching: Keep a foot of soil bare around the trunk. Beyond this, mulch with 6 inches of straw or 3 to 4 inches of a denser material such as shredded hardwood bark.

Pests: Codling moth, pear psylla, pear sawflies, pearleaf blister mites, and San Jose scale.

Diseases: Fire blight (*Erwinia amylovora*), pear scab (*Ventura pirina*), leaf blight, and fruit spot (*Fabraea maculata*).

PRUNING

After Planting: Choose well-positioned branches to keep as scaffold limbs, and thin poorly positioned growth. Head back the leader and branch tips.

Routine Pruning: Prune and train to a central leader or modified central leader. Because fire blight infections may require pruning off an entire branch, retain more scaffold branches than you would if it were an apple tree. Do not head back the tips of the fruiting shoots on cultivars that fruit here as well as on spurs. Be vigilant about training branches to promote wide angles; pears have a tendency to grow vertically.

Mature Plants: Remove growth that prevents air and light from getting into the center of the tree. Remove all diseased growth as soon as you notice it. Thin new laterals and poorly positioned and weak growth in late winter or early spring. Do not thin fruit unless set is unusually heavy. Thin old wood when the spurs on it are 7 or 8 years old.

HARVESTING

Fruiting: Fruit forms on 1- to 10-year-old spurs and also on the tips of lateral branches.

Years to Bearing: 4 to 7.

Harvest Season: August to October, depending on cultivar. For the best texture and flavor, pick before the fruit is fully ripe and ripen indoors or in a root cellar or refrigerator.

Yields: ½ to 1½ bushels for dwarfs, 2 to 4 bushels for standards.

Notes: Resistance to fire blight can be promoted by rootstock choice. 'Old Home' × 'Framington' ('OH × F') are the best known resistant rootstocks and can range in size from dwarfing to standard. Asian pears have the same culture as European pears, but because their chilling requirements are only 400 to 900 hours, they bloom extremely early. Consequently, they are appropriate only for Zones 5 to 9 and must be grown in sheltered areas in Zone 5. They also differ in pruning needs because they tend to grow more vigorously and generally require more pruning to keep them within bounds. Thin fruit to one per spur to promote the largest fruit size and best health.

The Bradford pear (shown far left) does not produce edible fruit. However, it is covered with beautiful white flowers in the spring, making this tree an ornamental asset to any landscape.

Diospyros virginiana, D. kaki

American persimmon, Oriental persimmon

Zones: American, 5 to 9; Oriental, 7 to 10.

Size: American, 30 to 40 feet tall, 30 feet wide; Oriental, 25 to 30 feet tall, 25 feet wide.

Flowers: Both American and Oriental: fragrant, waxy white, ½ to 2 inches wide, in summer.

Leaves: American: dark green glossy leaves are about 6 inches long and turn yellow in fall. Oriental: dark green glossy leaves are heart shaped, 5 to 7 inches wide, and turn brilliant yellow or orange in fall.

PLANTING

Exposure: Full sun.

Soil: Well-drained, moderate fertility. American cultivars tolerate a broad range of soil types, but Oriental cultivars prefer sandy loams. Neither type can tolerate soils that are rich in nitrogen; fertilize with 5 to 10 lbs. of compost in early spring each year.

Spacing: A minimum of 25 to 30 feet between trees.

Pollinators: Check with your supplier

CHAPTER 8

Diospyros species /**Persimmon** *continued*

because most American and some Oriental cultivars require a pollinator.

CULTURAL CARE

Watering: Apply 3 gallons of water per square foot of root area during the first year. After that, do not water if rainfall measures 1½ inches every two weeks. Supplement if natural rainfall is less than this, remembering that 3 gallons of water per square foot of root area equals 1½ inches of water.

Mulching: Leave 8 to 12 inches of soil bare around trunk. Mulch beyond that with 6 inches of straw or 3 to 4 inches of a denser material.

Pests: Scale, aphids.

Diseases: Anthracnose (*Colletotrichum* spp.).

PRUNING

After Planting: Retain well-positioned branches, and head back all retained limbs, including the leader. Thin poorly positioned growth.

Routine Pruning: Prune and train as for a central leader with six to eight scaffold branches placed evenly around the trunk. Head back limbs to promote branching and remove suckers. Remove all dead or weak growth.

Mature Plants: Continue routine pruning, thinning old growth and heading back branches to stimulate new laterals.

HARVESTING

Fruiting: Fruits form on 1-year old wood.

Years to Bearing: 2 to 3.

Harvest Season: September to October. Harvest American persimmons when extremely ripe and let soften indoors. Clip off Oriental fruits with stem attached and if the cultivar is non-astringent, eat as soon as you wish. If astringent, let ripen fully indoors. Fruits can freeze on the trees and still be harvested.

Yields: American, 1 bushel; Oriental, 1 to 2 bushels.

Notes: Persimmons make excellent espalier trees because they grow so slowly that it is easy to keep up with their pruning. They are also beautiful at any time of year, making them an ideal focal point for the yard.

Prunus domestica, P. salicina
European plum, Japanese plum

Zones: European: 4 to 9; Japanese 6 to 10.

Size: European, 1 to 20 feet tall, 10 to 20 feet wide; Japanese, 10 to 20 feet tall, 10 to 20 feet wide.

Flowers: Beautiful white or pink, ¾- to 1-inch-wide flowers bloom in early spring.

Leaves: Oval, 2 to 4 inch long leaves have toothed margins and may exhibit a purplish undertone. They turn yellow in fall.

PLANTING

Exposure: Full sun, ideally on a north-facing slope.

Soil: Well-drained, high-fertility. Europoean plums tolerate heavy clay soils, but Japanese plums prefer a lighter, more sandy soil.

Spacing: As far apart as mature trees are tall.

Pollinators: Check with your nursery for the best pollinators because most Japanese plums require a pollinator as do many European ones.

CULTURAL CARE

Watering: Plants require 1 to 1½ inches of water per week. Supplement if necessary, using 3 gallons of water per square foot of root area to supply 1½ inches of water.

Mulching: Leave 8 to 12 inches of soil bare around the trunk and mulch beyond this with 6 inches of a light mulching material such as straw or 3 to 4 inches of a denser material.

Pests: Aphids, plum cucurlio, red spider mites.

Diseases: Black knot (*Dibotryon morbosum*), plum dwarf (viruses), brown rot (*Sclerotinia laxa*), leaf spot (*Xanthomonas pruni*).

PRUNING

After Planting: Choose branches to retain for scaffold limbs, and thin all poorly positioned branches. Head back the leader and all retained branches to stimulate branching.

Routine Pruning: Prune and train European plums to a modified central leader form and Japanese plums to open center forms. On both types remove dead, weak, or poorly positioned growth. On Japanese plums especially, cut back overly long branches, and thin out excess branches that block sunlight.

Mature Plants: European plums require very little pruning once the framework is established aside from thinning suckers and water sprouts. Japanese plums produce lots of growth that you must thin. Allow 4 to 6 inches between developing fruit of Japanese plums, and thin European plums to no more than two on each spur.

HARVESTING

Fruiting: European plums fruit on 2- to 6-year-old spurs; Japanese plums fruit on 1-year-old wood and spurs a year or more old.

Years to Bearing: 3 to 4.

Harvest Season: July to September for most of the U.S.

Yields: 1 to 2 bushels for standards of both types and ½ to 1 bushel for dwarfs.

Notes: In areas where soils are typically boron-deficient, tissue-test European plums for this element every two years. If the element is low, carefully follow the lab recommendations for amending because boron is toxic in high concentrations. Japanese plums usually require 700 to 1,000 chilling hours, and European plums require slightly more, from 800 to 1,100 chilling hours.

Asimina triloba
Pawpaw

Zones: 4 to 8.
Size: 10 to 25 feet tall, 5 to 15 feet wide.
Flowers: Flowers have a strong odor that some people find offensive. They are tri-lobed, a brown-violet color, and bloom in very early spring.
Leaves: Oval leaves with smooth margins are medium green before turning yellow in fall.

PLANTING
Preferred Exposure: Full sun.
Preferred Soil and Fertility: Moist but well-drained, moderately fertile.
Spacing: 20 feet apart from one another and from buildings.
Pollinators: Wild and cultivated paw-paws can pollinate each other. Buy two cultivars if pawpaws do not grow wild in your neighborhood. If pollination is sparse, hand-pollinate or hang rotten meat in the trees to attract carrion-seeking flies which will stay to pollinate the pawpaws.

CULTURAL CARE
Watering: Pawpaws require a consis-tently moist soil. Apply at least 3 gallons of water per square foot every week that rain does not supply 1½ inches.
Mulching: Leave the area around the trunk bare to protect against rodents, and mulch beyond this with a deep, mois-ture-retaining mulch.
Pests: Pawpaws are still wild enough to have few problems.

Diseases: No diseases attack pawpaws growing in well-drained soils.

PRUNING
After Planting: Head back any broken growth when you plant but do not cut undamaged branches.
Routine Pruning: Thin weak, diseased, or damaged growth.
Mature Plants: Pawpaws require very lit-tle pruning. Thin growth that prevents light and air from the center of the plant and remove any weak branches.

HARVESTING
Fruiting: Fruit forms on 1-year old wood.
Years to Bearing: 6 to 8.
Harvest Season: August to September.
Yields: 1 to 2 bushels.
Notes: Uder-ripe fruit can be astringent or bitter. After picking, let fruits soften for a few days indoors. Flavor varies between plants. Choose a named cultivar to assure good fruit quality. If you have wild plants with a slightly bitter taste, make sweetened pies or puddings with the fruit.

Cydonia oblonga
Quince

Zones: 5 to 8.
Size: 10 to 15 feet tall, 10 to 15 feet wide.
Flowers: Lovely, magnolia-like flowers are white or pink, 2 inches wide, and bloom in spring.
Leaves: Thick, oblong, 4-inch-long, medium green leaves with smooth mar-gins are woolly underneath and turn yel-low in fall.

PLANTING
Exposure: Full sun.
Soil: Well drained, moisture-retentive, fer-tile with a pH of 6.5 to 6.8. Apply 5 to 10 lbs. of compost around each tree in early spring.
Spacing: Allow 15 feet between plants.
Pollinators: None required.

CULTURAL CARE
Watering: Quinces require an inch of water a week. Supplement with 2 gallons of water per square foot to make an inch of water.
Mulching: Leave 8 to 12 inches of bare soil around trunk. Beyond this, mulch with 6 to 8 inches of straw or 3 to 4 inches of a denser material.
Pests: Codling moth, Oriental fruit moth, and aphids.
Diseases: Fire blight (*Erwinia amylovera*), bacterial leaf blight (*Pseudomonas* spp.).

PRUNING
After Planting: Quinces can become bushes or open-center trees. If you want to grow them as bushes, head back the leader to a foot above the soil surface, and allow suckers to grow. If you're growing the plant as an open-center tree, choose appropriate limbs to retain, and thin the others.
Routine Pruning: For bushes, thin as little as possible, but remove diseased growth. Develop tree form as soon as possible.
Mature Plants: Do not thin fruit. Head back branches of trees and branches every few years to stimulate new shoots.

HARVESTING
Fruiting: Fruit forms on tips of the previ-ous year's growth.
Years to Bearing: 3 to 4.
Harvest Season: September and October
Yields: 1 bushel.
Notes: You must cook quinces to make them edible. Stew them with apples or make preserves or jelly with them. When purchasing trees, look for a vegetatively propagated, named cultivar to assure yourself of the finest fruit quality.

ELDERBERRIES are beautiful shrubs that can feed you or the neighborhood birds.

Soil. Like fruit trees, most fruiting shrubs require light, well-drained soils for root health. Exceptions to this rule include currants, gooseberries, blueberries, and cranberries, all of which can tolerate a heavier soil as long as it contains enough compost or organic matter so that oxygen supplies remain high.

Blueberries and cranberries differ from the majority of plants in their pH requirements. While a pH of 6.5 to 6.8 suits almost all the other plants you'll grow, these plants suffer in a pH higher than 4.5. Some Northeastern soils are naturally this acid, as shown by the numbers of wild blueberries growing on hills and at the edges of northern woodlands, but most garden soils are not. If you want to grow cranberries or blueberries, you'll

CHOOSING FRUITING SHRUBS

FRUITING SHRUBS ARE SOME of the most beautiful and useful plantings in your yard. When you plan your landscape, consider whether a fruiting shrub can supply the necessary form or color required for the design. For example, if you need a high hedge to buffer highway noises, try growing high-bush blueberries (*Vaccinium corymbosum*) or elderberries (*Sambucus canadensis*). Prickly shrubs such as gooseberries (*Ribes hirtellum*) can make a hedge that keeps deer and dogs from entering the yard, and half-high blueberries are wonderful foundation plantings in combination with some evergreen plants. Whatever your design, there is sure to be a way to fit fruiting shrubs into it.

Environmental Requirements

Fruiting shrubs vary as much in their requirements as fruit trees—and are as similar to each other. Almost all fruiting shrubs require full sun, although currants and gooseberries (*Ribes* species) can tolerate light afternoon shade if they are growing in a hot area. Good air circulation is imperative to prevent some fungal diseases which can be a problem. Whenever possible, site fruiting shrubs where the prevailing winds will blow through them to prevent moist air from settling around the leaves.

Site early-blooming plants, such as currants and gooseberries, on a north-facing slope to delay their bloom as long as possible, or place them in a protected spot where late frost is rare.

BIRD NETTING is essential if you want blueberries. Leave one bush without netting if you want to share.

ALL GOOSEBERRIES make wonderful pies and preserves but most people prefer the pink ones for eating fresh.

need to set aside a part of the yard where you can make the soil more acid.

The first step in this procedure is to have the soil tested by a good laboratory. When you send in the sample, let them know that you will be growing blueberries in the soil and would like a recommendation for sulfur rather than another acidifying material.

Till the soil, and apply the recommended amount of sulfur, working it into the top few inches. Mulch over this with pine needles or crushed pine bark, and let the soil sit under this mulch, replacing it as necessary to keep weeds from taking over the area. It may take as long as a year for the soil to become properly acidified. Keep testing through this time with a pH meter or litmus strips from the pharmacy. By the end of a year, the soil should be acid enough to plant.

In addition to increased acidity, cranberries require extremely moist soil. Site them where the water table is naturally high, and plan to keep them watered well at all times.

You do not have to flood them as commercial growers do as long as you maintain high moisture levels, particularly when berries are developing.

Supplying nutrients. Fruiting plants of all types require soils that are at least moderately fertile. As a general rule, apply an inch to 1½ inches of compost around the base of your shrubs every spring, shaking it down into the center of the stems if necessary and extending it several feet in all directions. Apply moisture-conserving mulches over the compost. If rodents are a problem, use fine-meshed screening around the bush to keep them from nibbling the bark. Bury the screening in a 6-inch-deep trench to prevent their burrowing under it.

Add specific materials such as rock powders, kelp, and alfalfa pellets to supply additional nutrients. Amend your soils before planting whenever possible. If you suspect nutrient deficiencies once the shrubs are planted and growing, send leaf samples to a lab that conducts tissue analysis. Use the table on page 29 to choose an appropriate nutrient source.

Time your fertilizer applications properly. Because compost contains relatively low amounts of immediately available nutrients, you can mulch around your plants with it any time during the growing season. However,

GROWING BLUEBERRIES

Blueberries require such acid conditions that you might not be able to grow them in your native soil. Instead, build boxes at least 3 feet x 3 feet x 3 feet, provide them with good drainage holes, and fill them with specially prepared, high acid soil. Mulch with pine needles, and check and adjust the pH each year.

THE TIME TO HARVEST BLUEBERRIES is when they are fully colored but before they become soft to the touch.

you'll need to take care with high-nitrogen materials such as fish emulsion, alfalfa pellets, and soybean meal. If you add high-nitrogen fertilizers in late summer, plants may put out a burst of new growth that is vulnerable to winterkill. It is best to wait until the danger of frost has passed to add a high-nitrogen fertilizer, and refrain from using such a fertilizer after mid-July.

Slow-release, natural sources of nutrients such as potassium, calcium, and phosphorous are generally added a year before planting a perennial crop such as a fruiting shrub. If you need to supplement after the plant is growing, apply nutrients in spring, and cover them with compost. Microorganisms in the compost will help to make the nutrients in these materials available to the plants and rainwater will wash the nutrients deep into the root zone. When you are liming prior to planting, add it in the fall, just under the cover crop or mulch you use to protect the soil over the winter.

When plants are severely nutrient-deficient, applications to the soil may take too long to be absorbed and become available. In these cases, amend the soil; then use a foliar feed to supply immediate nutrients.

Use foliar feeds in the early morning or on an overcast day to protect the leaves from burning under the droplets in bright light. Liquid seaweed, powdered kelp, and nettle and compost teas all make excellent foliar feeds. Both liquid seaweed and kelp minimize frost damage in the spring if they have been sprayed on the plant a day or two before the frost. Compost and nettle tea give plants increased resistance to disease, as discussed on page 296.

Powdered kelp is somewhat difficult to use as a liquid spray. You can keep it in solution by mixing it with an agri-

WELL-PLANNED BLUEBERRY PATCHES will provide you with fruit over several weeks' time.

cultural spreader/sticker that also helps materials adhere to leaves. Spreader/stickers are available from garden supply stores. Apply the kelp solution using a nozzle with large openings because its large particles can clog misting nozzles. If the kelp persists in clogging, filter it through a paper coffee filter before filling the spray container, and use the solids around the base of the bush or in the compost.

Routine Care and Special Needs

Fruiting shrubs tend to be easier to care for than fruit trees. In most cases, the pest pressure isn't as high, and it is easier to keep them disease-free. Pruning needs are lower, and the plants are more forgiving. But you can't just plant them and walk away without another thought.

Adequate soil moisture is crucial to fruit quality. Set up a rain gauge near the bushes, and monitor it.

Birds are likely to be the biggest problems for fruiting shrubs. Many people frighten birds away by suspending balloons painted to look like giant eyes from high stakes near the bushes, and others twist red and silver mylar tape through the bushes. Done well, the breeze will move the tape so that it looks like fire to a bird's eye. Some people report good results by hanging disposable aluminum pie pans in the bushes, and others say that birds will avoid the area if you set up perches that are covered in Tanglefoot™. The birds will be able to escape the sticky material but will develop an aversion to the area. These techniques have all been successful for many gardeners, but none of them is as foolproof as the traditional recourse—netting.

If birds are taking too much fruit, build an enclosure of 1x3 or 2x4 boards, and cover all sides and the top with bird netting. If the enclosure is at least 6 inches taller than the bushes, the birds will not be able to get to the fruit.

COMMON FRUITING SHRUBS

Fruiting shrubs are among the hardest working plants in the landscape. They provide year-round structure and deliver a delicious crop. Some fruiting shrubs are pretty enough to be used as specimens, while others make good hedges.

COMMON	BOTANICAL	ZONES	SOIL NEEDS	PRUNING NEEDS	FRUITING TIME	POLLINATORS Required
Blueberry, lowbush	*Vaccinium angustifolium*	3 to 8	Acid	Light	Late summer/fall	Yes
Blueberry, rabbiteye	*Vaccinium ashei*	6 to 9	Acid	Light	Late summer/fall	Yes
Blueberry, highbush	*Vaccinium corymbosum*	4 to 8	Acid	Light	Late summer/fall	Yes
Blueberry, half-high	*Vaccinium corymbosum*	4 to 7	Acid	Light	Late summer/fall	Yes
Cranberry	*Vaccinium macrocarpon*	2 to 6	Acid, moist	Light	Fall	No
Currant, black	*Ribes nigrum*	3 to 6	High fertility	Moderate	Summer	Yes
Currant, red & white	*Ribes silvestre & R. petraeum*	3 to 6	High fertility	Moderate	Summer	No
Elderberry, American	*Sambucus canadensis*	2 to 9	Deep, drained	Light	Late summer/fall	Yes
Gooseberry, European	*Ribes uva-crispa*	3 to 7	High fertility	Moderate	Summer	No
Gooseberry, American	*Ribes hirtellum*	3 to 7	High fertility	Moderate	Summer	No
Jostaberry	*Ribes x nidigrolaria*	3 to 7	High fertility	Moderate	Summer	No
Serviceberry	*Amelanchier spp.*	3 to 8	Well-drained	Light	Summer	No

PRUNING FRUITING SHRUBS

Most fruiting shrubs do not require intense pruning to remain healthy and productive. Bushes grow by developing new stems from the crown of the plant every year. Individual branches are not long lived, but the new growth every year means that the bush itself may be. As a gardener, your job is to remove old or diseased growth to make way for healthy new stems. In the case of fruiting shrubs, you'll also want to open up the center of the plant so that light and air can penetrate to the inside.

Fruiting shrubs vary in response to pruning, however. Even though you have the option of doing nothing more than thinning old growth from all of them, some respond to more-specialized pruning by giving higher yields of healthier fruit than might be possible if you simply let them grow as bushes.

After planting, there are two ways to handle a fruiting shrub. In the case of blueberries, cranberries, and serviceberries (*Amelanchier*), the best advice is to treat them as bushes and do as little pruning as possible. Thin out weak branches, and head back any damaged wood, always cutting to an outside bud. As the spring progresses, some of these bushes will bloom. Even though it may be hard to do

THIN OLD CANES by cutting flush with the soil surface. Do this work when the plants are dormant.

PRUNING RIBES

Pruning Ribes *species is very straightforward if you simply allow them to grow as bushes. As long as you keep up with this minimal work, the plants will continue to thrive and produce abundant fruit.*

In the third to fifth year, depending on the species, thin out the oldest stems.

The following year, repeat this process, always removing the stems that have borne fruit the longest.

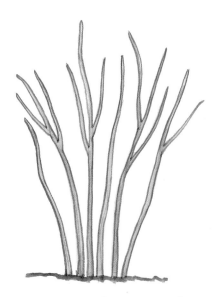

By continuing in this way, your plant will always have young, vital, fruit-bearing stems.

so, pinch off the flowers so that the plant can put all of its strength into root and shoot growth.

Shrubs are always pruned when they are dormant. After the first year, thin out weak or damaged growth and any branches that crowd the center of the plant. Otherwise, wait to do major pruning until the third or fourth year.

Highbush and half-high blueberries fruit on stems one to four years old. After that, productivity declines. Thin all five-year-old stems, cutting at the soil level. To keep the plant sturdy, head back all drooping stems and those that are less than ¼ inch thick. Always cut just above an outside bud or branch. Thin out twiggy growth and stems that crowd the center of the plant. If the plant has more than five fruit buds on each fruiting stem, head the stems back so that they don't carry more than this number. Even though the number of fruits will be fewer, the size of the berries will be larger.

Rabbiteye blueberries are pruned in a similar fashion except that you probably won't need to head back fruiting stems, because these plants are unlikely to have too many fruit buds on a stem. Also, rabbiteye plants are generally more vigorous and robust than highbush and half-high blueberries and usually do not need as many stems headed back or thinned.

Lowbush blueberries form new shoots from underground rhizomes as well as from buds on the branches. They will also form roots from the nodes of stems that lie on the ground. They fruit on one-year-old wood, and the biggest and best fruits come from shoots growing from the rhizomes rather than from aboveground wood. Prune to stimulate this kind of fruiting. The third year after planting, cut half of your plants to the ground while they are dormant. The half you didn't prune will set fruit that year. During the next dormant period, cut all the stems to the ground on the half of the plants that you allowed to fruit that year. Alternate pruning in this way to keep your bushes healthy and bearing well.

Pruning *Ribes* species. Currants, gooseberries, and jostaberries can be handled a number of ways. You have a choice of growing them as bushes, or "stools"; on a single stem or "leg"; and, except for black currants, as espaliered cordons.

PRUNING TO A LEG

Currants, gooseberries, and jostaberries all thrive when they are grown as a "leg," or on a single stem that you train to act as a trunk. This method is easy to do, but takes more time each year than growing plants as simple bushes.

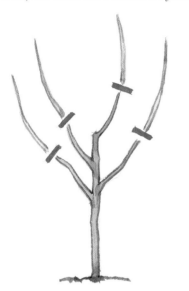

After developing the central stem and allowing four good branches to grow, head them back.

Each year, when the plant is dormant, head back the branches and remove any branches from the trunk.

To promote good growth, head back the tips of laterals on which fruit forms each year.

Remove 4-year old branches each year, and thin twiggy and poorly positioned growth.

Growing these plants as bushes is by far the easiest alternative. If you are a beginning fruit grower, this is probably the best choice you can make unless your landscape design demands a more formal-looking system. To grow the plants as stools, cut back all of the stems to two to four buds above the soil level just after planting. During the first year, the plant will develop branches from each of these buds, as well as new branches that originate underground.

When the plant is dormant, thin out any weak growth, and then thin the strong, upright growth so that only six or seven stems remain. Thin stems by cutting just at or slightly below soil level. In subsequent years you will repeat this dormant pruning, but in the third year you must thin out all the three-year old stems.

Pruning on a leg. To prune plants to grow on a leg, rub off all the buds on the bottom 6 inches or so of the central stem. Prune the plant during the dormant season almost as you would if it were a tree you were growing in a central leader design. First develop four or five branches as a permanent framework, and then head back the lateral branches that form on the framework when you prune each year. Thin out weak branches and twiggy growth in the center of the plant each year, and remove branches that are more than three years old.

In England, gardeners often train currants and gooseberries to cordons. As with other espalier systems, it is best to set up the trellis before you plant. Because you'll be tying the branches to lathing strips lashed to the wires, you should determine how many stems you're going to allow to develop beforehand. Prune off the unwanted growth, and tie the stems to the lathing strips as they grow.

ILLUSTRATED PLANT-BY-PLANT DIRECTORY OF FRUITING SHRUBS

Vaccinium angustifolium, V. ashei, & V. corymbosum

Lowbush, rabbiteye and highbush blueberries; half-high are cultivars of *V. corymbosum*

Zones: Lowbush, 3 to 8; rabbiteye, 6 to 9; highbush 4 to 8; and half-high 4 to 7.
Size: Lowbush, 1 to 3 feet tall, spread 5 to 8 feet wide; rabbiteye, 15 to 18 feet tall, 5 to 6 feet wide; highbush, 5 to 6 feet tall, 5 to 6 feet wide; half-high, 2 to 4 feet high, 2 to 4 feet wide.
Flowers: Pink to creamy-white, ½ inch long, urn-shaped waxy flowers form in clusters in early spring.
Leaves: Glossy, dark green leaves, sometimes with a reddish undertone, have smooth margins and pointed tips. They turn red before dropping in fall.

PLANTING
Exposure: Full sun for half-high and high-bush. Rabbiteyes can tolerate filtered shade in the afternoon in hot locations and lowbush cultivars prefer afternoon filtered light or moderate shade in the southern reaches of their range.
Soil: Consistently moist with high organic matter and extremely good drainage. The pH should range between 4.0 to 5.0

although rabbiteyes will tolerate 5.5 and somewhat drier conditions. Mulch with high-acid materials such as pine needles or oak leaves, and apply approximately ½ pound of rock phosphate and ½ pound of gypsum for every 10 row feet each year after all danger of frost has passed and soil is warming.
Spacing: Allow 8 feet between rows of lowbush, highbush, and half-highs and 5 to 6 feet between plants. The larger rabbiteye plants require a spacing of 8 feet in all directions.
Pollinators: Plant at least three different cultivars to ensure good pollination.

CULTURAL CARE
Watering: Lowbush, half-highs, and high bush plants require an inch to 1 to 1½ inches of water a week. Increase irrigation somewhat when fruits are plumping up. Rabbiteyes can tolerate less water—up to 1 inch per week.
Mulching: Apply a high-acid mulch such as pine needles or shredded hardwood tree leaves. Remove the old mulch each fall and compost it. Apply an inch of compost, and then mulch for the winter.
Pests: Blueberry maggot; cherry fruit-worm, birds.
Diseases: Mummyberry, stem canker.

PRUNING
After Planting: Prune as little as possible but remove flower buds.
Routine Pruning: In dormant season, remove damaged or weak growth. Thin center of plant to allow light and air into it. See page 246 for more information.
Mature Plants: Remove branches older than three years on half-high, highbush and rabbiteye plants. Cut half the plants of a lowbush planting to the ground each year, alternating sections of the planting. Do not prune off the tips of rabbiteye stems, because fruits form here.

HARVESTING
Fruiting: Fruits form on 1- to 4-year-old branches or spurs.
Years to Bearing: 4 to 5.
Harvest Season: Late summer to early fall.
Yields: 3 to 8 quarts for all types except lowbush; 2 to 4 quarts for lowbush plants.
Notes: Rabbiteye blueberries grow well in southern locations because they require only 100 to 500 chilling hours, depending on the cultivar. Highbush, half-high, and lowbush plants require 700 to 1,000 chilling hours.

Ribes species
Red and white currants

Zones: 3 to 6.
Size: 3 to 5 feet tall, 3 to 5 feet wide.
Flowers: Clusters of small greenish yellow to violet flowers, in early spring.
Leaves: Medium green, lobed leaves.

PLANTING
Exposure: Full sun in Zones 3 to 5, but filtered afternoon light in Zone 6.
Soil: Moist, well-drained, slightly acid with high organic matter. Each year, fertilize with 3 lbs. of soybean meal.
Spacing: 4 to 6 feet between plants, 6 to

8 feet between rows.
Pollinators: None required.

CULTURAL CARE

Watering: A minimum of an inch a week or 2 gallons per square foot of root area.
Mulching: 6 inches of straw or 3 to 4 inches of a denser material.
Pests: Currant borer, currant fruit fly.
Diseases: Anthracnose, leaf spot, powdery mildew.

PRUNING

After Planting: Head back to 2 to 4 buds.
Routine Pruning: See page 246.
Mature Plants: Maintain pruning design.

HARVESTING

Fruiting: Fruit forms on wood that is between 1 and 3 years old.
Years to Bearing: 2 to 3.
Harvest Season: Midsummer. Taste the bottom berry on a cluster to determine stage of ripeness.
Yields: 3 to 5 quarts per bush.
Notes: White pine blister rust depends on both black currants and pines for its life cycle and some states outlaw all Ribes species. Check with your state department of agriculture.

Sambucus canadensis
American Elderberry

Zones: 2 to 9.
Size: 6 to 12 feet tall, 5 to 6 feet wide.
Flowers: Fragrant, white in spring.
Leaves: Narrow, 6 inches long, oval.

PLANTING

Exposure: Full sun in Zones 2 to 5, fil-

tered afternoon shade in Zones 6 to 9.
Soil: Deep, fertile, well-drained soils with high levels of organic matter.
Spacing: 5 to 6 feet between plants.
Pollinators: Plant two cultivars.

CULTURAL CARE

Watering: 1 inch per square foot of root area each week.
Mulching: 6 inches of straw or 3 to 4 inches of a denser material.
Pests: Birds, elder shoot borer.
Diseases: Powdery mildew, stem and twig cankers.

PRUNING

After Planting: Prune as little as possible.
Routine Pruning: Keep center of plant open. Thin out weak or diseased growth.
Mature Plants: Thin out branches older than three years and thin suckers.

HARVESTING

Fruiting: Fruits form on tips of 1-year old wood and on 2-year old branches.
Years to Bearing: 2 to 4.
Harvest Season: Late summer to midfall.
Yields: 12 to 15 lbs.
Notes: Unlike gooseberries, they are nearly thornless, making picking easier. Fruits are larger than gooseberries, with a very similar flavor. Plants are hardy, pest and disease resistant, and high yielding.

Amelanchier spp.
Serviceberry, Juneberry, Saskatoon berry

Zones: 3 to 8.
Size: 6 to 40 feet tall, 4 to 20 feet wide.

Flowers: Small white flowers form in clusters in spring.
Leaves: Medium green leaves are oval-shaped with toothed margins and turn yellow before dropping in fall.

PLANTING

Preferred Exposure: Full sun but will tolerate partial shade, particularly in the southern reaches of their range.
Preferred Soil and Fertility: Well-drained of moderate fertility and organic matter content.
Spacing: As far apart as the mature plant will be tall.
Pollinators: None required.

CULTURAL CARE

Watering: 1 inch, or 2 gallons per square foot of root area, a week.
Mulching: Mulch with 6 inches of a light mulch such as straw or 4 inches of a denser material.
Pests: Largely pest-free except for fruit-eating birds.
Diseases: Largely disease free, although plants develop root rots.

PRUNING

After Planting: Prune as little as possible.
Routine Pruning: Prune bushy types by thinning out new growth during the dormant period to keep the center of the plant open. Remove weak growth.
Mature Plants: Prune to keep plants within bounds by thinning out suckers that travel too far from the mother plant. Head back drooping branches, and cut out growth more than 3 years old.

HARVESTING

Fruiting: Fruits on 1-year-old wood.
Years to Bearing: 2 to 4.
Harvest Season: Mid to late summer.
Yields: 4 to 6 quarts per plant.
Notes: No matter what kind of plant you buy, you can prune it to keep it a manageable size. Birds love these berries; to keep some for yourself, you'll have to net the bush.

CHOOSING FRUITING VINES

FRUITING VINES HAVE THE dual advantages of providing a dramatic focal point for your landscape and giving you high yields of truly delicious fruit. Depending on the vines you choose, you can grow them on decorative arbors along walkways, over the roof of an outdoor patio, up the wall of an outdoor shed, or on specially built trellises designed to give the highest yields of the healthiest fruit possible.

Fruiting vines consist of various kinds of grapes (*Vitis*) and kiwifruit (*Actinidia*). But despite the fact that all the common fruiting vines fit into one or the other of these categories, the range of fruit types and flavors is amazing. Grapes can be white, red, or purple, and meant for eating out of hand, juicing, turning into wine, or drying for raisins. The huge, flavorful muscadine grapes are common in the South, while California hosts most of the European and hybrid cultivars. American grapes (*V. labrusca* are grown in moderate climates from coast to coast.

Kiwifruits differ, too, depending on their species. You are probably familiar with the egg-sized, fuzzy brown fruit you see in the grocery store, but unless you know a fruit grower, you may not have seen or tasted one of the smaller, hardy kiwifruits. The grocery-store type, *Actinidia deliciosa*, requires a long frost-free season and is generally grown in Zones 7 to 10. In contrast, the hardy kiwifruits, *A. arguta* and *A. kolomikta*, tolerate conditions as far north as Zone 4 with winter protection. These kiwifruits differ from the more tender ones in other ways too. Their skin is smooth and edible and, even though their flavor is similar, they have a higher sugar content, and most people consider them superior for eating fresh.

USE GRAPEVINES IN THE LANDSCAPE by growing them on decorative arches or trellises.

Kiwifruit

Kiwifruit are native to China, Korea, Siberia, and possibly Japan. In the wild, these vines climb forest trees, often growing as high as 100 feet. During the decade between 1900 and 1910, enterprising plant explorers introduced kiwifruit to the United States, Europe, and New Zealand. Though the idea of these plants didn't really catch on elsewhere at that time, farmers in New Zealand set up commercial kiwifruit orchards in the late 1920s and 1930s. Beginning in the late 1960s, when kiwifruit imported from New Zealand began to be popular with the U.S. market, farmers in California planted their own kiwifruit orchards.

Kiwifruit plants are dioecious, meaning that they have male and female flowers on different plants. Home gardeners are usually advised to grow one male plant for every four females, but commercial growers use a ratio of 1:8. Kiwifruit flower early in the year when bee activity can be intermittent because of cold rainy weather. Commercial growers assure themselves of good pollination by keeping beehives in the orchards. The guaranteed presence of bees allows them the 1:8 ratio of male to female plants. If you live where bee populations are still high, you can follow their lead, but otherwise, stick to the generally recommended 1:4 ratio.

These plants are winter hardy down to 10°F, but the developing flower buds are damaged by temperatures of 30°F or lower. This damage can take place before the bloom is open. If you live where the frost-free period is less than 240 days, protect the developing buds by wrapping the canes in insulating material when temperatures dip during the late winter and early spring.

Young trunks and canes are also vulnerable to late-

KIWIFRUIT like these grow best in warm, Zone 7 to 10 locations.

winter and early-spring frosts. You can bury them, as described below for hardy kiwifruit plants, wrap them with insulating material, or use sprinklers for frost protection. Many gardeners have had good luck with growing the plants in 5-gallon buckets for the first year. The buckets are set outside during the first summer but are brought into a cool, dark, frost-free area once the plant has become dormant in the autumn. The following spring, the vine is transplanted where it will grow. In marginal areas where 240 frost-free days are not guaranteed, the vine and canes will have to be protected, as discussed above, for three or four more years, and the flower buds will always need protection.

Hardy kiwifruit are much easier to grow in most of the country. *A. arguta* plants are hardy to -25°F, while the even smaller *A. kolomikta* can tolerate temperatures as low as -30°F. Their wood is tender when it is young, so it is advisable to grow them in buckets for the first year or even two. In subsequent years, their survival is better guaranteed if they experience colder temperatures gradually. Because this is the usual fall pattern, providing gradual cooling will not often be a problem. In the few years when there is a sudden cold snap, protect the plants with blankets.

Despite the hardiness of the wood of the hardy kiwis, their flower buds can still be damaged by frosts. The usual recommendation is to grow these plants where there are 150 frost-free dates a year. Fortunately for gardeners in areas where frosts are likely in both May and September, you can have your choice of several protective techniques.

Many growers literally bury their vines for the winter. They dig a trench beside the vine, untie it from its trellis, and lay it down in the trench. They cover it with several inches of soil and then a deep layer of a protective mulch such as straw bales or shredded autumn leaves held down with tarps.

Grapes

Grapes have the distinction of being the most widely grown fruit in the world, but in most areas only one or two types are grown because of environmental constraints.

Choosing species and cultivars appropriate to your climate is important to your success with any crop, but this is especially true with grapes. Climate can determine disease resistance as well as whether your vines will be able to set fruit. The rule of buying local is a good one to follow when you are choosing grapes.

American grapes can tolerate conditions as far north as protected spots in Zones 4 and 5. The best-known cultivars that can withstand Zone 4 conditions are 'Canadice', 'Concord', and 'Reliance Seedless'. All three are resistant to some

GRAPES grow well in every area if you choose both species and cultivar wisely.

common diseases, and both 'Canadice' and 'Reliance Seedless' are red. The large white 'Niagara' and blue 'Mars' grow well in Zone 5 but do not fare well in Zone 4.

You should remember that, just as with kiwifruit, plants can survive a late frost but may not fruit that year. You can avoid problems by planting them in an area where late frosts are relatively uncommon and by protecting the flower buds as described for kiwifruit.

Muscadine grapes are also native to the United States, but are a different species than the grapes we call 'American'. Muscadines grow well from Zones 7 to 10, primarily in the Southeast. Their high resistance to pests and diseases makes them able to thrive in the high humidity levels in that area. Unlike other types of grapes, some of the best muscadines require a pollinator to set fruit. The vines commonly grow more vigorously too, so growers usually train them on a Munson trellis, as described on page 254.

The most cold-resistant cultivar is 'Carlos'. It will tolerate protected spots in Zone 6b, although it grows better in Zone 7 southward. 'Scuppernong' and 'Hunt' are well-known cultivars throughout the South, both because of their excellent flavor and because they are commonly grown together.

European grapes grow well in Zones 7 to 9, primarily in the lower-humidity conditions in California and the Southwest. Many of these grapes are used to make wine, but some, such as 'Thompson Seedless', are good table grapes.

In the late 1880s the grape phylloxera aphid attacked French vineyards, but not American grapes. Innovative breeders crossed European and American grapes. The resulting hybrids are grown as far north as Zone 5. 'Himrod' and 'Lakemont Seedless' are among the most popular of the hybrids because of their cold tolerance and because they have some of the disease resistance of their American parents.

PRUNING AND TRAINING FRUITING VINES

Fruiting vines are beautiful plants for covering arbors and roofs. Grown this way, the plants can give high yields of healthy fruit if you keep up with pruning and training. However, trellising them like this can make it harder to pay adequate attention to the vines. Several consequences are common. If the vine is growing in a marginal climate where you must protect flower buds from late frosts, there will be more years when you don't have fruit unless you plan in advance for protection. Diseases can be more common too. Most people who grow these plants on arbors and roofs are as interested in ample leaf cover as they are in fruit set, so humidity levels around the leaves are generally high. Some disease-resistant cultivars tolerate these conditions well, but others fall prey to fungi such as anthracnose or black rot.

When you are planning the location of your vines, consider the uses you want from them. If the decorative value of the vine is your primary interest, by all means grow them on an arbor or over a roof. However, if fruit is your primary concern, set up a freestanding trellis.

FRUITS GROWING ON AN OVERHEAD ARBOR must be harvested when ripe so that they don't drop onto the area below.

TRAINING GRAPES

European, American, and hybrid grapes are usually pruned to a four-armed Kniffen system. However, if space is tight, you can also grow them as a two-armed plant, or cordon. The basic pruning is the same whether you leave four arms or two.

Prune off all the lateral buds when you plant the vine.

Allow two buds to develop into arms where they meet the wire.

Head back lateral branches that form on the shoots and train the shoots over the wires. Allow two renewal buds to grow each year.

Grapes

Grapes require vigorous annual pruning and training. They require so much attention that they make a wonderful crop for people who love gardening work but a problem plant for those who do not.

The easiest and most common way to trellis European, hybrid, and American grapes is with the four-armed Kniffen system.

Set up the trellis before you plant. Use exterior-grade 4x4 or 6x6 posts, burying them below the frost line. Extend them 6 feet above the soil surface, and space them 6 to 8 feet apart from each other. Stretch 12-gauge wires from post to post at about 2 to 3 feet from the soil surface and at the top of the posts. Anchor the wires to strong stakes at each end of the trellis.

Plant each grape directly under the wire in the middle of the space between two posts. Prune back the vine to two buds near the bottom wire, and pinch off all the other buds. As the shoots develop from the two buds over the season, tie them to the wire without letting them twine around it.

The following late winter or early spring, while the plant is still dormant, select the shoot that seems the strongest

GRAPES grow as well when tied to a wooden fence as on any other trellis.

and most vigorous to become the trunk of the vine. Untie it from the bottom wire, and lead it upward to the top wire. Tie it to that support. Prune off the other shoot and any lateral branches that have formed, leaving two buds near both the top and bottom wires.

Allow four buds, two at the bottom wire and two at the top, to develop during the summer, but pinch off all those that grow from the top and center portion of the trunk. Allow a renewal bud to grow on each shoot near the wire.

During the dormant period, head back the shoots, or canes, to about ten buds. During the season, grapes will grow near the bases of shoots that grow from these buds. Allow the renewal buds to develop, too, because this is where fruiting shoots will grow the following year.

In subsequent years during the dormant period, cut back the canes where fruit formed the year before, head back the current year's fruiting canes to ten buds, and allow renewal buds to remain on the plant.

Muscadine grapes are generally grown with a Munson system. This style allows greater air circulation around the foliage, making it particularly appropriate for grapes grown in the humid Southeast.

Set up a T-bar trellis, as illustrated on page 254, with posts set 6 to 8 feet apart and Ts 3 feet long. Secure the 12-gauge wire 4 feet above the soil surface and on the top surfaces at the ends of the T bars.

Plant the grape under the center wire, between two posts, and cut it back to two buds. Allow these to grow during the season. While the plant is dormant, choose the shoot that will become the trunk, lead it to the wire, and tie it.

Allow two shoots to develop from the trunk, and tie them to the central wire as they grow over the summer. During the dormant period, head back the canes, allow two renewal buds to remain on the plant for the following year, and prune back any other growth.

Grapes form on one-year-old wood. Leave the shoots from which you want fruit to grow, and prune off all the others, always leaving two renewal buds.

TRAINING MUSCADINE GRAPES

Muscadine grapes are pruned and trained to a Munson system, primarily because the vines are heavy. This system allows greater air circulation, reducing the plants' vulnerability to the fungal diseases that are so prevalent in the regions where they grow.

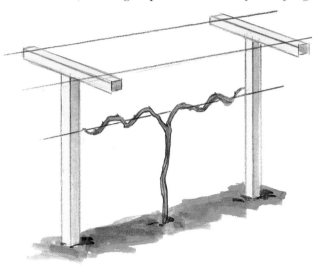

Prune the vine to two buds near the bottom wire after planting, and pinch off all other growth. Tie the shoots that develop to the bottom wire.

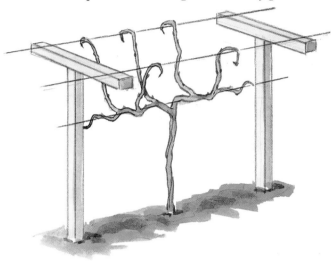

Drape the shoots that develop the following year over the top wires, spacing them well. Fruit will form on the laterals in the following year.

During the season, shoots will grow from the arms. Drape them over the top wires. Branches that grow from these shoots will form fruit the following year. Each year, allow two new shoots to form for the following year's fruit.

If you are growing a grape over an arbor, start it off as if you were growing it as a four-armed *Kniffen* system. However, rather than allowing fruiting canes to develop low on the trunk, pinch them off in favor of those growing near the top of the vine. Each year, allow renewal buds to form near the supporting trelliswork of the arbor, and prune off all the others.

Kiwifruit

The most practical type of trellis for a kiwifruit vine is a T bar, 6 feet high with 6 foot wide Ts. Bore holes in the crossbars, about a foot apart, and string 12-gauge wire through these openings.

Plant the vine under the center of the wire, and tie it to a support as it grows. Rub off any shoots that develop from the vine during the summer. When the vine reaches the height of the wire, pinch out the tip so that lateral buds will develop. Allow two buds to develop into shoots that

KIWI VINES make a lovely display in any yard.

you train as permanent cordons. Tie these along the wires so that they grow in opposite directions.

The shoots that grow from these cordons constitute the fruiting wood. Train them over the wires. Some will droop

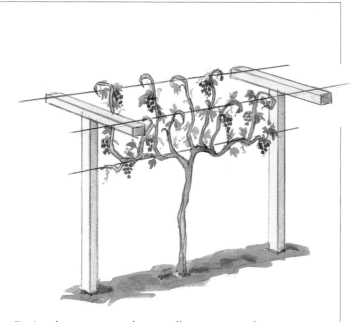

During the summer each year, allow two new shoots to form, and tie them to the support. Laterals growing from them will provide fruit the next year.

between wires, but this will not hurt the fruit quality.

Stimulate the fruiting wood when dormant by heading back the cordons to within 2 feet of where growth started the previous season. Thin the fruiting branches so that they are a foot apart along the cordon, and tie them to the outside wires of the trellis. In subsequent years, new lateral branches will grow from those that fruited the previous year, so leave them in place for two years, thinning only as necessary to keep the plant from becoming too congested.

When the cordons are about 7 feet long, shorten each cordon to where it started growth the year before when it was still dormant. Shorten each lateral branch to only 1½ feet long. Prune out all the fruiting arms, along with their lateral, sublateral, and sub-sublateral branches after their third year to let new fruiting arms develop.

Summer pruning is also necessary. Rub off shoots from the trunk and short shoots growing beyond the outside wires. If a shoot grows around other growth, prune it off.

Male plants are pruned even more severely. Just after they bloom, cut back all the shoots that flowered to a new shoot. This sometimes involves cutting away as much 70 percent of the plant each year, but it is necessary to keep the plant blooming well.

CARING FOR YOUR FRUIT VINES

CARING FOR YOUR FRUITING vines is part of pleasure of having them. Check them every day or each evening when you return from work. You'll want to be certain that they've had enough water, that growth is staying within bounds, and that all the growth looks healthy.

Fruit plants require high levels of balanced nutrition. If you use compost tea foliar sprays every month during the active growing season, you can add some nutrients and prevent many of the diseases that attack fruit vines. Similarly, liquid seaweed foliar sprays can supply trace elements and help to protect the plants against light frosts.

Foliar sprays will help keep the vines healthy, but even so, it is best to check the nutrient status by sending leaves to a lab for tissue analysis every three years. Let the lab know that you are working with organic fertilizers so that they will give you appropriate recommendations.

All through the season, monitor your vines closely for pests and diseases. If you catch these problems in the beginning, your control job will be easier and more pleasant. Check the fruiting vines directory, pages 256 and 257, for pests and diseases common to grapes and kiwifruit.

One of the best pest- and disease-control measures is good sanitation. As leaves drop in the autumn, rake them up and compost or destroy them. Protect the vines with screen mesh and white latex paint, and add new mulch over the root area once the top inch of the ground has frozen.

If you bury your vines for winter protection, dig the trench long before the ground is frozen. Wait until all the leaves have dropped, and rake them up from the area. Untie the vine carefully, and gently lower it into the trench. You may have to spade around one side of the root ball to give the vine a way of bending over. If so, pile a foot of soil over the upended roots, and then cover them with mulch.

TASTE THE BOTTOM grape of the cluster to judge whether the grapes are ripe. If it's sweet, cut the bunch from the vine.

ILLUSTRATED PLANT-BY-PLANT DIRECTORY OF FRUITING VINES

Vitis labrusca
Grapes, American

Zones: 5 to 9.
Size: 12 to 15 feet long, 3 to 5 feet wide.
Flowers: Clusters of inconspicuous small flowers bloom in spring.
Leaves: Large, lobed, dark green leaves usually have a waffled texture and turn yellow before dropping in autumn.

PLANTING
Exposure: Full sun, preferably on a south-facing slope with good air circulation and drainage.
Soil: Deep, well-drained soil with high fertility and organic matter content. Add 1½ to 2 lbs. of compost per row-foot in early spring each year.
Spacing: Allow 8 feet between plants, 9 feet between rows.
Pollinators: None required.

CULTURAL CARE
Watering: Plants require 4 gallons per square foot of root area every week from early spring until the fruits begin to color. After that, hold back on watering until the end of the season, unless natural rainfall is less than ½ inch per week. In that case, water deeply every 2 weeks.
Mulching: Rake off old mulch, along with fallen leaves, at the end of the sea-

son and mulch for winter protection. Remove winter mulch as soon as all threat of frost has passed.
Pests: Birds, grape berry moths and larvae, grape leafhoppers, grape mealybugs, Japanese beetles.
Diseases: Botrytis fruit rot, Pierce's disease, powdery mildew.

PRUNING
See page 252.

HARVESTING
Fruiting: Fruits form on 1-year old wood.
Years to Bearing: 2 to 3.
Harvest Season: Late summer to early fall, depending on cultivar.
Yields: 10 to 15 lbs. per plant.
Notes: Some of the new American cultivars have thinner skins than traditional Concords. When you pick for jams or jellies, gather the fruit before it is fully ripe. Underripe fruit makes a more flavorful product and contains high levels of natural pectin.

Vitis vinifera
Grapes, European and hybrid

Zones: 7 to 9.
Size: 12 to 20 feet long, 4 to 5 feet wide.
Flowers: Clusters of small, inconspicuous

flowers form in spring.
Leaves: Lobed and toothed, medium to dark green leaves have prominent veins and turn yellow before dropping in autumn.

PLANTING
Preferred Exposure: Full sun in an open site with good air circulation and drainage.
Preferred Soil and Fertility: Deep, rich soil with high levels of organic matter. Apply close to 2 lbs. of compost per row-foot every spring.
Spacing: Allow 6 to 8 feet between plants and 10 feet between rows.
Pollinators: None required.

CULTURAL CARE
Watering: Supplement natural rainfall if necessary to supply 2 inches, or 4 gallons per square foot of root area, of water each week from spring until the fruits start to color. After that, do not water unless there is a severe drought.
Mulching: Do not mulch for the first summer. For winter protection, pile 8 to 12 inches of straw or 4 to 6 inches of a denser material over the roots once the top inch of the ground has frozen. In spring, remove the mulch and do not add new material until midseason. Remove and compost old mulches when you rake up the leaves in autumn, and mulch again for winter protection.
Pests: Birds, grape berry moths and larvae, grape cane gallmakers, grape leafhoppers, grape mealybugs, grape phylloxera, Japanese beetles.
Diseases: Anthracnose, botrytis fruit rot, Pierce's disease, powdery mildew.

PRUNING
See page 252.

HARVESTING
Fruiting: Fruits form on 1-year-old wood.
Years to Bearing: 2 to 3.
Harvest Season: Late summer to fall.

Notes: Taste the bottom grape on a cluster before cutting it from the vine because grapes do not ripen once they are picked. Use the leaves to keep pickles crisp—add one leaf to every jar. Greek cookbooks give recipes for stuffed grape leaves.

Vitis rotundifolia
Grapes, Muscadine

Zones: 7 to 10.
Size: 12 to 20 feet long, 3 to 5 feet wide.
Flowers: Inconspicuous greenish flowers bloom in clusters in spring.
Leaves: Toothed leaves are medium green and 4 to 6 inches long. They turn yellow before dropping in autumn.

PLANTING
Exposure: Full sun.
Soil: Deep, well-drained, fertile with high levels of organic matter. Apply 1 to 2 lbs. of compost per row-foot every spring.
Spacing: 15 to 20 feet between plants and 15 feet between rows.
Pollinators: Check with the nursery for appropriate pollinators, and grow the plants within 50 feet of each other because they are wind pollinated.

CULTURAL CARE
Watering: Supply 2 inches or 4 gallons per square foot of root area every week from spring until the fruit begins to color. Do not water after this unless there is a severe drought. Do not wet leaves when watering.
Mulching: Do not mulch the first season

until late fall. Remove mulch in spring, and allow the soil to be bare until midseason. After that, mulch with 6 inches of loose material or 4 inches of a dense substance. Remove mulch in fall, and apply new material for winter protection.
Pests: Birds, grape berry moths and larvae, grape cane gallmakers, grape leafhoppers, grape mealybugs, grape phylloxera, Japanese beetles.
Diseases: Anthracnose, black rot, botrytis fruit rot, Pierce's disease, powdery mildew.

PRUNING
See page 252.

HARVESTING
Fruiting: Fruits form on 1-year old wood.
Years to Bearing: 2 to 3.
Harvest Season: Late summer and fall.
Yields: 8 to 16 quarts per plant.
Notes: Muscadine grapes form looser clusters than American or European cultivars. They make superb eating and can be used for juice, jam, or jelly.

Actinidia deliciosa, A. arguta and A. kolomikta
Kiwifruit, hardy kiwifruit

Zones: *A. deliciosa*: 7 to 10; *A. arguta* and *A. kolomikta*: 4 to 9.
Size: 15 to 30 feet long, 3 to 5 feet wide.
Flowers: In spring, cream-colored, fragrant, pretty flowers.
Leaves: Bronze or reddish green when young, turn dark green and somewhat

shiny as they mature. Leaves are oval-shaped with slightly toothed margins. Male *A. kolomikta* plants have variegated leaves of green, cream, and pink.

PLANTING
Exposure: Full sun for *A. deliciosa*. North of Zone 7, plant hardy kiwifruit on a north-facing slope in partial shade to protect them from winter injury.
Soil: Well-drained with high fertility and organic matter content with a pH between 5.0 and 6.5. Maintain high fertility with spring applications of 2 inches of compost over the root zone each spring. If necessary, add a balanced organic fertilizer as recommended by a soil- and tissue-testing lab.
Spacing: Allow 10 feet between plants and 15 feet between rows.
Pollinators: Even cultivars sold as 'self-fruitful' yield better with a male plant.

CULTURAL CARE
Watering: Water a minimum of 4 gallons per square feet of root area, or 10 feet in all directions from the base of the vine, each week. Do not wet foliage or fruit.
Mulching: Do not mulch during the first season until it's time to protect plants from winter injury. After that, wait to mulch until midseason each year.
Pests: Leaf roller caterpillars, soft scales.
Diseases: Botrytis blight, crown rot.

PRUNING
See Page 252.

HARVESTING
Fruiting: Fruits form on 1-year-old wood.
Years to Bearing: 3.
Harvest Season: Fall.
Yields: 5 to 10 gallons per plant.
Notes: Gather kiwifruits before the first frost, even though they taste best when allowed to ripen on the vine.

CHAPTER 8

CHOOSING BRAMBLE FRUIT

BRAMBLE FRUITS MAKE A wonderful introduction to the joys of growing your own fruit. They are extraordinarily easy to grow in most locations and yield large amounts of fruit for the space they take. Additionally, berries are one of the fruits that are so much better fresh-picked out of the garden that you'll wonder how you ever ate commercially produced fruit. Fortunately, it takes only a little work to see to it that you never do again.

Bramble fruits are wonderfully variable. The table on the next page lists only a few of the more than 250 known bramble species, but a cursory look tells you that no matter where you live, whether in the Florida Keys or the Arctic Circle, you can grow some bramble fruit. But despite the wide adaptation of the genus, you still have to take care when selecting the species and cultivars you'll grow because they are individually picky about their environments. In addition to referring to the table on the next page, check with area nurseries, gardeners associations, and neighbors to learn which cultivars are best adapted to your particular area.

Raspberry or Blackberry

From a gardener's point of view, the important difference between raspberries and blackberries comes down to the way the fruit separates from the bush. When you pick a raspberry, the central core of the fruit stays on the bush. In contrast, the central core comes along with a harvested

BRAMBLE CANES can grow against any support, as long as you keep them tied in place.

blackberry. Raspberries are also hardier than blackberries, growing well in Zones 3, 4, and the coldest areas of 5a, spots where blackberries suffer during cold winters. Blackberries tend to be shiny, too, while raspberries have a matte finish, sometimes with a grayish bloom. And lastly, all raspberries are self-fruitful, but some blackberries require pollinators. As always, check with your supplier when you buy the plants.

Summer or Fall Bearing

Bramble bushes grow a new set of canes, or stems, from the crown each year. The current year's set are called primocanes. They overwinter and resume growth in the spring. At this point, they are called floricanes.

Lateral branches growing from the floricanes produce the flowers and fruits on most bramble fruit. However, a few, generally called ever-bearing or fall-bearing, set fruit on the tips of the current year's primocanes as well as on laterals growing from the floricanes. 'Heritage', 'Fall Red', and 'Fall Gold' are all well-known and reliable fall-bearing types.

Most gardeners discover that they like growing brambles so much that they want to have both summer- and fall-bearing plants in the yard. The advantage to having some of each type is one of timing. The first crop of the fall-bearers comes in just about the same time the standard raspberries do, but because fruit is restricted to the tips of the primocanes, isn't as large. If you want to space your preserving jobs through the season, it is handy to have a large crop in both midsummer and fall.

A VARIETY OF BRAMBLE fruits is easy to grow in even a small backyard.

BRAMBLE BERRIES

GENUS & SPECIES NAME	COMMON NAME	NOTABLE CULTIVARS	ZONE	NOTES
Rubus albescens	**Asian Raspberry**		9 to 10	Best for Florida and other Zone 9 areas
Rubus arcticus	**Crimson Bramble**		1 to 4	Dark red fruit on truly cold-hardy plants
Rubus canadensis	**American Dewberry**		5 to 9	Purple fruit on nearly thornless canes
Rubus idaeus	**European Red Raspberry**		3 to 8	Includes both red and yellow types
Rubus idaeus var. *strigosus*	**American Red Raspberry**		4 to 7	Includes both red and yellow types
		'Latham'	3 to 8	July fruiting
		'Dormanred'	6 to 9	Best for southern conditions
		'Canby'	5 to 8	Nearly thornless, aphid immune, July fruit
Rubus occidentalis	**Black Cap Raspberry**		3 to 8	American native, some are purple
		'Royalty'	4 to 8	A purple hybrid of American & Black Cap
		'Black Hawk'	4 to 8	Somewhat virus resistant
Rubus phoenicolasius	**Wineberry**		5 to 8	Fine flavored, large fruit on erect canes
Rubus spp.	**Blackberry, Erect**		5 to 10	Many types are available
		'Darrow'	5 to 10	Best in Northeast
		'Dirksen'	5 to 10	Rust Resistant
		'Cheyenne'	6 to 10	Best for Gulf Coast and South
	Blackberry, Trailing		5 to 10	Must always be trellised
		'Cascade'	5 to 8	Best for Pacific Coast
Rubus ulmifolius	**Thornless Blackberry**		5 to 10	Grows best in southern zones
		'Perron Black'	5 to 8	Adaptable but do best from Zones 6-8
Rubus ursinus var. *loganobaccus* 'Logan'	**Loganberry**		5 to 9	A cross between raspberry and blackberry
Rubus ursinus var. *loganobaccus* 'Boysen'	**Boysenberry**		6 to 8	Derived from the hybrid Loganberry

Siting Your Brambles

Bramble berries can grow almost anywhere in the yard but will be easiest to care for if you can work on both sides of the planting. Commercial growers site them in open areas and orient the rows to run north and south, so they don't shade themselves. In Zone 7 and southward, blackberries can take a filtered shade in the afternoon, but farther north, plants will perform best with full sun.

If possible, site the plants where late frosts are unlikely and winter winds are moderated by trees or buildings. Gardeners living in Zones 5a to 3 who have no choice but to plant the brambles in cold, exposed frost-pockets may need to wrap the canes in burlap or bury them as described for kiwifruit, page 251.

No matter where you put your brambles, they will become a visual focal point. The only way to make them unobtrusive is to hide them behind a building or hedge. But inasmuch as this isn't always possible, try to find a place where you can use their growth habit to advantage. They can define an area of the yard or separate one spot from another. A small planting can even grow between seedlings of standard-sized trees.

Bramble berries are not very long-lived. In general, they remain healthy and productive for 10 to 15 years but eventually lose vigor because of the cumulative effect of the various viral diseases that prey on them. When you replant the fruit, you'll want to move them to an entirely different part of the yard so that the new bushes can avoid the diseases for as long as possible.

PLANTING, PRUNING, AND TRAINING BRAMBLES

ALL BRAMBLE FRUITS GROW best on a trellis. Some, such as trailing blackberries, absolutely demand it if the fruits are to be edible, but even plants that produce "erect" canes, which can grow without support, yield better and are easier to care for if you trellis them.

The three most common types of trellises for brambles include the T-bar trellis, the double-post-and-wire trellis, and the cable-and-post-fence support. Each of these supports can be used for any of the erect or semi-erect cultivars, but the cable-and-post-fence support is the most practical for the long canes of trailing blackberries.

Set up the trellis you plan to use before planting the berries. Spring planting, while the plants are still dormant, is generally recommended for bare-root plants in Zone 5 and northward. In Zone 6 and southward, plant while the canes are dormant in the spring or in the fall, at least a month before the ground freezes.

Plant the berry bushes slightly deeper than they were growing at the nursery. Space them as recommended in the bramble fruit directory, on page 262. If the tip of a cane looks damaged, head it back until you reach healthy tissue. Head back undamaged canes to a length of 6 inches to stimulate new growth.

WIRE SUPPORTS allow you to work with the plants from both sides and also provide excellent air circulation.

During the first year, summer-bearing cultivars will produce a healthy crop of primocanes—the stems that will become fruiting floricanes the following year. The fall-bearers will also produce primocanes, some of which may produce a small crop of berries the first year.

Depending on the type of trellis you have set up, your job during the first year will be to move the canes into position between or against the wires and tie them in place. Keep up with this throughout the season so that your fall work is minimal.

During the dormant season, thin the canes if they are growing more closely together than 6 inches, and head back the remaining canes. If you are growing a trailing blackberry, it is best to wrap the long canes around the top wire and head them back only a few inches. Head back the shorter, erect cultivars so that they are only a foot above the top wire.

There are two ways to handle the plants during the summer. You can tie the new primocanes to the bottom wire of your support until after the the floricanes are harvested, or you can divide the planting so that all the floricanes are trained to one side and all the primocanes to the other. Separating the canes in this way may seem like extra work, but it saves time and trouble in the long run, especially when you are picking and pruning old floricanes.

Once the floricanes have fruited, they will die. If you simply leave them in the plant, they inhibit air movement and provide a niche for some pests. Many gardeners suggest leaving them in place until late winter, but it is often preferable to prune them out in the fall. For one thing, they are easy to spot, and for another, you can open up the planting so that it is easier to mulch. But no matter when you thin, make all the cuts just above the soil surface. For sanitation's sake, remove the old canes from the area, and do not compost them. Once all the old wood has been removed, retie the primocanes. If you are doing this work during the dormant period, thin and head back the remaining canes as described above. However, if you prune out old wood in the fall, wait until late winter to thin and head back or you may encourage new, vulnerable growth.

Fall-bearers are sometimes pruned differently. If the canes have developed diseases or the planting has been neglected and is now too crowded, you have the option of cutting all the canes to the ground. If you plan to do this, you can prune in late fall, after the canes have become dormant, or wait until late winter. The plant will flower and fruit on the tips of the primocanes the following spring, and you'll have a chance to make the planting more manageable.

Watering and Routine Care

Brambles are among the easiest fruit to grow. Despite their susceptibility to various pests and diseases and their inevitable decline, you can count on 8 to 15 good years from a single planting if you take minimal care of them.

Water is imperative for bramble fruit. After you plant, soak the area thoroughly. Set up a rain gauge, and supplement rainfall so that plants receive at least an inch a week, or 2 gallons per square foot of root area. In subsequent years, do not irrigate while the fruits are developing unless there are drought conditions.

Drip irrigation is particularly useful for brambles. These plants are vulnerable to many fungi, particularly while they are fruiting, and wet leaves or berries can set the stage for an infection. If you do not have a drip system, hand-water rather than use a sprinkler. This allows you to direct the water to the soil rather than the plants.

Weeds can be a real menace to brambles. For one thing, it is difficult to stick your hand into the thorny canes to yank out the stray grass that might have found its way there. And, beside the brambles, the weeds can look so insignificant at first that you barely notice them.

Take warning—that single blade of grass or lonely bindweed stem can become a huge problem in years to come. Use a deep mulch all around the perimeter of the planting to keep grasses and other rhizome-spreading weeds from invading, and use whatever tool is necessary to dig out all the weeds, both annual and perennial.

Pests and diseases enjoy bramble berries as much as we do. It is unlikely that you will be able to keep your planting entirely free of pests, but you can minimize your troubles. Prevention is the key. Develop the habit of spraying plants with compost tea on a regular schedule to keep fungal problems at bay. Monitor plants closely, looking under the leaves as well as in growing tips and on the berries for signs of pests and diseases.

Many of the worst bramble diseases, such as the viruses, are spread by aphids. Habitat islands can be the backbone of your control system, but you may need to take other action in the early spring, before most of the beneficial insects are active. Monitor the plants carefully, and if you notice aphids, hand-squash them or use insecticidal soap to kill them. Early vigilance pays off later.

Good sanitation for brambles involves removing and destroying all the pruned cuttings, as well as dropped leaves and old mulch. You can do this work most efficiently in the autumn, after the plants have gone dormant but just before the ground freezes. Wait to remulch until the top inch of the ground has frozen.

In Zone 5 and northward, it is sometimes necessary to protect plants over the winter months. If you are growing a cultivar that is marginal in your area, you may need to set up a wind barrier in addition to providing a deep winter mulch.

PROPAGATING WITH SUCKERS

Bramble fruits propagate themselves by forming suckers from their far-ranging roots. If the plants are healthy, that is, if they do not have the viral diseases that aphids often transmit, you can transplant these to add to your planting.

In early spring, as soon as you can identify the suckers, dig them up. Take as large a root ball as possible and transplant as usual.

ILLUSTRATED PLANT-BY-PLANT DIRECTORY OF BRAMBLE FRUITS

Rubus spp.

Blackberry

Rubus idaeus

Raspberry

Rubus ursinus var. *loganobaccus* 'Boysen'

Boysenberry

Zones: Blackberry, Dewberry, and Loganberry, 5 to 10; Boysenberry, 6 to 8; Raspberry, 3 to 9.
Size: Erect cultivars, 5 to 10 feet long, 3 to 5 feet wide; Trailing cultivars: 15 feet long, 4 to 5 feet wide.
Flowers: Clusters of white or pink, five petaled, 1-inch wide flowers with prominent centers, bloom in spring.
Leaves: Dull green with three leaflets and toothed margins turn a dull red in the fall.

PLANTING

Preferred Exposure: Full sun. Protect from winds in Zones 6 and cooler.
Preferred Soil and Fertility: Deep, well-drained of average fertility and high organic matter. Apply 1 to 1½ lbs.

of compost per row foot in early spring each year.
Spacing: Erect cultivars, 3 to 5 feet between plants; trailing cultivars, 8 to 10 feet between plants.
Pollinators: Occasionally required. Check with your supplier.

CULTURAL CARE

Watering: Plants require an inch of water a week from spring to the time the fruit is coloring. Unless there is a severe drought, do not supplement natural rainfall from the time the fruit begins to color until it is harvested.
Mulching: Keep plants mulched to prevent weeds from growing in the area. Use newspaper or cardboard cov-

BLACKBERRY 'THORNFREE'

ered with straw or shredded hardwood bark. Remove mulch each fall and replace with clean material to help keep diseases in check.
Pests: Aphids, raspberry red-necked cane borers, two-spotted and European red spider mites, Japanese beetles, raspberry fruit worms.
Diseases: Anthracnose, botrytis fruit rot, crown gall, crumbly berry virus, mosaic virus, orange rust, powdery mildew, spur blight and verticillium wilt.

PRUNING

After Planting: Head back canes to 6 inches.
Routine Pruning: See pages 260 to 261.
Fruiting: Most brambles fruit on 1-year-old canes; some raspberry cultivars fruit in fall.
Years to Bearing: 1.
Harvest Season: July to fall, depending on species.
Yields: 1 to 8 quarts per plant, depending on species.

Notes: Taste-test for ripeness and harvest every other day during the season.

Boysenberries are a stabilized hybrid with blackberry, loganberry, and raspberry parents. They resemble blackberries and loganberries more than they do raspberries. They differ from blackberries in that they require a spacing of 8 feet between plants, they never require a pollinator, and their larger vines yield up to 8 quarts per plant.

Dewberries are one of the most distinctively flavored of the brambles—sweet with tart undertones. 'Carolina' is a cultivar that resists fungal leaf diseases.

Loganberries were bred from blackberries and raspberries in the 1880s. The first plants developed had fruit so tart that gardeners cooked it with sweeteners before eating. Today, however, improved strains are available. But it's important that you taste-test any fruit that you are interested in growing to be certain that you like the flavor. Loganberries resemble raspberries more than blackberries when it comes to the pests and diseases they attract.

STRAW makes the best mulch for strawberry plants. Garden centers usually carry it.

STRAWBERRY JARS add a festive note to your yard or patio while also making a good home for the berries.

STRAWBERRIES

EVERY GARDENER CAN GROW strawberries. Whether you garden on a balcony in the middle of Manhattan or on a farm in Iowa, there's an ideal strawberry for your circumstances.

Almost everyone is familiar with the traditional June-bearing strawberries. True to their name, they fruit just once a year, generally in June. Various cultivars of June-bearers are the fruit that most gardeners and commercial growers prefer.

Day-neutral, or everbearing, strawberries have become more popular during the last few years. Rather than bearing all their fruit at once, they produce small amounts all through the season with production peaks in June and August. On the downside, they are more attractive to one of the worst strawberry pests, the tarnished plant bug, than the June-bearers but they have several strong advantages. Gardeners can rely on the June-bearers for bumper crops to preserve and freeze and a patch of day-neutrals for a steady supply of through the season. And because these plants are less particular about day length, gardeners with

greenhouses can schedule their planting so that fruit is ripening just as the outside berries are coming into bloom.

The fruit of both June-bearers and day-neutrals is the size and shape that you imagine when you think of strawberries. In contrast, alpine strawberries are much smaller. They too are everbearing, but they produce fruit that tastes more like wild than cultivated strawberries, and their fruits are the size of a baby's thumbnail. Alpine strawberries can be grown from seeds rather than plants and thrive in hanging baskets filled with a humus-rich soil mix.

Choosing Cultivars

Once you start exploring the world of strawberries, you'll discover that there are literally hundreds of June-bearers available for most locations. Read the cultivar descriptions carefully; you will want to choose those with fine flavor rather than large size or good shipping qualities. In northern areas, you may also want to choose mid- and late-season types so you don't have to worry about protecting the plants from late spring frosts.

FAVORITE STRAWBERRY CULTIVARS

Choosing an appropriate cultivar can help to prevent problems. The better adapted a plant is to your area, the more likely it is to resist pests and diseases. The following list is by no means inclusive. Use it as a starting point, but ask friends, neighbors, the Cooperative Extension Service, and area nurseries for their favorite strawberries.

	ZONES	NOTES
ALPINE CULTIVARS		
'Baron Solemacher'	4 to 8	Grows well in pots anywhere
'Ruegen Improved'	5 to 8	The alpine most widely grown commercially
'Pineapple Crush'	5 to 8	A yellow fruit with good flavor
DAY-NEUTRAL CULTIVARS		
'Aptos'	6 to 9	Commonly grown in California and Arizona
'Fort Laramie'	3 to 8	A good choice for the North
'Ozark Beauty'	5 to 8	This plant is fairly disease-resistant and yields well
'Ogallala'	5 to 8	Tolerates dry conditions better than most
'Tristar'	5 to 8	Known for good flavor
'Tribute'	4 to 8	Resists most diseases and has good flavor
JUNE-BEARING CULTIVARS		
'Earliglow'	4 to 8	Disease resistant and matures early
'Cardinal'	4 to 8	Matures early and is common in the mid-Atlantic states
'Dunlap'	4 to 8	Tolerates a range of soils, including clays
'Kent'	4 to 8	Hardy to Zone 3 if protected; yields early
'Honeoye'	4 to 8	Widely grown commercially because it is disease resistant and has huge fruit; some consider it a bit bland
'Red Chief'	4 to 8	Hardy to Zone 3 if protected; resists most diseases, and matures midseason
'Sparkle'	4 to 8	A fine-flavored, late-season berry

PLANTING STRAWBERRIES

Strawberries are one of the easiest crops you can grow. However, to get the best possible fruit, you'll need to plan to move the crop every four or five years.

1 Prepare the soil well before you plant the berries. Adjust the pH, and work up to 4 inches of fully finished compost into the top few inches of the soil.

4 Mulch the plants, and cover them with row-cover material to protect them from late frosts while they are getting established.

Grow a nongrass cover crop in the area where you plan to grow your next crop of strawberries to avoid building high populations of cutworms or beetle grubs.

Tools and Materials: **Metal rake, trowel, row-cover material, bypass pruners, bird netting.**

2 Set out the plants at the spacing you have decided on. Soak the roots well before setting them out, and work on a cloudy day so they don't dry out.

3 Plant the strawberries at the correct depth. As shown in the inset, the crown should be just at the soil line, not above or below it.

5 Allow a maximum of two runners to set roots to avoid crowding in the planting. If this seems too dense, prune off some of the new plants.

6 Save some berries for yourself by covering them with bird netting when the fruit is ripe. Reflective tape and pie pans also deter birds.

CHAPTER 9

PREVENTING WEEDS, PESTS, AND DISEASES

*T*he secret of having a wonderful garden—productive, beautiful, and free
of weeds, pests, and diseases—can be
summed up by one word: prevention. With
a little foreknowledge about the problems
that can beset your particular plants in
your particular ecosystem, you can avoid
most of them.

You may never completely eliminate certain
weeds, pests, and diseases, but you can bring their
populations down to the point where they are relatively easy to control.

New gardeners usually have trouble believing
this, in large part because their soils are so far from
ideal that they experience lots of trouble. However,
with attention and care, it takes only a few years of
good gardening to bring most of your problems
under control. As you garden, mentally check your

TIDY GARDENS where plants have adequate space are easier to
keep healthy. Above: The green lacewing is a beneficial insect.

activities against these basic principles:

■ Encourage a diverse and complex group of
living creatures, from insects and microorganisms to
plants, birds, and frogs.

■ Plan so that a succession of both large and
small-flowered plants are in bloom at all times and
include members of the *Umbelliferae* and *Aster-
aceae* families in these successions. Both groups
attract many beneficial insects.

■ Build and maintain soil health by using
composts, organic mulches, cover crops and green
manures, and natural soil amendments such as rock
powders in an appropriate manner.

■ Avoid using materials such as herbicides,
synthetic fertilizers, or insecticides that disrupt the
natural system.

■ Avoid plant diseases by rotating crops,
choosing disease-resistant cultivars, and providing
the correct conditions for each plant you grow.

■ Provide the best possible environment for
every plant you grow, from soil characteristics to air
circulation and drainage.

■ Plant only as much as you can easily maintain, and design all gardens to be as easy to care for
as possible.

WEEDS

WEEDS CAN BE THE most troublesome gardening problem you'll experience, particularly during the first few years of your garden. You've no doubt heard the cliche about weeds being nothing more than plants "out of place." But no matter what your relationship to the weeds in your garden, you'll be able to control and, believe it or not, use them better if you understand them.

Gardeners are well served by learning about the remarkable reproductive capabilities of weeds. Vines such as poison ivy (*Toxicodendron radicans*) and morning-glory can send up new shoots from rhizomes that have traveled 20 feet from the mother plant, perhaps under a sidewalk or a concrete-block wall. Plants such as quack grass (*Agropyron repens*) and curly dock (*Rumex crispus*) can reproduce from a tiny piece of root as well as from seeds. And finally,

most weeds produce amazing numbers of seeds. For example, redroot pigweed can drop more than 100,000 seeds in a square foot area, and common mullein (*Verbascum thapsus*) routinely produces more than 200,000 seeds. Additionally, these seeds have a long period of viability. Once they are in the soil "seed bank," they remain ready to germinate for up to 50 years.

Weeds can tell you a great deal about your soil conditions too. Some, such as sheep sorrel (*Rumex acetosella*) thrive in acid conditions, others in alkaline soil; some, such as plantain, like compaction, while others prefer a loose, friable environment.

Weeds can be habitats for many of the beneficial organisms that you want to attract to your garden. If you have a weedy area with a collection of mints, some umbelliferous plants (those with an umbrella-shaped flower head, such as dill), and other good nectar-producing plants, you may not have to plant a habitat island. However, just as weeds can host beneficials, they can also host the pests and diseases that prey on your garden plants. For example, you will never be able to control the cabbage root fly maggot if you live next door to a field of wild mustard (*Brassica kaber*). Similarly, aphids can bring a virus from a wild cucumber to your cultivated plants.

Most of the plants gardeners call weeds are the first step in vegetative succession. One way or another, they are opportunists capable of thriving in hostile environments. This quality enables them to colonize areas that have suffered such things as fires, earthquakes, floods, or simply poor gardening practices. Depending on the season, it takes only a few weeks to months for weed seeds to germinate and take root in disturbed soils.

DEVELOP THE HABIT of clearing pulled weeds from the garden to keep them from rerooting.

SMART TIP
PUT WEEDS TO WORK

Use the fast growth of weeds such as lamb's-quarters to provide a quick green manure crop. Or take advantage of weeds with strong, deep roots like amaranth to break up hard pans, increase water movement through the soil, and expand the area that crop roots can penetrate. As long as you mow or till before the weeds set seed, you can benefit from this "free" crop.

TOOLS

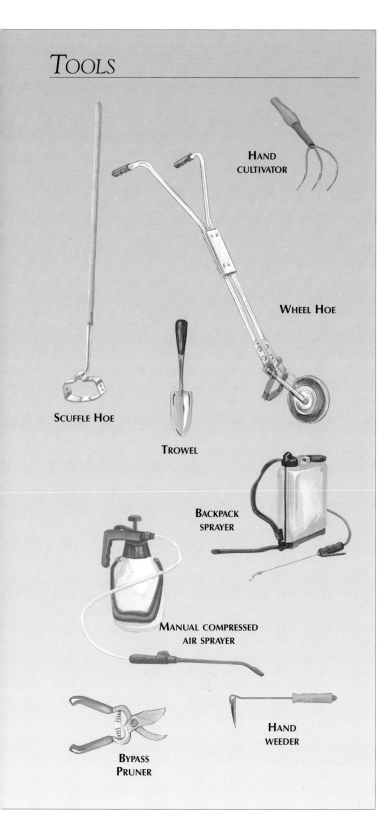

HAND CULTIVATOR

WHEEL HOE

SCUFFLE HOE

TROWEL

BACKPACK SPRAYER

MANUAL COMPRESSED AIR SPRAYER

BYPASS PRUNER

HAND WEEDER

REMEMBER TO DEADHEAD flowering plants such as chives and marigold to keep them from being next year's weeds.

The Weed Problem

The aforementioned concerns you may have for weeds aside, the major reason to try to eliminate weeds from your garden is competition. In comparison with weeds, most of our cultivated plants are weak creatures. Side by side, you can count on the weeds to take more than their fair share of space, both above and below ground. In the garden, space equals access to water and soil minerals as well as exposure to the sun.

Weeds can also ruin the look of a garden. If you've designed a bed and specified where various shapes and colors will go, you don't want a bunch of weeds—with their unruly colors and shapes—to take over the area.

Mulches reduce weed problems by blocking the light necessary for seeds to germinate or, in the case of materials such as sawdust, by robbing so much nitrogen from the soil as they are decomposing that weeds can't survive.

Living mulches, or low-growing companion plants that you seed between your ornamental plants or crop rows, can

CHAPTER 9

SMART TIP

COPING WITH WEEDS

When it comes to weeds, always look for the lazy way. If grasses threaten the edges of your flower gardens, put a layer of newspaper along the garden edge, and cover it with gravel or bark mulch. Any weed seeds that blow in and germinate will be much easier to spot and easier to pull. This kind of barrier can also be used under fences, beside buildings, and along the driveway.

also keep weeds down. Use this technique in paths in the annual garden or around perennials such as fruit trees. For example, after you plant a fruit tree, seed a foot of fava beans on the outside edge of the mound around it. The beans will block weeds from growing in the area and contribute nitrogen to the tree after they die and decompose.

Use companion plantings. In annual gardens where weeds have previously been a major problem, you can take advantage of natural plant antagonisms. Chemical compounds from some plants have an injurious, or allelopathic, effect on others. As discussed in Chapter 1, winter rye is often used to inhibit the growth of quack grass. Other allelopathic interactions include the effects asters have on ragweed and barley has on redroot pigweed, purslane, and ragweed.

Intensive planting schemes minimize weed problems. If plants are spaced so that they don't suffer from competing with each other but still shade the soil surface below them, weeds can't get a foothold once the cultivated plants mature. The spacing recommendations in the plant directories in this book are meant to give this kind of control.

Crop rotations also help with weed problems. If you have an area where weeds have built up over the season, it's wise to plant a heavily mulched crop in that spot the following year. Similarly, you can take advantage of beds that were mulched so heavily that no weeds grew by planting a crop that can't compete well against weeds, such as carrots, the next year.

CONTROLLING WEEDS

Sad to say, no matter how good your preventive measures, you're sure to face at least a few weeds every year. Again, your goal should be to control them with the least possible effort. With this in mind, try to:

■ Weed early and often. It's easier to remove tiny seedlings than foot-tall monsters.

■ Hoe or cultivate as shallowly as possible. Weed seeds buried in the soil will germinate if you bring them to the surface.

■ Mow or deadhead weeds or cultivated plants, such as dill or tansy, that can become weeds.

■ Remove most weeds from the garden after you pull or hoe them. Some, such as small-seeded galinsoga (*Galinsoga parviflora*), are capable of setting seeds after they have been pulled if they have flowers, while others, such as lamb's-quarters, can reroot easily.

■ Mow fields that host perennial weeds such as Canada thistle (*Cirsium arvense*) and common milkweed (*Asclepias syriaca*) every seven to ten days after the plants have formed blooms. Set the mower to cut very low. Eventually, nutrients stored in the roots will be exhausted, and the plants will die.

■ Use techniques appropriate to your circumstances to eliminate weeds before you plant. For example, stale seedbeds are ideal in annual gardens. Similarly, flameweeders can make growing weed-free carrots possible.

There is at least one "don't" to which you should pay attention when it comes to weed control.

■ Never till a patch of perennial weeds that can reproduce from the rootstock. Dandelions, quack grass, Canada thistle, and curly dock fit into this category, but some crop plants do too. Comfrey and Jerusalem artichokes can both take over a field in only a season. Instead, dig out the roots, mulch, or mow repeatedly.

A WHEEL HOE makes weeding between rows of plants a snap; the upright position eliminates the bending of hand pulling.

COMMON "BENEFICIAL" WEEDS

Identification is the first step in controlling weeds. This chart shows several common weeds and the benefits of keeping them in your garden. Some are medicinal, while others attract beneficial insects. Knowing the plant family and its life cycle may help you manage it. Life cycle and control systems often go together. For example, annuals are easy to pull if you do it early in the season, while many perennial weeds can be controlled by mulching them heavily for at least a year. Any gardener can tolerate a couple of stray biennial weeds as long as you never let them set seed.

Plantain/Plantago major

Broadleaf plantain takes the sting out of insect bites and soothes irritated skin. Made into an infusion, this perennial settles the stomach.

Lamb's quarters/Chenopodium

Lamb's quarters are a tasty and nutritious addition to salads when they are young. Keep this annual from seeding to prevent a weed problem.

Burdock/Arctium

Burdock is a medicinal plant that can easily become a weed. This biennial reproduces from seeds. Mow first year plants; pull them in year two.

Ramps/Allium tricoccum

Ramps, often called wild leeks, are a wonderful spring cooking green with an oniony flavor. To keep them from being weeds, dig and enjoy.

Milkweed/Asclepias speciosa

Milkweed reproduces by seeds as well as rhizomes. Pull to eliminate, but leave a few plants to feed butterflies and make pods for dried bouquets.

Tansy/Tanacetum vulgare

Tansy can be used to repel ants in the house, and the flowers can be dried for winter bouquets. But don't let it seed in the garden, or it will be a weed.

CHAPTER 9

ANIMAL PESTS

WILD ANIMALS CAN CAUSE a great deal of damage in your garden. Deer like the flavor of expensive daylilies as much as they like lettuce or broccoli; raccoons usually get the corn the night before you plan to harvest it; rodents kill unprotected trees and bushes; and birds eat everything from newly planted cover crops to fully ripened cherries.

Once again, prevention is the best recourse. Count yourself lucky if you have a dog that likes to spend the night outside and feels some territorial imperative to protect the garden. This is all it takes to discourage deer and larger rodents such as woodchucks, as well as rabbits. But those without dogs must take other action.

DEER lose their appeal about the time you find them munching on the tulips or dining on the daylililes.

EFFECTIVE FENCING

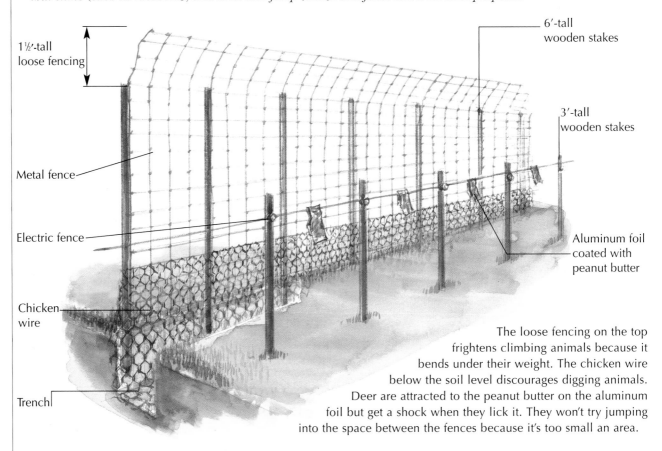

Fencing must protect the garden from animals that can burrow (such as groundhogs), those that climb (such as raccoons), and those that jump (deer). This fence serves all these purposes.

1½'-tall loose fencing

6'-tall wooden stakes

Metal fence

3'-tall wooden stakes

Electric fence

Aluminum foil coated with peanut butter

Chicken wire

Trench

The loose fencing on the top frightens climbing animals because it bends under their weight. The chicken wire below the soil level discourages digging animals. Deer are attracted to the peanut butter on the aluminum foil but get a shock when they lick it. They won't try jumping into the space between the fences because it's too small an area.

> ### SMART TIP
> #### CHANGE REPELLENTS FREQUENTLY
> No matter how dreadful your repellents smell, the deer will eventually get used to them. Combat this by leaving soap in place and adding and subtracting other repellents throughout the season.

Deer repellents have become big business. They work because their smell is offensive or frightening to deer. You can buy bottled coyote urine, garlic oil, or mixtures of fatty acids that deer find offensive. Each of these materials must be applied according to directions, and most of them must be reapplied after every rain.

Homemade repellents also work against deer. Try hanging deodorant soaps on 4- to 5-foot stakes on the perimeter of the garden. You can also hang cheesecloth filled with dirty human or dog hair on plants you want to protect. Let a few eggs rot, and then paint this material on stakes set around the garden. Like other odor barriers, you must reapply the rotten eggs after every rain.

Fences are the best protection against deer. In areas where deer pressure is especially high, some people totally enclose their garden plots with strong wire fencing, even extending it on the top edges to form a partial roof. A three-foot-high length of chicken wire, attached to the bottom of the fencing, keeps smaller animals out of the area.

Small Animals

Rabbits, mice, rats, and woodchucks will all be attracted to the lavish spread in your garden. Once again, both repellents and barriers are the most effective deterrents you can use aside from a vigilant dog or, in the case of mice and small rats, cats.

Unfortunately, these small animals aren't in the least deterred by the smell of human hair, rotten eggs, or soap. The smell of large predators does keep them out of the garden, though you'll probably find that fox urine is more effective than coyote. Some of the other commercial products that repel deer also repel rodents. Read labels carefully to discover whether the repellent you are considering is effective against rodents as well as deer, and to learn how to handle the product safely.

Depending on the size of the animal, fencing is only effective if it extends at least 2 feet below the soil surface

WOODCHUCKS, or groundhogs, have been known to burrow under black plastic mulch to reach some ripe winter-squash.

OPOSSUMS are unlikely to cause any damage in the garden. If you see one, let it be; it's likely to just go on its way.

as well as several feet above it. Groundhogs have no trouble plowing over or through a 3-foot-high chicken wire fence, for example, but rabbits can't jump that high. Groundhogs can burrow more than 2 feet into the soil, but a fence at this depth seems to discourage them.

> ### SMART TIP
> #### TRY SMOKE BOMBS FOR GROUNDHOG CONTROL
> Find all of the openings to the burrows, and plug them with rocks so heavy that the groundhogs can't move them. After this, place the smoke bombs in the two holes that seem to be the primary entrances of the burrow, and light them. The smoke drives the groundhogs out but does not kill them. Still, if this idea bothers you, try to protect your plants with barriers instead of bombs.

Some people trap groundhogs in large wire traps that do not kill them. If you choose to do this, investigate your options for releasing the groundhog in advance of catching it. Many states have laws forbidding the transport and release of wild animals.

Rats and mice aren't likely to eat herbaceous plants in your garden. Instead, they will munch on tree and shrub bark during the winter. Plastic tree guards and fine-mesh screening prevent rodent damage.

Raccoons

RACCOONS know when the corn is ripe. Keep them out of the garden if you want any for yourself.

Raccoons belong to the same family as bears. This fact only strikes you as odd if you have not yet engaged in a battle with a raccoon over your garden produce.

The most important thing to understand about a raccoon is that it has no fear of you. Big, fierce dogs frighten them, but they pay no mind to the ordinary retriever unless it threatens them. Be aware that rabies infections have been prevalent in raccoon populations for several years.

Perfectly healthy raccoons eat your corn at night. The old-time remedy is to plant the corn with winter squashes that vine around the stalks. Supposedly, the scratchy squash leaves will repel the raccoons. However, this is not always effective.

Powdered cayenne pepper, sprinkled on the corn silks, is also supposed to repel raccoons. With a couple of provisos, this does work. But don't sprinkle it onto the silks while the corn kernels are still developing, or it will sift between them, and your corn will taste really hot. Wait until the kernels are full size. Reapply after it rains.

Keeping birds out of the garden. Certain birds are among a gardener's best allies because they prey on so many pests, but others give you nothing but trouble. As you gain experience with your garden, you'll also learn which of the local birds to discourage.

The only way to keep birds out of the garden is by frightening them away, generally with visual cues. Try setting up a couple of plastic owls on stakes near areas you want to protect. Plastic snakes, even those made out of old hoses, also work. But even a bird is smart enough to figure out that a stationary owl or snake is not alive, so you'll need to change their location and position every day.

Scarecrows are really fun to make, but serve more often as perches than deterrents. Make one if you wish, but regard it as garden decoration rather than a serious bird deterrent.

BIRDS SUCH AS THIS BLACKBIRD love cherries and other small fruit. Net the plants to keep some harvest.

> ### SMART TIP
> #### USE CAUTION NEAR RACCOONS
> If you wake up to discover a family of raccoons on the back porch, pillaging your produce baskets, do not throw open the door to yell at them. Instead, turn on the radio with the volume as loud as you can take it. Arm yourself with a broom, and cautiously open the door, extending only the broom through it. Healthy raccoons will run away, alarmed by the noise, but animals that are developing rabies will attack the broom. Drop the broom, close the door, and call the state animal control department.

Bird and Animal Controls

Gardeners become quite ingenious when faced with the challenge of keeping animal pests away from their plants. Just a little research in garden supply catalogs and retail outlets will provide you with lots of tools to protect your harvests. These tools are inexpensive and easy to install; they are worth every penny and minute spent.

CAGES made of wire, netting, or floating row cover material can protect your fruit from the many birds that arrive to pick it.

WIRE NETTING OR FENCING can prevent cats from attacking one of their favorite foods and scratching posts—kiwi vines.

BLACK PLASTIC wrapped around this trunk may prevent rodents from stripping the bark. If the bark becomes too hot under the plastic, paint it white.

WHITE PAINT protects trunks from sunscald. Use white plastic wraps to protect against both rodents and possible sun damage.

INSECT AND MITE PESTS

ALMOST ALL GARDENERS HAVE trouble with one or another insect at some time. However, these problems are likely to be less frequent and less serious than most gardeners probably imagine. And a surprise waiting for gardeners new to working with biological controls is how much they will come to like the beneficial insects in their garden. Even people who have suffered all their lives from an aversion to spiders and other creepy, crawly creatures develop new feelings when they see them preying on plant pests. It's quite thrilling to see a wasp carry a caterpillar from the leaf of a broccoli plant or notice a syrphid fly larvae systematically eating its way through an aphid colony.

The best defenses against insect pests are those that occur naturally. Climate, weather, food sources, habitat, pathogens, predators, parasites, and parasitoids all fit into this category. Very often, these factors work so well that the entire drama of pest attack and natural control goes on without your even being aware of it.

Any organism's survival depends on climate and weather as well as its life cycle and the severity of its attack. For example, onion seedlings imported from Georgia may be carrying a pest nematode when they arrive in Vermont. If the soil is cold when the onions are transplanted, the nematodes may die, and if it is warm, they may thrive. But no matter how they fare during the summer, the nematodes are sure to die in the freezing fall and winter soil. And, you'll notice, for example, that pests such as cabbage root fly maggots are much worse in rainy springs than they are in hot, dry years, just as mites always take advantage of drought conditions.

NASTURTIUMS make excellent trap crops for aphids. Check under the leaves and in leaf axils frequently.

Common Beneficial Insects

No matter where you garden, tremendous numbers of beneficial insects live there too. Develop the habit of considering unknown insects innocent of preying on your plants until you have identified them. Those you can't identify are unlikely to be pests, predators, or parasitoids, but may be helping to transform dead organic matter into nutrient sources for your plants. The insects shown below are some of the most common beneficials in the garden.

Rotating crops is another way of manipulating insect habitats and food sources. If you deny a pest its food, it will try to find another host. Sometimes, this means flying to someone else's garden, but in other cases, the pest dies of starvation.

Insects are as vulnerable to microorganisms as are larger animals. Gardeners can buy many disease microorganisms specific to their pests, but in most environments, indigenous diseases also provide a great deal of control, most of it invisible to the gardener.

Similarly, you can purchase predators, parasites, and parasitoids. Many of these are incredibly effective, particularly in a greenhouse situation. But again, natural beneficials will always give more certain control than imported ones.

GALLERY OF BENEFICIAL INSECTS

Many beneficial insects look quite different at younger periods in their life that you might expect. Below, for example, are ladybugs in pupa cases and as larvae.

LADYBUG PUPAE   **LADYBUG LARVA EATING APHIDS**

Food sources and habitat go hand in hand because insects tend to live near, or on, their food sources. If you plant permanent habitat areas in your yard that include plants such as daisies, dandelions, mints, asters, sunflowers, yarrows, and a selection of umbelliferous herbs, you'll be furnishing both habitat and food for beneficial predators and parasitoids. In dry conditions, remember to provide water for the insects in an old pie pan. Put a few rocks in the pan to give them a spot on which to stand.

Complicating Factors

The goal of most ecologically sensitive gardeners is to develop such healthy garden ecosystems that natural controls do all of the pest control. Not only is this theoretically possible, there are many gardeners and farmers who have achieved it. However, it is unrealistic to expect your garden ecosystem to work this way from the beginning.

Two factors complicate the issue: imported insects and previous ecosystem disturbances. Insects that are indigenous to your area are part of the natural system, so they have at least one natural control. But insects imported from other places do not necessarily have any controls in their new location. This accounts for their ability to build high populations without the sort of checks that keep most indigenous insects within reasonable bounds. Some of the imported insects you will probably come to know well are cabbage moths, gypsy moths, and Japanese beetles.

The natural ecosystem has been disturbed, to one extent or another, almost everywhere that human beings live. This is inevitable and not worth bemoaning. Instead, you can take positive action by allowing a little wildness on the edges of your property. A more active approach is to use only "ecologically benign" materials in your garden.

Defining ecologically benign is tricky. For example, synthetic nitrogen fertilizers do not fit into this category because they short-circuit the series of transformations that nitrogen naturally goes through, thereby eliminating some of the niches required by some microorganisms. However, you may one day find yourself having to decide whether or not to spray copper or sulfur to control a plant disease. Because these materials are nutrients that are necessary to plant growth in small amounts, it could be that you will be helping to restore balance by spraying with them. However, you have to remember that copper and sulfur are necessary in only trace amounts and that overreliance on them as pest-control materials is sure to be disruptive. The best advice is to learn as much as you can about the pest or disease preying on your plants and then to apply that knowledge to prevent the problem. When prevention doesn't work, start with the least disruptive control system, and only move to stronger measures if the first controls don't work.

Preventing Pest Problems

Good cultural care and excellent garden sanitation form the backbone of an effective pest-prevention program. Practices such as choosing pest-resistant cultivars, timing plantings to avoid pest outbreaks, using barriers to prevent pest access to your plants, planting "trap" plants, and providing habitats for beneficial organisms are also important preventive measures.

Many pests are attracted to plants that are stressed. For example, you are likely to have trouble with aphids if your soil has too much nitrogen or if the plants are water stressed. Simply taking good care of your plants minimizes the chances of an aphid outbreak.

Sanitation is also imperative. For example, insects such as squash bugs overwinter as adults in garden debris. If you clean up the yard at the end of the season, you eliminate this habitat, making it more difficult for them to find a cozy winter home.

It's important to learn to recognize less familiar beneficials too. The larvae of both of the insects below prey on aphids and other soft-bodied pests.

NEWLY HATCHED LACEWING

SYRPHID FLY

CODLING MOTH TRAPS are baited with pheromones that attract the moths. Once inside, the moths cannot get out again.

If Disaster Strikes

No matter how good your pest preventive measures, your plants may still be attacked, particularly during the first few years while you are still building soil and ecosystem health. This can be a devastating experience, particularly if you don't know how severe the damage can eventually become.

After you experience the perfectly rational feelings of outrage, panic, horror, or sorrow, it's best to take a steady, calm approach to the situation. Identifying the pest is your first task. If the pest is not immediately apparent, look for it after dark. Check the damage it has caused against a list of likely culprits. (Cross-reference between "pests" in the individual plant directory entries and "hosts" in the pest entries.) Remember that pests such as mites and thrips are so tiny that you usually notice their damage before you see the pests. Similarly, you're likely to see the symptoms of viral diseases carried in by aphids or leafhoppers before you notice the insects themselves. In the case of under-

Most preventive measures tend to be fairly pest specific. You can't always find a pest-resistant cultivar any more than you can time every planting to avoid an insect. However, as you'll discover when you read the pest directory, pages 280 to 291, preventive measures exist for most pests.

INSECT LIFE CYCLES

All insects go through various stages in their lives. Some, such as the Colorado potato beetle and Japanese beetle, go through complete metamorphosis, while others, such as the squash bug and praying mantid go through incomplete metamorphosis. You will learn how to control them at various stages of their lifecycles.

PRAYING MANTID

COLORADO POTATO BEETLE

PRAYING MANTIDS are one of the many insects that go through incomplete, or gradual, metamorphosis. The foamy-looking structure on the left, above, is an egg case that contains hundreds of eggs. Nymphs, which resemble the adult insect, hatch from this case in appropriate environmental conditions. As the nymphs eat, they grow, eventually molting, or splitting out of, their exoskeletons three or four times, depending on the insect species. At the final molt, they have functional wings and reproductive organs.

COLORADO POTATO BEETLES make a good example of insects that go through complete metamorphosis. The adult beetles overwinter in the soil, and lay eggs in the early summer, as shown in the photo on the left, above. Tiny brick red larvae hatch from the eggs and begin eating. As they grow, they molt. They go through four instars, or periods between molts, before they form a pupa case in which they go through their complete metamorphosis. After a few days, they emerge as adult beetles that continue eating but also lay eggs.

ground pests, the first clues are usually wilted leaves and stunting.

Once you have identified the pest, you need to plan your response. If the infestation is just beginning, it may be that you can still use a preventive measure to minimize the damage. For example, if Japanese beetles suddenly appear on the roses, there is certainly time to set up a pheromone, or attractant odor, trap. Similarly, you can often cover plants with floating row covers if you do it when the first pests appear. But don't do this before carefully considering the situation. You might be able to keep striped cucumber beetles off the squash, but if you cover a row of flea beetle-infested arugula, you'll be making matters worse by enclosing the pests along with their food source.

Assess the potential damage before acting. To determine further action, you'll need to assess the potential damage. For example, arugula for salads can stand a few flea beetle holes, so there is no need to panic if the dam-

BEETLE BATTLE PADDLES

Flea beetle traps are easy to make. Attach large sheets of cardboard to two long stakes. Coat the cardboard with sticky Tanglefoot™ to trap the beetles.

FLEA BEETLES hop into the air when they think they're under attack. You can use this habit to catch them. Hold the traps beside the plants while you jostle them with your feet. The flea beetles will jump onto the traps.

SMART TIP

HAND PICKING AND SQUASHING

One of the most effective pest control methods is also the oldest — picking and/or squashing pests and their eggs. Whenever you are confronted with a large pest,

this is the first line of action. If you do it well enough, you'll keep populations down to a reasonable level. If you can't bear touching the pest, use a large leaf, kitchen tongs, plastic gloves, or a kitchen towel to protect your hands. Be prepared to kill the pests if you collect them, either by squashing, stomping on them, or by placing them in a bucket of water mixed with a poison such as gasoline or laundry bleach.

age is light. However, if there are more holes than leaf surface, you do have to take action. No matter what the pest, it's important to go through this kind of assessment. This will be difficult in your first years of gardening. However, with time and experience, you'll soon be able to judge likely damage quite accurately.

If potential damage is severe enough to warrant control, it's almost always best to begin by choosing the least ecologically damaging approach. Remember to allow sufficient time for the control to work before making a judgment about it. If the control doesn't stop the damage within four to five days, then it's time to step in with stronger measures. Check the directory section to learn the range of controls available for each pest.

Pest infestations usually build up over a few years. In the first year or two, damage and populations are light. But by year three, if you have not yet stepped in with preventive measures, pest populations and crop damage can become truly serious. It is sensible to evaluate all of the control techniques you use. You not only want to prepare for the coming year by taking preventive action before the pest appears, you also want to use the most effective control method of the previous year if your preventive measures fail.

ILLUSTRATED DIRECTORY OF PESTS, INCLUDING CONTROLS

Acyrthosiphon pisum (pea aphid), *Myzus persicae* (green peach aphid), *Dyasaphis plantaginea* (rosy apple aphid), *Macrosiphum euphorbiae* (potato aphid), *Brevicoryne brassicae* (cabbage aphid), *Aphis fabae* (black bean aphid), and many others

Aphid

APHIS FABAE

BREVICORYNE BRASSICAE

Appearance: Soft-bodied insects, most with two tubules, called cornicles, pro-truding from the posterior end. Antennae are long and positioned on the front on the head, between the eyes. Colors include green, pink, black, red, yellow and nearly clear. They release honeydew, a sweet sticky material. Sooty mold fungus can grow on honeydew, and ants feed on it, often "milking" aphids as well as protecting them as if they were a herd of cows.

Life Cycle: Gradual or "simple" metamorphosis, but complicated life cycle overall. In early spring, the first aphids hatch from eggs laid on woody perennials. These aphids, known as "stem mothers" give birth to live young, each of which is a female capable of giving birth to another generation of females, which in turn gives live birth to more females, all without benefit of male fertilization. When the weather is warm, a generation is born that includes winged females that fly to annual crops, many of which can be in your garden. In autumn, wingless males are born that mate with winged females. The females fly to perennial plants where they lay eggs capable of overwintering through the harshest conditions.

Hosts: Many, but particularly damaging to leafy crops, roses, apples, cabbage-family crops, citrus, brambles, and melons. Some species feed only on one host, some alternate between two species and others feed on a wide range of plants.

Damage: Aphids suck plant juices from their hosts, often transmitting virus diseases as they do. Some, such as woolly aphids (*Eriosoma langerum*) form galls on leaves, stems or buds of various plants. Others, such as the strawberry root aphid (*Aphis forbesi*) feed on the plant roots. Damage ranges from minor to lethal.

Prevention: Practice good cultural care, taking care to supply appropriate amounts of soil nitrogen and adequate moisture levels. Plant habitat islands, and interlant herbs such as dill and chervil with crops or ornamentals that attract aphids.

Controls: There are many natural controls including hard, driving rainfall as well as predators such as ladybugs, lacewings, syrphid fly larvae, and *Aphidoletes aphidimyza*. Parasitoids include braconid and chalcid wasps. Use dormant oil on fruit trees to control overwintering eggs. Hard water sprays can knock some aphids off plants. Insecticidal soap, superior oil, garlic oil, pyrethrins and rotenone, in order from least to most ecologically disruptive, can kill them.

Notes: If you hand-squash aphids when you first see them, you can get a surprising amount of control over the situation. Look for aphids in the growing tips as well as along the stems and on the undersides of leaves.

Rhagoletis pomonella

Apple Maggot

Appearance: Adults are dark-colored flies, about ¼ inch long, with yellow legs and dark-colored stripes across their wings. The larvae are small and white.

Life Cycle: Female flies pierce the fruit skin and lay eggs that hatch in five to seven days. Maggots hatch and tunnel their way through the fruit as they feed. Infected fruit often drops to the ground. The maggots crawl out of the fruit and into the soil, where they pupate. They overwinter as pupae and emerge as adults in mid-June to July to start the next cycle.

Hosts: Apple, crab apple, and blueberries are the primary hosts, but apple maggots will feed on cherries and plums too.

Damage: Feeding makes tunnels in the fruit and usually causes fruit to fall prematurely. Yields can be seriously depressed if infestation is severe.

Prevention: Careful sanitation is the best prevention. Pick up all dropped fruit as soon as you see it. Plant ground covers just beyond the watering mound to provide a habitat for ground beetles that feed on pupae.

Controls: Sticky red apple-maggot traps are available from most orchard suppliers. Hang at least one trap in every dwarf tree and up to six in a fullsize tree.

Notes: Commercial orchardists use the heaviest concentration of traps on perimeter trees.

Crioceris asparagi
Asparagus Beetle

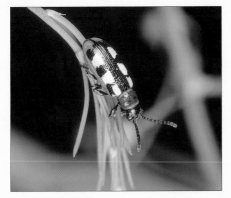

Appearance: The ¼-inch-long beetles are narrow, with shiny, metallic blue heads, a reddish margin on their wing covers and on their thorax, and a blue-black stripe down the central edges of the wing covers. The larvae are plump and gray with dark heads and legs. The shiny black eggs that adults lay in rows on the stems are easy to spot.

Life Cycle: Asparagus beetles hibernate as adults in the asparagus patch and emerge when the first spears are ready to harvest. They lay eggs which hatch within three to eight days. Larvae feed for about two weeks and then pupate in the soil. Adults emerge ten days later. In warm areas, there can be as many as five generations in a summer.

Host: Asparagus

Damage: Both adults and larvae feed on the tips, causing them to scar and turn brown. The larvae excrete a black fluid that stains the plant.

Prevention: Cover the asparagus patch with a row cover before spears emerge in spring, and leave the covers on until the end of harvest. At the end of the season, remove all the old spears.

Controls: Monitor for eggs, beetles, and larvae, and hand pick or squash. With diligence, you can control them all. If you are taking over a neglected patch, spray with pyrethrins when adults first emerge.

Notes: Spotted asparagus beetles (*C. duodecimpunctata*) emerge later in the spring, have black spots on reddish-brown wing covers, lay green eggs and are orange as larvae. Otherwise, the two beetles are very similar.

Delia radicum
(formerly *Hylemya brassicae*)
Cabbage Maggot

Appearance: Adults are gray flies about ¼ inch long, with long legs. The maggot like larvae are white or grayish and almost translucent.

Life Cycle: Adult flies emerge from the soil in spring, just about the time you transplant cabbage family seedlings. They lay eggs near host plants. After hatching, the larvae burrow into the soil where they feed on roots for three to four weeks before pupating. A second generation of adults emerges in two to three weeks. Depending on the length of the season, there are two to four generations a year. Pupae overwinter several inches deep in the soil.

Hosts: Members of the cabbage family.

Damage: Larvae eat roots, eventually killing the plant. The first symptom is wilting in the afternoon even when the soil is wet. Plants are also stunted and often show signs of nutrient deficiencies. Look for a reddish purple hue to the leaves.

Prevention: Rotate plants in the garden, making certain not to follow any cabbage family plants with others. Cover all seeded rows and transplanted seedlings with floating row cover materials immediately after planting. Bury the edges of the material or place a series of 2x4 boards on the edges so the low-flying adults flies cannot get under it. If the problems have been severe in the past, erect fences made of row-cover material all around the garden or cabbage family plants. Bury the bottom of the fence so the pests cannot fly under it. Secure the material to stakes with staples.

If you have only a few spring cabbage family plants, make 6-inch-square tar-paper guards for the plants. Cut a slit from one corner to the center so that you can slip it around the stem. Pull and destroy all affected plants as soon as you see damage, taking remaining soil from around the roots.

Controls: If you have only a few plants, mound diatomaceous earth and/or cayenne powder around the stems of unaffected plants to kill any larvae that may hatch. If damage is serious, drench the area with beneficial nematodes while the larvae are still active. If you miss this window, wait until the following spring

CHAPTER 9

and apply the nematodes when you first see damage.

Notes: In Zones 5 and northward, little damage occurs after June 15, so gardeners often plant of their cabbage-family crops to mature in the fall rather than the spring. Some growers report success with newspaper slurry. Make it by soaking strips of newspaper in water until they turn into mush. Apply a deep layer of this material around the stems when you transplant the seedlings. Larvae cannot burrow through it to the roots. Onion maggots (*D. antiqua*) are similar in all respects but their host and can be controlled the same way.

Psila rosae

Carrot Rust Fly

Appearance:. The ¼-inch adult fly is slender and is a shiny green-black with yellow legs and a reddish head. Larvae are white and maggot like, tapering at the ends.

Life Cycle: Adults emerge from the soil in early to mid-spring and lay eggs close to their hosts. Larvae hatch in a week to 10 days and burrow into the soil where they feed for three to four weeks. They pupate in the soil and a second generation of adults emerges about two weeks later. There are two to three generations in most of the United States. They overwinter as pupae in the soil.

Hosts: Primarily carrots, although they also attack celery, parsley, parsnips,

and weeds in the carrot family such as Queen Anne's lace.

Damage: Larvae feed on the root hairs before boring into the main root. They leave rusty-colored castings in their tunnels. Look for stunted or sick plants. In addition to harming the plants directly, they also leave openings for secondary organisms such as root-rotting fungi. Inspect all carrots destined for winter storage because they may carry maggots.

Prevention: Cover soil with floating row covers as soon as you plant carrots. Pull all carrots from the soil in the fall, and store, or if infected, destroy. Rotate umbelliferae crops.

Controls: Beneficial nematodes will attack the larvae. Apply them at the first sign of damage.

Notes: Once you learn the timing of the pest in your area, you can time your plantings to avoid egg-laying periods as much as possible. But don't give up the row covers if you have ever had damage.

Cydia pomonella

Codling Moth

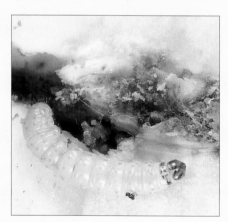

Appearance: The adult moths are grayish-brown. The wings, which measure approximately ¾ inch across when spread, are a warm brown with wavy patterns. The larvae are pinkish-white caterpillars with brown heads. They grow to about ¾ inch long. The flat-

tened white eggs are usually laid on the upper leaf surface but may also appear on twigs and fruit.

Life Cycle: Adults emerge in the early spring months, generally about the time the apples blossom. Female codling moths lay eggs that hatch within a week to ten days. The larvae burrow into the fruit, usually from the blossom end, and feed for between three and five weeks. They emerge from the fruit and crawl down the tree to pupate in niches in the bark or litter on the soil. There are between three and five generations a year, depending on the length of the season. The last generation overwinters as larvae in the soil and pupates in early spring.

Hosts: Apple, apricot, cherry, crab apple, peach, pear and plum.

Damage: Undamaged parts of the fruit are perfectly edible, but the tunnels they leave are generally filled with unappetizing brown-colored castings. They also open the way for secondary organisms.

Prevention: Native beneficial ground beetles prey on the pupae, so it's important not to use herbicides or other pesticides against codling moths that will kill the beetles. Trichogramma parasitic wasps attack the eggs, so grow small-flowered plants in the understory. In late winter, inspect the trees carefully. The cocoons are visible, so you can scrape them off the bark before spraying with dormant oil.

Controls: Sticky bands tied around the trunk can trap larvae on their way to pupate, and round red traps coated with sticky material can trap adults. If you have more than a couple of trees, use pheromone traps to monitor populations. Spray granulosis virus onto trees during the period when eggs are hatching. Twist-tie dispensers of sex pheromones disrupts mating by confusing males.

Notes: Do your best to control the first generation of codling moths so that the later generations will be smaller and less problematic. Practice good sanitation at all times, raking up fruit drops and fallen leaves immediately.

Leptinotarsa decemlineata

Colorado Potato Beetle

Appearance: The ⅓-inch long adults are domed beetles with ten dark lines running vertically on their yellow-orange wing shields. Their heads are generally more orange than their bodies. The larvae start out as tiny rust-colored grubs but soon develop into humpbacked orange grubs with a row of black spots on each side. They can grow to a half inch long. The yellow eggs, laid on end in clusters on leaf undersides, resemble those of ladybugs. Learn to tell the difference so you don't mistakenly kill one of their predators.

Life Cycle: Overwintering adults emerge from the soil in spring to eat the first potato shoots, mate, and lay eggs. The eggs hatch in four to nine days, larvae feed for two to three weeks, and then drop to the soil to pupate. In five to ten days, the second generation emerges and the cycle repeats. There are two generations in the North, three in the South. Adults and occasionally pupae overwinter in the soil.

Hosts: Potatoes, eggplant, tomatoes, nicotiana

Damage: Both adults and larvae eat huge amounts of leaf surface. A potato plant can lose up to a quarter of its leaves without having yields suffer, but it doesn't take long for beetles to go beyond this threshold.

Prevention: Rotate crops. Use straw mulch around potato plants. Cover plants with floating row covers. Encourage the ladybugs that eat the eggs by growing small-flowered plants at the end of the rows. Use white eggplant and nicotiana as trap crops to monitor populations.

Controls: Hand picking is the best control. Look for adults and eggs when the first shoots appear, and continue the search every other day on the leaf undersides. If you are uncertain whether the eggs belong to ladybugs or CPBs, place them in a jar with a cheesecloth cover and a wet cotton ball for humidity, and place the jar in a warm but shaded area. It will take only a few days for the larvae to hatch. Diatomaceous earth sprinkled on larvae kills them. *Bacillus thuringiensis* var. *san diego* kills first and early second instar larvae.

Notes: Commercial growers are reporting excellent control with a trench system. They dig 2-foot-deep, 1-foot-wide trenches around the potato plantings and line them with black plastic. When the beetles emerge from the soil in early spring, they walk rather than fly to their new hosts. If you have rotated crops, the beetles will fall into the trench on the way. The plastic is too slippery for them to climb, so they can't reach your plants.

Helicoverpa zea (formerly *Heliothis zea*)

Corn Earworm/Tomato Fruitworm

Appearance: Adults are tan with a wingspan of 1½ to 2 inches. The larvae are 1 to 2 inches long and can be light yellow, green, pink, or brown and have white and dark stripes along their sides. Their heads are yellow and their legs are black. Eggs are round, ribbed, whitish-green, and can be found on leaves or corn stalks.

Life Cycle: Adults emerge in early spring and fly long distances to find hosts. Females lay eggs on the tips of corn ears or near the stem end of tomatoes and peppers. Larvae hatch and tunnel into the ear or fruit where they eat for two to four weeks and then move to the soil to pupate. Adults emerge ten to twenty-five days later. Depending on location, there are one to four generations a year. The pupae overwinter in the soil.

Hosts: Corn, tomatoes, and peppers primarily, but they can also feed on beans, cabbage, okra, potatoes, squash, and sunflowers.

Damage: The larvae not only eat the corn kernels or tomato or pepper fruit but they also leave unappetizing castings behind. In tomatoes and peppers, the larvae may also eat the leaves and flower buds. On peppers, damage is sometimes unnoticeable until you cut open the pepper to find the castings and destroyed cells. Secondary disease organisms sometimes take advantage of the holes that the larvae leave behind.

Prevention: Do not put lights in the garden because you'll attract the moths. Use small-flowered plants on the edges of the corn patch or as companions to attract beneficial wasps, lacewings and minute pirate bugs. Avoid the first generation in northern zones by starting corn plants early under plastic tunnels or inside, in soil blocks or peat pots, and transplanting them to covered tunnels.

Controls: Handpick larvae if you see them on tomatoes and peppers. When corn silks are dry, apply 20 drops of mineral oil to the tip of each ear. You can also apply *Bacillus thuringiensis* var. *kurstaki* to ear tips.

Notes: Commercial growers often use pheromone traps to monitor populations, and time their sprays of neem or BTK. In home gardens, you can dig out the larvae from the tips of affected ears before they have a chance to tunnel far into the ear. If you grow early corn, be careful to monitor the peppers and tomatoes after the corn is gone because the moth will simply change hosts.

Diabrotica undecimpunctata howardii; Acalymma vittatum

Cucumber Beetle, Spotted; Cucumber Beetle, Striped

Appearance: Spotted cucumber beetle adults are greenish yellow with 12 black spots on their wing shields. They are about ¼ inch long and have orange thoraxes and black heads. The larvae, also known as southern corn rootworms, are slender with reddish brown heads. They have dark spots on the first and last segments. The ¼-inch eggs are laid in the soil at the base of the plants.

Striped cucumber beetles are yellow and elongated, also about ¼ inch long. They have black heads and three stripes on their wing shields. The larvae look like those of the spotted cucumber beetle. The eggs are orange and are laid in the soil at the base of the plants.

Life Cycle: Spotted cucumber beetles have one or two generations in the North but up to four generations in the South. Adults overwinter in plant debris and garden trash and emerge in spring to mate and lay eggs. Eggs hatch and feed for two to four weeks before pupating.

Striped cucumber beetles also over-

winter as adults, often in the grass. They feed on pollen for two weeks and then move into the garden to lay eggs. The larvae feed for two to six weeks and pupate in early August.

Hosts: Cucurbit (squash) family crops are the primary hosts of each, but spotted cucumber beetle larvae eat the roots of many plants, and the adults eat the leaves, flowers, and fruit of many plants. Larvae of striped cucumber beetles feed primarily on the roots of cucurbits, and adults feed on the leaves. Adults prey on tomatoes as well as cucurbits.

Damage: Root loss may stunt plants. Both striped and spotted cucumber beetles can transmit bacterial wilt and cucumber mosaic virus. Spotted cucumber beetle adults transmit brown rot of stone fruit.

Prevention: Rotate crops and practice excellent garden sanitation. Choose wilt- and mosaic-resistant cultivars of cucumbers, squash, and melons, when possible. Cover all plantings of cucurbits with floating row covers as soon as they are planted or transplanted. Mulch cucurbits with a deep layer of straw. Make second plantings of summer squash and cucumbers to prolong the harvest.

A{::}calymma vittatum

Controls: Use newspaper slurry around the base of all cucurbit plants. Apply beneficial nematodes at the base of cucurbit plants and along corn rows. If infestations are severe, spray pyrethrin as a last resort.

Notes: The three-lined potato bug (*Lema trilineata*) looks like a striped cucumber

beetle except for the color of its head. Rather than being black, its head is reddish orange. Their larvae look like Colorado potato bug larvae that have a fungus disease. They give this appearance because they coat themselves with their excrement. They do less damage than either cucumber beetles or Colorado potato beetles but are still pests. Handpick or squash the larvae.

Many, all *Lepidoptera* of either the *Euxoa* or *Agrotis* species

Cutworm

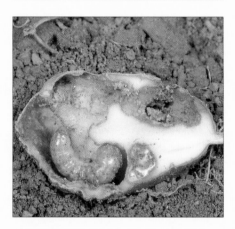

Appearance: Adults are brown or gray moths with wingspans from 1½ to 2 inches wide. Larvae are fat, greasy-looking, gray or grayish brown grubs with shiny dark heads.

Life Cycle: Adult moths lay eggs on grass stems or in the soil in midspring to early summer. The eggs hatch in five to seven days and the cutworms feed on their hosts for three to five weeks before pupating in the soil. Moths emerge in late summer to early fall. Some species overwinter as eggs and some as larvae.

Hosts: Many, including grasses as well as early vegetable and flower seedlings.

Damage: Cutworms do most of their work at night. Most curl around the stem of a plant and literally cut it off before feeding on the leaves, but some crawl up stems to eat individual leaves.

Prevention: Cutworms spend their days sleeping just under the soil near their hosts. Scrape the top layer of soil away to look for them. Three toothpicks placed around the stems protect seedlings. Cardboard collars are also useful, and newspaper slurry may prevent their being able to reach the soil surface.

Controls: On newly tilled ground where cutworm populations are likely to be high, mix bran with *Bacillus thuringiensis* var. *kurstaki* (BTK) and molasses, and spread this over the soil. Neem sprays and beneficial nematodes can also kill the larvae.

Notes: Before planting strawberries, treat the soil with the BTK mixture. Wait a few days to plant.

Ostrinia nubilalis

European Corn Borer

Appearance: Adult female moths have a wingspan of an inch wide. Their bodies are pale yellow-brown and they have dark zigzag patterns on their wings. The male moths are smaller and darker. The larvae are gray or tan with dark spots on the side of each segment. Their heads are brown. They grow up to an inch long. The white or tan eggs are laid in clusters on leaf undersides.

Life Cycle: Adult moths emerge in June and lay eggs. The eggs hatch in a week and the larvae feed for three to four weeks before spinning a cocoon in a cornstalk. Adults emerge in a week or two and repeat the cycle. Corn borers overwinter as larvae in the soil. There are one to three generations per year,

depending on locations.

Hosts: Corn, beans, peppers, potatoes, tomatoes, and small grains, and many flowers can also host the corn borer.

Damage: Caterpillars feed on leaves, tassels, and ears of corn. In general, young larvae feed on corn tassels before moving to feed on the ears. On other hosts, they feed on leaves and flowers.

Prevention: Good garden sanitation removes overwintering larvae; remove all corn stalks and compost in a hot pile. Plant corn cultivars that have tight husk covers, generally listed as resistant. Plant habitats to attract beneficial wasps and flies.

Controls: Apply mineral oil or *Bacillus thuringiensis* var. *kurstaki* to tips of ears. BTK and neem both control caterpillars on leaves of corn and other plants.

Notes: If problems are severe, consider removing tassels from half of the corn stalks. This leaves enough pollen to produce a good crop but removes many of the young larvae.

Several *Phyllotreta* and *Epitrix* spp.

Flea Beetle

Appearance: Adults are tiny, ⅛-inch long beetles that jump like fleas. They can be black, brown, bronze, or striped. The larvae are small, thin, white grubs with brown heads.

Life Cycle: Adults overwinter in the soil or in plant debris. In spring, they emerge and lay eggs near hosts. The larvae feed

on roots for two to three weeks before pupating in the soil. The second generation of adults emerges in two to three weeks and repeats the cycle. There can be up to four generations a year in warm climates.

Hosts: Almost all vegetables and many flowers and weeds.

Damage: You'll notice small round holes in leaves that the adults make. However, the root damage caused by larvae is just as damaging. Large transplants often live through the damage, but smaller seedlings can be killed.

Prevention: Use floating row covers on all vulnerable plants as soon as they are seeded or transplanted.

Controls: Capture adult beetles with Tanglefoot-coated cardboard paddles, as pictured on page 15. Beneficial nematodes will prey on the larvae. Pyrethrins kill the adult beetles.

Notes: Arugula is a favorite food for flea beetles. If you cannot grow early arugula that does not sustain heavy damage, try planting it in containers that you can set on a porch. Even so, you'd be wise to use row-cover material over the pots.

Acrididae family

Grasshopper

Appearance: Adults have 1- to 2- inch-long, narrow bodies colored brown to reddish yellow or green. Their hind legs are large and jointed for jumping. Their wings make a characteristic whirring sound when they fly. Eggs are laid in pods in the soil or weeds, generally in uncultivated ground.

Lifecycle: Grasshoppers hatch from their eggs in mid-May to July, depending on the species. Nymphs go through five instars and mature into adults in 40 to 60 days. They lay eggs that overwinter.

Hosts: Almost all plants

Damage: They eat enormous amounts of vegetation, particularly if they belong to a species that flies in a swarm. Many species migrate from field to field.

Prevention: Floating row covers will protect some crops from grasshoppers but cannot stop their feeding on tall crops.

Controls: *Nosema locustae* is a protozoan parasite of grasshoppers and locusts. It takes several years to become fully effective.

Notes: There are over 600 identified species of grasshoppers in the U.S. and southern Canada, but of these, only five species cause 90 percent of the damage. Other members of the *Acrididae* family include locusts, crickets, mantids, katydids, and walkingsticks. Locusts can be serious garden pests, and crickets do light feeding in the vegetable garden. The others are benign to gardeners.

Popillia japonica

Japanese Beetle

Appearance: Adults are metallic blue-green, ½-inch long beetles with bronze-brown wing shields. Their legs are long, tufted, and end in claws. The larvae are fat gray grubs with brown heads, often as large as ¾ inch.

Life Cycle: Larvae pupate in the soil in May and June, and adult beetles emerge in late June to mid-July. They eat foliage until late summer and then lay eggs under grasses. The eggs hatch and feed until colder weather. They burrow deep into the soil and remain dormant until spring. In the spring, they move to the root zone. First-year larvae feed all year and don't pupate until the second spring.

Hosts: Larvae feed on roots, especially grasses. Adults feed on many plants, particularly roses, grapes, and basil.

JAPANESE BEETLE LARVA

Damage: Adults skeletonize leaves, and if populations are high, can completely defoliate a plant in days. High populations of larvae can kill patches of lawn grasses.

Prevention: Floating row covers will protect particularly vulnerable plants, such as roses and basil, from adults. If problems are severe, don't grow extremely susceptible plants for a few years.

Controls: Handpick beetles in early to mid-morning, and destroy them. Set up traps far from the crops you are trying to protect. Neem, beneficial nematodes, and milky spore disease all kill larvae.

Notes: Milky spore disease is most effective in Zone 5b southward. It may take two years to see results, but many people report having to use it only once every 10 to 15 years. If you live in Zones 5a to 3, use neem or beneficial nematodes in late spring or late summer.

Cicadellidae family

Leafhopper

Appearance: Adult leafhoppers are small, ⅛ to ½-inch long, wedge-shaped and slender. Their wings are folded over their bodies. Some have bright red, brown, or yellow stripes; others are dull green or brown in color. All jump into flight. The larvae are wingless and run sidewise or hop rapidly when bothered. The tiny eggs are laid in plant tissue.

Life Cycle: Adult leafhoppers of many species become active in early spring. Depending on species, they may migrate from southern states northward as far as 200 to 300 miles. They lay eggs about the time the trees leaf out. The eggs hatch in 10 to 14 days, and the nymphs take two to eight weeks to mature, depending on

species and weather. There can be two to five generations per year. Most overwinter as adults, often migrating back to warmer climates, though some overwinter on wild plants. Other species overwinter as eggs.

Hosts: Almost all plants are prey to one leafhopper or another, but grasses, alfalfa, potatoes, roses, and grapes are particular favorites.

Damage: In addition to the damage they do by sucking out plant sap, most species transmit viral diseases, Even when they do not carry disease, they damage plants severely by injecting salivary substances which obstruct the vascular system of the plant.

Prevention: Plant habitat islands for their many natural controls, which include many beneficial wasps, big-eyed flies, damsel bugs, minute pirate bugs, lady beetles, lacewings, and spiders.

Controls: Dormant-oil sprays kill overwintering adults on fruit trees. First and second instar nymphs you can control with insecticidal soap, neem, or pyrethrins.

Notes: Do not grow potatoes or other particularly vulnerable crops near clover or alfalfa fields, because leafhoppers will migrate to the crop when the field is mowed.

Liriomyza spp., *Pegomya* spp.

Leaf Miner

Appearance: Adults are black and yellow flies, usually ⅛-inch long or less. Larvae are pale green, translucent maggots. Eggs are white, cylindrical and laid side by side in clusters on leaf undersides.

Life Cycle: Adults emerge from cocoons in early spring and lay eggs. The larvae hatch and tunnel into the leaves where they feed for one to three weeks. They pupate in the leaf or drop to the soil to pupate for two to four weeks. There are two to three generations per year, depending on location. They overwinter as pupae in cocoons.

Hosts: Many, including beans, beets, chard, columbine, lettuce, nasturtium, peppers, tomatoes, spinach.

Damage: Larvae tunnel through the leaves as they feed, making them unsightly. Most crops can tolerate a little damage, but if left unchecked, populations can become serious.

Prevention: Row covers over plants early in the season prevent adults from laying eggs. Search for egg masses and destroy them. Keep surrounding area clear of weedy hosts such as lamb's-quarters and dock. Plant habitats for beneficial insects.

Controls: Monitor, and handpick and destroy all affected leaves as soon as you see damage. If populations are high, spray neem onto the egg masses to control the pests. Tomatoes, beans, and chrysanthemums absorb neem through the roots. Soil drenches with neem kill the larvae on these plants.

Notes: Several natural controls are now available but they are expensive.

Many, including *Planococcus* spp. and *Pseudococcus* spp.

Mealybug

Appearance: Adult females have soft bodies covered with white powdery or waxy fluff. Under the covering, the oval bodies are pink. They are about ⅒ inch long, with two long filaments from the rear in some species. Males are small two-winged insects that go unnoticed. Nymphs resemble the females but are smaller. Eggs look like a tiny cotton ball on leaves, stems, or bark.

Life Cycle: In the South, mealybugs overwinter outdoors. In the North, they overwinter in greenhouses or homes. Most species overwinter at all stages of growth, both inside and out. Females can lay eggs at any time of year. Eggs hatch in ten days and the larval crawlers move to spots on the plant where they will stay and feed for as long as two months before becoming adults. They produce from 3 to 5 generations a year outdoors and more inside.

Hosts: Many, particularly citrus trees, avocados, grapes, and houseplants.

PSEUDOCOCCUS CITRI

Damage: Both adults and nymphs suck plant juices. In large populations, they can severely weaken the plant. Like aphids, they excrete honeydew onto leaves where sooty mold can grow.

Prevention: Beneficial wasps.

Controls: Insecticidal soap is sometimes effective. If affected plants tolerate superior oil applications, spray twice, at two week intervals. Purchase mealybug (*Cryptolaemus montrouzieri*) to control mealybugs on trees and grapes outdoors.

Notes: If you have only a few mealybugs on houseplants, dip a cotton swab in rubbing alcohol and dab it on each pest. Or, remove them from stems with a narrow blade.

Epilachna varivestis

Mexican Bean Beetle

Appearance: Adult beetles look like yellow to copper-colored lady bugs with 16 black spots. The spots are arranged in three rows across the wing shields. Larvae are elliptical, spiny but soft-looking, yellowish orange and about ⅓ inch long. The yellow eggs are laid upright in groups of 40 to 60, usually on leaf undersides.

Life Cycle: Adults overwinter in garden debris. They emerge from early to midsummer and feed for two weeks before they lay eggs. Larvae hatch in five to fourteen days and feed for two to five weeks before pupating in a case attached to the bottom of a leaf. Adults emerge in a week and begin the cycle again. There can be between two and four generations a year.

Hosts: Beans of all types.

Damage: Larvae and adults feed from leaf undersides, skeletonizing the leaves. High populations kill plants, but even low populations cut yields.

Prevention: Plant resistant cultivars. Cover beans with floating row covers. Plant insect habitats to feed beneficials. Practice good garden sanitation at the end of the season.

Controls: Handpicking the first beetles and squashing egg masses often keeps populations under control. Commercially available spined soldier bugs (*Podisus maculiventris*) are effective. If populations become too large to control by handpicking, spray neem every week for two to four weeks.

Notes: When beetles first emerge from their pupae cases, they are a solid yellow, with no spots.

Members of the *Coccidae* family

Scale

Appearance: Adults are hard shelled and gray, yellow, white, reddish, or purplish brown, about ⅒ inch long. They crawl as nymphs but settle into one spot as adults. Adults secrete a waxy armor around themselves in a circular or oyster-like shape. Female soft scales are oval or round, ⅒ to ⅛ inch long. The males are tiny yellow-winged insects that are rarely noticed. Nymphs are mobile and somewhat fuzzy looking but the adult females are sedentary and shinier.

Life Cycle: Outdoors, most scales overwinter as nymphs or eggs on tree bark. After mating, females either lay eggs or give birth to live young, depending on species. Some lay as many as 2,000 eggs throughout their lives. Nymphs take a month or so to develop into adults. Depending on location, there can be between two to six generations a year.

Hosts: Citrus, palms, roses, currants, grapes, raspberries, many ornamental shrubs, and many tropical houseplants.

Damage: All stages of scales suck plant sap, causing leaves to yellow and drop. If populations are high, plants can be killed. Soft scales secrete honeydew, thus providing a habitat for sooty mold fungi.

Prevention: Natural controls include many beneficial wasps and predatory beetles, so habitat plantings near susceptible plants can help to keep populations under control.

Controls: When possible, prune and destroy branches that are severely infested. Wash soft scales from plants with a soft cloth dipped into Insecticidal soap. Rinse to protect stomates from clogging. During winter, spray dormant oil. If plants will tolerate it, spray summer oil during the summer.

Notes: If houseplants are infested, try washing scales off the plants, but if that doesn't work, make a tight-fitting cover of floating row cover material to enclose the plant. Buy either *Chilocorus nigritus* or *Lindorus lophanthae*, both predatory beetles, and release them onto the enclosed plant.

Members of the *Mollusca* class

Slugs and Snails

Appearance: Slugs are ⅛ to 6 inches long, depending on age and species. They are gray, tan, green, or black with two long tentacles, topped with eyes, on the tops of their heads. Snails are like slugs with shells. Both leave a slimy trail of mucus as they travel. The jellylike eggs are clear, oval, or round and are laid in masses under rocks or debris.

Life Cycle: Both slugs and snails overwinter in garden debris and emerge in early spring. They lay eggs that hatch in 2 to 4 weeks. They grow for 5 months to two years before becoming adults. Many live for several years.

Hosts: Many, but slugs are particularly damaging to seedlings in the vegetable and flower gardens, and snails are often a serious problem on citrus trees.

Damage: Although both slugs and snails eat more dead and decaying material than they do live tissue, they can cause tremendous losses in the garden. They scrape huge holes in foliage, stems and flowers of many garden plants.

Prevention: Birds, garter snakes, lizards, and toads all prey on slugs, while fireflies eat their eggs. Permanent sod areas and stone mulches provide habitat for these predators. A wide border of wood ashes or diatomaceous earth around the garden may keep slugs and snails from entering it. Renew the material after every rain. Copper screening or flashing gives them a small electrical shock and can also be used to exclude them from an area.

Controls: Handpick and destroy all the slugs you see. Leave wooden boards at least 4 inches wide or upturned grapefruit rinds out at night to trap them. Check the traps early in the day and destroy any slugs you find. Bury tin cans to their lips and fill them with beer or moistened dog food. Check for slugs in the cans several hours after dark and again before first morning light; slugs in the beer traps will have drowned.

Notes: Researchers are working to develop efficient breeding and collection methods for a nematode that targets slugs. Watch organic-grower suppliers for notices about this control.

Members of the *Tetranychidae* family

Spider Mites

Appearance: Adults are tiny spider-like creatures less than ⅕ to ⅟₅₀ inch long. While adults have eight legs, the youngest nymphs, visible only with a hand-lens, have only six. Most species are reddish brown, yellow, or green and some have two dark spots on their backs. Eggs are too small to see but are laid at the base of plants or on leaves and buds. Spider mites leave fine webbing on leaf undersides and between leaves and stems.

Life Cycle: Adult mites overwinter in garden debris or litter in a hedgerow. They resume activity in spring, mate, and lay eggs. The entire life cycle can take place in only a few days, depending on the temperature, but in most situations, nymphs require five to seven days to mature. Indoors or in greenhouses, they remain active all year.

Hosts: Many, but warm weather vegetables such as beans, melons, and tomatoes as well as fruit trees, berries, and ornamental plants, including houseplants, are their favorites.

Damage: Mites suck plant sap, weakening, stunting, and even killing their hosts. Look for yellow speckled areas on leaves and then search for the fine webbing. Severely damaged tissue turns brown and dry looking.

Prevention: Predaceous mites control pest mites, often without your knowl-

edge. Mites eat and reproduce more in hot, dry conditions, so keeping humidity levels high can minimize damage.

Controls: Predatory mites are available from many biological control suppliers. When you call, describe the environment the mites are living in, from types of plants to temperature and relative humidity ranges,. The supplier can choose the appropriate mite for your conditions. On fruit trees, dormant oil sprays kill overwintering eggs. As a last resort, spray superior oil, neem, insecticidal soap or pyrthrins during the season.

Notes: There are a number of pest mite species. Citrus mites, European red mites, rust mites, spruce spider mites, and two-spotted spider mites can all be controlled with particular species of predatory mites. If predatory mites are present, avoid using any of the pesticides listed above because they kill the predatory mites as well as they kill the pests.

Many, including *Philaenus spumarius*, *Cercopidae* spp., *Stictocephala* spp.

Spittlebug/Froghopper

Appearance: The first thing you'll notice about spittlebugs is the white bubble that the nymphs create. Adults are oval-shaped, about ¼ to ½ inch long, and tan, brown, or black. The nymphs are yellow to green and look similar to the adults but lack wings. The eggs are white or tan, and are laid in rows on stems.

Life Cycle: Spittlebugs overwinter as eggs

and hatch in early spring. Nymphs feed for six to seven weeks, gradually developing into adults. Adults feed from midsummer to fall, when they lay eggs.

Hosts: Many, but strawberries and legumes are particular favorites.

Damage: Both adults and nymphs suck plant sap. If populations are low, damage will be light. However, if there is an infestation, they can severely weaken and even kill host plants.

Prevention: Natural controls such as damsel bugs and minute pirate bugs usually keep populations under control. If your garden is close to a hay field, cover the strawberries and any small plants with row-cover material before the hay is cut.

Controls: Spray nymphs off plants with a hard water spray or squash.

Notes: Buffalo treehoppers (*Stictocephala bubalus*), another type of spittle bug, are serious pests of young fruit trees. This insect lays eggs in a series of crescent-shaped slits in the tree bark in pairs. The nymph, which hatches in spring, drops to the ground and feeds on grasses as well as tomatoes, potatoes, and many ornamentals before returning to the trees to lay eggs. When populations are high, young trees suffer from the many cuts into their bark which also open the way for pathogenic organisms.

Anasa tristis

Squash Bug

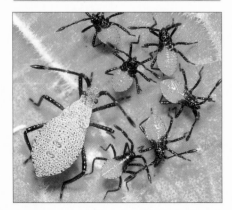

Appearance: Adults are oval-shaped and black or brown with yellowish-orange

areas on the margins around their abdomens. They are about ⅝ inch long. When threatened, they give off a disagreeable odor.

The pale green nymphs have long, dark legs. As they mature, their bodies become darker, and they look as if they are covered with a slate gray powder. The eggs are yellow when they are first laid in groups on the undersides of leaves but turn copper or brick red as they mature.

Life Cycle: Adults overwinter in garden debris or under boards or other refuse as protection against the weather. The insects become active in spring, eat voraciously, and lay eggs in groups on the undersides of leaves. Eggs hatch in approximately one to two weeks, and nymphs feed and grow for between four and six weeks before maturing into adults. There is only one generation a year, no matter the location.

Hosts: All members of the cucurbit family except pumpkins are hosts.

Damage: Both adults and nymphs suck plant sap. The affected shoots and leaves blacken and die; severely infested plants become so compromised that they do not produce fruit.

Prevention: Choose resistant squash cultivars. Cover all cucurbits with floating row-cover material until the plants flower. If the populations of squash bug have been high, leave the covers in place and hand-pollinate the flowers. Remove weeds in the cucurbit family from your property.

Controls: Handpick adults and nymphs off plants, and search for and destroy any egg masses you might find under the leaves. Place boards on the soil surface next to plants, and lift them to discover adults every morning. You should use Sabadilla sprays only as a last resort.

Notes: Early control of the eggs usually takes care of any problem you may have with this pest for the remainder of the year. If problems with the squash bug are severe, however, make certain to rotate crops far from last year's plantings, or do not provide a host for this pest for at least a year.

Thrips angusticeps

Thrips

Appearance: Adults are tiny, ¹⁄₅₀ to ¹⁄₂₅ inch long, narrow yellowish/brown or black insects with narrow wings. The nymphs are light green or yellow and smaller, and resemble the adults.

Life Cycle: Adults overwinter in sod, garden debris, or bark, becoming active in very early spring. They lay eggs in plant tissue; eggs hatch in 3 to 5 days. Nymphs feed for 1 to 3 weeks and then migrate to the soil where they remain quiet for a week or two before their final molt into adults. There can be many generations a year and in greenhouses, they remain active at all times.

Hosts: Many, including all types of ornamentals as well as onions, cabbage, lettuce, and fruit trees.

Damage: Both adults and nymphs suck plant juices, usually giving a silvery streaked appearance to the affected plant parts. When populations are high, plants can be stunted or show distorted growth. Flowers are often damaged and fruit shows silvery scars or round pale spots.

Prevention: Plant habitat islands for the many beneficials that prey on thrips. These include minute pirate bugs, lacewings, and lady beetles.

Controls: Outside, spray dormant oil on fruit and ornamental trees. Neem, insecticidal soap and pyrethrins all kill thrips and can be used as a last resort. In greenhouses, monitor populations with blue or yellow sticky traps. If you catch more than a couple in 24 hours, purchase predatory mites or minute pirate bugs. Lacewing and ladybug larvae can also prey on thrips but only if they run short of aphids.

Notes: Thrips are an inevitable fact of life in any greenhouse that is built directly on soil were grass once grew. Remove all plants from the greenhouse for a month during the summer so that the thrips will die of starvation.

Members of the *Aleyrodidae* family

Whiteflies

Appearance: Adults are pure white moth-like insects with a powdery coating on their wings. They are only ¹⁄₂₀ inch long. They feed on leaf undersides but fly into the air when they are disturbed. Nymphs are called scales because they resemble that insect. They are tiny, translucent, or whitish green and are usually found on leaf undersides. Eggs look like minuscule dots of yellow or gray. With a hand lens, you can see that they are cone-shaped.

Lifecycle: In warm climates, whiteflies remain active all year. The females lay eggs that hatch in only two days. Nymphs are mobile for the first two instars but become sedentary at the end of the third instar period and exude a waxy material around their edges during the fourth instar. In a few days, they molt into adults. The life cycle takes twenty-five days to complete but in most environments, there are usually whiteflies at every stage.

Hosts: Many, but citrus trees, foliage houseplants and members of the solanaceous family are particularly vulnerable to whiteflies.

Damage: Both adults and nymphs suck plant sap. Severely infested plants weaken and die. Whiteflies also spread many viral diseases and excrete honeydew, giving sooty mold a host.

Prevention: Plant habitats for beneficial wasps and predatory beetles. Use row covers over susceptible garden plants.

Controls: Monitor populations with yellow sticky traps. In greenhouses you can vacuum up these pests. When the pests fly into the air, suck them up. *Encarsia formosa*, a beneficial wasp, is commercially available and can be encouraged to live in the greenhouse year round if there is a warm habitat with small-flowered plants. If all else fails, try garlic oil, insecticidal soap, neem or pyrethrin sprays on leaf undersides.

Notes: Although whiteflies overwinter only in frost-free areas, they migrate each spring to more northern locations. If you have had trouble with them, set out yellow sticky traps near susceptible plants early in the season. Watch the traps to know when you should begin control.

Limonius spp.

Wireworm

Appearance: Adults are brown or black click beetles, about ⅓ to ¾ inch long. When they are upside down, they make a clicking sound as they flip upright. The larvae are wormlike and segmented, with tough-looking, shiny, coppery brown skin. They can grow to ½ inch long.

Life Cycle: Adults lay eggs around plant roots in early spring. The larvae hatch in three to ten days and feed on plant roots from two to six years. They pupate in late summer and overwinter as adults.

Hosts: Almost all vegetables, but wireworm damage is most severe on root crops and corn as well as ornamental bulbs and corms.

Damage: Wireworms eat roots and bore into bulbs, tubers, and corms. Not only does this injure the plant, it also allows pathogenic organisms a pathway into the tissue. Adult beetles feed on leaves and flowers but do not cause much damage.

Prevention: Time plantings to avoid the worst damage. Since wireworms feed close to the surface only when the soil is cool in spring and fall, late-planted corn, carrots, and potatoes are less likely to sustain damage.

Controls: Trap the worms before planting susceptible crops in areas known to have wireworms. To trap the worms, buy a 50-lb. sack of potatoes. Cut the tubers into thick slices and bury the cut edges an inch or two in the soil near susceptible plants. Lift the tubers every few days and remove and kill the wireworms that you find. Beneficial nematodes control wireworms.

Notes: Wireworm populations are apt to be high during the first few years after a lawn or sod area has been turned into a garden. If you see a great many wireworms while you are doing the initial soil preparation, leave the soil bare for the first season, and till or cultivate the area every week to ten days to allow birds to prey on the wireworms.

PEACH LEAF CURL is a common disease that can often be prevented with compost tea sprays during the summer.

GOOD SANITATION and crop diversity help to keep your garden free of both pests and diseases.

DISEASES

PLANT DISEASES can be as emotionally devastating to a gardener as they are physically devastating to a plant. Fortunately, this is one area where good soil management and cultural care show dramatic results. Armed with a little knowledge, you can make a big difference in a single year. What's more, the cumulative effects of building good soil drainage and organic matter content will result in fewer and fewer diseases every year.

Plants develop diseases in much that same way as people do, with one important difference. While you have a lymphatic system that busily sends white blood cells out to disable invading pathogenic organisms, plants do not. Instead, they rely on microorganisms in the soil around them for protection. In some cases, the microbes produce antibiotics that the plant actually takes in through the roots, but more often the drama takes place in the soil. There, the natural order decrees that all organisms are part of a food chain. If there is a huge population of pathogenic organisms, it won't be long before there is also a huge number of the organisms that consider them dinner.

Bacteria, fungi, viruses, and viruslike organisms all cause plant diseases. Destructive nematodes are also discussed as diseases since they cause many of the same effects.

Bacteria

Disease-causing bacteria enter plants through natural openings such as the stomates as well as through wounds. They cause three major types of plant diseases: wilting, galls, and tissue death. Wilting occurs when bacteria living in the vascular system build to such high populations that they clog the vessels, preventing water and nutrient movement to the affected portions of the plant. Bacteria that cause galls stimulate unnatural growth patterns of selected cells. Spots, rots, and internal blights are all examples of tissue death, or necrosis.

PLUM CHERRY BACTERIAL CANKER has caused dieback on this peach plant.

Fungi

Fungi cause the same sorts of symptoms—wilts, galls, or smuts, and tissue death. Because fungi cause the majority of plant diseases, it's wise to begin your search for a causal organism by looking in this category.

Fungi have enormously complicated life cycles. Unlike bacteria, most of which are simple cells that reproduce by cell division, the majority of fungi carry out both asexual and sexual reproduction. Rather than seeds, they make spores. There are many types of spores. Summer spores, which are the product of asexual reproduction, are capable of infecting plant tissue as soon as they are released. This means that an infection on a lower leaf can release spores that will blow to higher leaves or to those on a nearby plant and infect them immediately. Other spores, called resting spores, are capable of remaining dormant but alive for as long as 20 years. For the most part, these are formed sexually, so they can carry a more diverse genetic code than the summer spores. Some fungi, notably those that cause rust diseases, have five different spore forms. Additionally, rusts such as the cedar-apple rust require two different hosts, and take two years to complete their life cycle.

The fungal body is composed of branching tubes called *hyphae.* The outer walls of these tubes contain chitin or cellulose to make them a bit rigid. They grow at their tips. Ther mycelium is a group of hyphae and the thallis is a group of mycelium.

Rather than forming spores, some fungi reproduce by

CEDAR APPLE RUST forms galls on cedar trees. Check your trees in the late summer to find these tell-tale signs and prune off any galls you find.

CEDAR APPLE RUST spots on a crabapple leaf.

ORANGE BLIGHT can disfigure rose hips; it also weakens the plant.

creating a thickened section of a hypha. We call this a sclerotia. Sclerotia are formed asexually but are capable of overwintering or surviving other harsh conditions.

Spores called zoospores swim by moving a whiplike tail through dew or soil water, but most spores float through the air or are carried along by running water or on tools, hands, insect feet and mouth parts, or fur. Some fungi live their entire lives in the soil, attacking the underground parts of a plant; others may overwinter in the soil and live on above-ground tissues during the growing season, while still others spend their entire lives above ground.

Viruses

Viruses are the third major cause of plant diseases. Symptoms include yellowing, stunting, and abnormal growth patterns. Mosaics are a good example of the kind of yellowing viruses cause, but ring spots and a generalized paleness can also occur. Stunting can be localized or general and malformations include everything from relatively minor leaf rolls to such dramatic effects as witches brooms or shoestring leaves. Even though they are obligate, meaning that they can live and reproduce only on living tissues, most viruses remain capable of infecting plants for as long as 50 years. They can hang out in dead plant material or simply in the soil. Many of them withstand both freezing and boiling temperatures. This is why you never put a virus-infected plant in the compost pile.

While wind and water carry many bacteria and fungi to plants, insects and gardeners are responsible for the majority of viral infections in the garden. Insect carriers, called vectors, generally inject the virus as they feed on the plant. Gardeners transmit viruses by touching plants. Even a light touch can bruise a plant, leaving an opening through which viruses can enter, and unless you have just washed your hands, it's possible that viruses are riding around on them.

Nematodes

Destructive nematodes pierce plant tissues with their stylets. Some exude digestive juices that rot plant tissue so that they can take up the nutrients, while others release compounds that stimulate abnormal growth such as galls. They carry many viral diseases, and the holes they make allow secondary pathogens such as fungi and bacteria to enter the plant.

Nematodes are obligate organisms, but if they do not have a host, they can remain dormant for up to 30 years. In cold climates, they overwinter as eggs or larvae, but in warm conditions, they simply carry on their life cycle. They often come into a garden on new plants, even those from respected nurseries. Soil and running water can also carry them. Beneficial nematodes prey on them as do many other organisms in a fully finished compost.

Lifestyles. Organisms can live on dead or living material. It's helpful to understand how the particular pathogen your plants are hosting works; this information can help you prevent infection.

Saprophytic organisms live only on dead material. True saprophytes are responsible for a great deal of the decay in your compost pile and on the soil surface, but some fungi are saprophytic in action. Rather than waiting until a plant has died to begin to digest it, they release a toxin that kills the cells it touches. After the cells are dead, they ingest the nutrients and move on to kill and eat more tissue. Some fungi even use this technique to enter a plant.

Facultative organisms can live on dead or living material. During the summer, they may inhabit your tomato plants, for example. When frost comes, the tomatoes will die and their chemical composition will change radically. But facultative fungi simply change their diet accordingly. After spending the winter feeding on the dead tomato stalks, they release spores that can infect the living seedlings you've just transplanted to the garden. Needless to say, rotating crops can minimize this kind of reinfection.

Obligate organisms, as defined above, prey on living tissues. All viruses fit into this category, but some fungi do, as well. In the case of viruses, the organism forms crystals

AIR CIRCULATION is high in this garden, making it more difficult for some fungal diseases to germinate.

CHAPTER 9

SMART TIP

SANITATION IS A POWERFUL WEAPON

Crop rotation and sanitation both eliminate niches for disease organisms. A simple practice such as taking weeds to the compost pile as soon as you pick them is enormously effective in preventing plant diseases. Wipe the soil from all your tools after using them, and pick up old pots and flats right away. If you are removing diseased leaves from a plant, pop them into a plastic bag as soon as you collect them so that you don't spread spores while walking out of the garden.

that can remain capable of infecting new tissue when they encounter it, while fungi form resting spores.

Most fungi enter plants through natural openings, although the saprophytic fungi poison their way in, and others literally bore through the cuticle. After germinating, their first hypha glues itself to the leaf just far enough from the tip to give good leverage. The tip then pushes itself into the leaf. Once inside, it separates from the outside portion and forms a protective covering to prevent other organisms from entering through the hole it has made.

Prevention

Preventing plant diseases is easier by far than trying to kill them once they are in the garden. Fortunately, good gardening practices form the platform of disease prevention. Fast soil drainage is essential, so you should remember not to compact the soil by stepping on it. Because most fungal spores germinate in a film of water, it's also best to locate plants where the prevailing breeze will blow over the leaves. You'll notice that plants arrange their leaves so they never touch each other. Take your lead from nature, and thin often enough so that leaves of adjacent plants never touch.

Choosing disease-resistant plants is also crucial. In some cases, you can buy seeds or planting stock that is certified to be disease-free. This is particularly important with potatoes, strawberries, bramble bushes, and other fruit plants. If you save your own seeds, treat them to kill any diseases they may be carrying.

Provide balanced nutrition and organic matter. These two factors cannot be emphasized enough. Balanced nutrition and high levels of organic matter help to protect plants.

Not only is a healthier plant more resistant to a disease, but organisms living in organic matter attack and kill many pathogens. You may notice, for example, that tilling in a cover crop in the spring can significantly decrease disease incidence in the area.

Recent research indicates that living mulches and cover crops decrease disease incidence on tomatoes, potatoes, and corn. In the trials, vetch was used between rows of tomatoes and potatoes, while annual white clover was seeded between corn rows.

And last but not least, make the following an iron-clad gardening rule: never go into the garden when the plants are wet. If you simply must pick some parsley and can stay on the grass while you do so, OK, but otherwise, stay out. This rule is particularly important with beans, tomatoes, basil, and squash-family plants.

Identifying the problem. When you research control methods for various diseases, you have to know what the disease is before you can determine how to prevent and control it. The disease directory, pages 297 to 303, lists many of the most common plant diseases in the U.S. and southern Canada. If you can't find the problem here, consult the Cooperative Extension Service or neighboring gardeners.

HORSETAIL, or equisetum, makes an excellent disease preventive tea.

NETTLE TEA

Nettle tea is effective against most diseases. Make it by covering 2 to 3 pounds of young stinging nettle plants with 5 gallons of water in a bucket with a lid. Let it sit at temperatures of about 60°F for a week or two. Strain it and dilute with 5 parts of water to every 1 part of tea. The dreadful smell is normal. Like compost tea, it only works as a preventive measure and should be sprayed on susceptible plants every week to ten days before they contract a disease. Because nettle tea contains high levels of nitrogen and other nutrients, it is best used on crops with high nitrogen demands.

Preventive Sprays

Compost tea is now widely recognized as an excellent preventive measure against many fungal diseases. Universities all across the country are replicating the trials that demonstrated this and, as every year goes by, adding new diseases to the list of those affected. Any compost works, as long as it is fully finished and was made from a wide variety of materials. However, to be effective, the tea must be used between the fifth and fifteenth day after the compost was first added to the water.

Compost tea. To make compost tea, suspend a burlap sack or old pillow case containing one shovelful of finished compost in a bucket holding 5 gallons of water. Let the pillow case sit in the bucket of water for five to fifteen days, and strain the tea through several layers of cheesecloth before using it. If you have leftover tea, use it as a liquid fertilizer.

Equisetum tea. This is a better choice for plants that suffer if their nitrogen content is too high. Buy or gather non-fruiting stems of common horsetail (*Equisetum arvense*). Boil 4 ounces of the stems in a gallon of rainwater or non-chlorinated spring water for 20 minutes. Do not dilute before using it. Like compost tea and nettle tea, this tea must be sprayed as a protective measure before diseases strike.

After-the-Fact Controls

Fortunately, there are also materials that kill or inhibit diseases after they have attacked plants. Of these, baking soda is the least environmentally disruptive. Mix it at the rate of 1 to 2 tablespoons per gallon of water. Individual entries in the disease directory, pages 297 to 303, indicate diseases for which it is effective.

Fine or superior horticultural oil. Sometimes called hort oil, this is also an excellent control. In some cases, it is mixed with baking soda (2½ teaspoons of superior oil, 1 tbsp. baking soda, 1 gallon of water), but in others, it is used alone.

Mineral controls. Minerals used to treat diseases include copper, sulfur, and bordeaux mix. Orchardists also use lime-sulfur mixtures during the dormant season to control both pests and diseases.

Sulfur. This mineral kills fungi and all sorts of mites, both beneficial and destructive. It is available as a dust that has been mixed with 1 to 5 percent talc or clay; "wettable" sulfur, which is finely ground before being mixed with a wetting agent; and colloidal sulfur, which is meant to be mixed with a small amount of water and used as a paste over plant wounds. For most gardeners and most applications, wettable sulfur is the most practical form of this control agent. Again, avoid the dust. Not only will it drift to other parts of the yard, it can injure your lungs, eyes, and skin. Wear protective clothing and goggles when you spray.

Sulfur can injure plant tissue. Do not apply sulfur within a month of using any oil on your plants, because the oil will increase its potency so much that it burns the leaves. High temperatures also make it too potent. Do not use it if daytime temperatures are 90°F or above. Use only plastic sprayers with it, and remember to rinse them well, including the nozzle, after every use.

Copper. By itself it is insoluble, so it is usually available as copper sulfate. Again, buy wettable powder or a liquid concentrate rather than the dust. Copper is a skin and eye irritant, so you should wear protective gear, including gloves and goggles, when spraying. Copper kills fish.

Bordeaux mix. This control is a mixture of copper sulfate and hydrated lime. Like copper, it controls fungi, but it is slightly stronger. It is most often used on fruits. As with all other materials, you must follow the directions on the label carefully to avoid problems.

DIRECTORY
CONTROLS

um

they form spores tha⌐
hosts. The hyphae f
peg to enter the p⌐
are released duri⌐
diately infective
Transmission:
spread on sp⌐
plants, parti⌐
carry the in⌐
seeds.
Prevention and ⌐
Remove all infecte⌐
and compost only in a⌐
in the garden when plants a⌐
when they are wet. Practice excelle⌐
den sanitation. Allow enough space
between plants for good air circulation;
use copper fungicides as a last resort.
Notes: Don't wait for pink spores to suspect anthracnose, because they may not
appear until the whole fruit or leaf has
disintegrated. Spores germinate in a film
of water when temperatures range
between 59°F and 77°F.

Venturia inaequalis
Apple Scab

Range: Humid areas of the U.S. and
southern Canada.
Hosts: Apple, pear, crab apple, and
hawthorn trees.

⌐: This fungus produces light
⌐y spots on the undersides of
⌐aves and fruits. The spots
⌐ a velvety olive green and then
⌐late colored before turning metallic
⌐. Leaves drop prematurely. Fruit
⌐y also be cracked, deformed, or rus-
⌐ed, meaning that rough patches on
⌐e skin are russet colored. Apple scab
rarely kills the tree but can disfigure or
ruin the fruit. If the disease is
unchecked, trees can be weakened.
Life Cycle: The fungal mycelium overwinters on old leaves that were infected
the previous season. In the spring,
spores form and ripen just as the petals
are falling. Once in tissue, the fungus
produces spores in a matter of days to
weeks. Spores formed during the summer are immediately infective.
Transmission: When spring rains drip on
leaves that were infected the previous
season, the spores shoot into the air.
Wind carries them to new tissues.
Prevention and Control: Choose resistant
apple cultivars such as 'Freedom', 'Lib-
erty' and 'Sweet 16'. Space trees far
enough apart so that air circulates freely
around them. Practice excellent sanitation through the season. Spray sulfur
onto the trees before a rainy period and
again just afterward, from the time that
buds begin to break until a month after
petal fall. If spots appear after this point,
spray sulfur again.
Notes: Commercial growers use Mills
Charts, available from any growers supply house, to determine the likelihood
of apple scab outbreaks. This chart lists
the number of hours at various temperatures that leaves and fruit must be wet
in order for the apple scab spores to germinate and penetrate the plant tissue.
This information helps you to time
sprays appropriately and eliminate
unnecessary spraying.

CHAPTER 9

Erwinia spp., *Pseudomonas* spp.
Bacterial Soft Rot

Range: Throughout the U.S. and southern Canada.

Hosts: Many, including numerous flowers and both fresh and stored vegetables.

Description: This bacteria kills tissues by exuding enzymes that decompose the material between cell walls. The bacteria feed on the released nutrients. To the gardener, the first noticeable symptom is a small, water-soaked spot. As the infection spreads, tissues become dark and slimy and give off a foul odor. This disease usually makes flowers or other plant parts unusable. If it attacks early enough, it can kill the plant. However since it's more likely to strike in midsummer, plants may not die until frost.

Life Cycle: The soft rot bacteria overwinter on plant debris in the garden and non-decomposed organic matter in the soil.

Transmission: These soilborne bacteria travel to new plants with soil water and can also be carried along by root maggots or on tools.

Prevention and Control: Planting in well-drained soil and allowing good air circulation can cut incidence of this ubiquitous bacteria. Do not work in the garden when plants are wet. When you water, take care to water the soil, not the plants; soaker hoses are the most effective way to do this. But if you must water with a sprinkler or watering can, do it early in the day so leaves can dry quickly.

Notes: Most people become familiar with this bacteria when it infects vegetables stored for too long in the refrigerator. The infection looks slightly different on different plants but it always smells bad once it has advanced.

Pseudomonas spp., *Xanthomonas* spp.
Bacterial Leaf Spot

Range: Throughout the U.S. and southern Canada.

Hosts: Many, including fruit of tomatoes, sweet peppers, squash, and cucumbers; flowers such as begonias, geraniums, and hyacinths; and the leaves of many woody shrubs and trees.

Description: The first symptoms of this disease are small, water-soaked spots on leaves or flowers. The spots may be

trans
and
tion
angu
veins
dark
Some
the s
know
Life
infec
seed.
grow
Trans
trave
or on
The
natur
borne
befor
bacte
other
Preve
susce
tivars
preca
by di
bleac
excel
the y
infect
you r
the p
enoug
On o
cially
weath
becor
spray
sulfat
Notes
pers,
translu
diseas
dark a
them
soon a
them
post a

Botrytis allii, B. cinerea
Botrytis Blight, Gray Mold

Range: Throughout the U.S. and southern Canada.

Hosts: Almost all plants are susceptible

Description: The first symptoms are pale, water-soaked spots on leaves, flowers, or stems. They turn a soft gray or tan and look almost velvety. Affected tissue eventually breaks open to allow the fuzzy gray spores to emerge.

Life Cycle: *Botrytis* overwinters on plant debris. In spring, spores form in response to warm wet weather. Once inside the host, the fungus produces immediately infective spores as well as the sclerotia, which overwinter and can also remain dormant for many years.

Transmission: Wind and water carry the ubiquitous botrytis spores.

Prevention and Control: Remove all blossoms on soft-flowered plants such as begonia and geranium as soon as they fade. Plant only in well-drained soil, and space to allow good air circulation. Remove and destroy infected plant parts as soon as you notice the spots to keep the disease from spreading. Practice excellent garden sanitation.

Notes: Fermented nettle sprays, sprayed every two to four weeks before the plants are infected, can sometimes prevent this disease. Let about two lbs. of fresh nettles soak in a covered 5-gallon bucket filled with water for five to ten days. Strain out the leaves and dilute to a 1:5 solution before spraying on your plants. this spray smells bad, but its benefits are worth it.

Gymnosporangium juniperi-virginianae
Cedar-Apple Rust

Range: Northeastern and Midwestern US; southeastern Canada.

Hosts: Apple trees and eastern red cedars

Description: Small yellow spots form on leaves and fruit of apple trees. As the spots age, they turn brown and sunken, often forming bulls-eyes with green or brown centers and yellow halos. Affected fruit can show distorted growth. Raised orange spots develop when the fungus is producing spores. On cedars, the first symptoms are greenish brown swellings on the needle tips. During the second year, the swellings turn into hard brown galls up to 2 inches wide. When spores develop, they create bright orange gelatinous masses on the galls. Damage ranges from cosmetic to ruinous on apples. Both plants can be weakened by it.

Life Cycle: This fungus is dependent on both of its hosts through its life cycle. The fungus spends two years on cedars and produces spores in warm rainy weather of the second spring. The spores infect apple leaves where the fungus grows and creates spores that infect cedars.

Transmission: Wind and air currents move spores from the cedars to the apples. The spore masses that apples form are attractive to insects that move them around from place to place on the apple tree. Spores formed on apples are also moved by air currents and wind to nearby cedars.

Prevention and Control: Choose resistant apple cultivars such as 'Empire', 'Redfree' and 'Stayman'. Remove and destroy infected leaves or fruit when you see the very first spot.

Notes: This disease is easiest to notice on cedar trees. Look for galls several times each year and prune off and destroy any that you might find.

Agrobacterium tumefasciens
Crown Gall

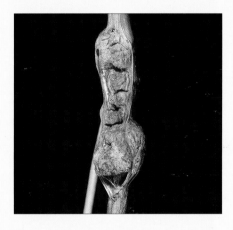

Range: Throughout the U.S. and Canada.

Hosts: Many, but roses, fruit trees, brambles, grapes, and tomatoes are particularly susceptible.

Description: Galls form on the stems or trunks near the soil line, and growth is distorted. Long before that, leaves turn yellow and wilt easily and branches begin to die back. As the galls enlarge, the cell walls of the plant break open and release more nutrients for the bacteria to feed on. Crown gall can eventually kill the plant.

Life Cycle: These bacteria overwinter on infected tissue, particularly the roots. Once inside a plant, they grow and reproduce. They can remain in soil for several years without a host.

Transmission: Splashed water carries these bacteria from one host to another. They enter plants through wounds and less frequently, natural openings.

Prevention and Control: Before planting newly purchased, susceptible plants, soak their roots in a solution containing *Agrobacterium radiobacter,* a beneficial bacteria that preys on the crown gall. If plants contract the disease, dig them up, taking the soil that surrounds the roots.

Notes: Crown gall is most likely to come onto your soils along with purchased plants. When you buy nursery stock, examine all the roots carefully, looking for abnormal growth patterns. Do not plant anything that looks suspicious.

Erwinia amylovora
Fire Blight

Range: Throughout North America.

Hosts: Apples, pears, plums, raspberries, hawthorns, roses, and many ornamental woody plants are the most frequent hosts.

Description: Leaves, flowers, and young shoots suddenly wilt in late spring. The shoots droop, and infected flowers look wet and then turn brown and shrivel. Leaves curl upward and turn black or brown but remain hanging on the plant. Infected fruit is dark and shriveled but also remains on the tree. As the disease spreads, large cankers form on the branches or trunk. These cankers begin by looking wet and then turn dark. The disease is called fire blight because

branches, leaves, and fruit look scorched by fire. Damage on mature plants is usually controllable; young plants may be killed from it in a season or two.

Life Cycle: Fire blight bacteria overwinter on infected twigs and at the edges of cankers. Warm wet spring weather breaks the bacteria's dormancy, and it resumes growth and reproduction. The bacteria generally become dormant in late summer.

Transmission: The bacterial ooze of fire blight is attractive to many insects that spread it as they move among plants. Rain and splashing water also transmit it.

Prevention and Control: Do not over fertilize, particularly with high nitrogen materials because excesses favor the growth of this disease. During the season, prune out all infected growth as soon as you see it, well before the shoots look fire-blackened. Inspect dormant plants carefully. If you find them, cut affected branches back at least 6 to 12 inches below the infection site. If fire blight has been present in your plantings, spray susceptible plants with streptomycin during blossoming and again seven to ten days later.

Notes: More than one pruner has spread fire blight through an entire planting. Remember to sterilize all your pruning tools with a 10-percent laundry bleach solution or 100-percent alcohol between each cut, no matter what the season.

Many viruses
Mosaic Virus

Range: Throughout North America

Hosts: Almost all plants are affected by at

least one of the mosaic viruses

Description: Mottled leaves are the first symptom of mosaic viruses. Distorted growth, stunting, and a generalized yellowing can also occur. In tomatoes, the leaves are cupped and puckered and there may be yellow areas on the fruit.

Life Cycle: Viruses remain inactive but viable in dead tissue for as long as 50

years. When they encounter a suitable host and environmental conditions, they become active. Rather than reproducing themselves, they stimulate the plant cells where they are present to produce more viruses.

Transmission: Most viruses are transmitted by insects, although gardeners spread their fair share too.

Prevention and Control: Vigorously growing, robustly healthy plants can sometimes resist a virus, so good cultural care is imperative. Resistant cultivars of many species are available. Floating row covers over susceptible plants exclude the insects that carry viruses. If you see a plant with a virus, immediately dig and destroy it.

Notes: Viruses can become inactive in extremely hot weather, making the plant appear to have outgrown the disease. This is not true; infected plants must still be removed and destroyed. Viruses easily live through composting and freezing temperatures. Some can even live through boiling. This is the reason that you are advised to put all virus-laden plants in plastic bags destined for the landfill rather than the compost pile. Smokers can transmit Tobacco Mosaic Virus (TMV) to their plants. Avoid problems by washing hands in skim milk before going into the garden.

Aphelenchoides spp, and *Meloidogyne* spp.

Nematodes, foliar and root knot

Range: Foliar nematodes live in all parts of the U.S. and warmer regions of Canada but root knot nematodes do not survive well north of Zone 5b.

Hosts: Foliar nematodes are most troublesome on chrysanthemums, strawberries, phlox, dahlias, primroses, and asters. Root-knot nematodes infect almost all vegetables, fruit trees, and ornamental plants.

Description: Foliar nematodes generally attack lower leaves first. They feed between the veins, making affected areas yellow before they brown and die. Root knot nematodes live on plant roots. They secrete toxins that stimulate the root cells to enlarge abnormally, making knots on the tissue. Plants are stunted and yellow as a consequence of losing root area. If infection is severe, plants can die.

Life Cycle: Nematodes can remain viable but dormant in the soil or crop debris. Warm weather stimulates them to become active again. They can be mobile in water films, both above and within the soil, so they can travel to search for an opening to enter the plant. They reproduce sexually, and a female can lay thousands of eggs in her lifetime.

Transmission: Generally water and soil-borne although gardeners can carry them from one place to another with dirty tools and infected seedlings often bring them onto land.

Prevention and Control: To prevent foliar nematodes, examine all purchased nursery stock carefully and do not plant any that look sickly. If symptoms appear on a garden plant, pick off and destroy all infected tissue and rake the surrounding soil clear. In serious cases, dig and remove the plants. Root knot nematodes can be killed if you cover-crop the garden with 'Nemagold' marigolds. Chitin, a compound found in insect exoskeletons and crab shells, is available from some organic-supply houses, and is an effective control. Beneficial fungi in compost prey on nematodes, so problems are rare in well-composted soil. Drenching the soil with neem sometimes controls them, but beneficial nematodes provide the best control.

Notes: Do not compost nematode-infested plants or soils because they often live through the composting process.

Erysiphe spp, *Sphaerotheca* spp. and many others

Powdery Mildew

Range: Throughout the U.S. and southern Canada.

Hosts: Many, but cabbage-and squash-family crops, legumes, peppers and many ornamentals are particularly susceptible.

Description: White mycelium grow on the surface of the plant and are quite visible. The powdery look is given by spores growing from the mycelium. The disease usually starts with round white dots on undersides of older leaves. The spots enlarge and coalesce until both sides of the leaf are covered. Leaves become pale and then brown and dry. On ornamentals the disease usually causes cosmetic damage; yields of all fruiting plants are severely cut.

Life Cycle: Powdery mildew fungi overwinter as sexual fruiting bodies on crop debris or as mycelium on ornamental plants. In spring, spores infect new tissues by sending penetration pegs through the cuticle. They directly absorb the cell sap. It only takes a week for an entire cycle to take place, from germinating spore to spore-producing mycelium.

Transmission: Primarily wind-borne. In the North where powdery mildew does not always survive, most infections are due to spores that travel on winds from more southern states. These fungi do not need a water film to germinate.

Prevention and Control: Choose resistant cultivars whenever possible. Space plants well to allow good air circulation. Practice excellent garden sanitation. Compost tea sprays used at intervals of 7 to 14 days through the season will often prevent infections. Baking soda and/or baking soda and superior oil sprays kill the fungi.

Notes: Different powdery mildew species infect legumes, cabbage family plants and those in the Asteracae (formerly Compositae) family, so you can follow one of these groups with another even if powdery mildew was present. However, the same species that infects hollyhocks, sunflowers, and phlox also infects the squash-family plants.

Pseudomonas spp.

Pseudomonas Leaf Blight, Bacterial Blight

Range: Throughout North America.
Hosts: Legumes, as well as many woody plants, particularly fruit trees and roses.
Description: The first symptom you see will be pale spots on leaves, shoots and flowers in early spring. The spots enlarge and darken. Tissues die and flowers, branches, and leaves eventually drop. On branches, dark-colored streaks form on the bark, and cankers may develop. A dark gummy material oozes from the cankers. If cankers have been present during the preceding winter, they will enlarge rapidly just about the time that buds break in the spring. If the disease is not checked, it can kill the plant.
Life Cycle: This bacteria overwinters in infected tissue. They are dormant when they are cold but can become active anytime the weather warms for a few hours.
Transmission: Wind, rain, and insects spread the bacteria to new sites. They enter the plant through natural openings and wounds.
Prevention and Control: Fertilize only as needed because excess nitrogen stimulates this bacteria. Do not prune plants in wet weather. If infection strikes a woody plant, prune affected wood back at least six inches below the infection site, and spray the cut with an antibiotic. Sterilize pruning tools with a 10 percent laundry-bleach solution between cuts. Spray an antibiotic, available from orchard supply houses, before buds swell in the spring. If all else fails, spray copper or lime-sulfur just about the time the buds swell but before they break.
Notes: On peas and beans, this disease is most likely to occur on late summer plantings. Drape floating row cover over the plants to protect them from wind-borne spores.

Aphanomyces spp., *Fusarium* spp., *Pellicularia filamentosa*, *Phoma apiicola*, *Phytophthora* spp., *Pythium* spp. and *Rhizoctonia* spp.

Root Rot

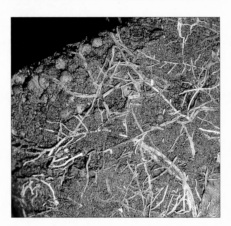

Range: Throughout the U.S. and southern Canada.
Hosts: Almost all plants
Description: Root rot fungi kill seedlings as well as established plants. The first symptoms of root rot diseases are hard to detect; plants just don't look as vigorous and healthy as they should. It doesn't take long for more severe effects to become apparent. Plants wilt easily, even when soil is wet, leaves yellow, growth is stunted, and young plants usually die. Older plants may suffer for a long time before succumbing to the disease.
Life Cycle: Root rot fungi overwinter on crop debris or remain dormant as resting spores. When the soil begins to warm in the spring, they infect new tissues. Many of these fungi produce swimming spores that are chemically attracted to roots. Some produce resting spores that can remain viable in the soil for 10 or 15 years without a host.
Transmission: Spores may travel through the soil solution or be carried by splashing water.
Prevention and Control: Plant only in well-drained soils, and space plants widely enough to facilitate air circulation. Do not overwater seedlings. In greenhouses or other starting facilities, keep air circulation high, using a fan, if necessary. Do not apply excess nitrogen.
Notes: Root rot fungi are in all soils, so good cultural care is the only recourse. If you are like most gardeners, you will lose very few plants to them as long as you use good gardening practices.

Many fungi, including *Puccinia* spp. and *Uromyces* spp.

Rust

Range: All regions of the U.S. and southern Canada.
Hosts: Almost all plants are susceptible to one or another of the rust fungi.
Description: Slow growth and a general unhealthiness are the first signs of a rust infection. Though these can be subtle symptoms, as soon as the fungus produces its brightly colored spores, the problem will be obvious. Depending on the species, the spores can be rust colored, yellow, orange, or reddish brown. In most cases, the spores form on leaf

undersides, so look here if a plant seems less healthy than it should be. Rust won't kill a plant for many years but can seriously weaken it.

Life Cycle: Rust fungi can produce as many as five different types of spores and some, such as cedar-apple rust, require two hosts to complete their life cycle. Most overwinter in a dormant state but spring weather stimulates spore production. Depending on the species, they may take two seasons to produce spores.

Transmission: Primarily wind-borne although insects and rain can also spread the spores.

Prevention and Control: Keep nitrogen levels adequate but not excessive. Keep air circulation high around plants by proper spacing and pruning. Pick off and destroy any infected tissue. Spray sulfur on young spots of rust to kill spores.

Notes: Pines and asters are alternate hosts for *Coleosporium asterum* rust, and corn and *Oxalis* species such as the common weed woodsorrel are alternate hosts for *Puccinia sorghi* rust. If either of these organisms becomes a problem in your garden, you will need to eradicate the spore-producing lesions on the alternate host to eradicate the disease.

Cladosporium cucumerinum, *Streptomyces scabies*

Scab

Range: In all areas of the U.S. and southern Canada except the southwestern US.

Hosts: *Cladosporium cucumerinum*

infects only cucurbits while *Streptomyces scabies* infects beets, cabbages, carrots, eggplants, spinach, onions, parsnips, potatoes, and turnips.

Description: Warty-looking scabs form on the skins of infected tubers, roots, and fruits. Though the damage can be only skin-deep in the case of tubers and roots, it opens the way for secondary infection. On squash-family plants, the first signs of the disease are angular spots on the leaves. On the fruit, the scabs can be superficial or the stem ends can rot.

Life Cycle: The fungi that cause scab overwinter on crop debris. In spring, spores form and spread to new plants.

Transmission: *S. scabies* is soilborne, while *C. cucumerinum* is airborne and travels to new plants with the breezes.

Prevention and Control: Choose resistant cultivars. When growing potatoes, do not apply noncomposted animal manures or lime the soil before planting. Acid conditions discourage this fungi. Apply compost to the area the year before you plant and cover-crop with hairy vetch the preceding fall.

Notes: *S. scabies* can remain dormant without a host for many years, so rotations must take this into account. Four or five year rotations are usually sufficient to escape infection.

Septoria spp.

Septoria Leaf Spot

Range: Throughout North America.

Hosts: Various species infect celery,

tomatoes, potatoes, peppers, eggplant, cucurbits as well as many ornamental plants.

Description: The first symptoms of septoria infection are spots which appear on the lower leaves. The first spots are small and yellow, often with a halo of brown or gray tissue around them. As they age, they enlarge and finally turn dark brown or reddish brown. At this point, they are usually surrounded by a yellow halo. Black spores are visible in the center of the spots. Infections of septoria leaf spot move from the bottom leaves of the plant to those higher up. Severely infected leaves drop off, and if the disease is left unchecked, the plant can die.

Life Cycle: *Septoria* fungi overwinter in crop debris and infected seeds. The warm, wet spring weather stimulates spore production. Many generations of septoria fungi are produced in one season.

Transmission: Both water and air-borne but most infections come from rain or irrigation water which splashes the spores onto leaves.

Prevention and Control: Allow four-year rotations of susceptible plants, particularly celery and tomatoes. Do not work in the garden when it is wet. Spray plants with compost tea every seven to ten days as a preventive before infection strikes.

If you save tomato seed, treat it with a hot-water bath at 122°F for approximately 25 minutes before you plant it. If septoria appears in the garden, pick off all infected tissue immediately, and rake up the dropped leaves. If the infection is serious, spray copper once or twice, at a seven-day interval.

Notes: Seeds infected with septoria usually die before they emerge from the soil or shortly afterwards. Although this kind of damage is fairly painless to a gardener, the more serious effect is that the fungus has had a chance to reproduce and can lie in wait for other susceptible hosts.

GLOSSARY

Acidic Soil pH that is less than 7.0 (neutral); acid soils tend to be deficient in phosphorus and sometimes contain excess manganese and aluminum.

Aerial rootlet. Aboveground structure on the stems of certain vines such as English ivy; attaches and anchors the vine to its support.

Alkaline. Soil pH that is above 7.0 (neutral); alkaline soils tend to lack manganese and boron.

Allelopathic. The injurious effect that some plant compounds have on other plants.

Alpine plant. A plant that grows above the tree line in mountainous areas; often cultivated in rock gardens.

Annual. A plant that germinates, grows, flowers, produces seeds, and dies in the course of a single growing season; a plant that is treated like an annual and grown for a single season's display.

Antidesiccant. A commercial product applied to leaves to form a protective barrier, usually against wind, which causes drying.

Auxins. Chemical compounds that promote shoot growth and root formation.

Bt (*Bacillus thuringiensis*). Naturally occurring pathogen that is toxic to insect larvae but not harmful to other organisms; various strains are sold commercially.

Beneficial insects. Insects that are considered "helpful" in the garden because they kill pest insects. Examples: ladybugs and tachinid flies.

Beneficial nematodes. Commercially available, microscopic worms used to control soil-dwelling insect pests. Once inside the host, they infect it with lethal bacteria.

Biennial. A plant that flowers, produces seeds, and dies in its second growing season.

Black spot. Fungal disease that attacks roses, causing dark, rounded areas on foliage.

Bordeaux mix. A pesticide that is a mixture of copper sulfate and hydrated lime. Like copper, it controls algae and fungi, but it is slightly stronger. It is most often used on fruits. As with all other materials, you must follow the directions on the label carefully to avoid problems.

Botanical poisons. Plant-derived pesticides, including rotenone, pyrethrum, sabadilla, ryania, neem, garlic, and nicotine. Because these substances kill beneficial insects (and fish, in the case of pyrethrum) as well as pests, they should be used only as a last resort.

Broadcast seeding. A planting technique that involves randomly scattering seeds over prepared soil rather than sowing in rows. Most often used with small plantings of crops such as carrots, beets, radishes, and salad greens.

Bud union. The area where top growth is joined to a rootstock.

Calyx. The outer segments (usually green) that surround a flower bud.

Capillary action. Upward movement of water through the soil, and into the root zone.

Chilling hours. Plant requirement for a specific period below 45°F in order to break dormancy in spring.

Cloche. A transparent or translucent cover used to protect plants from the cold.

Collar. The area of a tree where a main branch meets the trunk or a side branch meets a main branch.

Cold frame. A low, boxlike structure with removable glass or plastic cover, used to protect plants from the cold.

Companion planting. Positioning plants in the garden to take advantage of their influence on neighboring plants. Can be used to stimulate growth or to ward off pests or disease.

Compost. A humus-rich, organic material formed by the decomposition of leaves, grass clippings, and other organic materials. Used to improve soil.

Compost tea. Liquid made by steeping compost in water; used as a fertilizer or treatment for fungal diseases on plants.

Conditioning. Process for drying herbs completely before long-term storage; involves transferring them from one jar to another every three to four days, boosting air circulation.

Corm. A bulb-like, underground structure used primarily for storing food.

Cover crop. A crop such as oats or winter rye planted in late summer or fall, then tilled under in early spring to prevent erosion. Also adds nutrients and organic matter to the soil.

Crop rotation. A system for varying the type of plant grown in a given area over time, avoiding the depletion of soil nutrients and minimizing soilborne insect and disease problems. Usually done on a cyclical basis: e.g., four different crops grown in a plot over a four-year period.

Cultivar. A cultivated variety of a plant, often bred or selected for some special trait, such as double flowers, compact growth, cold hardiness, or disease resistance.

Damping off. A fungal disease that kills seedlings shortly before or after germination. Can be prevented by ensuring good air circulation.

Day-neutral. Refers to strawberry cultivars that produce small amounts of fruit throughout the season rather than a single large crop in June.

Days to maturity. The number of days required for a crop to reach the point where harvest typically begins. Numbers listed on seed packets can refer either to the number of days from direct seeding (such as for beans, corn, squash, and other crops typically sown directly in the garden) or to days from transplant (such as for tomatoes, peppers, broccoli, and others generally started indoors).

Deadhead. To remove old flowers during the growing season to prevent seed formation and to encourage the development of new flowers.

Decoction. Herbal preparation made from fresh, crushed roots simmered in water for 20 to 30 minutes.

Determinate tomatoes. Vines grow to a given height and then stop. Most of the fruit is produced and ripens at one time.

Diatomaceous earth. The fossilized remains of ancient marine organisms, sold as a control for soft-bodied insect pests, such as aphids and slugs.

Dioecious. Male and female flowers occur on different plants. For fruiting, plants of each sex must be within pollination range. Example: kiwi vine.

Direct-seed. To plant seeds outside where they will grow.

Divide. To propagate a plant by separating it into two or more pieces, each of which has at least one bud and some roots. Used mostly for perennials, grasses, ferns, and bulbs.

Dormant oil. A type of horticultural oil sprayed on dormant plants to control insect pests.

Double dig. To work soil to a depth that is twice the usual by digging a trench, loosening the soil at the bottom of the trench, then returning the top layer of soil to the trench. This produces a raised bed with a deep layer of loose, fluffy soil.

Dusts. Nonpoisonous, contact pesticides such as diatomaceous earth, montmorillonite, finely ground rock powers, and ordinary dust from garden soil. They dehydrate insects, especially soft-bodied larvae. Must be reapplied frequently.

Espalier. The training of a plant to grow flat against wires, often against a wall or framework. A plant so trained is called an espalier.

Exudant. Substance released from a plant, potentially affecting other plants, as well as insects and microorganisms.

Fertilizer. An organic or mineral material, such as fish emulsion, used primarily to provide nutrients for plants. All commercial fertilizers are required by law to state the minimum amount of nutrients supplied; for example: 5-1-2 (5 percent nitrogen, 1 percent phosphorus, and 2 percent potassium).

Fish emulsion. A natural, liquid fertilizer made from fish. The primary nutrient is nitrogen, but this fertilizer also supplies phosphorus and potassium.

Floricanes. Two-year-old, flowering and fruiting canes of bramble bushes.

Flushing. Rinsing seeds in water several times a day to encourage germination.

Focal point. A garden or landscape element—usually a plant or plant grouping—that draws the attention of viewers.

Genus. The plant classification that groups related species linked by a range of common characteristics.

Graft. To artificially attach one or more plant parts to another.

Green manure. A fast-maturing leafy crop, such as buckwheat, rye, or clover, generally planted in early spring then turned under later in the season. Adds nutrients and organic matter to the soil.

Harden off. To gradually acclimate indoor seedlings to outside conditions before transplanting.

Hardiness. A plant's ability to survive the winter without protection from the cold.

Hardiness zone. Geographic region where the coldest temperature in an average winter falls within a certain range, such as between 0° and –10°F.

Hardwood cutting. Mature wood (deciduous or evergreen), usually taken at the end of the growing season for the purpose of propagation.

Heading cut. Pruning cut that removes end growth of stems or branches. Encourages new growth below the cut.

Heating hours. Plant requirement for a specific period above 65° F in order to thrive and, in some cases, to produce mature fruit.

Heirloom flowers and vegetables. Varieties grown from seed that has been saved from one plant generation to the next. Plants of each generation carry genetic traits similar to their parents.

Heeling in. Temporary planting until a plant can be placed in the desired location.

Herbaceous. Perennial plants that die back to the ground each fall, then grow back again each spring.

Holdfast. Disk-shaped structure on the stems of certain vines (such as trumpet vine or Virginia creeper); secretes an adhesive substance that allows the vine to attach to its support.

Horticultural oil. Hydrocarbon-based pesticide derived from petroleum, plant fat, or animal fat. When sprayed on plants, it kills insects by smothering them or disrupting their metabolism. Use only in cool, shady conditions with low to moderate relative humidity.

Humus. The complex, organic residue of decayed plant matter in soil.

Hybrid. A plant resulting from a cross between two parents that belong to different varieties, species, or genera.

Hyphae. Threadlike structures that make up fungus. A group of interwoven hyphae is called a mycelium.

Indeterminate tomatoes. Varieties that produce vines that continue to grow for the life of the plant.

Infusion. Very strong tea made by pouring boiling water over herbs and steeping in a covered container for at least 20 minutes.

Inoculant. Nitrogen-fixing bacteria sold as a powder that is dusted over bean and pea seeds before planting to boost yields.

Insect growth regulators. Chemical compounds that control insects pests by mimicking or interfering with the hormones that regulate their development. Used mostly by commercial growers and orchardists; not commonly available to home gardeners.

Insect pheromones. Chemical signals given off by insects to attract other insects, usually for mating. Commercially sold, pheromone-baited traps are often used in orchards to monitor or trap pests, disrupt their mating, or lure them to poison baits.

Insecticidal soap. Soap-based pesticide used as a spray; fatty acids kill insects by eroding their cell walls. Relatively benign because it kills only the insects that it touches.

Interplant. To combine plants with different bloom times or growth habits, making it possible to fit more plants in a bed, thus prolonging the bed's appeal.

Layering. A propagation technique that involves burying a small portion of a growing branch to encourage root formation. After roots form, the new plant can be separated from the parent plant.

Limb up. To remove a tree's bottom limbs, allowing more light into a landscape.

Loam. An ideal soil for gardening, containing organic matter and a balanced range of small to large mineral particles.

Long-day/short-day cultivar. Describes onion cultivars, based on their relative need for darkness each night in order to form bulbs. Long-day cultivars do best in the North, where summer days are longer than 12 hours. Short-day cultivars are better suited to the South, where summer days are 12 hours.

Microbial pesticides. Naturally occurring pathogens, such as milky spore disease of Japanese beetles and the many strains of *Bacillus thuringiensis*, used to control pest insects. Most affect only larval stages, so application must be carefully timed and repeated. They degrade quickly in sunlight.

Microclimate. Local conditions of shade, exposure, wind, drainage, and other factors that affect plant growth at any particular site.

Milky spore disease. A commercially available microbial pesticide used to control Japanese beetles.

Molt. To split and shed the exoskeleton—a development stage for insects.

Monoecious. Having both male and female flowers on the same plant. Example: squash.

Open pollinated. Plants grown from seed produced by parents that are genetically similar, but not identical, to each other. Second-generation plants carry the characteristic traits of their parents. These varieties are sometimes called heirlooms.

Organic matter. Plant and animal residues, such as leaves, garden trimmings, and manure, in various stages of decomposition.

Pathogen. Disease-causing microorganism.

Peduncle. A flower stalk.

Perennial. A plant that lives for three or more years and generally flowers each year. By perennial, gardeners usually mean herbaceous perennial, although woody plants such as vines, shrubs, and trees are also perennial.

Perfect flower. Having both male and female parts within the same bloom. Example: tomato.

pH. Measure of acid/alkaline balance in soil that affects the availability of plant nutrients, such as phosphorus and potassium. Seven is neutral on the pH scale.

Phytotoxic. Poisonous to plants.

Primocanes. First-year stems, or canes, of bramble bushes. They generally do not bear fruit until the following year, except on "ever-bearing" varieties, which may fruit on the first year's growth.

Rachis. An extension of the petiole that supports leaflets of compound leaves.

Repellents. Strong-smelling substances, such as deodorant soap, garlic oil, or fox urine, used to deter deer, rabbits, and other animal pests.

Rhizome. A horizontal underground stem, often swollen into a storage organ. Both roots and shoots emerge from rhizomes, generally branch as they creep along. They can be divided to make new plants.

Rooting hormone. Substance used to promote the growth of roots on plant cuttings.

Rotenone. A broad-spectrum pesticide made from the roots of the rotenone plant. This kills almost all insects (beneficials and pests), so it should be used only as a last resort. Breaks down after a few hours of exposure to sunlight.

Row cover. A translucent woven cover used to protect crops from cold and/or insect pests, while letting in light and water. The lightweight material usually rests directly on plants; edges of the cover are secured with soil, rocks, or pins.

Scarify. To scratch or nick a seed coat to encourage germination.

Scree. Gravelly soil, such as is found on mountainsides; also used for growing alpine plants in rock gardens.

Self-incompatible. Describes flowers that contain both male and female parts but that require pollen from another flower for fertilization.

Self-wrapping. The tendency of some cauliflower cultivars to produce leaves that shield the developing head from sunlight.

Semi-ripe cutting. Stem tip growth (usually 3 to 4 inches) taken in early summer for the purpose of propagation.

Sepal. Individual segment of a calyx—the leafy covering that surrounds a flower bud.

Sheet mulching. Covering the surface of the soil with layers of organic material, such as newspaper, compost, and straw. Often used to convert a lawn area into a garden area, while improving the underlying soil.

Soil amendments. Organic or mineral materials such as peat moss, perlite, or compost, used to improve the soil or benefit microbial life.

Soil structure. Refers to the way soil particles group together and to the size and number of air spaces between particles.

Soil texture. Describes the relative amounts of sand, silt, and clay in soil. Influences the availability of air, water, and nutrients for soil life, including plant roots.

Spur. A short branch that produces flower buds and fruit on a fruit tree.

Stipule. Appendage at the base of a leaf of certain plants, such as roses.

Stool. Plant form in which currants, gooseberries, and other bush fruits are grown as multistemmed shrubs.

Stratify. To subject seeds to fluctuating temperatures or to a period of freezing to encourage germination.

Succession planting. A technique in which an early, fast-maturing crop, such as lettuce or peas, is followed by another crop during the same growing season. Boosts productivity per square foot of growing space.

Superior oil. A type of horticultural oil used to kill insect pests on plants during the growing season. Also called "refined" or "fine" oil.

Swale. Low-lying land area that serves as a drainage channel for rainwater.

Tender. Describes a plant that is damaged by cold weather.

Thin. To remove weak or crowded seedlings, branches, or fruits.

Thinning cut. Pruning to remove an entire branch or stem by cutting back to the trunk, main branch, or ground. Used for removing weak or poorly positioned growth.

Tiller. Garden device used to cultivate soil. Also refers to the new, offset growth that emerges from the crown of a grass plant.

Tuber. A swollen, underground portion a stem or root, used to store food.

Umbelliferous. Plants, such as dill, fennel, anise, yarrow, and coriander, that have umbrella-shaped flower heads.

Water rose. A nozzle that disperses water through many holes, thereby reducing the force of a single stream.

Windscreen. A structure, such as a wooden frame covered with burlap, used to protect plants from damaging winds.

INDEX

PLANT INDEX

Note: Page numbers in **bold type** indicate plant profiles, which always contain photographs. Page numbers in *italic type* indicate additional photographs or illustrations.

PHOTO CREDITS

Key: T-Top, B-Bottom, C-Center, L-Left, R-Right

strom R Alan and Linda Detrick/Photo Researchers **p. 70:** T Walter Chandoha; B Photos Horticultural. **p. 72:** T Neil Soderstrom; B Walter Chandoha **p. 73:** All Walter Chandoha **p. 74:** L John Eastcott/Yva Momatiuk/Photo Researchers; C Derek Fell; R Alan and Linda Detrick/Photo Researchers **p. 75:** L D. Cavagnaro; C Alan and Linda Detrick/Photo Researchers; R Derek Fell **p. 76:** L Derek Fell; C Emily Harste/Bruce Coleman; R Derek Fell **p. 77:** L Michael Gadomski/Photo Researchers; C Derek Fell; R Geoff Bryant/Photo Researchers **p. 78:** L H. Reinhard/Okapia/Photo Researchers; C Walter Chandoha; R Derek Fell **p. 79:** L John Glover; C Geoff Bryant/Photo Researchers; R D. Cavagnaro **p. 80:** L Walter Chandoha; C Geoff Bryant/Photo Researchers; R Alan and Linda Detrick/Photo Researchers **p. 81:** L Derek Fell; C, R D. Cavagnaro **p. 82:** L D. Cavagnaro; C Derek Fell; R Jeff Lepore/Photo Researchers **p. 83:** L, R John Glover; C Scott Camazine/Photo Researchers **p. 84:** L D. Cavagnaro; C Gail Jankus/Photo Researchers; R Derek Fell **p. 85:** L Geoff Bryant/Photo Researchers; C Derek Fell; R D. Cavagnaro **p. 86:** L Alan and Linda Detrick/Photo Researchers; C D. Cavagnaro; R D. Cavagnaro **p. 87:** L Neil Soderstrom; C Derek Fell; R Walter Chandoha **p. 88:** T Photos Horticultural; B Alan and Linda Detrick/Photo Researchers **p. 89:** Derek Fell **p. 90:** Walter Chandoha **p. 91:** Michael Thompson **p. 92:** L Neil Soderstrom; C, R Derek Fell **p. 93:** L Neil Soderstrom; C Derek Fell R D. Cavagnaro **p. 94** All D. Cavagnaro **p. 95:** L Derek Fell; C Jane Legate/The Garden Picture Library; R Jerry Pavia **p. 96:** L Jerry Pavia, *Bonners Ferry, ID*; C Neil Soderstrom R S. Nelson/Bruce Coleman **p. 97:** L Derek Fell; C James Carmichael/Bruce Coleman; R John Glover **p. 98:** L Jerry Pavia; C Rex Butcher/Bruce Coleman; R Neil Soderstrom **p. 99:** L Jerry Pavia; C Neil Soderstrom R Michael Thompson **p. 100:** L, C D. Cavagnaro; R Derek Fell **p. 101:** Inset D. Cavagnaro; L, C Derek Fell; R John Glover **p. 102:** T Neil Soderstrom; BL Derek Fell BR John Glover **p. 103:** L Neil Soderstrom; R D. Cavagnaro **p. 104:** L Neil Soderstrom; C D. Cavagnaro; R John Glover **p. 105:** L, C Derek Fell; R D. Cavagnaro **p. 106:** L Alan and Linda Detrick/Photo Researchers; C, R Jerry Pavia **p. 107:** D. Cavagnaro **p. 108:** Roger Harvey/Garden World/Photo Horticultural **p. 109:** B Photo Horticultural; T D. Cavagnaro **p. 110:** L Neil Soderstrom; **C** Bob Gibbons/Holt Studios/Photo Researchers; R Jerry Pavia **p. 111:** All Jerry Pavia **p. 112:** L Derek Fell; C Jerry Pavia; L John Glover **p. 113:** TL Jerry Pavia; TR Neil Soderstrom; B Box D. Cavagnaro **p. 114**: John Glover **p. 115:** John Glover **p. 116:** John Glover **p. 117:** Wayside Gardens *courtesy* **p. 118:** Walter Chandoha **p. 119:** All Neil Soderstrom **p. 120:** D. Cavagnaro **p. 121:** Holt Studios/Photo Researchers **p. 122:** T John Glover; B Jerry Pavia **p. 123:** TR Jerry Pavia; CL John Glover/The Garden Picture Library; BR Jerry Pavia **p. 124:** Jerry Pavia **p. 125:** Michael Thompson **p. 126:** John Glover **p. 127:** T Rosalind Creasy B Mayer/Le Scanff/The Garden Picture Library **p. 129:** All Derek Fell **p. 133:** All Neil Soderstrom **p. 134:** Rosalind Creasy **p. 135:** Rob Cardillo, *Ambler, PA* **p. 137:** John Glover **p. 138:** L J S Sira/The Garden Picture Library; R Derek Fell **p. 139:** L John Glover; R Jerry Pavia **p. 142:** All Derek Fell **pp. 144-145:** L Michael Thompson; C Rosalind Creasy; R Derek Fell **p. 146:** L John Bova/Photo Researchers; C John Glover; R Jerry Pavia Inset Jerry Pavia **p. 147:** L, R, Inset Derek Fell; C Walter Chandoha **p. 148:** L Michael Gadomski/Photo Researchers; C Jerry Pavia; R Walter Chandoha **p. 149:** L John Glover; R Jerry Pavia **p. 150:** Walter Chandoha **p. 151:** Walter Chandoha **p. 152:** L D. Cavagnaro; R John Glover **p. 153:** Carole Ottesen, *Potomac, MD* **p. 154:** Walter Chandoha **p. 155** All Walter Chandoha **p. 156:** Derek Fell **p. 157:** Derek Fell **p. 160:** D. Cavagnaro **p. 161:** TL D. Cavagnaro; TR Walter Chandoha; BL, BR Derek Fell **p. 162:** Derek Fell **p. 165:** Neil Soderstrom **p. 166:** TL, BC Walter Chandoha; TC Neil Soderstrom; TR John Glover; C Derek Fell **p. 167:** T D. Cavagnaro; B Marianne Majerus/The Garden Picture Library **p. 168:** TR , L D. Cavagnaro; BR Derek Fell **p. 169:** D. Cavagnaro **p. 170:** All Neil Soderstrom **p. 171:** All Neil Soderstrom **p. 172:** L, TC Derek Fell; R Jerry Pavia; BC D. Cavagnaro **p. 174:** L Derek Fell; R Alan and Linda Detrick/Photo Researchers **p. 175:** L, C Derek Fell; R D. Cavagnaro **p. 176:** Derek Fell **p. 177:** All Derek Fell **p. 179:** Derek Fell **p. 180:** TL, TR , BC, BR D. Cavagnaro; TC Derek Fell; BL Holt Studios/Photo Researchers **p. 182:** TL, TR , BL, BR Derek Fell; TC, BC D. Cavagnaro **p. 183:** T Derek Fell; B D. Cavagnaro **p. 184:** Jerry Pavia **p. 185:** TL D. Cavagnaro; TC, CL, CC, BC Derek Fell; TR, CR, BC Neil Soderstrom **p. 187:** L D. Cavagnaro; R Neil Soderstrom **p. 188:** L Derek Fell; R D. Cavagnaro **p. 189:** L D. Cavagnaro; R Derek Fell **p. 190:** T D. Cavagnaro; B Neil Soderstrom **p. 191:** Derek Fell **p. 192:** All Derek Fell **p. 194:** Walter Chandoha **p. 195:** John Glover **p. 196:** T J S Sira/The Garden Picture Library; B John Glover/The Garden Picture Library **p. 197:** Walter Chandoha **p. 198:** Photos Horticultural **p. 199:** L Lynne Brotchie/The Garden Picture Library; R John Glover **p. 200:** T Photos Horticultural; B Derek Fell **p. 201:** John Glover **p. 202:** All Photos Horticultural **p. 203:** T Photos Horticultural; B PW Flowers/The Garden Picture Library **p. 204:** T Mayer/Le Scanff/ The Garden Picture Library; B Walter Chandoha **p. 205:** L D. Cavagnaro; R Jerry Pavia **p. 206:** L, R, C D. Cavagnaro **p. 207:** L D. Cavagnaro; R Susan Roth,

Stony Brook, NY **p. 208:** L Jerry Pavia; C , R D. Cavagnaro **p. 209:** L, C Jerry Pavia; R Derek Fell **p. 210:** L D. Cavagnaro; R Jerry Pavia **p. 211:** L, C, R D. Cavagnaro; Inset Jerry Pavia; R D. Cavagnaro **p. 212:** L, R D. Cavagnaro; C Neil Soderstrom; **p. 213:** All Jerry Pavia **p. 214:** L Charles Mann, *Santa Fe, NM;* C Derek Fell R John Glover **p. 215:** L, C D. Cavagnaro R Derek Fell **p. 216:** L Charles Mann; C Jerry Pavia; TR D. Cavagnaro; BR Derek Fell; **p. 217:** L Jerry Pavia; R Derek Fell **p. 218:** Mayer/Le Scanff/The Garden Picture Library **p. 219:** Linda Burgess/The Garden Picture Library **pp. 220-221:** T to B John Glover; Walter Chandoha **pp. 222-223:** TL Crandall and Crandall; BL Photos Horticultural; BC, BR, TR John Glover **p. 224:** John Glover **p. 226:** Walter Chandoha **p. 228:** All Walter Chandoha **p. 229:** L Photos Horticultural; R Walter Chandoha **p. 230:** T Derek Fell; B Crandall and Crandall **p. 231:** T Lamontagne/The Garden Picture Library; B Michael Thompson **p. 232:** John Glover **p. 233:** T Crandall and Crandall; B D. Cavagnaro **p. 234:** Howard Rice/The Garden Picture Library **p. 235:** L John Glover; R Kaj Svensson/Science Library/Photo Researchers **p. 236:** H. Lange/Okapia/Photo Researchers **p. 237:** T Bob Gibbons/Holt Studios/Photo Researchers; B Jerry Pavia **p. 238:** L Jerry Pavia; R Michael Gadomski/Photo Researchers **p. 239:** L Southern Living/Photo Researchers **p. 240:** W. Weisser/Bruce Coleman **p. 241:** T Richard Parker/Photo Researchers; B Jerry Pavia **p. 242:** T Lamontagne/The Garden Picture Library; B Photos Horticultural **p. 243:** J S Sira/The Garden Picture Library **p. 244:** T Derek Fell; B Walter Chandoha **p. 245:** T Walter Chandoha; B Photos Horticultural **p. 248:** L Jerry Pavia; R Walter Chandoha **p. 249:** L Gilbert Grant/Photo Researchers; R Erwin and Peggy Bauer/Bruce Coleman Inc. **p. 250:** T Derek Fell; B Michel Vard/The Garden Picture Library **p. 251:** D. Cavagnaro **p. 252:** Photos Horticultural **p. 253:** Walter Chandoha **p. 254:** Derek Fell **p. 255:** D. Cavagnaro **p. 256:** L Walter Chandoha; R L & D Klein/ Photo Researchers **p. 257:** L Neil Holmes/ The Garden Picture Library; R Photos Horticultural **p. 258:** T John Glover; B D. Cavagnaro **p. 260:** D. Cavagnaro **p. 262:** All D. Cavagnaro **p. 263:** L Friedrich Strauss/The Garden Picture Library; R Photos Horticultural **p. 264:** T Derek Fell; B Walter Chandoha **p. 265:** TL, TR Derek Fell; BL Neil Soderstrom; BR Catriona Tudor Erler **p. 266:** Walter Chandoha **p. 267:** Hans Pfletschinger/Peter Arnold **p. 268:** Derek Fell **p. 269:** Walter Chandoha **p. 271:** Neil Soderstrom except BR E&P Bauer/Bruce Coleman **p. 272:** Kevin Schaffer/Peter Arnold **p. 273:** T Joe McDonald/Bruce Coleman; B Neil Soderstrom **p. 274:** L Nicole Duplaix/Peter Arnold; R Photos Horticultural **p. 275:** TL Marijke Heuff/The Garden Picture Library; TR , BL, BR Photos Horticultural **p. 276:** T Jerry Howard/Positive Images; BR, BL Hans Pfletschinger/Peter Arnold **p. 277:** L, R Hans Pfletschinger/Peter Arnold **p. 278:** T Photos Horticultural; B last on right Neil Soderstrom; last two left to right Hans Pfletschinger/Peter Arnold **p. 279:** Neil Soderstrom **p. 280:** TL, BL Nigel Cattlin/Holt Studios/Photo Researchers; BR E.R. Degginger/Photo Researchers **p. 281:** All Nigel Cattlin/Holt Studios/Photo Researchers **p. 282:** All Nigel Cattlin/Holt Studios/Photo Researchers **p. 283:** T John Mitchell/Photo Researchers; B J.H. Robinson/Photo Researchers **p. 284:** L, C Scott Camazine/Photo Researchers; R Nigel Cattlin/Holt Studios/Photo Researchers **p. 285:** L Len McLeod/Holt Studios/Photo Researchers;B Nigel Cattlin/Holt Studios/Photo Researchers; R Martin Wendler/Okapia/Photo Researchers **p. 286:** L Ken Brate/Photo Researchers; C Dwight Kuhn; TR Harry Rogers/Photo Researchers; BR Runk and Schoenberg/Grant Heilman **p. 287:** L, R Nigel Cattlin/Holt Studios/Photo Researchers; C Harry Rogers/Photo Researchers **p. 288:** L Harry Rogers/Photo Researchers; C Michael Gadomski/Photo Researchers; R Nigel Cattlin/Holt Studios/Photo Researchers **p. 289:** L, C Alan and Linda Detrick; R James Robinson/Photo Researchers **p. 290:** L Harry Rogers/Photo Researchers; R Nigel Cattlin/Holt Studios/Photo Researchers **p. 291:** L J.H. Robinson/Photo Researchers; R L. West/Photo Researchers **p. 292:** TL Walter Chandoha; TR Zara McCalmont/The Garden Picture Library; BR Photos Horticultural **p. 293:** BL S.J. Kraseman/Peter Arnold; TR, CR Walter Hodge/Peter Arnold **p. 294:** Jerry Pavia **p. 295:** Walter Hodge/Peter Arnold **p. 297:** L E. R. Degginger/ Bruce Coleman; F Crandall & Crandall **p. 298:** L Phil Degginger/Bruce Coleman; TC Dan Curavich/Photo Researchers; RC Nigel Cattlin/Holt Studios/Photo Researchers **p. 299:** L, R Nigel Cattlin/Holt Studios/Photo Researchers; C Alan and Linda Detrick/Photo Researchers; R Nigel Cattlin/Holt Studios/Photo Researchers **p. 300:** L Derek Fell; C, R Nigel Cattlin/Holt Studios/Photo Researchers **p. 301:** L Kathy Merrifield/Photo Researchers; C M.H. Black/Bruce Coleman; Nigel Cattlin/Holt Studios/Photo Researchers **p. 302:** L, C Nigel Cattlin/Holt Studios/Photo Researchers; R Phil Degginger/Bruce Coleman **p. 303:** L Holt Studios/Photo Researchers; R Phil Degginger/Bruce Coleman.

Illustration Credits

All of the illustrations in this book were created by Mavis Augustine Torke except for those noted here: pp. 13, 23, 42, 57, 60-61, 117, 137, 153, 197: Todd Ferris; pp. 44, 143, 224-227, 230, 246-247, 252-255: Michele Angle Ferrar; pp. 140-141: Terese Nicole Green

Have a home gardening, decorating, or improvement project? Look for these and other fine Creative Homeowner books wherever books are sold. . .

An impressive guide to garden design and plant selection. More than 600 color photos. 320 pp.; 9"×10"
BOOK #: 274615

Lavishly illustrated with portraits of over 100 flowering plants; more than 500 photos. 208 pp.; 9"×10"
BOOK #: 274032

A four-season step-by-step guide to growing flowers. Over 500 photos & illustrations. 224 pp.; 9"×10"
BOOK #: 274791

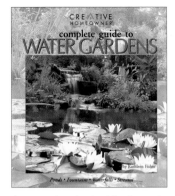

A comprehensive tool for the aspiring water gardener. Over 400 color photos. 208 pp.; 9"×10"
BOOK #: 274452

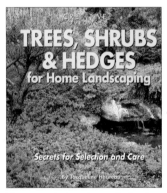

How to select and care for landscaping plants. Over 500 illustrations. 208 pp.; 9"×10"
BOOK #: 274238

Create more beautiful, healthier, lower-maintenance lawns. Over 300 illustrations. 160 pp.; 9"×10"
BOOK #: 274359

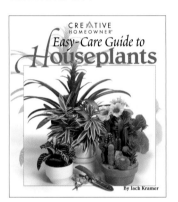

Complete houseplant guide 200 readily available plants; more than 400 photos. 192pp.; 9"×10"
BOOK #: 275243

Four Regions: Northeast (274618); Mid-Atlantic (274537); Southeast (274762); Midwest (274385). 400 illustrations each.

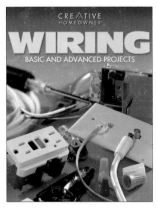

New, updated edition of best-selling house wiring manual. Over 700 color photos. 256 pp.; 8¹⁄₂"×10⁷⁄₈"
BOOK #: 277049

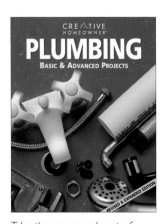

Take the guesswork out of plumbing repair. More than 550 illustrations. 176 pp.; 8¹⁄₂"×10⁷⁄₈"
BOOK #: 277620

How to create kitchen style like a pro. Over 150 color photographs. 176 pp.; 9"×10"
BOOK #: 279667

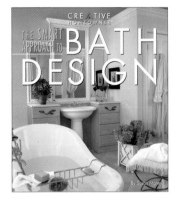

All you need to know about designing a bath. Over 150 color photos. 176 pp.; 9"×10"
BOOK #: 287225

For more information, and to order direct, call 800-631-7795; in New Jersey 201-934-7100.
Please visit our Web site at www.creativehomeowner.com